Motivation to Learn

From Theory to Practice

THIRD EDITION

Deborah Stipek
University of California, Los Angeles

ALLYN AND BACON
Boston • London • Toronto • Sydney • Tokyo • Singapore

Senior Vice President, Publisher: Nancy Forsyth
Series Editorial Assistant: Cheryl Ouellette
Senior Marketing Manager: Kathy Hunter
Composition Buyer: Linda Cox
Manufacturing Buyer: Suzanne Lareau
Cover Administrator: Jenny Hart
Production Administration: Rosalie Briand
Editorial-Production Service: Spectrum Publisher Services

Library of Congress Catalog Card Number: 97-77132

Printed in the United States of America

10   9   8   7   6   5   4   3   2   02   01   00   99   98

Contents

Preface   xi

CHAPTER 1   **Profiles of Motivation Problems**   1

DEFENSIVE DAVE   1
HELPLESS HANNAH   2
SAFE SALLY   4
SATISFIED SANTOS   5
ANXIOUS ALMA   6
CONCLUSION   7

CHAPTER 2   **Defining and Assessing Achievement Motivation**   9

DEFINING ACHIEVEMENT MOTIVATION   9
  Theoretical Framework   9
  Is Motivation in the Person or the Environment?   13
IDENTIFYING MOTIVATION PROBLEMS   14
  Observing Behavior   14
  From Identifying to Explaining   15
  High Achievers Are Not Invulnerable   16
  Looking Beyond the Student   16
  Grade Differences in Motivation Problems   17
CONCLUSION   18

CHAPTER **3**   **Reinforcement Theory   19**

THEORY   19
IMPLICATIONS FOR EDUCATIONAL PRACTICE   22
Token Economies   23
Problems with Reward and Punishment   25
Effectiveness of Rewards   26
Accessibility of Rewards   26
Rewarding Desired Behavior   27
Negative Effects of Rewards on Behavior   28
Short-Lived Effectiveness   29
Effects of Punishment   30
Summary   31
PRAISE   31
CONCLUSION   34

CHAPTER **4**   **Social Cognitive Theory   39**

INTRODUCING COGNITIONS   39
Self-Efficacy in Bandura's Social Cognitive Theory   41
Sources of Self-Efficacy Judgments   42
Consequences of Self-Efficacy   43
Summary   44
SELF-REGULATION   44
Cognitive Behavior Modification   45
Self-Recording   46
Self-Instruction   47
Self-Reinforcement   48
Metacognitive Strategies   49
CONCLUSION   51

CHAPTER **5**   **Cognitive Theories Applied to Achievement Contexts   53**

ATKINSON'S EXPECTANCY *x* VALUE THEORY   53
ROTTER'S SOCIAL LEARNING THEORY   57
Control = Strategy + Capacity   59
Measuring Locus of Control   59
Classroom Contexts and Beliefs about Control   60
WEINER'S ATTRIBUTION THEORY   61
Antecedents to Attributions   62
Attribution Dispositions   62
Measurement   64

Consequences of Attributions   65
 Expectations   **65**
 Helplessness   **65**
 Emotions   **68**
CONCLUSION   69

CHAPTER   **6**   **Perceptions of Ability   73**

WHAT IS "ABILITY"?   74
COVINGTON'S SELF-WORTH THEORY   75
 Avoiding Negative Implications of Failure for Ability   77
 Success without Learning   80
 Summary   80
GENDER DIFFERENCES IN SELF-PERCEPTIONS
 OF ABILITY   81
AGE-RELATED CHANGES IN SELF-PERCEPTIONS
 OF ABILITY   82
 Classroom Practice Effects   84
FRAME OF REFERENCE   86
ASSESSING ABILITY PERCEPTIONS   88
CONCLUSION   92

CHAPTER   **7**   **Maintaining Positive**
Achievement-Related Beliefs   93

EFFECTIVE CLASSROOM PRACTICE   94
 Tasks and Assignments   94
 Goals   96
 Evaluation   98
 Giving Help   102
 Direct Statements   104
 Classroom Structure   106
COMPREHENSIVE PROGRAMS   109
 Mastery Learning Programs   109
 Cooperative Incentive Structures   112
CONCLUSION   115

CHAPTER   **8**   **Intrinsic Motivation   117**

COMPETENCE MOTIVATION   118
 Principle of Optimal Challenge   119
 Emotional Reactions to Mastery   119

Effects of the Social Environment   120
Self-Perceptions of Competence and Intrinsic Motivation   121
NOVELTY   122
SELF-DETERMINATION   123
Summary   123
ADVANTAGE OF INTRINSIC MOTIVATION   124
Learning Activities Outside of School   124
Preference for Challenge   124
Conceptual Understanding   124
Creativity   125
Pleasure and Involvement   125
INTRINSIC MOTIVATION AND EXTRINSIC REWARDS   126
Controlling versus Information Function of Rewards   128
INDIVIDUAL DIFFERENCES   129
Measures of Individual Differences in Motivation   130
Age-Related Changes   132
CONCLUSION   134

CHAPTER **9**   **Values, Goals, and Relationships   137**

SELF-DETERMINATION AND
   INTERNALIZED MOTIVATION   138
Measures of Internalized Motivation   140
Summary   140
EXPECTANCY *x* VALUES   140
Effects of Values   142
From Where Do Achievement Values Come?   143
Age-Related Changes   144
Measures of Values   145
Summary   145
GOAL THEORY   146
Implications of Task Goals   146
Risk Taking and Challenge Seeking   147
Focus of Attention   147
Learning Behavior   148
Attributions   148
Emotions   149
Learning   149
Are Performance Goals All Bad?   150
Beyond Achievement   150
Ethnicity, Culture, Values, and Goals   151
Assessing Students' Achievement-Related Goals   152
Summary   152

RELATIONSHIPS   153
   Consequences of Relationships   156
   Assessing Teacher–Student Relationships   157
   Age-Related Shifts   157
   Summary   159
CONCLUSION   159

CHAPTER **10** **Maximizing Intrinsic Motivation, Mastery Goals, and Belongingness   161**
THE TEACHER'S TASKS   161
TASKS   162
   Summary   171
EVALUATION AND REWARDS   171
   Summary   176
CONTROL   176
   Summary   181
CLASSROOM CLIMATE   182
CONCLUSION   185

CHAPTER **11** **Achievement Anxiety   187**
MEASURING ANXIETY   188
ANXIETY AND ACHIEVEMENT   190
   Preprocessing and Processing   191
   Output   191
   Summary   192
ORIGINS OF ACHIEVEMENT ANXIETY   192
SUBJECT MATTER ANXIETIES   194
   Mathematics   194
   Writing   195
MINIMIZING THE NEGATIVE EFFECTS OF ANXIETY   197
   Preprocessing   198
   Processing and Output   198
   Alleviating Test Anxiety   200
CONCLUSION   201

CHAPTER **12** **Communicating Expectations   203**
WHAT ARE TEACHERS' EXPECTATIONS BASED ON?   204
   Teachers' Self-Efficacy   206
STABILITY OF EXPECTATIONS   207

HOW DO TEACHERS' EXPECTATIONS AFFECT
STUDENT LEARNING?   208
   Teacher Behavior Toward High- and Low-Expectancy Students   208
      Well-Meaning But Counterproductive Teacher Behaviors   210
      Ability Grouping and Tracking   212
DO TEACHERS TREAT GIRLS AND BOYS
DIFFERENTLY?   213
STUDENTS' PERCEPTIONS OF TEACHERS'
EXPECTATIONS   215
AVOIDING THE NEGATIVE EFFECTS OF
EXPECTATIONS   217
CONCLUSION   220

CHAPTER   **13**   **Real Students, Real Teachers, Real Schools   221**
OUR FIVE CHILDREN   221
   Dave   221
   Hannah   223
   Sally   224
   Santos   225
   Alma   226
IT IS HARDER THAN IT SOUNDS   227
   The Undermining Effects of Students   227
   Different Students, Different Needs   228
   Giving Up Control   229
   Knowing Students   230
   Self-Monitoring   230
   Everything Is Related to Everything Else   230
BEYOND THE CLASSROOM   231
   Support for Risk Taking   231
   Cooperation and Collaboration   232
   Time   232
   Autonomy   232
   School Policies   233
CAN IT BE DONE?   234

Appendix 2–A: Identifying Motivation Problems   237

Appendix 3–A: External Reinforcement: Teacher Self-Reports   239

Appendix 3–B: Observations of Teachers' Uses of Praise   242

Appendix 7–A: Evaluating Your Practices   244

Appendix 10–A: Evaluating Your Tasks 246

Appendix 10–B: Evaluating Your Evaluation 247

Appendix 10–C: Evaluating Control 248

Appendix 11–A: Strategies for Reducing Anxiety 249

**Appendix 12–A: Questions for Teachers to Ask to Help
Them Monitor Behavior Toward High and Low Achievers** 250

References 251

Author Index 289

Subject Index 299

Preface

Why do some students approach school tasks eagerly and work diligently on school assignments, while others avoid schoolwork or work half-heartedly? Why do some children enjoy learning in and out of school and take pride in their accomplishments, while others rarely seek opportunities to learn on their own and are anxious and unhappy in school? These are motivation questions that have important implications for learning.

Motivation is relevant to learning because learning is an active process requiring conscious and deliberate activity. Even the most able students will not learn if they do not pay attention and exert some effort. If students are to derive the maximum benefits from school, educators must provide a learning context in which students are motivated to engage actively and productively in learning activities.

PURPOSE

This book gives readers a thorough understanding of motivation theories and research and an appreciation of their implications for educational practice. The focus is on classroom learning, but attention also is given to how strategies used to motivate students in school affect students' motivation to engage in intellectual activities outside of school. A primary goal is to demonstrate how achievement motivation theory and research can be used to help teachers develop autonomous, self-confident learners who value and enjoy learning both in and out of school and throughout their lives.

Terms are clearly defined so that a reader unfamiliar with psychological theory and the academic research literature can understand the concepts used. All new terms introduced in the book are summarized in a table at the end of each chapter. Personal anecdotes and classroom observations are used to make the book more enjoyable to read.

This book also contains many specific and practical examples of how principles based on research and theory might be applied in the classroom. Charts, checklists, and questionnaires have been added to this edition in the form of tables and appendices to assist teachers in assessing their own students' motivation and in monitoring their own practices. In addition to a greater emphasis on classroom practice, this edition discusses current practical issues related to culture, ethnicity, and gender more than the previous editions. The book can be useful to individuals anticipating a teaching career as well as to practicing teachers; it also could serve as a supplementary textbook for a course on teaching methods.

Because the book provides a broad overview of theory and research on achievement motivation, which is a central area of educational psychology, it could serve as a supplementary text in a survey course on educational psychology or as the primary text in a course on achievement motivation. The literature review is obsessively thorough and has been significantly updated in this edition.

ORGANIZATION

The third edition is organized somewhat differently from the first and second editions and contains one entirely new chapter.

Chapter 1 describes hypothetical children with motivation problems that are commonly encountered in classrooms. A profile of each student's behavior in the classroom is used to make these common motivation problems vivid. The hypothetical students are referred to in subsequent chapters, more in this edition than in previous editions, as concrete examples to illustrate theoretical constructs, research findings, and appropriate interventions.

Chapter 2 has been substantially reorganized. It begins with an overview of the theoretical frameworks used by achievement motivation researchers and discussed in this book. This chapter also provides a brief history of these frameworks and discusses the links between them and their implications for how motivation problems are conceptualized, assessed, and remediated. The second half of the chapter discusses issues related to the identification of motivation problems in students.

Chapter 3 reviews traditional reinforcement theory and gives examples of the effective application of reinforcement principles to maximize student effort in the classroom. A detailed analysis of effective and ineffective praise illustrates some of these principles. The potential negative effects of over-reliance on extrinsic reinforcement are also considered.

Social cognitive theory, focusing on Bandura and the concept of self-efficacy, is discussed in Chapter 4. This chapter also reviews several approaches to fostering self-regulation in students, including cognitive behavior modification and teaching metacognitive strategies for learning and monitoring understanding.

Cognitive theories of achievement motivation, including Atkinson's expectancy *x* value theory, Rotter's locus of control theory, and Weiner's attribution theory are described in Chapter 5. Chapter 6 focuses on cognitions directly related to ability. It begins with a discussion of different conceptions of ability, then describes Covington's self-worth theory, and summarizes research on gender and age differences in children's perceptions of their academic ability.

Chapter 7 provides a clear set of principles for classroom practice that can be derived from the theory and research reviewed in previous chapters on students' achievement-related beliefs. The principles have been rephrased in this new edition to be concrete and practical.

The concept of intrinsic motivation is introduced in Chapter 8, and research on the effects of extrinsic rewards on intrinsic motivation is reviewed.

Chapter 9 is an entirely new chapter that summarizes research on goals, values, and relationships in the classroom. The section on goals makes a distinction between performance goals (e.g., look smart, gain approval, get good grades) and learning goals (e.g., develop understanding and mastery), and then broadens the discussion to include recent research on social and personal responsibility goals. The section on values reviews theory and research based in self-determination theory, with a focus on the internalization of adult values, and in Eccles' expectancy *x* value theory.

Chapter 10 summarizes, again in more concrete and practical terms than in the previous edition, the implications for classroom practice of theory and research on intrinsic motivation, goals, values, and relationships.

The causes and consequences of achievement anxiety for learning and performance in achievement contexts are discussed in Chapter 11. Here, specific recommendations are made for alleviating the negative effects of anxiety in the classroom. Research on ways that teacher expectations affect students' own beliefs about competence and learning is described in Chapter 12.

The practical implications of achievement motivation research and theory are integrated in Chapter 13, by discussing remedies to the problems of the hypothetical children described in the first chapter. Two entirely new sections were added to this final chapter. The first section discusses some of the complexities and obstacles teachers face in their efforts to increase student motivation. The second steps back to examine teachers and classrooms in a larger school context, and discusses ways in which school-level practices and policies can support or undermine teachers' efforts to apply the principles of good classroom practice discussed in the book.

ACKNOWLEDGMENTS

I am extremely grateful to Laura Weishaupt for her careful and speedy editing, to Cristina Moreira for checking and rechecking references, and to my students,

Patty Byler, Elham Kazemi, Rosaleen Ryan, Julie Salmon, and Melinda Wagner, for their assistance with updating the book and for their friendly, constructive feedback. I also thank the reviewers of the text: Helene Anthony, Moorhead State University and Myron Dembo, University of Southern California, Los Angeles.

Profiles of Motivation Problems

Like cold and flu symptoms, motivation problems come in many shapes and sizes. But some combinations of problems are more common than others. This chapter describes typical motivation "syndromes"—patterns of beliefs and behaviors that inhibit optimal learning. No child you meet will look exactly like any of the five hypothetical children described here. Indeed, these children are in some respects caricatures. But these vignettes should remind some readers of real children they have observed or taught. Later chapters discuss the causes of the problems described here and ways to improve the motivation and learning of children like these five.

DEFENSIVE DAVE

Dave is one of the worst students in his fourth-grade class. Poor performance, as far as Dave is concerned, is highly likely. So he puts his energy into preventing anyone from interpreting his poor performance as evidence of a lack of ability. Unfortunately, the strategies he uses to avoid looking dumb prevent him from developing his competencies.

Dave's strategies, usually missed by the teacher, are clever. For example, one morning Dave is working on an assignment to answer ten questions about a story the children were supposed to read. The teacher shifts her attention from one child to another, monitoring each student's work to the best of her ability while answering questions. Dave asks the teacher several questions, but he is careful to give her the impression that he is working diligently to answer most of the questions on his own. Actually, he receives the rest of the answers by asking classmates or by copying his neighbor's paper. Thus, Dave manages to complete the assignment without reading or understanding the story.

That afternoon the teacher asks students to take out yesterday's assignment, which required the use of a dictionary. Dave makes a show of looking through his desk for an assignment that he knows, his teacher knows, and his classmates probably know he has not completed.

During a social studies test Dave sharpens his pencil twice, picks up an eraser that has fallen to the floor, and ties his shoelaces. He makes no attempt to conceal his lack of attention to the questions. To the contrary, he seems eager for everyone to notice that he is not trying. The teacher publicly reminds him several times to get to work, giving Dave and his classmates the message that if he tried, his performance, which will otherwise inevitably be poor, might be better. This, of course, is exactly the interpretation Dave desires.

Dave's strategies serve their purpose, at least in the short term. He manages to complete some assignments with a respectable, if not an excellent, level of performance. By fooling around while he is supposed to be taking tests (when other strategies, such as cheating, are not available), he at least avoids appearing dumb, the logical conclusion associated with poor performance and high effort. By not trying, he creates an alternative explanation for failure, leaving open the question of whether he would have done well on the test if he had tried.

The tragedy is that Dave's ingenious efforts to avoid looking dumb are self-defeating. He makes little progress in mastering the curriculum, and failure becomes increasingly inevitable. Eventually Dave will give up trying to preserve the image of himself as a capable person, and he will resign himself to the status of one of the "dumb" kids in the class. If he continues this self-destructive game, he will soon look like Helpless Hannah, who does not even try to look competent.

HELPLESS HANNAH

Hannah has been sitting at her desk for nearly half an hour doing, as far as the teacher can tell, nothing. The teacher urges Hannah to try one of the arithmetic problems she is supposed to be working on. "I can't," claims Hannah without even looking at the problem to which the teacher is pointing. She adds, "I don't understand what I'm supposed to do." The frustrated teacher replies, "But I just went over a problem like it on the board—weren't you listening?" "I don't understand," Hannah repeats. The teacher goes through a long-division problem step by step, asking Hannah questions along the way. Hannah answers most of the questions correctly. She obviously has at least some understanding of the problem. "See, you know how to do these kinds of problems," the teacher observes. "Why don't you try one on your own now?" "I don't know how," Hannah stubbornly declares. "But you knew the right answers to my questions," the teacher responds. "You were helping me," Hannah readily replies. Not to be fooled, the teacher concludes firmly, "I think you know how to do these, and I want you to try some of the problems."

The teacher has the last word and turns her attention to another student, leaving Hannah alone with her arithmetic problems. Later, she passes by Hannah's desk and finds no progress. The scene just described is repeated, as it has been so many times that year, and the end result is an exasperated teacher and a student who interprets the teacher's despair as confirmation of her own lack of competence.

Hannah is a classic example of what researchers refer to as *learned helplessness*. Her academic performance is uniformly poor, and she is regarded by her classmates as one of the "dummies." She has developed a firm view of herself as incompetent and unable to master any new academic material. Failure is inevitable, so "why try?" she reasons.

Hannah makes little academic progress and is more than a grade behind in most academic subjects, but she is not disruptive. She is not socially integrated into the classroom and therefore does not have the option of spending her time socializing. She is not an aggressive child, and rather than acting out, calling attention to herself, or interfering with her classmates, she sits quietly, spending much of her time gazing into space. She also makes few demands on the teacher. Hannah perceives no reason to ask questions because she does not expect to understand or to be able to make use of the answers.

There are many variations of learned helplessness in students. Some of the students who have given up trying to gain respect through their academic performance turn to other domains for recognition. They may become the class clown, the bully, or the tease. Or, especially as they approach adolescence, they may engage in more serious antisocial behavior to gain respect in a peer group that publicly rejects academic achievement. It is unusual for the academically "helpless" child to turn to legitimate ways of demonstrating competence, such as athletics, music, or other activities. For some children, the feeling of incompetence is so profound that they assume that there is simply no domain in which they can excel.

School offers little joy for students like Hannah. Their days are characterized by hopelessness, despair, and probably, because they spend little time working on academic tasks, boredom. They are often shunned by their classmates and sometimes ignored by their teachers—an understandable response considering the intractability of helpless students.

Because they rarely try, helpless students rarely succeed. Their repeated failures confirm their perceptions of themselves as incompetent. When they do succeed, they are quick to deny responsibility. They attribute their success to some variable over which they have no control—an easy problem, the teacher's help, or even luck. The logic is elegantly consistent; the consequences are devastating.

Luckily, pure cases of learned helplessness are rare; weak versions are more common. Learned helplessness is, however, the motivation problem most resistant to change by even the most clever and persistent teacher. Obviously, it is best to prevent it from developing. But teachers in later grades have no control over their students' experiences in earlier grades, and children like Hannah occasionally appear in their classes.

SAFE SALLY

In her senior year of high school, Sally's SAT scores are in the top 5 percent of her class. This does not surprise her teachers because she is a "straight A" student. In many respects, Sally is a perfect student—well behaved, dependable, and highly motivated. A superficial look at her would reveal no motivation problems.

But despite Sally's high academic performance, she is an underachiever. She is motivated, but only to achieve high grades and the accompanying respect of her teachers. She perceives a "B+" as a disastrous blemish on her record, something to be avoided at all costs.

A careful look at Sally's perfect record reveals a series of courses that offered little challenge. She is taking the high-achievement class in English, but the teacher of this course is well known for giving every student in the class an "A," as long as the work is done reliably. She took only the required science courses, and she enrolled in the calculus course but dropped it after getting a "C+" on the first weekly quiz.

Sally religiously follows directions for every assignment. She is tuned in to her teachers and has an astonishing ability to predict what material will be stressed on tests. Sally overstudies for every test, repeatedly reviewing the text and memorizing every possible fact that she might be asked to recall. She rarely reads anything that she is not required to read for a course.

Sally is anxious, but her anxiety is not debilitating within the context of the intellectual demands she allows herself. She is constantly reinforced by teachers for her achievements, and she appears to be academically self-confident. She enjoys the respect of her classmates and is socially active.

What is unfortunate for Sally is that she does not allow herself to be challenged. She systematically takes the safe route in all of her academic endeavors. In her classes she learns only what she is told to learn, in ways she expects to be evaluated. The notion that learning has some intrinsic value aside from being a means to good grades and external recognition simply does not occur to her. Working methodically within the guidelines and structure given to her, she makes no effort to be creative.

Sally ignored the school counselor's suggestion that she take the advanced courses required for acceptance at a selective university. She lacks self-confidence in her academic skills and prefers not to risk failure. The self-confidence she displays in her own high school is, in a sense, illusory. Sally knows that she is "smart enough" to excel in the carefully chosen not-too-demanding courses she takes, but she is not at all sure she can handle a more challenging academic experience. She does not know the true boundaries of her competencies because she never tests them.

Sally will no doubt excel in college, and she will probably perform well in a responsible, albeit unintellectually challenging, job. But she will not, as an adult, stretch her knowledge and imagination. Learning, for Sally, is what you do in school. It has instrumental but no intrinsic value. It brings "As," but no joy or excitement. Learning means memorizing somebody else's ideas, not developing her own. Sally's potential for creative thinking will never be tapped.

SATISFIED SANTOS

Santos is the seventh-grade class clown. He is one of the first to arrive at school in the morning, and he often fools around with classmates on the school grounds long after school is over. He seems to enjoy school, is popular with peers, and only occasionally gets into trouble for his pranks.

Santos is a likable student, but has frustrated many of his teachers. He is a "C+/B−" student who could easily be earning "As." His scores on standardized aptitude tests consistently show that he is capable of achieving considerably more than most of his classmates, and he occasionally demonstrates this unusual aptitude. On those rare days when he pays close attention, Santos is frequently the only student in the class who can answer a difficult question. His potential is also evident when he becomes seriously involved in a project, such as the prize-winning model of the solar system that he presented to his science teacher after several weeks of intense effort.

Typically, Santos shows little interest in schoolwork. Threats of bad grades have no effect because he is quite satisfied with a grade that he can achieve with little effort. He usually finishes his work, but he never does more than the minimum. He makes it a rule never to study for a test because he knows that he can pass most tests simply by paying marginal attention in class. Santos knows he is smart, but he is not inclined to show off. He is not interested in gaining his peers' respect by demonstrating academic excellence, and he is not interested in gaining his teachers' respect at all. He is motivated to stay out of trouble—at least most of the time. Consequently, he does what is required to keep teachers "off his back."

At home Santos spends hour after hour playing intellectually demanding computer games. Santos is also interested in science. He reads every book on space that he can find, and often he surprises his science teacher with comments that demonstrate sophisticated understanding—usually on topics that are not part of the science curriculum. His performance on topics that are covered in his science class is typical of his performance in all his other courses—he does exactly what he needs to do to avoid getting into trouble. Reading science fiction novels is another great love of his, and he has written several short stories himself. Although he has some talent for writing, it is rarely evident in school assignments.

Santos's teachers know that he could do better in school. Each new teacher goes through essentially the same series of strategies. Noting his half-hearted efforts with assignments, teachers first encourage him to spend a little more time on his schoolwork to achieve higher grades. But Santos is unresponsive to this strategy because high grades simply do not have the same value for him that they have for some other students, and poor grades are not perceived as punishment, unless they dip below his "C+" threshold of acceptability.

Santos sees no reason to push himself with school-related work. He enjoys intellectual challenges, but on his own terms. If his current interests happen to overlap with course requirements, he excels at school. More typically, his intellectual life is outside of the classroom and his life in the classroom is not intellectual.

Students like Santos are seen at all grade levels, although they are common in junior high school. They frustrate parents and teachers alike. In contrast to Hannah, who convinces her teachers that she really cannot learn, Santos's teachers know that he has the ability to excel. But conventional strategies to motivate students like Santos are ineffective.

ANXIOUS ALMA

Alma is in the eighth grade. She is an average student in most subjects but she is doing poorly in mathematics. Tests often are turned in with many unanswered problems. Sometimes correct answers had been written but were erased. Alma occasionally spends math period in the nurse's room, claiming a headache, stomachache, or some other ailment that miraculously disappears about the time her math class ends.

For the first few weeks of the semester, Alma's math teacher frequently asked Alma questions in an attempt to elicit her participation and to assess her understanding of the concepts that were explained to the class. But she usually refused to participate, and the teacher, sensing that Alma was uncomfortable when questions were addressed to her publicly, stopped trying to engage her in class discussion.

In contrast to her class performance, assignments that Alma can take home are often returned completed and mostly correct. The teacher knows from conversations with Alma's parents that she does her homework on her own. Her math teacher is puzzled by her reticence in class because she knows from Alma's homework assignments that she could figure out the answers if she tried.

Alma lacks self-confidence and apparently finds that refusing to answer a question is less threatening than risking a wrong answer. It is difficult for her to concentrate on math problems in class because she is distracted by her concerns about failure. However prepared Alma may be for a test, as soon as it is in front of her, she panics. She cannot remember the simplest procedures that she knew well the evening before. When the teacher asks her a question in front of the class, she is conscious of the other students' evaluative gazes and cannot concentrate on the question itself.

Alma will get through eighth-grade math with a passing grade, partly because she can compensate for her poor test scores and class performance with complete and correct homework, but she will take only the mathematics courses required to graduate. If she goes to college, she will major in an area that does not require any math. For the rest of her life she will claim, if the subject comes up, that she has no aptitude for numbers.

CONCLUSION

The following chapters provide a theoretical framework for understanding the kinds of motivation problems presented by these five children. They also discuss research that can be used to guide educational practices that will prevent and even reverse them. School learning is emphasized, but attention is also given to how strategies that are used to motivate students in school affect students' motivation to engage in intellectual activities outside the classroom. The goals in the practices recommended are for students to exert maximum effort on academic tasks in the classroom, but also to seek and engage in challenging learning activities outside of school and throughout their adult lives.

Defining and Assessing Achievement Motivation

DEFINING ACHIEVEMENT MOTIVATION

This book is about behavior in achievement contexts. The problems described in Chapter 1 occur in regular classrooms. But achievement contexts can be found anywhere—on the playing field, on the stage, or in an art studio, a kitchen, or even a garden. The standards, even the definitions of success, vary. In sports success usually means performing better than others, although it can also be defined in terms of personal improvement. Success for the pianist might be measured in the length of applause, for the hostess in the amount of food the guests consume, and for the surgeon in the survival of her patients. This book focuses primarily on school contexts, but most of the issues discussed apply to any context that involves some standard against which performance can be measured—any situation that offers the opportunity to succeed or fail.

Theoretical Framework

A number of psychological theories are discussed to help us think about achievement motivation. Theories of motivation are created to explain and help predict and influence behavior. If we can explain why individuals behave the way they do in achievement settings we might be able to change their behavior. Why does Defensive Dave (see Chapter 1) pretend to be working when he is not, and how can we get him to exert genuine effort on school tasks? Why does Satisfied Santos (see Chapter 1) put so much more effort into intellectual activities outside of school than in school? What can be done to engage his interest in the school curriculum? Why does Safe Sally (see Chapter 1) avoid challenging work, and what can we do to get her to push herself closer to the limits of her ability?

The theories discussed in this book are coherent systems of constructs (psychological variables). Rules link constructs to explain a broad set of behaviors that affect learning outcomes. The theory one chooses for thinking about motivation has implications for how motivation is defined, how it is measured, and how problems are identified and corrected. Some of the theories discussed in this book contradict each other; they both cannot be "right." More often different theories are compatible because they account for different aspects of achievement motivation or focus on different causes of behavior.

Over time, psychological theories are often modified in response to research evidence on their usefulness in predicting and changing behavior. New theories also are developed, and different theories become prominent at different times. In general, the psychological theories that have been used to explain behavior in achievement contexts have shifted in the last three decades from a focus on observable behavior to a focus on psychological variables—such as beliefs, values, and goals—that can be inferred from behavior but cannot be observed directly. The central differences and similarities among the theories discussed in this book are outlined briefly in the following.

Reinforcement theory, which dominated the educational literature through the 1960s, conceptualizes motivation entirely in terms of observable behavior. According to traditional reinforcement theory, individuals exhibit a particular behavior in achievement or other settings because they have been reinforced (rewarded) for that behavior in the past. Accordingly, students who are rewarded (e.g., with good grades) for working hard on school tasks and persisting when they face difficulty will continue to work hard and persist in the future.

Reinforcement theory was originally derived from drive theories, which assumed that reinforcement necessarily involved the reduction of basic biological needs (e.g., hunger, thirst; Hull, 1943, 1951). Applications to achievement contexts, however, assume that other consequences (e.g., teacher praise) take on reinforcing properties, and therefore can influence behavior because they previously were associated with the reduction of basic drives. Traditional reinforcement theory is considered "mechanistic" because it is not concerned with beliefs, feelings, aspirations, or any other psychological variable that cannot be observed directly.

This theory has clear implications for how motivation is conceptualized and measured. Motivation is not considered a quality of the person, but a set of behaviors and their contingencies (i.e., whether they are rewarded or punished). Any attempt to explain, predict, or influence motivation would involve measuring behavior and examining the consequences of the current and desired behaviors. A reinforcement theorist who wanted Dave to exert more effort, for example, first would examine Dave's behavior closely. What does he do when the teacher gives him an assignment? What happens to him (what are the consequences) when he spends 20 minutes sharpening his pencil and arranging his desk? What happens on those, perhaps rare, occasions when he completes tasks efficiently? The next step would be to adjust the environmental consequences so that the undesirable behaviors (wasting time) were punished, or at least not rewarded, and the desired behaviors (getting to work and completing tasks) were rewarded.

In the 1960s, most motivation theorists found such mechanistic assumptions about behavior unsatisfactory, and began to explore psychological variables that are not observable directly. *Cognitive motivation* theorists do not rule out external reinforcement as a cause of achievement behavior. They claim, however, that cognitions (beliefs), such as expectations, "mediate" the effect of rewards. Thus, for example, they claim that students work hard because their past experiences lead them to expect hard work to be rewarded in the future, not because they have been rewarded for working hard in the past.

A motivated person, therefore, is conceptualized as someone with cognitions or beliefs that are associated with constructive achievement behavior. Although expectations have been especially prominent, cognitive motivation theorists are also interested in the mediating effects of other beliefs associated with expectations—such as perceptions of one's ability, perceptions of one's control over achievement outcomes, and perceptions of the causes of achievement outcomes (referred to as "attributions").

Cognitive motivation theorists would not be satisfied by merely observing behavior and its consequences. They would want to assess students' beliefs about the consequences of behavior and causes of performance outcomes. And their intervention would be aimed at changing maladaptive beliefs. An effort to get Helpless Hannah (see Chapter 1) to exert effort with school tasks, therefore, might begin with an interview to ascertain her perceptions of her competencies (i.e., does she think she is incapable of completing school tasks? if so, which ones?), then trying to increase her perceptions of her competencies and thus her expectations for success on tasks she could, if she tried to, complete. (This may also require changing tasks so that they are appropriate for her skill level.) An interviewer might ask Dave what he thinks would happen if he tried hard to complete a task and was not able to do it. If he expected negative consequences (e.g., teacher disapproval, ridicule from his classmates), the interviewer might try to change his expectations by reassuring him that his fears are not well founded. (Some discussions with classmates may also be necessary.)

Cognitive motivation theorists do not assume that beliefs are based entirely on previous experiences with the contingencies (e.g., reward and punishment) to their own behavior. People's expectations are based on many factors—for example, observations of what happens to others when they behave a particular way, or even simply what they are told. When teachers call attention to the consequences of students' behaviors ("Table 3 can go to recess because they have cleared their desks and are sitting quietly") and when they promise rewards ("if you finish all your work before recess I'll let you go out early"), they are using cognitive motivation theory—they are attempting to influence behavior by influencing expectations about the consequences of desired behaviors.

Atkinson (1964) also emphasized expectations as explanations of achievement behavior, but he added values as another explanatory variable. In his *expect-*

ancy x value theory, exerting effort and persisting with a task requires more than expecting to be able to complete it; the task must also have some value attached to it. Atkinson conceptualized value narrowly, in terms of pride in success and shame in failure. Other theorists have considered values more broadly, such as in terms of how important academic achievement is to students' self-concept and how useful particular kinds of achievement are in their lives outside of school (Eccles et al., 1983).

Researchers and teachers working from an expectancy *x* value theoretical framework, therefore, would need to measure students' perceptions of the value of rewards in any effort to predict or change behavior. Dave's teacher might try to find out whether Dave expects his effort with school tasks to lead to pride or shame, and then try to make sure that pride is more likely (e.g., by giving him tasks with which he is sure to succeed, by making sure that put-downs from classmates are not allowed). Santos's teacher might try to increase the value Santos places on doing well in school by giving him examples of the long-term accomplishments or privileges of people who perform well in school.

Intrinsic motivation theorists are also concerned with emotional as well as cognitive aspects of motivation, although they stress different emotions than expectancy *x* value theorists. Intrinsic motivation theory is based on the assumption that humans are naturally motivated to develop their intellectual and other competencies and that they take pleasure in their accomplishments (White, 1959). Part of the value of striving to achieve something is the intrinsic pleasure one experiences from developing an understanding and mastery of it. Intrinsic motivation researchers have examined factors that foster or inhibit human beings' intrinsic desires to engage in intellectual tasks.

Motivation is usually measured by intrinsic motivation theorists in terms of individuals' voluntary activities. Thus, to assess students' intrinsic motivation to read, these theorists might find out how much they read on their own, when there is no external reward (e.g., a good grade) for doing so and no punishment (e.g., a bad grade) for not reading. To determine an intervention for children who are not intrinsically motivated to engage in intellectual activities, intrinsic motivation theorists would determine whether factors (e.g., feelings of control and competence) that research has shown to support intrinsic interest are present, and then manipulate those factors to increase intrinsic interest (e.g., provide students with more autonomy, or make sure they can succeed with tasks and will feel competent).

Although intrinsic motivation theorists emphasize feelings of enjoyment, *self-worth* theorists are concerned with feelings of being valued. Covington (1992) proposed that students are naturally motivated to preserve a sense of personal worth, in their own and in others' eyes. To the degree that one's value in a particular educational context is based on academic competence, individuals will seek opportunities to demonstrate their competencies and, like Dave, they will avoid situations that may lead to a judgment of incompetence. Self-worth theorists, therefore, might assess students' perceptions of the criteria for others' positive regard and their beliefs about what strategies will achieve that regard. Interventions might be aimed at making sure that they are supported and admired for trying, regardless of the outcome of their efforts.

Recently, *goal* theorists have pointed out that individuals may engage in the same behavior for different reasons, and that the reason for engaging in a task is just as important as the level of effort expended, the degree of persistence, or any other observable behavior. Sally's goal is to get good grades. As a consequence, she does only what is likely to contribute directly to grades. Another student might work to meet the school's minimum requirement for being on the football team (and stop working when this minimum requirement is achieved). Santos never works hard on academic tasks because his goal is to enjoy himself. Dave engages in behaviors that achieve his goal of avoiding embarrassment or looking stupid. According to goal theorists, interventions designed to change such maladaptive behaviors would require changing students' goals.

That children often have different goals than the teacher was illustrated in research by Wentzel (1989, 1991) in which she asked high school students how often they tried to achieve a set of twelve goals while they were in class. "Making or keeping friends" ranked the highest for students with average GPAs and second highest (after "having fun") for the lowest achieving students. Only the highest achieving students ranked "learning" above friends as a frequent goal in school.

Is Motivation in the Person or the Environment?

For reinforcement theorists, motivation is not in the person; it is in the environment. Changes in a person's behavior are produced by changing contingencies in the environment. Some theorists conceptualize achievement motivation as a stable trait—something that an individual has either a lot or a little of and that is only modestly changeable. For example, in Atkinson's theory, achievement motivation is, in part, conceptualized as an unconscious trait (the motive to achieve success) that develops early in life as the result of certain parenting practices. Thus, experiences in early childhood are assumed to play a continuing and pervasive role in individuals' responses to achievement situations.

Other theorists conceptualize achievement motivation as a set of conscious beliefs and values that are influenced primarily by recent experiences in achievement situations (e.g., the amount of success or failure) and variables in the immediate environment (e.g., the nature and difficulty of tasks). A student's behavior when working on geography may differ from her behavior when working on algebra because of differences in her past performance in these two subjects, or because of differences in the teachers' instructional approaches.

Most theories allow for change in achievement behavior, implying that teachers have considerable opportunity to influence students' motivation to achieve in school. According to most theories, students are not limited by the level of motivation inculcated in them by their parents. Parents are influential, but teachers control most aspects of instruction as well as the social climate of the classroom, and can therefore improve their students' motivation.

The remainder of this book is about the theories of motivation previously mentioned, the research based on them, and the practical implications of theory and research. Although most people are not knowledgeable of these psychological theories, everyone makes assumptions about why people behave the way they do, and their efforts to change others and even their own behaviors are based implicitly on the theories this book describes. This book, therefore, acquaints readers with the formal language and details of psychological theories that should already be a part of their naive explanations of behavior. A good understanding of these theoretical frameworks will make readers better, more thoughtful observers and predictors of behavior, and more effective in their efforts to change their own and influence others' motivation in achievement contexts.

Regardless of the theoretical orientation we take, our ultimate goal is to affect behavior. Before examining the theories in greater depth, we need a behavioral basis for judging when there is a need for intervention or changes in practices, and for evaluating whether changes made have had a positive impact. We make an abrupt turn, therefore, from a theoretical to a behavioral analysis of achievement motivation.

IDENTIFYING MOTIVATION PROBLEMS

Observing Behavior

Whatever the cause of students' motivation problems, they usually manifest themselves in behavior. The first step, therefore, is to observe student behavior systematically. To provide a rough index of the degree and nature of students' motivation, Appendix 2–A lists behaviors that can be observed directly. Although motivation theorists and educators have varying interpretations of the behaviors in this list, and varying beliefs about which behaviors are most important, most would agree that all the behaviors listed are desirable and their absence, particularly of the first twelve, signals a problem.

Teachers should observe all students, including those who are achieving relatively well. Students should be observed in different subject areas, in a variety of contexts, and performing a variety of tasks. Some students work diligently in small groups but never finish tasks that are designed to be done individually. Some students work best in structured learning situations, others in unstructured situations, and so on. These differences will not be identified if students are observed in only one learning context. Analysis of these variations can provide hints about the causes of motivation problems and likely solutions.

It is important to examine evidence of students' emotional expressions as well as their behaviors. Do students approach tasks enthusiastically—do they smile, get excited, or even cry out occasionally when a major breakthrough is achieved? Or do they look depressed, bored, or anxious? Do they express pride in their achievements? Do they appear embarrassed or humiliated when they answer a question incorrectly? Emotions are important determinants of behavior and they can reveal a great deal about students' motivation.

From Identifying to Explaining

Although essential, even careful observations are usually insufficient to diagnose problems and they need to be supplemented with other strategies. Discussions with individuals or small groups of students can be revealing if teachers encourage and do not penalize students for honesty and openness. Teachers are often surprised to hear some of their high-performing students claim that they do not like schoolwork and work hard only to achieve extrinsic rewards or to avoid parental sanctions. Some lower achieving students, who teachers assume do not care about academic success, occasionally confess to being discouraged or fearful of failure and in other ways provide important information that can be used to design interventions. The teacher who is interested in assessing motivation problems in the class as a whole also can give students questionnaires to complete anonymously. Examples of questions that can be asked in discussions or on questionnaires are provided throughout this book.

The importance of going beyond observable behavior was demonstrated in a study by Peterson and Swing (1982), in which some elementary school-age students who looked as if they were listening faithfully to a mathematics lesson reported in subsequent interviews that they were actually thinking of other things. They claimed, for example, to be worrying about whether they would be able to solve the problems and whether they would be among the last to finish. Students' responses to questions about their thoughts during the time they were supposed to be working on the task predicted their achievement better than observers' judgments regarding their levels of attention. Not surprisingly, children who claimed they were thinking about strategies to solve the problems performed better than those who claimed to be thinking about whether they could solve them.

This finding should not be surprising. What adult has not been guilty of feigning attention at a teachers' meeting or during a sermon at church or synagogue while planning the evening's dinner menu or fantasizing about an upcoming vacation? What college student has not pretended to be taking notes in a lecture while writing a letter to a friend? Adults sometimes have elaborate strategies for looking attentive, and so do children. With a large group of students to observe, it is often difficult for the teacher to see through these ruses. Because we cannot observe children's thoughts, the most careful observations of a student's work habits will not be sufficient to identify motivation problems.

This book helps teachers to identify and remedy motivation problems stemming from unobservable thoughts and feelings, such as levels of self-confidence, expectations for success, interest in academic work, feelings of autonomy, achievement anxiety, and fear of failure. Even if motivation problems are apparent from overt behavior, remedies require accurate diagnoses. Strategies for identifying the causes of maladaptive behavior are described to help teachers in this important process.

High Achievers Are Not Invulnerable

Teachers are usually aware of the motivation problems of relatively low achievers. Motivation problems in high-achieving students, like Sally, who are not realizing their potential for intellectual development often go unrecognized. This is because teachers usually assume that students who do well in school do not have motivation problems. They rate students like Safe Sally high in motivation and view them as desirable students.

Studies of student motivation challenge this assumption. Phillips (1984), for example, studied 117 fifth graders who were above the 75th national percentile on the Stanford Research Associates (SRA) achievement tests. Twenty-three of these students seriously underestimated their actual levels of performance, set low achievement standards for themselves, and persisted less with tasks than the high achievers in the sample who had high perceptions of competence. By setting low standards and giving up easily, these high-ability students were not living up to their learning potentials. (See also Kolb & Jussim, 1994; Phillips & Zimmerman, 1990.)

It is easy to overlook relatively high-achieving students who are not performing at their capacity. Teachers who have as many as twenty-five or even thirty-five students in a class generally believe that their primary responsibility is to make sure that all students master the basic curriculum. As long as students consistently finish their work and are not disruptive they are not considered to be problems. That some students finish assignments in half of the allotted time often goes unnoticed. This is especially true in classes where there are many students who are having difficulty mastering the assigned material and who lay significant claims on the teacher's attention. Consequently, the "B+" student who could be getting "As," and the student who gets "As" without really trying are less likely to be noticed or to be perceived as problems than students who are barely passing. It is, therefore, important to scrutinize all students for motivation problems.

Looking Beyond the Student

What are seen as students' motivation problems are often problems with the achievement context. If more than a few children are exhibiting problems, it is useful to examine factors in the educational program and the social context of the classroom that might not be fostering positive motivation. Student motivation is strongly affected by the nature of instruction and the tasks given—for example, whether tasks are clear, involve active participation, are personally meaningful, and are at the appropriate level of difficulty. Students' motivation is also affected by the social context—for example, whether students feel valued as human beings, are supported in their learning efforts by the teacher and their peers, and are allowed to make mistakes without being embarrassed. Motivation problems that are observed in students' behaviors, therefore, often actually reside in the educational program.

Often an analysis of the fit between the student and the instructional program is required to understand motivation problems. This is because a program that is highly motivating for one student is not necessarily effective for another. For example, a student like Sally who is used to working for grades may not work at all in a classroom in which grades are not given. A student like Santos, who is motivated only to do the work he chooses, may work effectively in a classroom that allows a great deal of choice and autonomy, but not in a classroom that is very teacher directed. Identifying motivation "problems," therefore, requires a complex analysis of students, the educational context, and their interactions.

Grade Differences in Motivation Problems

Underachievement in the early elementary grades (i.e., kindergarten and first grade) usually has different causes than it does in later grades. Some young children do not work effectively on school tasks because they are having difficulty adapting to the new social context. Young children usually have not had experience in formal academic settings. Some have difficulty sitting still for more than a few minutes. They may also be easily distracted because they are not accustomed to the stimulation of many other children and activities. Some young children, who are used to being able to choose their activities, are unenthusiastic about accepting constraints the teacher sets.

Although some children in kindergarten and first grade have difficulty following directions and completing tasks, most are eager, self-confident learners (although not necessarily on the tasks the teacher provides). Helpless Hannahs, Defensive Daves, and Anxious Almas are rare in the early elementary grades. Indeed, most young children have unrealistically high expectations about their ability to complete tasks (see Stipek, 1984a, 1984b; Stipek & Tannatt, 1984).

By second or third grade some students lose self-confidence, become anxious in learning contexts, and consequently engage in activities that inhibit rather than facilitate learning. Thus, although the kinds of adjustment problems that very young children have usually disappear with time and experience in a school setting, other problems emerge.

The older the child, the more serious the consequences of motivation problems. For the first 6–9 years of school, students have little choice in their educational curriculum. Because there are not many tasks they can avoid, children's motivation problems are often revealed in low-effort expenditure, poor attention, or inappropriate behavior. High school students have more choice in the type and difficulty level of the courses they take, and even in whether they remain in an educational context at all. Like Sally, older students can avoid certain courses, or school itself. Thus, while the fifth grader who lacks self-confidence in mathematics may "forget" to do her homework, the older student may not take any courses in mathematics.

Although the immediate consequences of motivation problems in the early grades of school may be less serious than in later grades, children's early experiences in school appear to put them on a pathway that becomes increasingly difficult to change. Children's school performance as early as kindergarten is highly predictive of their performance much later (Luster & McAdoo, 1996; Stevenson & Newman, 1986), and a major predictor of dropping out is failure in elementary school (Brooks-Gunn, Guo, & Furstenberg, 1993; Ensminger & Slusarcick, 1992). Motivation orientations that develop early on no doubt play a role in this stability. Indeed, some analysts consider low perceptions of competence resulting from early school failure as a major cause of dropping out of high school (Finn, 1989). Achievement motivation, therefore, has serious and life-long implications.

CONCLUSION

Careful observation of students' behaviors is a critical first step to enhancing student motivation in achievement contexts. Thorough observations in variable contexts, supplemented with interviews and analyses of the educational program, are necessary to identify and understand motivation problems.

Psychological theories provide a coherent set of constructs and principles that can guide this analysis. Theories provide a framework for understanding, predicting, and changing behavior in achievement contexts. They also provide a framework for conducting research, which can be used to guide decisions about practices that will enhance student motivation. The remainder of this book is about how theory and research can be used to inform decisions about educational practice.

Reinforcement Theory

Reinforcement theory was developed to explain all human behavior, not only achievement-related behavior. But a great deal has been written about the application of reinforcement theory to classrooms. Indeed, for many years a reinforcement model of motivation dominated the educational psychology literature. This chapter describes the theory and its applications in achievement settings. In the last section, praise is discussed in some detail to illustrate the principles for effective use of reinforcement.

THEORY

Reinforcement theorists assume that behavior is caused by events external to the person and can be understood in terms of simple laws that apply to both humans and animals. According to the **law of effect,** behavior is determined by its consequences. Responses become more probable as the result of some consequences and less probable as the result of others. Thorndike (1898) derived this principle from his observations of food-deprived cats placed inside a box with food outside. In their attempts to escape, the animals eventually, by accident, would operate a device that released the door, allowing them to consume the food. The animals subsequently operated the device more and more rapidly when placed in the box. Thus, an accidental behavior that originally had very low probability occurred with increasing frequency as a result of its consequence.

Skinner (1974) elaborated on the law of effect proposed by Thorndike by systematically manipulating consequences and studying their effects on behavior. He defined consequences that increased the probability of behaviors on which they were made contingent as **positive reinforcers,** and consequences that reduced the probability of behavior as **punishments. Negative reinforcers** are consequences that increase the probability of a behavior by taking something away or reducing its intensity.

Although originally derived primarily from research on animals, reinforcement theorists assume that these principles apply to humans as well. Consider, for example, a teacher who wants to increase the amount of attention a child pays to her directions. This child likes **social reinforcement** (reinforcers that are linked to social approval, e.g., teacher smiles, verbal praise) and dislikes missing recess. If she praises the child (positive reinforcement), or stops frowning (negative reinforcement) when he pays attention, the child is more likely to pay attention in the future. If the teacher cancels the child's recess (punishment) when he is inattentive, his inattention will decrease.

Reinforcers and punishments are defined strictly in terms of their effects on behavior and cannot be identified independently of these effects. What is a positive reinforcer for some, therefore, may be punishment for others. An opportunity to perform in front of the class may be a real treat for an outgoing, self-assured student and would serve as a positive reinforcer. The same "opportunity" may serve as punishment for a student who is shy or lacks self-confidence.

Consequences can become reinforcing by being linked to other consequences that are already reinforcing. These are called **secondary reinforcers.** Consider grades, for example. Grades have little effect on most kindergartners who have not learned their value. But kindergartners who bring home "As" are likely to be praised by their parents and possibly even given tangible rewards. As a result of being paired with consequences that are already reinforcing, "As" take on reinforcing qualities that are independent of the rewards with which they were originally paired.

This process also works for punishment. Most young students value teachers' positive attention, but after the first few grades of school, children who appear to be the teachers' pets are sometimes teased or rejected by classmates. What once served as a positive reinforcer becomes punishment by being linked to an undesirable consequence. Therefore, a child who previously sought teacher approval may cease engaging in behaviors that gain teacher attention.

If a previously reinforced behavior ceases to be reinforced, its rate of occurrence decreases; the desired behavior becomes **extinguished.** Thus, for example, if the attention of the boy described previously does not continue to be reinforced, he will stop paying attention (i.e., attention will be extinguished). Although a reinforcer needs to be contingent on a desired behavior from time to time, reinforcers do not have to follow every occurrence of the behavior. To the contrary, behaviors that are reinforced **intermittently** or partially (rather than every time the desired behavior occurs) actually take longer to extinguish when reinforcement ceases altogether.

Another reinforcement principle explains the conditions under which behavior that has been reinforced will occur. Skinner found that unrelated external cues became signals for the availability of reinforcement or punishment. For example, if a rat is reinforced for pushing a lever only when a particular type of light is on, the rat will begin to push the lever when the light is turned on and will not push it without the light. The light, according to Skinner, serves as a **discriminative stimulus,** and the lever-pushing response is under **stimulus control.** Thus, according to the principle of stimulus control, stimuli that become associated with consequences can cause behavior, and this behavior may occur only in the presence of those stimuli. The stimuli that are present when reinforcement occurs serve as a "signal" for the consequences of the behavior.

The principle of stimulus control applies to humans as well as rats. For example, a teacher standing in front of the classroom may cause students to pay attention if, in the past, students were rewarded for paying attention or punished for not paying attention when the teacher stood in front of the class. A change in the stimulus, such as a substitute teacher or a student standing in front of the class, may not cue students to pay attention because these individuals previously were not associated with positive reinforcers or punishment. This principle may explain why discipline sometimes deteriorates when the teacher leaves the room for a few minutes or when a substitute takes over a class.

Fortunately, it is not necessary to reinforce positively every desired behavior. The effects of positive reinforcement on one response **generalize** to similar responses. In essence, reinforcement for a particular behavior affects not only that behavior but also a class of behaviors. For example, the probability of a student paying attention during a social studies lesson may be increased by rewarding him for paying attention during a mathematics lesson. A child who is punished for disrupting the class by throwing paper airplanes, as a consequence, may be less likely to disrupt the class by other means as well as by the specific behavior for which the punishment was received.

As mentioned in Chapter 2, reinforcement theory is considered "mechanistic" because no reference is made to such unobservable variables as choice, beliefs, expectations, or emotions (Graham & Weiner, 1996). The emphasis is placed exclusively on the environment and observable behaviors. A strict reinforcement theorist, such as Skinner (1974), assumes that individuals' behavior at any given time is determined fully by their reinforcement history and the contingencies in the present environment. Thoughts and feelings are irrelevant. According to the reinforcement theory, we should look only at the environment to understand behavior, not to inner thoughts such as self-perceptions of competence and expectations for success, or to emotions such as fear and anxiety.

Strict reinforcement theorists, therefore, do not consider motivation as a characteristic of the individual. Individuals are considered "motivated" only inasmuch as they exhibit behaviors that are believed or known to enhance learning, such as paying attention or working on assignments. Faced with a student who is not working in school, a reinforcement theorist asks, "What's wrong with the environment?" rather than "What's wrong with this student?" The only way to change a student's behavior is to change the reward contingencies (consequences to behavior) in the classroom.

IMPLICATIONS FOR EDUCATIONAL PRACTICE

The educational implications of reinforcement theory for maximizing desired learning behaviors are straightforward. The teacher makes positive reinforcers contingent on desired behavior and punishments contingent on undesired behavior. The process of using reinforcement principles to change behavior is referred to as **behavior modification.** The simplicity of this theory is no doubt a major reason for its long-standing central role in educational psychology and widespread classroom application. (See Sulzer-Azaroff & Mayer, 1986, and Walker, Greenwood, & Terry, 1994, for discussions of the use of behavioral strategies in the classroom.)

The teacher's first task is to determine what constitutes rewards and punishment for any given student. To do this, teachers can try to make different consequences contingent on behavior, observe students' responses to each, and continue to use those that increase desired behavior and decrease undesired behavior. Rewards that are common in American classrooms include praise, good grades, public recognition, and privileges. Disapproval, bad grades, public humiliation, and staying after school are commonly used as punishment. I also have observed teachers who provide students with the opportunity to clean the blackboard, do extra challenging math problems, and read a poem to the class contingent on some desired behavior. In one kindergarten class I visited, the teacher explained that the children were being especially good because homework was given only to the students who behaved well all day!

Teachers sometimes make positive reinforcers and punishment contingent on the whole class behaving or not behaving a particular way. This can produce peer pressure for desirable behavior. For example, a teacher might make a popcorn party on Friday afternoons contingent on the class completing all their work and make a shortened recess for the whole class a result of too many students failing to pay attention during a lesson.

Reinforcement affects a particular behavior only if it is contingent on that behavior. The teacher, therefore, must reinforce only desirable behavior and ignore or punish undesirable behavior. Clearly, if maximum learning is the goal, behaviors that enhance learning need to be reinforced and behaviors that inhibit learning need to be ignored or punished. Accordingly, students should be reinforced for paying attention to the teacher or the present task, persisting with tasks that are difficult, selecting challenging tasks, completing tasks, and engaging in other behaviors that enhance learning. Such behaviors as inattentiveness, giving up quickly, selecting very easy tasks, or turning in incomplete assignments should be ignored or punished. Teachers also may reinforce helpfulness, generosity, picking up trash, or other socially desirable behaviors.

Rewards and punishment might be used to change the behavior of some of the children described in Chapter 1. According to reinforcement theory, a teacher who wants to increase Safe Sally's risk taking should make positive reinforcers contingent on her initial approach to challenging learning situations rather than on performing well. A different strategy would be required to improve Helpless Hannah's behavior. For Hannah, rewards need to be contingent on completing assignments.

This approach, however, can work only if Hannah actually completes an assignment. What can a teacher do if a desired behavior never occurs? This problem is particularly serious for students who almost never engage in desired behavior. To address this problem, individuals using reinforcement methods have developed a strategy called **shaping.** Skinner used this strategy to teach pigeons to play Ping-Pong. Needless to say, if Skinner had waited for his pigeons to begin a game of Ping-Pong to allow him to reinforce their behaviors, he would have had a long wait. Instead, he began by giving a pellet of food to the pigeon for performing the first behavior in a sequence of behaviors required for playing Ping-Pong. When that initial behavior began to occur frequently, he was able to reinforce the pigeon for the second behavior in the sequence, and so on.

This same strategy can be used to shape behavior in a child. The teacher first makes clear to the child what the desired behavior is and then begins reinforcing any behavior that approximates it. If a troublesome student looks in the teacher's direction, the teacher may praise him for paying attention. Presumably the student, as a result of the reinforcement, will look more often in the teacher's direction. The teacher then may praise the student for maintaining a gaze in his direction for more than 1 minute and gradually increase the length of time required for reinforcement. Thus, the teacher "shapes" the student's actions in the direction of the desired behavior—paying attention to him for an extended period of time.

Because she has become completely disengaged from classroom activities, shaping would probably be necessary to get Hannah to finish assignments. The teacher might begin by praising her for opening her book and taking out her pencil after an assignment is given. This, according to reinforcement theory, should increase the probability of her preparing to work on assignments. The teacher then could praise Hannah only for actually beginning the assignment (e.g., doing a few problems), and then "up the ante"—praise her for persisting with an assignment. If praise serves as a positive reinforcer for Hannah, she eventually should complete an assignment—which the teacher also can reward.

Token Economies

In some classrooms teachers have developed elaborate **token economies**—formalized systems of behavior modification. The essential components of a token economy are (1) tokens (that can be exchanged for a reward), (2) target behaviors, (3) rules for earning and losing tokens, and (4) "back-up consequences" for which tokens can be exchanged. Tokens can be anything that is easily counted: points, play money, chips, stars, or check marks. They have no inherent value; rather, their worth is based on their ability to be exchanged for valued "back-up conse-quences," such as candy, toys, trinkets, money, extra recess, or movies. Although token economies have been used primarily to improve social behavior—such as talking out of turn, refusing to sit down, and poor attendance—they also have been used to improve assignment completion and accuracy. A token economy can be implemented with one student, a small group of students, or the whole class.

For programs designed to reduce undesirable behaviors (e.g., talking out of turn), students initially are given a set of tokens and have to give back a prespeci-fied amount for engaging in each undesirable behavior. In programs designed to increase desirable behaviors (e.g., completing assignments), students are given tokens for exhibiting the target behavior.

All programs include specific rules for earning or losing tokens, which may be simple or complicated. Systems can be created to increase a single behavior or a combination of behaviors. For example, the teacher who desires to increase both task completion and task accuracy may allow students to earn one token for com-pleting an assignment and two for completing it with 80 percent accuracy. A vari-able number of tokens may be earned for different degrees of accuracy.

A program developed by Cohen (1973) for a difficult group of adolescent boys in a residential home illustrates how token economies are implemented (see also Blue, Madsen, & Heimberg, 1981). Most of the students in Cohen's study had dropped out of school and many had been found guilty of crimes. They were given points that could be exchanged for goods, services, and special privileges, such as recreational time in a lounge, books, magazines, extra clothing, mail-order supplies, a private shower, or a private room for sleeping and entertaining. (This list demonstrates the importance of tailoring reinforcers to the particular indi-viduals whose behavior one desires to change.) Reinforcement was made contin-gent on academic achievement and behaviors presumed to enhance achievement. Despite a long history of failed attempts to increase the motivation of these boys, their academic achievement improved dramatically under this token economy system.

Another form of a token economy is illustrated by Alschuler's (1968) perfor-mance contracting. In one program, students were advanced $2,000 in play money. Students determined their own performance goals, which they stated in a written contract. The higher the goals, the greater the payoff; students lost money for not meeting their goals, or for turning in assignments late. Consequently, un-realistically high goals generally resulted in losses and unnecessarily low goals resulted in very low payoffs. The system, therefore, encouraged moderate risks to produce the greatest amount of learning. In one study of fifth graders, Alschuler observed an average gain of 3 years of growth on standardized mathematics tests in 1 academic year.

Different procedures for implementing token economies are required for students of different ages. High school students may be able to comprehend com-plicated systems and delay exchanging tokens for the back-up consequence for a relatively long period of time. Young children cannot understand or analyze complicated systems, and they are likely to lose interest in the tokens if the exchange is delayed more than a few days.[1]

Token economies initially were developed primarily as a procedure of last resort with clinical, frequently institutionalized populations. They now have been applied to less severely disturbed populations and children in regular classrooms. Studies have examined the effectiveness of token economy programs in changing behavior, such as attention and persistence with tasks. Most studies find that tangible rewards, systematically applied, can produce major behavior changes, even in the most recalcitrant subjects (see Abramowitz & O'Leary, 1991; Kazdin, 1975; O'Leary, 1978; Williams, Williams, & McLaughlin, 1991).

Research on the maintenance and generalization of desired behaviors in token programs is less positive. Kazdin (1988), Kazdin and Bootzin (1972), and O'Leary and Drabman (1971) reviewed data that assess how well behavioral changes are maintained after token programs are withdrawn, and how well the desired behaviors generalize to other settings in which tokens are not administered. They conclude that although effects are sometimes evident a few years after the program is concluded, removing the tokens often leads to a rapid return to **baseline behaviors** (behaviors preceding the implementation of the token economy program). They also report that behavior outside of the setting in which the tokens were given (sometimes referred to as "transfer") generally is not affected by the token economy (see also Kohn, 1993). These and other limitations of external reinforcement are discussed next.

Problems with Reward and Punishment

Teachers usually find that the promise of a reward or the threat of punishment can affect most children's behaviors in the classroom. Behavioral methods have been particularly successful with children who behave extremely maladaptively in school settings. Indeed, it is hard to imagine a well-functioning classroom in which desirable behaviors are not reinforced in some way and undesirable behaviors are not ignored or at least occasionally punished.

But research on the use of rewards to control student behavior suggests that rewards should be used thoughtfully and sparingly. Inappropriate application of reinforcement principles can affect behavior adversely; overdependence on rewards and punishment to influence achievement behavior can have long-term negative effects on student motivation (Kohn, 1993). We now turn to a summary

---

[1]I discovered the importance of frequent exchanges when I tried to implement a token economy to motivate my 5-year-old daughter to get dressed for school in the morning. She was allowed to put a star on a calendar each day that she was dressed by 7:30 A.M. I explained that when she earned twenty stars I would take her to a toy store and she could pick out a toy. The implementation of the star system had an immediate and dramatic effect on her behavior, but after about 1 week she lost interest in the stars and we returned to our daily morning conflict. Twenty days without linking the stars to a tangible reward was simply too long.

of some of the problems that teachers need to consider when using rewards and punishment.

EFFECTIVENESS OF REWARDS

Consider first the problem of finding an effective reward. Rewards used in most American classrooms are not universally effective. Grades, for example, are not effective for some children in early elementary school because these children find no intrinsic value in them. Unless the value placed on grades by teachers is reinforced by parents and peers, even older students are unlikely to work for such a symbolic reward. For some students good grades are not sufficiently desirable to inspire high effort. Satisfied Santos (see Chapter 1), for example, is satisfied with a grade that requires a level of performance below what he could achieve with a little more effort; for him, higher grades are not reinforcing. The teacher who perseveres in promising good grades as a reward for positive achievement behaviors, and in threatening bad grades for negative ones, will not obtain desired behaviors in students like Santos.

The effectiveness of grades and other symbols of high performance as reinforcers declines for some students during adolescence. In early adolescence peer approval becomes increasingly important and adult approval less critical. Unless peer acceptance, to some degree, is associated with high achievement, as has been found in studies of younger children (e.g., Leonard, Reyes, Danner, & de la Torre, 1994), grades may not have value. For rebellious or alienated adolescents who explicitly devalue success in school, high grades may be perceived as embarrassing—a punishment, rather than a reward.

Likewise, some consequences that the teacher administers as punishment actually serve as reinforcers. For example, some students desire any form of teacher or peer attention, including negative attention (e.g., threats, nagging, teasing). For these students, a reprimand, which the teacher believes serves as punishment, actually reinforces undesirable behavior.

Recall that Cohen (1973) used private showers, magazines, and clothing, not good grades, to reinforce achievement behavior among delinquent boys. In a residential center such tangible rewards may be available and appropriate, but in most regular schools they are not. Alternatives to grades—such as candy and even money—are sometimes used, but there are obvious problems with using such reinforcers in regular schools, regardless of how effective they might be.

ACCESSIBILITY OF REWARDS

If grades are based on competitive criteria (and they usually are), high grades will not be earned by all students. By definition, all students cannot be above average. Moreover, students begin classes with varying levels of preparation, and some students learn new concepts more quickly than others. A few students, such as Hannah, will find that they cannot get a high grade, regardless of how hard they work. Defensive Dave (see Chapter 1) doubts that he can earn good grades, and thus does not exhibit the behaviors his teachers desire. Other students, like Santos, will find that they can get a respectable grade with little effort. Then there are students like Sally for whom only "As" work as rewards, and who avoid situations in which an "A" is not ensured—the very situations that would enhance their competencies the most.

The threat of a bad grade (which for some is a "D" and for others an "A–") will not affect the behavior of students who believe that bad grades are unavoidable, whatever they do. The promise of a good grade will not increase the effort of students who believe that they will achieve a good grade whether or not they exert much effort. This principle holds for any reward that can be earned easily by some children and only with great difficulty (or not at all) by others.

The principle applies to rewards that have become common in American schools as incentives for academic achievement, including academic awards, "student of the year," vouchers for toys or hamburgers, and scholarships (Webb, Covington, & Guthrie, 1993). Such rewards will motivate only the students for whom the reward is genuinely accessible, sometimes a very small proportion and often those who are already working hard.[2] There are also problems of timing. Many rewards, such as scholarships for college, are too far in the distant future in the minds of most children to motivate the kinds of daily activities (e.g., finishing homework, studying for tests) that are required to achieve the reward.

Perceived unavailability of positive reinforcers explains why teachers often get a false impression that a student does not desire conventional rewards. Teachers often express dismay at a student's apparent unwillingness to engage in behaviors that will be positively reinforced. I have heard teachers complain: "I have told him over and over that if he would just put a little effort into his work he could get good grades; he just doesn't seem to care one way or the other." Careful observations of these troublesome students often reveal that they virtually never receive positive reinforcement, even when they do exert a little effort. Many actually care a great deal and would be delighted to receive teacher praise or good grades, but they perceive neither of these positive reinforcers as being genuinely available. It is not uncommon for such students to resort to alternative, and often undesirable, means of gaining recognition. Misbehaving to get negative teacher attention is not their preferred mode of operation; it is used as a last resort.

REWARDING DESIRED BEHAVIOR

Another problem with relying on reinforcement is that only observable behavior can be reinforced. Some "behaviors," such as attention, are not entirely observ-

---

[2]An analogous argument could be made for merit pay for teachers. If it is available only to a small percentage (e.g., 5 percent), most teachers would not perceive merit pay to be realistically available. Therefore, it would not serve to motivate most teachers. Individuals must perceive that reinforcement genuinely is available to them for it to have any positive effect on their behavior.

able. As mentioned in Chapter 2, students can look as if they are engaged intensely in intellectual tasks while they actually are reliving the home runs they made at recess or planning their strategies for asking a particular girl to go to the junior prom. Teachers directly can reinforce students for looking in their direction, but it is difficult to reinforce students for listening or thinking about the information. Teachers also can reinforce observable outcomes, such as good performance on a test, that are usually associated with paying attention. But if the student had cheated, or guessed, or did not have to study to do well, the teacher will inadvertently reward cheating, guessing, or low effort. And, consistent with reinforcement theory, studies show that rewarding performance that required low levels of effort fosters relatively low levels of effort (Eisenberger, 1992).

If the teacher's goal is to increase effort, then effort must be rewarded. Studies have shown that rewarding serious effort and high (but achievable) levels of performance enhances effort and the quality of performance (Eisenberger, 1992). But effort, like attention, is not easy to assess in a classroom with many students. Teachers usually are not able to observe the level of effort directly, and even when they can, students (e.g., Dave) can be very skillful at giving a false impression of intense effort. To make accurate judgments teachers need very good observation skills (and eyes in the back of their heads). Most of the time effort has to be inferred from performance, which to be accurate requires a very good knowledge of students' skill levels. It is often difficult to distinguish poor performance despite high effort from poor performance caused by low effort. As a consequence, for some children punishment follows high effort and, as reinforcement theorists claim, their effort decreases.

NEGATIVE EFFECTS OF REWARDS ON BEHAVIOR

In several studies rewards have been shown to have negative effects on individuals' willingness to attempt challenging tasks. In one study, for example, some children were offered an extrinsic reward for correct answers and others were not. Subjects who were offered extrinsic rewards chose significantly less difficult problems than subjects who were not offered rewards for correct answers (Harter, 1978b). Thus, under the reward condition children were less likely to select a challenging problem. Or, as Kohn (1993) pointed out, if children are offered a pizza for reading a certain number of books, how likely are they to select long, difficult books, and how carefully are they likely to read whatever they choose? (See Chapter 10 for further discussion of these effects.)

Extrinsic rewards can have negative effects on teachers' as well as students' behaviors. Garbarino (1975) described a study in which sixth-grade children served as tutors for first-grade children. Tutors who were offered rewards for their success in tutoring exhibited a more "instrumental" orientation toward their pupils. They were more demanding and critical, and created a more negative emotional atmosphere in the tutoring setting than tutors who were not offered rewards. The rewards presumably caused these sixth-grade tutors to focus exclusively on their students' performance. Tutors consequently neglected behaviors such as nurturing and giving encouragement that may have seemed unnecessary, but actually would have helped them accomplish their goals.[3]

SHORT-LIVED EFFECTIVENESS

A fifth problem with external reinforcement is that its effectiveness is often short lived. Rewards may be effective in eliciting desired behaviors, but if the only reason for engaging in a behavior is to obtain a reward, the behavior will occur only under reward conditions. Indeed, evidence discussed in Chapter 10 suggests that under some circumstances when a reward is given, and then later withdrawn, the desired behavior occurs even less frequently than it would have occurred if no reward had ever been offered.

This limitation in the use of external reinforcement becomes increasingly important as children advance in school. The curriculum in the early elementary grades generally is broken down into small units with frequent opportunities for positive reinforcement. Most assignments are completed in less than half an hour and are reviewed by the teacher soon after. In the upper grades, assignments are generally larger, less frequent, and span a longer time period. Compare, for example, typical language arts assignments for elementary versus high school students. The younger students may, in 1 day, be given as many as three short assignments for which they can receive reinforcement (e.g., a grade, a star, or teacher praise). High school students are more likely to be asked to write a theme based on assigned reading once every week or two. Consequently, although young children can be reinforced for every subcomponent of an academic task, older students must go through many steps without any reinforcement (i.e., they must read the assigned literature, think about it, make an outline, write, and perhaps rewrite the theme). The older student is not rewarded for the several intermediate tasks that are required to complete the assignment.

For students who enter college, many rewards (e.g., obtaining a degree, admittance into graduate school, getting a good job) are far removed from the immediate situation requiring achievement behaviors. Even within a given course, a midterm and a final examination are often the only "products" of a semester of academic labor that the professor sees. Consequently, they are the only opportunities students have to be reinforced. The promise of such distant rewards will not be effective for students who are accustomed to being reinforced daily for every academic effort.

Reinforcing behavior also conveys the message that the behavior is not worth doing for its own sake. Consider the different messages given by the

---

[3]It is possible that rewards to teachers made contingent on the achievement test performance of their students also can result in an "instrumental" orientation—a focus on behavior directly and obviously related to achievement test performance (e.g., drill and practice), and a neglect of variables, such as a positive social environment and opportunities to engage in creative problem solving, that may not enhance achievement directly, but in the long term may be extremely important.

teacher who tells students that they will be allowed to spend 15 minutes at the computer if they finish their math assignment versus the teacher who announces that students who complete their 15 minutes on the computer can go to recess early. The former teacher is much more likely than the latter to foster the perception that computers are fun.

Providing positive reinforcements for all intellectual activities in school ultimately can undermine students' desires to be involved in any nonschool-related learning activities. I once gave a copy of *Tom Sawyer* to an eighth-grade boy. He graciously accepted the gift, but added that he already had written a book report for his English class that semester so he would not be reading the book until the next semester. It apparently did not occur to him that a book could be read for reasons other than getting a grade in school. Sally is another example of a student who has learned to participate in learning activities only for extrinsic rewards. She does not engage in learning activities outside of the classroom unless the end results are graded or are likely to bring some kind of social recognition. Even the novels she selects to read over the summer are on the high school reading list and may be included in the English curriculum the next year.

EFFECTS OF PUNISHMENT

When the carrot approach is ineffective, it is natural to turn to the stick. Fear of punishment, such as public humiliation or low grades, can motivate positive work behaviors, but it also can cause anxiety and alienation, which hinder learning. Many children, such as Dave, spend considerably more energy trying to avoid punishment than they do trying to understand the curriculum or learn new skills. For example, they avoid volunteering answers for fear of being criticized. Some students turn in completed assignments with answers that they know are incorrect rather than attempting to figure out the right answers; they have learned that punishment is more severe for not turning in an assignment on time than for poor performance. Other students, like Anxious Alma (see Chapter 1), become paralyzed by their fear of humiliation or low grades.

Astute classroom observers have described these and other more elaborate measures that some children take to avoid punishment (e.g., Covington, 1992; Covington & Beery, 1976; Holt, 1964; see Chapter 6). Most of these behaviors accomplish the student's immediate goal, but they are self-defeating in the long run because they do not promote learning.

Since the mid-1980s, there has been a proliferation of school-, district-, and even statewide sanctions for poor academic performance or attendance (Webb et al., 1993). Many states have "no pass/no play" rules requiring a certain level of school performance to participate in sports. Some states also are implementing "no pass/no drive" regulations that preclude poorly performing students from obtaining a driver's license. There is, as far as I know, no evidence on the effects of these policies on students' academic effort and school achievement. They have considerable face value, but their limitations and drawbacks need to be weighed against whatever positive effects are expected. The no pass/no drive law has the same limitation as rewards that come late in the educational game; they may be too far off to motivate day-to-day behaviors necessary for school success. Playing sports is often the only reason some relatively poor-performing students stay in school, and the no pass/no play rule effectively could push out some students who otherwise might have persisted to graduate, learning something if not excelling, and keeping the door open for further education.

Students need to be made accountable for their work, and there should be some consequences for low effort, but punishment has to be used judiciously for the positive effect to outweigh the negative effect. And, to the degree possible, punishment should not be given for poor performance if there is evidence that the student has done her best. Research suggests also that some punishments work better than others. For example, reprimands given calmly, firmly, consistently, and immediately have been found to be more effective than those that are emotional or delayed (Abramowitz & O'Leary, 1991).

Summary

Applying the reinforcement theory effectively in the classroom requires considerable thought. In addition to making sure that reinforcement and punishment are implemented in the most effective ways, teachers need to be vigilant about possible inconsistencies between the behavior they desire and the reinforcement contingencies in their classrooms. A teacher once told me that he valued individual initiative and creativity and was disappointed that his students were passive and conforming. His students' behaviors, however, were predictable from his grading system, which was incompatible with the values he espoused. Students lost points by failing to follow arbitrary rules, and their grades were determined almost entirely by accuracy. There were no rewards for personal initiative or creativity. To the contrary, students could be punished for straying slightly from, or even going beyond, the teacher's directions.

It is useful for teachers to reflect on the kinds of rewards and punishments they use, the behavior on which these consequences are contingent, and the degree to which they are available to all students. Appendix 3–A is designed to help teachers in this reflective process, which occasionally will reveal inconsistencies between values and actions.

Praise is featured in the next section because it is the most common reward used in educational settings, and because it illustrates the problems, limitations, and practical implications of using reinforcement effectively.

PRAISE

Brophy (1981) defined praise as "reactions that go beyond simple feedback about appropriateness or correctness of behavior" (p. 5). Simply indicating to a student that her answer is correct would not be considered praise. Congratulating the student for a right answer, or saying, "good job," or "you're really good at this" are examples of praise. Praise serves as a reinforcer for most students, especially very young children. According to the principles of reinforcement theory, behaviors followed by praise should increase in frequency.

Like other types of reinforcement, however, praise is not valued universally by psychologists. Kamii (1984) suggested that praise, as it commonly is used, may discourage children from developing personal criteria for judging their own work and may lead to dependency on adult authority figures. Schwartz (1996) claimed that praise sends a message that adults "are always passing judgment on children's work and ideas and . . . are the ones to decide if things are good or bad" (p. 397). Others have claimed that because learning is intrinsically rewarding, praise is at best superfluous and can interfere with the natural disposition to learn (Kohn, 1993; Montessori, 1964; see also Chapter 8), or that it can interfere with the goal of genuine achievement, if given too freely (Damon, 1995). Another objection concerns the differential status it creates between the person giving the praise and the person receiving it, which teachers who desire a more egalitarian relationship want to avoid (Brophy, 1981; Kohn, 1993). The remainder of this chapter discusses how to use praise in a way that effectively minimizes the kinds of negative effects previously mentioned.

Consider first the principle that reinforcers, including praise, must be contingent on the behavior the teacher desires to maintain or increase. Brophy (1981) claimed that praise often is not contingent on good performance or even on high effort, especially among teachers who have low expectations for student learning and of students who are typically poor performers. Anderson, Evertson, and Brophy (1979) found, for example, that the rate of praise following reading turns containing mistakes was slightly higher than the rate of praise following errorless reading turns. No doubt, teachers use praise to encourage poorly performing students to try harder. But if praise is not contingent on high effort or good performance, it will not increase the likelihood of either one. If poor performance is just as likely to be praised as good performance, or if students are praised regardless of their effort, students learn that praise is not based on anything they do and they discount it.

Praise also must be credible to be effective. Praise that is not contingent on effort or good performance, is not backed up, or is contradicted by nonverbal, expressive behavior is not believable. Brophy, Evertson, Anderson, Baum, and Crawford (1976) found that troublesome students sometimes received as much verbal praise as successful students. Aspects of the teachers' nonverbal behaviors, such as stern or distracted expressions on their faces, however, often indicated negative emotions or that the teachers really were not paying attention while they were praising students.

Praise given noncontingently and praise lacking in credibility, under certain circumstances, actually can have negative effects on students' self-confidence. Praise for succeeding with a very easy task, for example, may be interpreted as an indication that the teacher has a low perception of the student's ability (Meyer,

1982, 1992). This interpretation is understandable in light of evidence that teachers tend to reward high effort (Covington & Omelich, 1979b). Thus, if a teacher praises a student, presumably she believes the student exerted some effort, and high effort to succeed on an easy task suggests low ability. (See Chapter 12 for further discussion of the paradoxical effects of praise.)

In contrast to older children and adults, who sometimes see negative implications in praise, research suggests that young children are more oriented toward pleasing adults, are more responsive to praise, and tend to accept it at face value (Meyer, 1992; Meyer et al., 1979; Stipek, 1984a). A compelling demonstration of this is seen in a study by Meid (1971) in which 6- and 10-year-old children were given either high-, medium-, or low-objective information (i.e., scores) for their past performance, and either praise, no comment, or a mildly negative comment. The younger children's expectations for performance on a subsequent task were based entirely on the social, verbal feedback, even when it conflicted with the objective feedback. The older elementary school-age children took both objective feedback and social feedback into account in their expectancy statements.

Although children in the elementary grades may accept praise at face value, young children who are praised when they have not exerted some effort will learn that effort is not necessary for reinforcement. There are, therefore, negative consequences to indiscriminate praise, even for very young children.

Praise can be used to inform students of the teacher's standards and to focus their attention on particular aspects of their performance. The elementary teacher who says, "I like the way your letters are all in between the lines," or "What nice, neat handwriting," is providing information on what she values. This information function is best accomplished with praise that is specific and informative. A general "good job," is appreciated by most students. But more informative praise (e.g., "Your paper is well organized, clearly written, creative, persuasive, well researched, and neat") provides information on the teacher's standards and guidance for future assignments.

Praise also can orient students toward particular kinds of standards. Praise that focuses students' attention on their own improvement or effort (e.g., "Your handwriting has improved"; "You obviously put a lot of time into this"; or "I think you really are beginning to understand this material") is better than praise that encourages social comparison (e.g., "This is one of the best papers in the class"). The former sets a high personal standard that all students can achieve. All children can improve, and if they are praised for improvement, they must continue to progress to receive further praise. Children who are praised for relative performance need to continue to perform better than classmates, which for some children is impossible and for others requires neither effort nor improvement.

Praise for outcomes that are achieved with little effort gives students the message that effort is not valued. This is unproductive because optimal performance requires effort. Praise should be given, therefore, only for outcomes that require some effort to achieve, and it sometimes should be given for effort alone, regardless of the outcome.

Students should be encouraged to work for their own purposes, not to please the teacher or for external rewards. Comments such as, "You're really getting good at figuring out these problems," are better than "I'm really pleased at how well you are doing." The first focuses the student's attention on skill development, the latter on external approval.

Table 3-1 is Brophy's (1981) summary of effective versus ineffective ways to use praise. Most of these principles apply not only to praise, but also to any form of external reinforcement.

It is difficult for teachers to monitor how they use praise because usually it is given spontaneously in the context of complex interactions in the classroom. It is useful, therefore, for teachers to have an aide, another teacher, or a parent observe them and give feedback. The form in Appendix 3–B is provided to help in this process.

CONCLUSION

Reinforcement techniques are used in virtually all classroom settings. When teachers praise students, give grades or gold stars, put students' papers on public display, or require students to stay after school for disruptive behavior, they are applying principles of reinforcement theory. The same is true for parents who praise children for cleaning their rooms and deny privileges for breaking rules. The basic notion that positive reinforcement increases the frequency of desired behavior and punishment decreases the likelihood of undesirable behavior underlies all of these techniques. (See Table 3-2 for a summary of terms.)

Reinforcement strategies can be very effective in influencing students' behaviors and are invaluable tools in educational settings. In particular, promising a reward is useful in getting children to try something they believe they will not like or will not be able to do, or to engage in an activity that simply cannot be made intrinsically interesting.[4]

Although strict reinforcement theorists would not discuss the effects of rewards on students' thoughts, less traditional theorists might point out that rewards have the added value of conveying the teachers' values. By observing which behaviors are rewarded and which are not, students learn what behaviors the teacher believes are important. Thus, for example, students get a different message in classrooms in which the teacher rewards effort and persistence regardless of the outcome than they get in classrooms in which the only thing that counts is

---

[4]My daughter was frustrated with how long mathematics assignments took because she had not memorized the multiplication tables. This was despite my efforts to make practicing multiplication interesting. I finally resorted to the most tangible of rewards—money! I'm not recommending it, unless all else fails, but in her case it was very effective.

the end result. For those of us who believe that values are important and that children often emulate and internalize the values they see in significant adults, this is an important process. (See Chapter 9 for a more extended discussion of values.)

But, as we have seen, there are costs associated with overreliance on reinforcement as a means of motivating behavior. Chapter 4 describes more recent theoretical developments as well as new classroom applications that are designed to maximize the benefits of reinforcement while minimizing these costs.

TABLE 3-1   Guidelines for Effective Praise

Effective Praise

1. Is delivered contingently.
2. Specifies the particulars of the accomplishment.
3. Shows spontaneity, variety, and other signs of credibility; suggests clear attention to the student's accomplishment.
4. Rewards attainment of specified performance criteria (which can include effort criteria).
5. Provides information to students about their competence or the value of their accomplishments.
6. Orients students toward better appreciation of their own task-related behavior and thinking about problem solving.
7. Uses students' own prior accomplishments as the context for describing present accomplishments.
8. Is given in recognition of noteworthy effort or success at difficult (for this student) tasks.
9. Attributes success to effort and ability, implying that similar successes can be expected in the future.
10. Fosters endogenous attributions (students believe that they expend effort on the task because they enjoy the task and/or want to develop task-relevant skills).
11. Focuses students' attention on their own task-relevant behavior.
12. Fosters appreciation of and desirable attributions about task-relevant behavior after the process is completed.

Ineffective Praise

1. Is delivered randomly or unsystematically.
2. Is restricted to global positive reactions.
3. Shows a bland uniformity which suggests a conditioned response made with minimal attention.
4. Rewards mere participation without consideration of performance processes or outcomes.
5. Provides no information at all or gives students information about their status.
6. Orients students toward comparing themselves with others and thinking about competing.
7. Uses the accomplishments of peers as the context for describing students' present accomplishments.
8. Is given without regard to the effort expended or the meaning of the accomplishment (for this student).
9. Attributes success to ability alone or to external factors such as luck or easy tasks.
10. Fosters exogenous attributions (students believe that they expend effort on the task for external reasons—to please the teacher, win a competition or reward, etc.).
11. Focuses students' attention on the teacher as an external authority figure who is manipulating them.
12. Intrudes into the ongoing process, distracting attention from task-relevant behavior.

TABLE 3-2   Summary of Terms

Term	Definition	Example
Law of effect	Principle of reinforcement theory in which behavior is assumed to be determined by its consequences	Students complete assignments because this behavior is rewarded
Positive reinforcer (rewards)	A consequence that increases the probability of the behavior on which it is made contingent	Good grade; star; teacher praise; teacher attention
Punishment	A consequence that decreases the probability of the behavior on which it is made contingent	Bad grade; loss of privilege; public criticism
Negative reinforcer	A consequence that increases the probability of a behavior if terminated or diminished	Teacher's angry stare; social isolation
Social reinforcement	Positive reinforcer linked to social approval	Praise; smile; pat on the back
Secondary reinforcers	Consequences that take on reinforcement properties by being paired with primary reinforcers	Grades (originally paired with praise)
Extinction	The termination of a behavior as the result of terminating positive reinforcers	Students stop doing homework when teacher stops giving stars for completed homework
Intermittent (partial) reinforcement	The reinforcement of some but not all occurrences of a response	Teacher praising some but not all correct answers
Discriminative stimulus	A stimulus that acquires the ability to control behavior because of its association with reinforcement or punishment	Teacher standing in front of the classroom
Stimulus control	Behavior is influenced by the presence of a stimulus that has previously been associated with reward or punishment	Students become quiet when the teacher enters the room
Generalization	The principle that a behavior will or will not occur because a similar behavior has been positively reinforced or punished	A student who is praised for neatness on a math assignment writes her spelling words neatly

(continued)

TABLE 3-2 *(Continued)*

Term	Definition	Example
Behavior modification	The process of using reinforcement principles to change behavior	Calling on a student when she raises her hand to answer a question and ignoring her when she calls out an answer
Shaping	Providing reinforcement for behaviors that increasingly approximate the desired behavior	Praising a child for opening a book, then for beginning, and then for completing assignments
Token economy	A system in which individuals receive or lose tokens that can be exchanged for a reward	A poker chip is earned for every assignment completed, and later exchanged for added recess
Baseline behaviors	Frequency of behavior previous to intervention designed to increase or decrease it by reward or punishment	Proportion of homework assignments completed before a token economy intervention is implemented

Social Cognitive Theory

INTRODUCING COGNITIONS

Bandura (1977a, 1977b, 1986) recognized the powerful effects of reinforcement and punishment on individuals' behaviors, but objected to the notion that individuals are regulated entirely by external forces—that they are passive respondents to environmental contingencies. As an alternative to strict reinforcement theory, he developed a social cognitive theory in which cognitions are assumed to mediate the effects of the environment on human behavior. According to Bandura, individuals' expectations regarding reinforcement for a behavior are more important than whether they previously have been reinforced for it. He claimed, furthermore, that reinforcement history does not have a direct effect on individuals' cognitions. Rather, it is filtered through personal memory, interpretations, and biases. Social cognitive theorists, therefore, portray individuals as actively processing events and developing expectations regarding reinforcement, rather than as automatically behaving according to previous reinforcement contingencies. This chapter summarizes the basic elements of social cognitive theory. Consistent with the theory's emphasis on an individual's personal agency, it also describes applications of reinforcement theory that are designed to help students learn to control their own behaviors and enhance their learning.

Studies on the importance of expectations and beliefs found that when individuals are not aware of the contingencies of reinforcement, their behavior is not affected by it (Dulany, 1968), and if individuals are led to believe that previously reinforced behavior will not be reinforced in the future, they will not engage in such behavior (Estes, 1972). Beliefs about future reinforcement appear to be more important determinants of behavior than actual reinforcement histories.

Social cognitive theorists assume that even personal experience with reinforcement and punishment is not required for behaviors to be manifested. This assumption solves a problem that strict reinforcement theorists have in explaining new behavior. According to traditional reinforcement theory, individuals' behaviors are determined by their own reinforcement histories. Children attend to the teacher and complete assignments because they have been reinforced for these behaviors in the past. Reinforcement theorists rely on the principle of shaping to explain how children "learn" new behaviors, behaviors that previously have not been reinforced. But this explanation is not entirely satisfying because it would be too cumbersome for every behavior to be shaped by reinforcing successive approximations.

Bandura and Walters (1963), therefore, proposed that individuals sometimes exhibit behaviors because they observe other individuals being reinforced for these behaviors. They refer to this process as **vicarious learning.** This process is illustrated in a classic study by Bandura (1965). Children were shown one of three versions of a 5-minute film that depicted aggressive responses to toys, including hitting and throwing objects at a Bobo doll. In the first version shown to one group of children the child was rewarded by an adult for the aggressive behavior; in the second version the child was punished; and in the third version there was no adult reaction. After they had viewed a version of the film, children secretly were observed in a room that contained the same toys shown in the movie. Children who viewed the rewarded model were most likely to repeat the model's aggressive behavior; children who viewed the punished model were least likely to repeat the behavior, with the third group falling in between. Thus, the likelihood of them demonstrating the behavior was a function of the reinforcement contingencies of the child they had observed in the film.

Note that all children were equally capable of reproducing the aggressive behavior, but they differed in the degree to which they actually manifested it. This distinction between acquiring a behavior and manifesting it in action—between learning and performance—is made by social cognitive theorists, but not by traditional reinforcement theorists.

Principles of vicarious learning are used frequently in elementary school classrooms. It is common for teachers of young children to reinforce one or a few children for a behavior that they desire in all children: "I like the way Jackson began working on his assignment right away"; "Table 5 is ready and can go to lunch." The effect can be dramatic. Before the children from table 5 reach the door, children at the other tables are likely to have ceased talking and put on their most angelic expressions.

Bandura (1986) also departed from strict reinforcement theory in stressing the importance of personal evaluation as a means of positive reinforcement. He claims that most people value the self-respect and self-satisfaction derived from a job well done more highly than material rewards. Thus, achieving a personal goal or meeting a personal achievement standard, and experiencing the accompanying self-satisfaction, can serve effectively as reinforcement.

Goals or intentions also play a central role in social cognitive theory. One way to influence students' behaviors is to influence their goals. When individuals commit themselves to goals, discrepancies between their goals and their accomplishments create self-dissatisfaction, which serves as an incentive for enhanced effort. The feeling of satisfaction for achieving a goal serves as a reward, which in turn increases future effort.

Social cognitive theory also portrays individuals as active agents in their behaviors. According to Bandura (1977b, 1986), the capacity to use symbols—especially language—provides humans with powerful tools for dealing with their environments and a means of controlling their own behaviors. Consequences of behavior have lasting effects on other behavior because they are processed and transformed into symbols. It is such cognitive representations of behavior and its consequences that guide future behavior. For example, a red light signals that you will be hit by another car (or you will get a traffic ticket) if you pass through the intersection, so you stop. Children in a classroom in which the teacher dismissed the quietest table first may quiet down quickly before recess in the future because they have a cognitive representation of the teacher's previous reaction.

The cognitive capacity for symbolic representation and forethought (e.g., of goals and expectations) also allows people to sustain effort over a long period of time. Thus, by keeping their goals in mind, students who aspire to mastering skills or obtaining high grades can continue to exert effort without regular reinforcement. With age comes increased capacity for symbolic thought and a longer time perspective, and consequently the ability to sustain effort for longer periods of time. Thus, although the second grader should be able to keep working until recess without some consequence to his behavior, a college student is expected to be able to sustain effort until the end of the semester.

Another way humans use their representational abilities to exercise self-control is by arranging the environment in a way that produces the behavior they desire. Setting an alarm clock to wake up at a particular time is a simple example. Making a reward (e.g., a chocolate chip cookie) contingent on a particular behavior (e.g., finishing a homework assignment) is another way of regulating one's own behavior. According to social cognitive theory, students can shape their own experiences—including the frequency and nature of reinforcements—in academic contexts by choosing which courses to take, which assignments to do, or which strategies to use to complete an assignment.

Self-Efficacy in Bandura's Social Cognitive Theory

Bandura (1986) claimed that no cognition affects human behavior more than people's judgments of their capabilities to achieve certain goals. **Self-efficacy,** in Bandura's theory, pertains to individuals' personal judgments of their performance capabilities for a particular type of task at a particular point in time and is closely linked to expectations for success (i.e., "Am I capable of succeeding at this task?"; Bandura, 1977a, 1977b, 1982a, 1982b, 1986, 1993, 1995, 1997; Schunk, 1989a, 1989b, 1994; Zimmerman, 1995). Efficacy, in Bandura's theory, is related to concepts of competence (discussed in Chapter 6), but unlike global perceptions that apply to many situations, self-efficacy usually refers to specific judgments in specific situations. (See Bandura, Barbaranelli, Caprara, & Pastorelli, 1996, for an example of assessing generalized, although domain-specific, self-efficacy.) There is some evidence that self-efficacy may be a more powerful predictor of academic performance than more general perceptions of academic competence (Pajares, 1996; Pajares & Miller, 1994).

SOURCES OF SELF-EFFICACY JUDGMENTS

According to Bandura there are four principal sources of information for self-efficacy judgments in academic situations—actual experience, vicarious experience, verbal persuasion, and physiological arousal.

Actual experience, especially past successes and failures, is an important source. Typically, successes raise efficacy appraisals and failures lower them. There is not, however, a simple relationship between objective experience and self-efficacy judgments. Self-efficacy judgments involve inferences, which are influenced by prior beliefs, expectations, difficulty of the task, amount of effort expended, amount of external help provided, and other factors. For example, success will not contribute to perceptions of efficacy if the individual perceives the task to be easy or if the individual did not think that much effort had been put forth (Earley & Lituchy, 1991). Perceptions of the cause of outcomes also affect subsequent self-efficacy judgments. A person like Helpless Hannah (see Chapter 1), who is convinced of her academic incompetence, may attribute success to some external factor, such as help from another or good luck. The success, consequently, does not engender feelings of efficacy.

Vicarious experiences affect self-perceptions of efficacy. For example, children sometimes can become persuaded that they are able to perform a task after watching another child of the same age complete the task. I observed this when I taught swimming lessons. Individual lessons often were not as effective as group lessons for young children because seeing a peer execute a behavior (e.g., swim across the deep end, dive off the diving board) often convinced children that they could do the same—a sense of efficacy that I, as an adult, could not engender as readily by modeling the same behaviors. Bandura (1986, 1992b) pointed out that vicarious experiences are most influential in situations in which individuals have little personal experience with the task.

Schunk and Hanson (1985) conducted a study that demonstrated the value of having children observe other children who successfully complete a task. Children who were having difficulty with subtraction observed either a same-sex peer or a teacher demonstrate mastery. Children observing a peer had higher self-efficacy for learning the procedure, as well as better mastery following a subsequent training intervention, than did those observing a teacher.

Verbal persuasion constitutes the third factor that influences, albeit more modestly, self-efficacy judgments. A teacher or parent sometimes can persuade children that they are able to achieve some goal. Verbal persuasion is not likely to be effective unless it is realistic and reinforced by real experience. But in some circumstances, encouragement (e.g., "Try it, I know you can do it") can bolster a child's self-confidence for a new task, especially when given by a credible person.

The final factor affecting self-efficacy judgments is *physiological arousal.* Consider, for example, that Anxious Alma (see Chapter 1) notices that her palms are sweaty and her heart is beating rapidly while she is taking a math test. If a high state of anxiety has affected her performance negatively in the past, she may lose confidence in her ability to perform in this instance. The lowered perceptions of efficacy, in turn, can increase her anxiety, and consequently interfere with her ability to demonstrate what she understands.

CONSEQUENCES OF SELF-EFFICACY

Perceived efficacy can affect individuals' behaviors, thoughts, and emotional reactions in achievement settings. People tend to avoid tasks and situations that they believe exceed their capabilities, and they seek out activities they judge themselves capable of handling (Bandura, 1977a, 1986, 1993). Individuals relatively high in self-efficacy set higher goals (Locke & Latham, 1990, 1994; Zimmerman & Bandura, 1994; Zimmerman, Bandura, & Martinez-Pons, 1992), choose more difficult tasks (Sexton & Tuckman, 1991), and persist longer with tasks, even when perceptions of efficacy are experimentally induced (Bouffard-Bouchard, 1990; see also Berry & West, 1993; Multon, Brown, & Lent, 1991; Zimmerman, 1995). Research has shown that self-efficacy judgments are even predictive of career choices (Hackett, 1995; Hackett & Betz, 1992).

Self-efficacy beliefs also affect students' thoughts and behaviors while they work on tasks. Students who are not confident that they can complete a task often become anxious and preoccupied with feelings of incompetence and concerns about failing, especially when they are being evaluated. In contrast, students who are convinced of their competence are task-oriented—they can concentrate on problem-solving strategies (Bandalos, Yates, & Thorndike-Christ, 1995; Bandura, 1981, 1986, 1992a, 1993; Bouffard-Bouchard, Parent, & Larivee, 1991; Zimmerman, 1995). A study by Pintrich and De Groot (1990) illustrated the value of high self-efficacy. They found that self-efficacy was associated strongly with constructive cognitive strategies and self-regulated learning (e.g., a student's attempts to make connections between textbook and classroom instruction, rereading material, making outlines), independent of prior achievement (see also Bandura, 1992b; Berry & West, 1993; Bouffard-Bouchard, 1990; Locke, Frederick, Lee, & Bobko, 1984; Meece, Wigfield, & Eccles, 1990; Pajares & Miller, 1994; Pintrich, Roeser, & De Groot, 1994; Randhawa, Beamer, & Lundberg, 1993).

Judgments of self-efficacy while solving a problem or completing a task also are associated with positive emotional experiences, which in turn foster future attempts at mastery. Consider the novice skier who finally makes a successful run to the bottom of a hill. He is likely to want to go right back up the hill, or possibly even a steeper hill, as a consequence of this success and the positive feelings it engendered. School tasks, such as solving a difficult algebra problem, also can engender positive feelings of efficacy. The student who solves a difficult problem should feel efficacious and be more eager to make future attempts.

These consequences of high self-efficacy—willingness to approach and persist with tasks, reduced fear and anxiety, a focus on problem-solving strategies, and positive emotional experiences—affect achievement outcomes (see Zimmerman, 1995, for a review). This was demonstrated in a study by Collins (1982). Students who ranked low, average, and high in mathematical skills were identified first on the basis of scores on standardized tests. Within each skill group students with higher self-efficacy solved more problems correctly and chose to rework more problems that they had missed than did students with low self-efficacy. Thus, self-efficacy predicted achievement behavior and performance over and above actual skill level in all three groups. These studies clearly point to the importance of fostering self-efficacy in learning situations.

Summary

Social cognitive theorists do not dismiss the effects of reinforcement and punishment on behavior, but they do not believe that direct behavioral contingencies are the only factors affecting behavior. Social cognitive theory includes individuals' thoughts—especially their expectations related to the likelihood of rewards—as mediators of behavior. Such thoughts are assumed to be influenced by observations, persuasion, and even physiological arousal, as well as by personal experiences with reinforcement and punishment.

Individuals are considered to be active agents in their behaviors in social cognitive theory. Cognitive representational abilities liberate humans in the sense that they can manipulate their own stimulus conditions. Thus, individuals can arrange the environment to maximize the chances that desired responses will occur. Social cognitive theory, accordingly, has inspired the development of a variety of techniques that can help individuals regulate their own behaviors. The next section on self-regulation summarizes strategies that have been developed to help individuals play an active, constructive role in their own learning.

SELF-REGULATION

The behavioral change strategies discussed next are referred to as **cognitive behavior modification** (CBM) because behavior is assumed to be mediated by cognitions. Sometimes they also are referred to as "self-management" approaches because individuals are invited to play an active role in managing their own behavioral changes. The final section of this chapter describes additional strategies for involving individuals in regulating their own learning. Because these strategies focus less than CBM or self-management on overt behavior and more on active thought processes that can enhance learning, they are referred to as **meta-cognitive strategies.**

Cognitive Behavior Modification

Hallahan and Sapona (1983) define CBM as "the modification of overt behavior through the manipulation of covert thought processes" (p. 616). (See also Hughes, Korinek, & Gorman, 1991; Shapiro & Bradley, 1996; Shapiro & Cole, 1994.) CBM is similar to approaches based on strict reinforcement theory in that it is designed to change overt behavior and assumes that reinforcement principles are operating. It is different because the treatment involves modifying a person's cognitive operations to achieve a change in his behavior. It is also different in that it is not regulated entirely by some outside source. When CBM approaches are used, the teacher is not the only determiner of reinforcement contingencies or the sole dispenser of rewards, as is the case with behavior modification programs such as token economies. Cognitive behavior modification requires individuals to take responsibility, either by monitoring their own behaviors, setting their own goals and standards, or administering their own rewards (Meichenbaum, 1977).

Personal involvement is believed to have numerous advantages over external monitoring and reinforcement. There are problems with external reinforcement that personal responsibility can resolve. It is difficult for teachers to monitor and reinforce many students' behaviors at one time, and students are less likely than teachers to miss their own reinforcement opportunities (Fantuzzo & Polite, 1990). Furthermore, when rewards and punishment always are administered by an external agent, that agent may become a discriminative stimulus, and thus a necessary cue for the performance of the desired behaviors. The behavior, there-fore, will not occur when the external agent is absent. As mentioned in Chapter 3, this is why classroom discipline can break down the moment the teacher leaves the room.

Desirable behaviors should be maintained longer after contingent rewards are withdrawn when students are involved in regulating their own behaviors than when they are not involved. Personal involvement should enhance understanding of the relationship between environmental events and behavior, and therefore will result in more generalization outside of the setting in which the rewards are given. In general, CBM is believed to result in less reliance on external agents to control behavior (Mace & Kratochwill, 1988; Shapiro & Cole, 1994), although some CBM advocates claim that ultimately all behavior is controlled by the contingen-cies of external reward or punishment (Mace, Belfiore, & Shea, 1989).

Shapiro and Cole (1994) distinguished between two types of self-manage-ment interventions: (1) *contingency-based* approaches, which target the con-sequences of behavior (e.g., self-monitoring/recording, self-evaluation, self-reinforcement); and (2) *cognitive-based* approaches, which focus more on the antecedents for behavior (e.g., self-instruction, stress inoculation, social problem solving). Three of the most commonly used approaches—self-recording, self-reinforcement, and self-instruction—are described next to illustrate CBM strategies.

SELF-RECORDING

One simple method that has been used to help children begin to take responsibility for their own behaviors is to have them keep a record of it. Self-recording has been found to influence behavior, even without tangible reinforcements—an outcome referred to as **reactivity** (Kirby, Fowler, & Baer, 1991; Lalli & Shapiro, 1990; Mace et al., 1989).

Children may be asked to record the duration of an activity, frequency of a particular behavior, task completion, or the level of performance (see Hughes et al., 1991; Kirby, Fowler, & Baer, 1991; Mace & Kratochwill, 1988; Shapiro & Cole, 1994). For example, students may record how long they read at home each evening, each time they bring their homework home, each time they begin an assignment without asking the teacher to repeat the instructions, or each time they complete an assignment on time. Or they may record how many spelling words they practice or spell correctly on quizzes, how many math problems they complete independently, or how many pages they read.

Time-sampling methods also have been used. Kern, Dunlap, Childs, and Clarke (1994), for example, increased task engagement and decreased disruptive behavior by having children record, on sheets placed in the corner of their desks, whether they were or were not "on task" when a bell sounded at 5-minute intervals. Methods as simple as touching a child on a shoulder can be used as cues (Maag, Rutherford, & DiGangi, 1992).

What is recorded depends on the problem. A child who is not doing assignments at all might benefit from keeping track of assignments completed and not completed. A child who usually finishes assignments but not carefully should record error rates or some other index of quality. A predetermined performance standard has been shown to enhance the effectiveness of self-monitoring (Kazdin, 1974), presumably because it gives children a particular goal toward which to work. A few researchers also have found that self-monitoring is more effective in increasing desired behaviors than in decreasing undesirable behaviors (e.g., Litrownik & Freitas, 1980).

Self-recording can be done in a variety of ways. One of the simplest is to have students make a mark on a sheet of paper every time they engage in some behavior, and endeavor to increase the number of marks from week to week. Some CBM researchers have taped paper to children's desks to record behavior. Shapiro (1984) described "countoons"—simple stick figure drawings that represent the specific behavior to be self-monitored. Children place a tally mark next to each picture when the behavior occurs. It is sometimes useful to have students graph their "scores" (Thoresen & Mahoney, 1974; see Shapiro, 1984, for examples). Some children are encouraged and excited when they see the line in the graph going up or down, depending on whether they are trying to increase or decrease the behavior.

Teachers can encourage personal responsibility by allowing students to set their own goals for improvement. For example, students may decide how many math problems they will do each day or how many words they will spell correctly on the next spelling test. Students may choose even the area in which they would like to improve their behavior. Personal choice and goal setting engage students' involvement and interest and gives them more responsibility for their own behaviors.

Personal goal setting also helps students learn how to set realistic goals, an important skill in achievement settings (see Schunk, 1990, 1995). Many students begin by setting goals that are either too easy or too difficult to achieve. Initially, teachers usually need to help students adjust their goals. Charting goals along with actual behavior shows them how close their progress is to their goal. If they are working hard but not meeting their goals, they may need to make them more realistic.

If goals are set too high, students simply will become discouraged when they do not reach them. Teachers should encourage students like Hannah, who are doing very poorly in school, to set modest goals at first, such as simply remembering to take home their homework or spelling more than half of the vocabulary words right. Once they have met the modest goals, the standards can be raised. Better performers, such as Safe Sally (see Chapter 1), need encouragement to set ambitious goals. Research has shown that maximum learning occurs when goals or standards are raised gradually as a function of students' past performance (Locke & Latham, 1994; Masters, Furman, & Barden, 1977).

O'Leary and Dubey (1979) pointed out that self-recording may be effective primarily for students who already want to engage in the desired behaviors. Evidence for this comes from numerous studies on smoking behavior. Lipinski, Black, Nelson, and Ciminero (1974), for example, found that self-recording decreased smoking in subjects who volunteered for an experiment to reduce smoking, but not for subjects who volunteered for a general experiment that involved smokers. Self-recording, therefore, may be effective only for students who genuinely desire to change their behaviors. It may, for example, help an easily distracted student who is motivated to finish assignments, but not a student like Satisfied Santos (see Chapter 1), who does not care whether he completes his work.

SELF-INSTRUCTION

Meichenbaum (1977) suggested that speech can be used to regulate one's own behavior or to solve problems. Adults, for example, might talk out loud to direct their own behavior on a new or difficult task, such as preparing a complicated recipe or assembling a piece of furniture. The notion that language can be used to control one's own behavior—a key assumption of social cognitive theory—is based on cognitive behavior theories of Russian psychologists Vygotsky and Luria. Vygotsky (1962, 1978) and Luria (1961) believed that language is responsible for humans' abilities to control their own behaviors. Unlike animals, humans can use language to plan and direct their actions before implementing them.

A number of researchers have observed that children with learning problems often lack two kinds of skills: **metacognitive skills** (e.g., awareness of what capabilities, strategies, and resources are needed to perform a task effectively) and **self-regulation skills** (e.g., planning, evaluating effectiveness of ongoing activities, or remediation; Hallahan & Sapona, 1983). These skills can be enhanced by helping children to become more cognizant of the demands of a task and to monitor their use of strategies better. One approach that has been used is teaching children to verbalize instructions (see Lenz, 1992; Shapiro & Bradley, 1996; Shapiro & Cole, 1994).

Swanson and Scarpati (1985, p. 30), for example, taught students to use a set of written instructions with prompts to improve their learning strategies: (1) "How do I understand the passage before I read it? First, I need to look at the title, then skim the passage for new words and circle them. Second, I need to underline people's names and words that show action"; (2) "I need to ask myself, 'Who, what, where, and how?' before I read" (see also Mahn & Greenwood, 1990).

The results of research on whether the effects of self-instruction on behavior persist and generalize to other situations are mixed (e.g., Hughes et al., 1991; Mahn & Greenwood, 1990; Meichenbaum & Asarnow, 1979; Robertson & Keely, 1974; Shapiro & Bradley, 1996). Hughes et al. (1991) suggested that self-instruction may increase self-confidence, and Kamann and Wong (1993) proposed that encouraging "self-talk" can reduce anxiety in learning disabled students. Some teachers, however, find these techniques, which usually require one-on-one interactions with the student, time consuming and the speak-aloud requirements uncomfortable for students (Wood, Rosenberg, & Carran, 1993).

SELF-REINFORCEMENT

Another way to help students control their own behaviors is to involve them in selecting and administering their own reinforcements. According to social cognitive theorists, self-reinforcement increases performance mainly through its motivation function. By making self-reward conditional on attaining a certain level of performance, individuals create self-inducements to persist with their efforts until their performance matches the prescribed standard (Bandura, 1977b). Self-reinforcement is an example of **reciprocal determinism** in social cognitive theory. Individuals exercise control over the environment, which in turn influences their own behaviors. Examples of self-reinforcement are promising oneself a piece of cake for finishing some predetermined amount of work (i.e., revising a section in a book chapter), or a vacation for not smoking for a specified length of time.

Children have been taught to engage in self-reinforcement, usually in combination with self-instruction techniques (Hughes et al., 1991). For example, in a study by Bornstein and Quevillon (1976), the experimenter modeled self-reinforcement by initially taking M & Ms for appropriate behavior (e.g., paying attention), and then by praising himself with "I'm doing a good job."

A practice common in elementary school classrooms is to give children opportunities to engage in desired activities (e.g., playing with a puzzle or game, using a listening center, or playing with the pet gerbil) when they finish their assigned work. This is a form of self-reinforcement when children can choose the specific activities and administer their own rewards. A common problem with this practice is that the reward may be realistically available only to a small subset of relatively fast workers. As a consequence, it will be motivating only for these students (usually those who need an external incentive the least).

Another potential problem with making one set of activities contingent on completing another is that it gives an implicit message to students that the assignment that is reinforced is undesirable, and the activities that serve as reinforcement are desirable. As noted in Chapter 3, the teacher who tells students they can read, play with the gerbils, or work on the computer when they finish their math assignment gives the message that the math assignment is not interesting or worth doing in its own right.

A few classroom studies in which children determined the standards for their self-reinforcement have found that children tend to select lenient performance standards (Rosenbaum & Drabman, 1979; Wall, 1983). If self-reinforcement is used, it might be necessary to have some incentive for selecting stricter standards. Research also suggests that publicly stated standards are more effective than private ones (Hayes et al., 1985). Studies documenting a fair amount of cheating (e.g., administering unearned rewards; Speidel & Tharp, 1980) suggest that some monitoring is required.

The CBM strategies described have been used primarily with children who have special learning disabilities, and have focused on observable behavior. The metacognitive strategies described next have been used to assist nondisabled as well as disabled students to improve their learning, and often involve cognitive processes that cannot be observed directly.

Metacognitive Strategies

Walking out at the end of a lecture, I realize I cannot remember a word that was said. I ask a colleague about an article he just read, and he has difficulty summarizing even the main points. My daughter stares at me blankly when I complain that she did not clean her room as I had asked. We all have experienced this gap between hearing or reading the surface structure of words and actually processing the information contained in them. I "listened" to the lecture, my colleague "read" every word of the article, and my daughter "heard" my request. But to process and remember the information we would have had to use more active cognitive strategies.

Active learning, or "metacognitive" strategies, can be used to regulate one's learning. Researchers have investigated many kinds of self-regulated learning strategies—including planning and goal setting, asking questions and testing for understanding, reflecting on new material, searching for main ideas, making connections to what one already knows, making inferences and predictions and checking to see whether they are correct, taking and organizing notes, keeping records, practicing problems, rehearsing, and creating mnemonics for memory. Many studies have investigated the value of teaching these skills directly (Hattie, Biggs, & Purdie, 1996; see also Schunk & Zimmerman, 1994).

Students who use these kinds of strategies in educational contexts learn more (Zimmerman & Martinez-Pons, 1986), but not everyone uses them. Research indicates that individuals are most likely to use such active learning strategies when they believe that the task is interesting or important and when they believe that they are capable of mastering the present task (i.e., when their "self-efficacy" is high; see Borkowski & Thorpe, 1994; Meece, 1994; Paris & Oka, 1986; Pintrich & De Groot, 1990; Pintrich & Schrauben, 1992; Pintrich et al., 1994; Schunk, 1994; Wigfield, 1994b; Zimmerman & Martinez-Pons, 1992).

But even when there is a will, some children lack the way. Metacognitive strategies that support self-regulated learning often need to be taught. Wang and Palincsar (1989) recommended embedding instruction on metacognitive skills into the regular instruction, rather than doing it as a separate curriculum (see also Brown & Pressley, 1994; Palincsar & Brown, 1984, 1987; Paris, Cross, & Lipson, 1984). Their recommendation is supported by research that indicates that training implemented in the context of teaching content is more effective than training provided in a counseling or remedial center as a "general or all-purpose package of portable skills" (Hattie et al., 1996, p. 130). Studies also find that students need to be taught how to apply new skills to material that is substantially different from the material used to train the skills (Hattie et al., 1996), and they need to understand the basis of how a strategy works and when it is appropriate to use it.

Wang and Palincsar (1989) suggested a set of strategies teachers can use to implement effective teaching of metacognitive strategies (see also Brown & Pressley, 1994; Graham & Harris, 1994). Initially, teachers need to assess the cognitive strategies their students currently use in learning situations. The simplest strategy is to ask them directly—for example, "What did you do to learn your spelling words, or to figure out how to complete the science experiment?" They then suggest introducing a cognitive strategy and explaining its usefulness. This is followed by modeling its use and engaging students in guided practice. Teachers need to provide "expert scaffolding"—assisting students at first by giving them reminders, directions, and hints, and then slowly withdrawing their assistance. The last step is to give students opportunities to apply and practice these strategies independently.

CONCLUSION

Social cognitive theory represents a significant departure from strict reinforcement theory by including cognitions as mediators of behavior. It also reflects a trend away from depicting individuals as passive organisms that emit only those behaviors for which they have been reinforced and toward viewing individuals as active, thinking, and self-regulating. Achievement motivation research, therefore, now focuses more on how to develop both the will and the metacognitive skills students need to play their parts effectively than on the conditions of the environment that produce particular behaviors.

As was shown previously, self-efficacy is a necessary ingredient in the will to engage actively in learning; individuals must believe that the strategies available to them actually will achieve their goals. Chapter 5 discusses other cognitive beliefs that affect students' motivation to learn.

Evolving from social cognitive theory are specific strategies, such as cognitive behavior modification, that are designed to help students control their own behaviors. Proponents of CBM claim that because cognitions mediate behavior, intervening in children's cognitions—helping them become self-conscious, to "think about" their behaviors—is an effective way to change behavior. The developers of the CBM procedures described in this chapter hope that they can help teachers spend more time teaching and that they can ensure the maintenance of the desired behavior when children are not being monitored by adults and when external reinforcement is not available.

Research implementing CBM procedures suggests that they may be superior to behavior change programs that rely entirely on external reinforcement, and they actually may increase independence and self-confidence (Hughes et al., 1991). It is still an open question whether they are effective, in the long run, without being accompanied by contingent reinforcement (Hughes et al., 1991). Teachers also sometimes view the intervention as too time consuming (Wood et al., 1993), and there remain many questions about its generalizability and applicability to regular classroom environments (Graham & Wong, 1993). Given these questions and limitations, it is important to explore other motivation systems that exist in learning contexts, such as those that are described in Chapters 8 and 9.

TABLE 4-1   Summary of Terms

Terms	Definition
Vicarious learning	Engaging in a behavior as a result of observing the consequences to another individual engaging in it
Self-efficacy	Personal judgments of performance capabilities on a particular task at a particular point in time
Cognitive behavior modification (CBM)	Strategies for changing behavior that involve changing beliefs and expectations and a more active role of the person whose behavior is being changed
Metacognitive strategies	Cognitive strategies used to enhance one's own learning—such as goal setting, planning, note taking, rehearsing, making mnemonics, checking for understanding, and making and testing inferences and predictions
Reactivity	Behavior change that occurs as the result of self-recording behaviors
Metacognitive skills	Awareness of what capabilities, strategies, and resources are needed to perform a task effectively
Self-regulation skills	Regulating one's own behavior (e.g., planning, evaluating the effectiveness of ongoing activities)
Reciprocal determinism	Individuals exercise control over the environment, which in turn influences their own behaviors

Cognitive Theories Applied to Achievement Contexts

Like social cognitive theory, the three cognitive theories discussed in this chapter emphasize cognitions or beliefs as mediators of behavior. For all three theories, changes in behavior are assumed to require changes in cognitions. Reinforcement and punishment may affect those cognitions, but the cognitions, not the consequences of the behavior, are what make the difference.

The theories differ, however, from social cognitive theory and from each other with regard to the particular beliefs they emphasize. Bandura's social learning theory, described in Chapter 4, focuses on self-efficacy. Atkinson's expectancy x value theory focuses on expectations for success, a cognition similar to self-efficacy, and also on achievement-related emotions (pride and shame); Rotter's social learning theory emphasizes beliefs about the contingency of rewards; and Weiner's attribution theory is concerned with beliefs about the causes of achievement outcomes and attendant emotions. These theories also differ in how much they emphasize stable dispositions. Atkinson and Rotter both consider stable individual differences as determinants of behavior, whereas Weiner emphasizes the effects of the immediate context.

Each of these three theories is described in the following sections. Some mention is made of practical classroom implications of the theories, but this topic is addressed in more detail in Chapter 7.

ATKINSON'S EXPECTANCY x VALUE THEORY

Atkinson's (1964) primary goal was to predict whether an individual would approach or avoid an achievement task. He conceptualized achievement behavior as being a conflict between a tendency to approach tasks and a tendency to avoid tasks. These two opposing tendencies are strengthened or weakened by stable individual differences in values and by expectations about the likelihood of accomplishing a particular goal. Emotions are central to many of the constructs (psychological variables) in Atkinson's theory.

Consider first the stable factor affecting the tendency to approach tasks. Atkinson proposed that an unconscious **motive for success (MS),** or **need to achieve (Nach),** directs individuals toward achievement tasks. The motive for success represents a relatively stable disposition to strive for success, conceptualized in expectancy x value theory as a "capacity to experience pride in accomplishment" (Atkinson, 1964, p. 214).

The motive for success usually is measured by the Thematic Apperception Test (TAT), in which individuals are shown ambiguous pictures and are asked to describe what is happening. It is assumed that subjects "project" their own achievement values into their interpretations of the pictures. Their responses are scored according to the amount of achievement-striving content in their descriptions (i.e., references to accomplishments, achievement concerns, goals, expressions of achievement-related affect). Use of a projective test reflects a Freudian view that motivation is unconscious and expressed in fantasy (McClelland, 1961).

The **motive to avoid failure (MAF),** conceived of as a capacity to experience shame given failure, is the unconscious, stable factor that directs individuals away from achievement tasks. It generally is operationalized (measured) as anxiety aroused in testing situations.

Any achievement-related activity is assumed to elicit both positive (hope for success) and negative (fear of failure) affective anticipations. What determines an individual's behavior is the relative strength of these two anticipations, in which emotions play a central role.

According to Atkinson's theory, individual differences in both of these stable motives (to achieve success and to avoid failure) can be traced to parents' child-rearing behaviors. Children whose parents encourage their achievement efforts and provide opportunities for them to demonstrate competence should have a relatively high motive to achieve success. In contrast, children whose parents punish their achievement efforts should develop a strong motive to avoid failure. Thus, emotional associations to achievement situations (e.g., pride in accomplishment, shame in failure) are assumed to be formed during early childhood but are evoked later in achievement contexts.

These proposals have not held up well in empirical tests. Some studies indicate that early independence training (Winterbottom, 1958) and high expectations (Rosen & D'Andrade, 1959) foster a strong achievement motive in children; however, these findings have been inconsistent. (See V. C. Crandall, 1967; V. J. Crandall, 1963; and Trudewind, 1982, for reviews.)

Although Atkinson assumed that the motives to strive for success and to avoid failure are unconscious, he also believed that individuals' behaviors in achievement situations are influenced by their conscious beliefs about those particular situations. These situational variables, such as the unconscious motives previously discussed, direct individuals toward or away from achievement tasks.

Two conscious variables are believed to direct individuals toward achievement tasks—the **perceived probability of success (Ps)** and the expectations of pride, which Atkinson refers to as the **incentive value of success (Is).** According to expectancy *x* value theory, individuals who expect to succeed (believe that the probability of success is high) at a particular task are more likely to approach it than individuals who are less certain about their chances for success.

Atkinson argued that greater pride is experienced following success with a difficult task (i.e., a task with a low probability of success) than following success with a task having a high probability of success. Thus, an "A" in a difficult course has a higher incentive value than an "A" in an easy course. Because anticipated pride is determined entirely by the perceived probability of success, the two situational variables in this model can be reduced to one (represented in the formula, $Is = 1 - Ps$).

Two situational variables also inhibit achievement efforts—perceptions of the **probability of failure (Pf)** and the anticipation of shame, which Atkinson refers to as the **incentive value of failure (If).** Shame is believed to be greatest following failure of very easy tasks, tasks that have a high probability of success, and least following failure of very difficult tasks. According to expectancy *x* value theory, a "C" in physics might be less humiliating than a "C" in a course that is considered less difficult (e.g., education). Thus, again, because one of these situational variables (If) is determined by the other (Pf), they can be reduced to one $(If = 1 - Pf)$.

In summary, the tendency to approach tasks is determined by an unconscious stable factor (i.e., motive for success or need for achievement) and two conscious situational factors (i.e., expectations for success and anticipated pride). The tendency to avoid tasks is determined by an unconscious stable factor (i.e., fear of failure) and two conscious situational factors (i.e., expectations for failure and anticipated shame). These two motivation tendencies—to approach and to avoid tasks—are represented as opposing forces. **The resultant tendency to approach or avoid an achievement activity (TA)** is a function of the strength of the tendency to approach (TS) minus the strength of the tendency to avoid failing (TAF) the task. If the tendency to approach is stronger, the individual will approach the task; if the tendency to avoid is stronger, the individual will avoid it. Atkinson combined these factors into a mathematical equation:

$$TA = TS - TAF$$
$$TA = (MS \times Ps \times Is) - (MAF \times Pf \times If)$$

To illustrate how the formula works let us try to predict whether Anxious Alma or Satisfied Santos (see Chapter 1) is more likely to approach a mathematics task. Alma's motive to avoid failure (MAF) is much higher (e.g., +5) than Santos's (e.g., +1) because she has a high capacity for experiencing shame related to failure; Alma's motive for success (Ms) is somewhat higher (+4) than Santos's (+2). Their expectations of success (Ps) and failure (Pf) for the task are about the same (70 percent chance of success, 30 percent chance of failure); thus the incentive value of success (pride they expect to experience if they succeed at this particular task) is the same (Is = 1 − 0.70 = 0.30), as is the incentive value of failure (shame they expect to experience if they fail; If = 1 − 0.30 = 0.70). Note that the negative feelings expected for failure are stronger than the positive feelings expected for success. This is because the task is relatively easy (with an anticipated 70 percent chance of success). Which child, according to Atkinson's formula, is most likely to approach (TA) the math task?

Alma: TA = (4 × 0.7 × 0.3) − (5 × 0.3 × 0.7) = 0.84 − 1.05 = −0.21
Santos: TA = (2 × 0.7 × 0.3) − (1 × 0.3 × 0.7) = 0.42 − 0.21 = +0.21

Although Alma's motive to achieve success is higher than Santos's, she is less likely to approach the task because her motive to avoid failure is so much higher. Indeed, according to the formula, she is more likely to avoid than to approach the task (indicated by the negative TA), whereas Santos is more likely to approach the task than to avoid it.

The evidence on how effectively this mathematical model predicts behavior in achievement situations is mixed. There is, however, some evidence suggesting that by measuring the components included in the model, and by combining them according to Atkinson's equations, modestly accurate predictions sometimes can be made regarding individuals' engagement in achievement tasks, the difficulty levels of the tasks they choose, their levels of aspiration or willingness to take risks, and their persistence in completing difficult tasks. (See Weiner, 1980a, 1992, for reviews of this research.)

There are many problems with Atkinson's model, which may explain why it has had only modest success in predicting behavior, even in highly controlled laboratory circumstances. The two major variables in the model, motive for success and motive to avoid failure, are difficult to measure. Also, the incentive values of success and failure are determined fully by the probability of success, regardless of the importance of the task. Consequently, if the probability of success with a puzzle and on a National Merit Test is the same, success with these two tasks is assumed to generate the same amount of pride. Intuitively, it seems that a greater amount of pride would be aroused in the latter than in the former situation, but the model does not differentiate tasks as a function of their importance to the performer.

The model also assumes that task value is associated inversely with the probability of success—that individuals value success with tasks that they expect to fail more than with tasks with which they expect to succeed. This is a very narrow definition of value, and most research that assesses values using a broader definition suggests the opposite, that individuals value tasks for which they believe they have high competence (e.g., Eccles & Wigfield, 1995; Wigfield & Eccles, 1992; see Chapter 9).

Despite these and many other problems, Atkinson made a major contribution to achievement motivation theory. By including expectations and emotions as factors that influence achievement behavior, he paved the way for future cognitive motivation theorists who have built on some of his basic notions. By elaborating on Atkinson's proposals, more recent cognitive theorists have developed models that have greater relevance to classroom practice.

ROTTER'S SOCIAL LEARNING THEORY

Recall that reinforcement theorists believe the frequency of a behavior (e.g., paying attention to the teacher, approaching tasks, completing tasks) depends on whether the behavior has been rewarded in the past. Like Bandura, Rotter (1966, 1975, 1990) proposed that it is not the reward itself that increases the frequency of a behavior, but an individual's beliefs about what brings rewards. If individuals do not believe that the rewards they receive are caused by aspects of their personal characteristics or behaviors, rewards will not influence their future behaviors.

Consider, for example, good grades, which have reinforcement value for most students (Santos being the exception). According to strict reinforcement theory, any behavior (whether it is studying or carrying a rabbit's foot) that preceded a good grade should increase in frequency. Rotter's more cognitive social learning theory predicts that increased studying or rabbit foot carrying would occur only if the person believed that her behavior caused the good grade. For instance, consider a student who worked hard on a paper and received an "A." If all students in the class received "As" on their papers, he may believe that the teacher gives "As" indiscriminately, regardless of the quality of work that is done or the amount of effort exerted. This student may not work as hard on papers in the future because he does not believe that rewards ("As") are contingent on his behavior.

Rotter, like Atkinson and Bandura, assumes that expectancies (both generalized and specific) of reinforcements and the value of reinforcements determine behavior. He conceptualized value, however, more broadly than Atkinson; reinforcement value in Rotter's theory is linked not only to the probability of success, but also to a person's needs and to associations with other reinforcements. Thus, an "A" in chemistry may have particularly high value for a college student hoping to become a doctor because it is perceived to be associated with another reinforcement: being accepted to medical school. This student's effort in her chemistry class, therefore, is determined by her expectation that hard work results in valued reinforcement.

Expectancies are based on subjective perceptions of the probability that a behavior will be reinforced. Thus, a rumor that a teacher is biased against girls, never gives "As," or is unpredictable in her grading can affect students' expectancies, and thus their behaviors, even if the rumor is fictitious.

Expectancies in a particular situation are determined not only by beliefs about reinforcement in that situation, but also by generalized expectancies based on experiences in other, similar situations. Rotter refers to individuals' generalized beliefs regarding the contingency of reinforcement as **locus of control (LOC).** *Internal locus of control* refers to the belief that events or outcomes are contingent on one's own behavior or on a personal characteristic, such as ability. The belief that events are caused by factors beyond the individual's control (e.g., luck, chance, fate, biased others) has been labeled *external control.* Thus, although Atkinson focused on individuals' expectations for reward, Rotter was concerned with their beliefs about what causes them to receive or not to receive rewards and the implications that these beliefs have on their expectations.

Some classroom conditions are more likely to result in external loci of control than others. For example, students are most likely to develop an external locus of control in situations in which rewards (e.g., grades) are not tied closely to skills or performance. If very lenient or very difficult standards are used, so that different levels of performance result in similar rewards, or if rewards are given variably in conjunction with the same performance (e.g., three errors result in an "A–" one time and a "B" the next), students may perceive rewards to be unrelated to their performance. This is why consistency and clarity in grading and giving rewards is critical to students' perceptions of control.

Students also bring to each new class their own generalized belief systems developed from past experiences in achievement situations. For instance, students who repeatedly have experienced failure regardless of the amount of effort they have exerted often develop the belief that success is not contingent on effort. This generalized belief may override contrary information in any specific situation. Thus, students such as Helpless Hannah (see Chapter 1), who come to believe that hard work will not be rewarded (e.g., by a good grade), are likely to exert little effort, even in situations in which their effort actually would lead to success.

Once such beliefs are developed they are difficult to change (Schmitz & Skinner, 1993). A few success experiences may not convince a child such as Hannah that rewards really are contingent on effort. Firm in her belief that she can do nothing to achieve success, Hannah is likely to interpret any positive outcome as the result of good luck, an easy task, or even the teacher's mistake. She tenaciously may hold to her belief that effort does not lead to success, despite contradictory evidence. This is why occasional experiences of success frequently do not encourage greater effort in students such as Hannah.

Rotter's theoretical work has spawned an extensive empirical literature linking students' academic achievements with their locus of control (for reviews, see Lefcourt, 1976, 1992; Skinner, 1995; Stipek & Weisz, 1981), and researchers have examined associations between perceptions of control and achievement behavior, such as effort and persistence (e.g., Patrick, Skinner, & Connell, 1993; Schmitz & Skinner, 1993). Rotter's distinction between the beliefs that rewards are contingent (internal) or not contingent (external) on individual characteristics or behavior has important educational implications, but practical classroom application requires certain refinements, some of which are discussed next.

Control = Strategy + Capacity

Skinner (1990, 1995; Chapman, Skinner, & Baltes, 1990) made a distinction that is not in Rotter's theory between **strategy (means–ends) beliefs** and **capacity (or agency) beliefs.** Strategy beliefs are conceptions about the extent to which certain strategies or means are sufficient to cause particular ends (e.g., "Will I get an 'A' if I understand everything in this book on motivation?"). Capacity beliefs refer to the extent to which a person has access to those means (e.g., "Am I able to understand this material?"). Logically, a perception of control requires both beliefs, although Skinner noted that individuals sometimes do not reason logically. (See Weisz, 1986, and Weisz and Stipek, 1982, for a similar distinction between contingency and competence.)

This distinction is useful in diagnosing and remedying motivation problems. One student, for example, may think that she has the capacity to master motivation theory, but is unsure how the professor grades (i.e., low-strategy beliefs). Her sense of control could be increased by clarifying the grading criteria. Another student may clearly know the criteria for a good grade, but may believe that he lacks the capacity to achieve those criteria. The remedy here is to persuade him that he can, perhaps by providing additional assistance.

Measuring Locus of Control

According to Rotter, locus of control is a relatively stable trait and can be measured by a questionnaire. He developed the internal–external (I–E) control scale, which, using a forced-choice format, pits an internal belief against an external belief. The items are classified into six subcategories: academic recognition, social recognition, love and affection, dominance, social–political beliefs, and life philosophy (Rotter, 1966). Note that in this scale locus of control is operationalized very broadly as general beliefs about controlling rewards that exist in many domains of life.

Several scales have been developed for use with children, and some focus on control over outcomes in achievement contexts (see Weisz & Stipek, 1982, for a review). One measure frequently used to assess children's perceptions of control in achievement situations is the Intellectual Achievement Responsibility (IAR) scale, developed by Crandall and associates (Crandall, Katkovsky, & Crandall, 1965; Crandall, Katkovsky, & Preston, 1962). The IAR scale has the advantage of systematically dividing questions between positive and negative outcomes. This is an example of a positive outcome: "When you do well on a test at school, is it more likely to be (a) because you studied for it (internal response), or (b) because the test was especially easy (external response)?" Children who deem positive outcomes to be contingent on their own behaviors have relatively high internal scores on the success subscale. In contrast, children who think that negative outcomes are contingent on their own behaviors have relatively high internal scores on the failure subscale.

This distinction, made in the IAR, between perceptions of control over success and failure is important. Consider Hannah, for instance; she accepts full responsibility for her failures, believing that they result from her low ability. She also believes that her rare successes are caused by external factors such as luck. Hannah has an internal locus of control with regard to failure and an external locus of control with regard to success. Some students have the opposite causal beliefs; they accept responsibility for success and assume that some external factor (e.g., a biased or unfair teacher) caused them to fail.

Connell (1985) developed a measure of locus of control that makes even finer distinctions than the IAR. Children respond to questions concerning their perceptions of control with regard to cognitive, social, and physical outcomes. Within each of these domains, subscores provide information on the degree to which children believe that they or other powerful persons (e.g., parents, teachers, popular peers) control outcomes and the degree to which they do not know why certain outcomes occur.

Skinner, Chapman, and Baltes (1988; see also Little, Oettingen, Stetsenko, & Baltes, 1995; Schmitz & Skinner, 1993) developed a measure that reflects their own conceptualization of perceived control with respect to school performance. Five types of means to achieve success or avoid failure are included: effort, ability, powerful others, luck, and unknown causes. For each of these five means there are questions pertaining to means–ends (strategy) beliefs (i.e., assumptions about the effectiveness of these means in bringing about desirable outcomes) and agency (capacity) beliefs (i.e., perceptions of personal access to the means).

Classroom Contexts and Beliefs About Control

Skinner (1995) recommended structure (rather than chaos)—that is, clear expectations and contingencies in responses to behavior—to foster in students the belief that they exercise control over their own rewards.[1] Note that clarity and consistency are not the same as rigidity, but some degree of structure and predictability is critical. In addition to making the contingency of rewards clear, fairness and consistency in implementing the advertised contingencies are important.

Clarifying the means to classroom rewards, however, does not guarantee perceptions of agency or capacity. Some students who very clearly understand the criteria for good grades still consider themselves to be unable to achieve these criteria. This requires making rewards genuinely accessible to all students.

---

[1] I discovered the hard way how easily students' beliefs in their ability to control rewards can be undermined. In an effort to reduce graduate students' obsessions with grades, I discouraged inquiries about grading criteria for my seminar—promising that if they focused on mastering the material good grades would follow. My intentions were good, but I underestimated the strength of good grades as a valued reinforcement. Among the many unintended consequences of my reluctance to discuss grading criteria were high anxiety and resentment. By giving students unclear contingencies of reinforcement—about the means to their desired end (an "A")—I received less effort from them than I would have if I had provided clear contingencies.

WEINER'S ATTRIBUTION THEORY

In some respects attribution theory is a refinement and elaboration of Rotter's concept of locus of control, yet it also reflects a significant departure from social learning theory. A primary difference is that attribution theorists, unlike social learning theorists, assume that humans are motivated primarily to understand themselves and the world around them—to "attain a cognitive mastery of the causal structure of [the] environment" (Kelly, 1967, p. 193).

Attribution theorists assume that individuals naturally search for an understanding of why events occur, especially when the outcome is important or unexpected (Weiner, 1992). Thus, the student who expects to do well but does poorly on a test will try to answer the question, "Why did I fail that test?" In a sense, attribution theory turns locus of control theory on its head. Whereas locus of control theorists study individuals' expectations related to future events, attribution theorists study perceptions of the cause of events that have already occurred.

Perceptions of the cause of outcomes are referred to as **causal attributions.** Outcomes typically studied in achievement contexts involve performance on tasks or tests. The most common attributions for performance outcomes are *ability* ("I did well because I'm smart"; "I did poorly because I'm dumb") and *effort* ("I did or did not study"; Weiner, 1992). Other attributions also are made—"I was lucky"; "The task was easy"; "The teacher explained things badly"; "My friend or parent helped me prepare"; "I didn't feel well"; "I was tired or hungry"; and so on—but these attributions are less common. Some perceived causes are highly idiosyncratic. Indeed, very creative attributions for poor performance often are offered as excuses (e.g., "I was distracted by the coughing of the girl in front of me"; "I was hit in the head at football practice and had trouble concentrating").

Weiner (1979, 1985, 1986, 1992, 1994) claimed that the specific causal attributions are less important in determining achievement behavior than the underlying dimensions of the attributions. The causal dimensions he described represent an elaboration and refinement of Rotter's internal–external locus of control dimension. Weiner noted that whether a cause is perceived as "internal" or "external" does not tell the full story, especially if the goal is to predict behavior in achievement situations. He claimed, for example, that effort and ability attributions, which are both internal and are treated equivalently by Rotter, have different behavioral implications. Most individuals see effort as being controlled by the individual, whereas most do not see ability as being controllable. Ability also generally is perceived as a relatively stable cause, whereas effort varies with the situation. Consequently, Weiner distinguishes between different internal causes of achievement outcomes with regard to their stability and controllability. The control and stability dimensions that Weiner added to Rotter's original internal–external dimension allow much more specific behavioral predictions from beliefs about the cause of reinforcement (i.e., success). (See also Graham, 1994.)

Thus, from Rotter's single internal–external locus of control dimension, Weiner developed three separate dimensions: locus, stability, and control. As in

Rotter's theory, *locus* refers to the source of the cause, that is, whether the outcome is contingent on an individual's characteristics or behavior ("internal") or on some "external" variable. The *stability* dimension differentiates between causes on the basis of their duration. Ability, for example, usually is considered to be relatively stable over time, whereas effort, luck, or mood can change at any moment. The *control* dimension concerns the degree of control an individual has over the cause. We control how much effort we exert, whereas presumably we have no control over how lucky we are.

An individual's own interpretation, not the interpretation of the attribution theorist, influences the individual's behavior in an achievement situation. Luck, for instance, could be perceived by some as being a relatively stable quality (i.e., "I am a lucky or unlucky person").

Antecedents to Attributions

Researchers have identified several factors that affect individuals' perceptions of the cause of achievement outcomes. *Consensus* information (i.e., information about how well others performed) is associated with the locus dimension of causal attributions. If all students in a class receive the same high grade, an external attribution (e.g., easy task or easy-grading teacher) is likely to be made. If only one student receives a good grade, that student is likely to make an internal attribution for her performance (e.g., high ability, studying).

Consistency is associated with the stability dimension. Outcomes that are consistent with previous performance (e.g., "I have always failed in the past, and I failed again this time") are likely to be attributed to stable causes, such as ability. Conversely, outcomes that are inconsistent with previous outcomes are most likely to be attributed to unstable causes, such as effort, luck, or an unusually hard or easy task.

Weiner's focus on the situational factors that affect students' attribution judgments is one of the major differences between his and Rotter's analysis of achievement-related cognitions. Rotter emphasized generalized beliefs that develop from experiences in achievement settings and are assumed to hold regardless of situational factors.

Attribution Dispositions

A few attribution researchers, however, have studied relatively stable individual differences in individuals' tendencies to attribute achievement outcomes to one cause versus another (e.g., Fincham, Hokoda, & Sanders, 1989; see Graham, 1991, for further discussion). These researchers conceptualize attributions, as Rotter conceptualized locus of control, to some degree as a generalized set of relatively stable beliefs that evolve from previous experiences and socialization.

They have studied several factors contributing to attribution dispositions—including past performance, culture, gender, and teachers' attitudes and behaviors.

Studies have shown that students who have a *history of poor performance*, such as Hannah, are more likely to attribute success to external causes and failure to a lack of ability than students who have a history of good performance (Butkowsky & Willows, 1980; Greene, 1985; Marsh, 1984a; Stipek & Hoffman, 1980). Consistent with this research are findings that children with mental retardation and learning disabilities, who presumably experience failure frequently, are more likely to blame themselves for their failures than normally developing or achieving children (see Licht, 1992, in press).

Past performance also affects attribution dispositions indirectly through the perceptions of competence that students develop. Thus, students who, because of repeated failures, develop perceptions of themselves as being academically incompetent, interpret achievement outcomes as being consistent with this view. Failure is attributed to their lack of ability and success is attributed to some external cause (e.g., an easy task; Ames, 1978; Marsh, Cairns, Relich, Barnes, & Debus, 1984).

There is also evidence for *cultural differences* in beliefs about the causes of achievement outcomes. Japanese and Chinese have been found to attribute outcomes more to effort and less to ability than Americans (Chen & Stevenson, 1995; Chen & Uttal, 1988; Holloway, 1988; Holloway, Kashiwagi, Hess, & Azuma, 1986; Lee, Ichikawa, & Stevenson, 1987; Stevenson, Lee, & Stigler, 1986; Tuss, Zimmer, & Ho, 1995). This emphasis is consistent with traditional Asian philosophy that assumes malleability in humans and stresses the importance of striving for improvement. Culturally different beliefs about the causes of achievement outcomes suggest that these perceptions, to some degree, are socialized. Parents and teachers within our culture, therefore, may influence children's perceptions of the cause of achievement outcomes.

Gender differences also are found commonly in attribution research. Many studies have found that females were less likely than males to attribute success to their own high ability and more likely to attribute failure to low ability (Cramer & Oshima, 1992; Dweck & Reppucci, 1973; Eccles et al., 1983; Nicholls, 1975, 1979a, 1980; Parsons, Meece, Adler, & Kaczala, 1982; Stipek, 1984c; see Sohn, 1982, for a meta-analysis). Gender differences are more prominent in domains such as math and science, which are stereotyped more often as "male domains." In a study of fifth- and sixth-grade students, for example, I found that in math girls were more likely to attribute failure to their lack of ability and less likely to attribute success to their ability than were boys; in contrast, there were no differences in boys' and girls' perceptions of the cause of achievement outcomes in spelling (Stipek, 1984c; see also Gitelson, Petersen, & Tobin-Richards, 1982; Ryckman & Peckhan, 1987; Stipek & Gralinski, 1991).

Many researchers have suggested explanations for the observed gender differences in attribution patterns. For instance, girls' attribution biases have been linked to low confidence in ability (Frieze, 1975) and to low expectations for success (Deaux, 1976). These perceptions are not easy to explain, given girls' relatively good performance.

Measurement

Weiner emphasized situation-specific attributions that can be measured by asking open-ended questions (e.g., "Why did you do well or poorly on your spelling test?") or by providing a set of options (e.g., effort, ability, task difficulty) and asking the respondent to rate the importance of each cause. Other researchers have assessed students' generalized perceptions of the cause of academic outcomes. In some studies they ask subjects to rate the causes of an outcome experienced by a hypothetical person described to them in a story. It is assumed that subjects project their own beliefs about the causes of academic outcomes in their ratings. In other studies students are asked to think about their own past academic outcomes. Table 5-1 is an example of how students' beliefs about the causes of outcomes might be measured. The questions easily could be adapted to apply to a

TABLE 5-1 Measure of Attributions for Performance on Academic Tasks

Rate the importance of each explanation.	Not at all a reason				An important reason
When you do well in school, is it usually because					
You studied hard?	1	2	3	4	5
You studied the right things?	1	2	3	4	5
You are smart?	1	2	3	4	5
The teacher explained things well?	1	2	3	4	5
You were helped by someone?	1	2	3	4	5
The work was easy?	1	2	3	4	5
When you do poorly in school, is it usually because					
You did not study much?	1	2	3	4	5
You did not study the right things?	1	2	3	4	5
You are not smart?	1	2	3	4	5
The teacher did not explain things well?	1	2	3	4	5
You were not helped by anyone?	1	2	3	4	5
The work was hard?	1	2	3	4	5

particular outcome (e.g., the student's grade on a test) or to outcomes in a particular subject area. (See Weiner, 1983, for a discussion of measurement issues.)

Consequences of Attributions

The consequences of attributions are what make them relevant to discussions of motivation in the classroom. Different dimensions are associated with different kinds of consequences.

EXPECTATIONS

Performance expectations usually rise following success and fall after failure. Motivation theorists refer to these expectancy changes as **typical shifts.** Attribution theorists have shown that typical shifts occur only when a stable attribution for past performance is made (see Weiner, 1980a, 1992). This is because past outcomes attributed to unstable causes do not have clear implications for future performance. The stability dimension, therefore, is associated with performance expectations.

Generally, it is assumed that effort attributions are more constructive than most other attributions for learning, in part because of the implications effort attributions have for expectations about future performance (Weiner, 1994). Effort usually is considered unstable. Students who attribute past failure to low effort, therefore, can hope for success in the future (assuming that they are willing to exert greater effort). Students who attribute past failure to low ability (in the sense of a stable trait), however, are not as likely to exert effort on future tasks because without the prerequisite ability they cannot expect success.

An effort attribution is also desirable when success occurs. The perception that effort is an important cause of success implies that the student possesses the required ability, but acknowledges that success is not achieved without some effort. In contrast, attributing success solely to ability can have negative effects on behavior in achievement situations. When students succeed without trying very hard, they may come to believe that effort is not needed for success. Therefore, they will not try very hard on future tasks, and, as a result, they will perform at levels below their true capabilities.

HELPLESSNESS

Attributing failure to causes that the individual does not control can lead to maladaptive behavior referred to as **learned helplessness.** Learned helplessness was first investigated in animals by Seligman and Maier (1967). Dogs were placed in a situation in which nothing they did prevented them from receiving a mild shock. The dogs soon became passive in the "helpless" situation, making no attempts to avoid being shocked, even when they were placed in a situation in which they could avoid it. Other dogs who previously were able to prevent shock by their own behaviors quickly learned the avoidance strategy. The authors claim that the animals in the helpless situation became passive because they perceived the environment to be unresponsive to (or not contingent on) their own behaviors.

Learned helplessness in achievement situations occurs when students—usually those who have experienced a great deal of failure, such as Hannah—believe that there is nothing that they can do to avoid failure. When they do fail, helpless children typically attribute the failure to their low ability, which they believe they cannot control (Dweck & Goetz, 1978). These students exert little effort on school tasks and give up easily when they encounter difficulty. They are unresponsive to teachers' exhortations to try and generally seem disengaged from classroom activities. Many studies have demonstrated the debilitating effects of a low-ability attribution for failure on subsequent performance (see Weiner, 1994). Table 5-2 lists additional behaviors associated with learned helplessness and can be used to identify children who have developed such maladaptive beliefs.

Much of the research on learned helplessness in achievement settings has been done by Dweck and her colleagues. In an early study, Dweck and Reppucci (1973) assessed connections between children's beliefs about the cause of achievement outcomes and their reactions to failure. In this study, children were given a questionnaire. Those children who indicated that they believed that controllable factors, such as effort, determined achievement outcomes tended to persist at an experimental task even after experiencing failure. The performance of children who indicated that they tend to blame their failures on uncontrollable factors, such as the difficulty of the task or their lack of ability, deteriorated under failure conditions; these children gave up quickly when they encountered difficulty on the experimental task (see also Diener & Dweck, 1978). Licht and Dweck (1984)

TABLE 5-2 Behaviors Suggesting Learned Helplessness

◆ Says, "I can't."

◆ Does not pay attention to teacher's instructions.

◆ Does not ask for help, even when help is needed.

◆ Does nothing (e.g., stares out the window).

◆ Does not show pride in successes.

◆ Appears bored and uninterested.

◆ Is unresponsive to teacher's exhortations to try.

◆ Is easily discouraged.

◆ Does not volunteer answers to teacher's questions.

◆ Does not interact socially with classmates.

likewise found that the performance of children who minimized the role of effort in achievement outcomes (i.e., helpless children), unlike that of children who emphasized effort, deteriorated when they encountered a confusing paragraph inserted into a text. Thus, in both studies the two groups of children behaved very differently in the same achievement situation, and their behaviors were related directly to their perceptions of the cause of achievement outcomes.

Diener and Dweck (1980) demonstrated that beliefs about the cause of achievement outcomes also affect children's reactions to success. They found that children who tended to attribute success to uncontrollable causes underestimated their number of successes, overestimated their number of failures, tended not to view their successes as indicative of ability, and tended not to expect success in the future. These studies illustrate how generalized beliefs can supersede situational variables.

Licht and Dweck (1984) suggested that high-achieving girls may be particularly vulnerable to learned helplessness. They found, in the study previously described, that the higher boys rated their intelligence, the less debilitated they were by the confusing paragraph. In contrast, girls' ratings of their intelligence tended to correlate negatively with their performance in the confusing condition. That is, the girls who considered themselves to be bright (and by objective evidence were relatively bright) were most debilitated by the confusing paragraph. The authors proposed that attribution tendencies may contribute to girls' lower participation in higher levels of mathematics because in math, more than in most other subject areas, students encounter tasks that, at first, may be difficult or confusing. These are the conditions that are most likely to elicit helpless behavior.

Although learned helplessness is more common among low-achieving children, it can be seen even in children who perform relatively well in school. Even children identified as being gifted are not immune to maladaptive attributions and feelings of helplessness (Cramer & Oshimar, 1992). Indeed, gifted children may be especially vulnerable because parents, usually proud of their children's special academic talents, sometimes have exceptionally high expectations that the children feel incapable of fulfilling. Children who regard any performance that is below parents' expectations as failure, and who do not believe that they can meet those expectations, may stop trying altogether. Gifted children also can develop learned helplessness as a result of being moved to a special class for gifted children. A child who is accustomed to being the highest achiever in a regular class may not adjust easily to performing at a comparatively lower level among other gifted children. A lower standing in the gifted class can cause feelings of failure and a belief that no amount of effort will ensure success (which the child defines as being one of the best in the class). This belief presumably explains why Safe Sally (see Chapter 1) dropped out of her calculus class after getting a "C+" on the first quiz.

Clearly, it is best to prevent children from developing an attribution pattern that results in helpless behaviors. As we saw with Hannah, such an attribution pattern is difficult to reverse. Children can fall into self-perpetuating cycles in which they attribute failure to causes over which they have no control, do nothing to avoid failure in subsequent situations, and consequently fail again, thus confirming their perceptions of themselves as being low in competence—and so the cycle continues. In Chapter 7, strategies for preventing attributions associated with helpless behavior and for altering maladaptive attribution patterns when they occur are discussed.

EMOTIONS

Weiner and his colleagues have examined the effects of different causal attributions on individuals' emotional reactions to their own as well as to others' achievement outcomes (see Graham & Weiner, 1993; Weiner, 1980b, 1985, 1986, 1992, 1994, 1995). In a series of studies using adult subjects, Weiner, Russell, and Lerman (1978, 1979) found that some emotions occur strictly as a function of outcome, regardless of an individual's perception of the cause of the outcome. Thus, students are happy when they succeed and sad when they fail, regardless of their attribution for the cause of their success or failure. Other emotions are tied to specific attributions. Students claim to feel surprised when they attribute success or failure to luck, grateful when they attribute success to someone else's help, and guilty when they attribute failure to a lack of effort. Pride and shame occur only when one's own outcome is attributed to some internal cause. For example, a student who attributes success to her own hard work and ability is more likely to be proud of herself than a student who attributes success to help received from another individual. Personal failure attributed to internal causes such as lack of effort or ability, similarly, is more likely to result in feelings of shame than failure blamed on external causes (e.g., an unfair teacher, interfering noise while taking a test). Studies show that children even as young as 3 years of age show more pride when they succeed on difficult tasks (for which they can take personal responsibility) than when they succeed on easy tasks (which should engender an external, task difficulty, attribution; Lewis, Allessandri, & Sullivan, 1992). (See also Mone and Baker, 1992; Niedenthal, Tangney, and Gavanski, 1994; Numi, 1991; and Van Overwalle, Mervielde, and De Schuyter, 1995, for research on attribution–emotion linkages.)

Consider, for example, a situation in which a student receives the only "A" in the class versus a situation in which everyone in the class receives an "A." In the former case, the student is likely to attribute the successful outcome to his own behavior or disposition; in the latter case, the student is likely to attribute the successful outcome to an indiscriminate teacher or an easy test. The student who makes the internal attribution should feel more pride than the student who makes an external attribution. Consider next the student who knows before she begins a multiple-choice test that she did not study for the test and has not mastered the material. She nevertheless does fairly well on the exam by guessing and attributes her successful performance to good luck. Because an external attribution is made, she may experience relief and happiness, but not pride (unless she sees good luck as a personal characteristic or something she controls).

These emotional consequences of attributions have important practical implications. The anticipation of feeling proud can sustain a student's effort on a difficult task, just as the anticipation of feeling ashamed can inhibit a student from approaching an achievement task (Atkinson, 1964; Weiner, 1980b, 1985, 1986). Weiner (1992) claimed that guilt, which is associated with low-effort attributions for failure, is a more desirable negative emotion than shame, because guilt engenders a desire to make amends (and therefore increases effort in the future), and shame engenders a desire to withdraw. He further claimed that internal attributions for success are associated with self-esteem. The attribution analysis, therefore, explains why success with easy tasks, which is likely to be attributed to an external rather than an internal cause, does not engender pride or increase self-esteem.

Support for some of the proposed effects of emotions on achievement behavior comes from a study by Covington and Omelich (1984a), in which college students' guilt about their performance on one midterm was associated with enhanced effort and performance on the next midterm, and humiliation for previous performance was associated with subsequent decreased effort and performance.

Links between attributions and emotions also have implications for how individuals respond to others' behaviors. Weiner (1992, 1994) pointed out that attributing a student's failure to an uncontrollable cause, such as poor health, poor English language skills, or poor ability, produces sympathy, whereas anger is the more likely response to failure the teacher attributes to controllable causes, such as low effort or sloppiness. Studies have shown that children as young as 6 years of age understand that people experience anger when they attribute a negative outcome to a controllable cause, such as low effort, and by 9 years of age they associate pity with attributions to uncontrollable causes (e.g., a disability or lack of intelligence; Graham, Doubleday, & Guarino, 1984; Weiner, Graham, Stern, & Lawson, 1982; see also Butler, 1994). Children's own judgments about the causes of their performance, therefore, may be affected by the teacher's or their parents' emotional reactions; a teacher's response of anger to low performance may foster a belief that the outcome was caused by low effort (a controllable cause), and a sympathetic response may foster a belief that the outcome was caused by low ability (an uncontrollable cause; Graham, 1984a, 1984b, 1990; Graham & Weiner, 1993). (See Chapter 12 for a more extended discussion of ways in which teachers convey their perceptions of the cause of students' performance through their emotional expressions.)

CONCLUSION

Like Bandura's social cognitive theory, Atkinson's, Rotter's, and Weiner's theories all represent a significant departure from strict reinforcement theory. Reinforcement theory is "mechanistic" in that it does not incorporate beliefs, values, expectations, emotions, or anything else that is not observable directly. Cognitive theorists, such as those reviewed in this chapter, consider unobservable thoughts and feelings to be important factors in understanding achievement behavior. Reinforcement theory focuses on the individual's environment, specifically the contingencies of reinforcement. Cognitive theorists focus on the individual's *interpretation* of the environment.

Chapter 6 focuses on individuals' beliefs about their competencies. This particular judgment underlies, to some degree, the cognitions (e.g., expectations for success, perceptions of control, perceptions of the cause of outcomes) emphasized in the achievement motivation theories previously discussed.

TABLE 5-3 Summary of Terms

Term	Definition
Expectancy x Value Theory	
Motive for success (Ms)/ need to achieve (Nach)	Unconscious disposition to strive for success
Motive to avoid failure (MAF)	Unconscious disposition that directs individuals away from achievement tasks
Perceived probability of success (Ps)	Individuals' expectations regarding the probability of success on a task
Incentive value of success (Is)	Amount of pride anticipated—inversely related to the perceived probability of success
Perceived probability of failure (Pf)	Individuals' expectations regarding the probability of failure on a task
Incentive value of failure (If)	Amount of shame anticipated—inversely related to the perceived probability of failure
Resultant tendency to approach or avoid an achievement activity (TA)	The strength of the tendency to approach a task minus the strength of the tendency to avoid a task
Locus of Control Theory	
Locus of control (LOC)	Beliefs about whether reinforcement is contingent on one's behavior or characteristics
Strategy (means-ends) beliefs	Beliefs about the extent to which certain strategies or means are sufficient to cause particular ends
Capacity (agency) beliefs	Beliefs about the extent to which a person has access to those means
Attribution Theory	
Causal attributions	Perceptions of the cause of outcomes
Typical shifts	Performance expectations rise after success and fall after failure
Learned helplessness	Unwillingness to try as a consequence of a belief that rewards are not contingent on one's behavior

Perceptions of Ability

$\mathbf{P}$erceptions of ability play an important role in all cognitive theories of achievement motivation. Confidence in one's ability is critical to self-efficacy in Bandura's social learning theory. In Atkinson's theory, individuals who believe they are competent at performing a task should perceive their probability of success as being high and, consequently, they should be more likely to approach the task than individuals who believe they lack the necessary competencies. In Rotter's locus of control theory, individuals who believe that they are academically competent are more likely to believe that they control rewards associated with academic success (that they have the capacity to achieve the performance on which rewards are contingent). And, in Weiner's attribution theory, individuals who consider themselves competent at a task probably will attribute success to their ability and effort, and attribute failure to some other cause; in contrast, those who think they are incompetent will attribute failure to lack of ability and will search for an external explanation for success. Consistent with these theoretical analyses, many studies have shown that perceptions of ability influence information seeking, task choice, intended effort, persistence, thoughts and feelings while working on tasks, evaluations and attributions about one's performance, and ultimate achievement (see Byrne, 1996; Eccles, Wigfield, & Schiefele, in press; Hattie, 1992; Marsh, 1990; Meyer, 1987; Miserandino, 1996).

Deci, Ryan, Connell, and their colleagues proposed that individuals have a fundamental need to see themselves as being competent (Connell, 1991; Connell & Ryan, 1984; Deci & Ryan, 1985). And Covington (1992) claimed that in this culture self-confidence in one's intellectual competence is fundamental to a sense of self-worth.

Many behaviors designed to promote perceptions of competence, such as exerting effort to be competent, are adaptive. But many other behaviors directed at this purpose actually inhibit the development of genuine competencies. This chapter describes some of the maladaptive strategies individuals use to maintain perceptions of competence when it is threatened. Gender and age-related differences that have been found in research on self-perceptions of ability also are discussed, as well as potential effects of school practices, such as ability grouping and tracking. Finally, strategies for assessing students' self-perceptions relative to their competencies are provided. First, however, we need to consider carefully what we mean by "ability."

WHAT IS "ABILITY"?

Dweck and Elliott (1983) claimed that adults use two different concepts of ability (see also Cain & Dweck, 1989; Dweck & Bempechat, 1983; Dweck & Leggett, 1988). According to an **entity** concept, ability is a stable trait. An entity theory, such as the notion of an intelligence quotient (IQ), also is associated with assumptions that ability is distributed unevenly among individuals (i.e., some have more of "it" than others) and that it is a general trait that affects learning and performance in various domains.

According to an **instrumental–incremental** concept, ability consists of "an ever-expanding repertoire of skills and knowledge . . . that is increased through one's own instrumental behavior" (Dweck & Bempechat, 1983, p. 144). Ability, by this definition, is more task specific and is developed through study or practice. One's ability in one area is not necessarily relevant to her ability in another area.

Most adults use both conceptions, sometimes with regard to the same skill area. For example, occasionally when I play tennis and am especially discouraged after a poor performance, I believe that I am constitutionally uncoordinated and incapable of ever learning to play the game. I am convinced that no amount of practice will result in any significant improvement. But when I am more optimistic, perhaps encouraged by an unusually patient opponent, I believe that with a little practice, my game will improve. The former view is an example of an entity theory of tennis ability; the latter illustrates an instrumental–incremental theory.

Dweck and her colleagues claimed that students' concepts of intellectual ability have important implications for their behaviors in achievement contexts. The goal of students who accept entity concepts is to look smart, regardless of how much is learned. (See Chapter 9 for further discussion of student goals.) Those who are fairly confident about their ability seek opportunities to demonstrate it, but, like Safe Sally (see Chapter 1), they tend to select tasks in which there is no risk of failure, never testing the limits of their abilities. Studies have shown that when such students encounter difficulty, their self-efficacy plummets. Students who have an entity concept of ability but lack confidence in their own ability avoid achievement situations, especially those in which their lack of ability would be revealed. If they are given a choice of tasks, they may select very easy or very difficult tasks so that failure is not necessarily attributable to low ability. If students may not choose which tasks they perform, as is usually the case in school, they, like Helpless Hannah (see Chapter 1), often develop learned helplessness (Burhans & Dweck, 1995).

The goal of children who develop instrumental–incremental concepts of ability is not to look smart, but to be smart by increasing their skill levels. When they fail, they assume that practice and effort will increase their chances of future success. Such children select moderately difficult tasks from which they are likely to learn more than they would learn on very easy tasks that require little effort or very difficult tasks that may be impossible to complete. They show evidence of mastery-oriented behaviors rather than helplessness, thus intensifying their effort, using effective strategies, and persisting when they encounter difficulty (see Burhans & Dweck, 1995).

Research suggests that teachers, like students, differ in the degree to which they see intellectual ability as being stable, or malleable and expanding. Midgley, Feldlaufer, and Eccles (1988) found, moreover, that teachers who consider math ability to be a fixed trait perceived themselves to be less efficacious and had stronger needs to control student behavior than did teachers who believed that math ability can readily be changed. This study demonstrated how important it is for teachers to monitor their own beliefs and the effects these beliefs have on their instructional strategies.

Dweck's distinction between a concept of ability as a stable trait versus as a skill that can be developed has implications for how effort is viewed. According to an entity definition, effort has limited potential for increasing ability, and under certain circumstances it can undermine one's image of being capable. This is because effort and ability are assumed to be related inversely; if two people achieve the same level of performance, the person who exerts less effort is considered to be more capable. If you are an entity theorist, claiming that you did not study for a test is a good way to look smart; if you do not do well, you can attribute your poor performance to low effort rather than low ability. If you do well despite not studying, you look very smart.

Unfortunately, this kind of reasoning can lead to behaviors that have more serious consequences than misleading friends on how much you studied. Covington and his colleagues have studied the maladaptive strategies that students sometimes use to "look smart."

COVINGTON'S SELF-WORTH THEORY

Self-worth concerns people's appraisal of their own value. It is similar to such concepts as self-esteem and self-respect. A fundamental assumption of Covington's self-worth theory is that humans naturally strive to protect their sense of self-worth when it is threatened, such as in the case of public failure (Covington, 1984, 1985, 1992; Covington & Beery, 1976). Consistent with this assumption, research indicates that individuals often take more responsibility for their successes than for their failures (Miller & Ross, 1975). And, as we will see later, students employ creative strategies to maintain a sense of worthiness when they face failure in school.

Covington and his colleagues believed that individuals' emotional reactions in achievement situations are influenced strongly by the implications that the outcomes have for their own and others' perceptions of their ability—that is, whether outcomes make them look competent or incompetent (using Dweck's entity definition of ability; see Covington & Omelich, 1981). Thus, failure engenders shame and distress the most when it appears to reflect low ability, and least when it can be attributed to some other cause. Affective reactions associated with low-ability judgments should be more negative for entity than for incremental theorists because a judgment of low ability has more profound and long-term implications for the former than for the latter (i.e., "It is something about me that I cannot do much to change").

Children like Defensive Dave (see Chapter 1), who are not confident that effort will result in success, are in a real bind. If they try but fail, they provide unambiguous evidence that they lack ability. If they do not try, they have an alternative explanation for their failures, but because effort also is valued and rewarded in most classrooms, they risk disapproval and punishment (Blumenfeld, Hamilton, Bossert, Wessels, & Meece, 1983; Eswara, 1972; Rest, Nierenberg, Weiner, & Heckhausen, 1973; Weiner, 1994, 1995). Thus, although failure with high effort engenders more shame or humiliation for students, failure with low effort elicits the most disapproval from teachers. This is why Covington and Omelich (1979a) referred to effort as a "double-edged sword." And it is why teachers' and students' goals sometimes conflict with each other. Teachers want to maximize student effort, and students want to maximize perceptions of their ability, which sometimes means that they do not try.

Self-worth theory is relevant to school because in most educational settings academic performance is the dominant criterion for evaluation. Ability in the sense of a stable trait often is perceived to be a critical ingredient for academic success, which generally is valued in this culture. And students' judgments of their academic competence are associated strongly with assessments of their general self-esteem (see Wigfield, Eccles, & Pintrich, 1996). Some antiacademic success values that some adolescents develop, at least in part, may reflect an unconscious effort to maintain self-esteem after they decide that academic success is not achievable. Their antiacademic posture may be partly a defensive attitude of last resort, rather than a genuine choice.

The strong link between self-perceptions of ability and of self-worth can be problematic for all students. Covington pointed out that a competitive educational setting precludes success for many students. Because everyone cannot be a relatively high performer, some students' self-worth is inevitably threatened. When the number of rewards and other indicators of ability (e.g., high grades) are restricted by reliance on a normal curve, then one person's success is achieved at the expense of another's. Even if grading is not done on a normal curve, a competitive atmosphere causes students to take classmates' performance into consideration when evaluating their own performance.

According to Covington, typical American classrooms threaten students' self-worth. In most schools rewards that symbolize success (e.g., good grades) are based on relative performance, thus guaranteeing failure for some students. Goals are determined by the teacher and, because some students face goals that are too difficult for them, genuine effort will not be rewarded. Even if the teacher attempts to individualize goals, because of the competitive nature of most classrooms, students attend to their classmates' accomplishments and often strive to keep up with them—regardless of whether their classmates' achievements represent realistic goals for them.

The emphasis on ability as being an important attribute in this culture, the impossibility of all students succeeding, and the value placed on correct responses force students such as Dave to develop strategies to protect themselves from the negative implications that failure usually has for one's ability. Most of these strategies, vividly described in Covington and Beery (1976), are self-defeating. This is why some theorists refer to them as "self-handicapping" (Riggs, 1992). A few of the more common strategies are described next.

Avoiding Negative Implications of Failure for Ability

Students can avoid school failure, to some degree, by minimizing participation. Being absent, especially on the day of the big test, is not uncommon. Not volunteering answers to questions in class is less drastic.

But students in most classrooms cannot escape some level of participation. Therefore, they must resort to more subtle methods of avoiding failure, or in those cases in which failure is unavoidable, resort to sidestepping a low-ability attribution. The student's task is to engender attributions for failure that do not have negative implications for ability.

For example, some students simply do not try—or at least they try to make people think that they do not try. Performance with no effort provides no information about students' abilities because no one can determine what they would have accomplished had they exerted more effort. This common strategy is seen in elementary grades as well as in college classrooms. Some students publicize their refusal to work and downgrade the importance of studying. Teachers often are frustrated and puzzled by such behavior, but obstinate refusal to exert any effort has its own logic. It achieves the short-term goal of avoiding a low-ability attribution for the failure.

Sometimes students will give the impression that they did not try, even though they did (Jagacinski & Nicholls, 1990). They claim they did not study for a test, or they guessed on all the questions, even though they actually exerted considerable effort. Strategies designed to influence others' perceptions are referred to by social psychologists as "self-presentational strategies," for **impres-**

sion management (Midgley, Arunkumar, & Urdan, 1996; Midgley & Urdan, 1995).

There are risks, of course, when such strategies are employed. As mentioned previously, teachers expect students to try, and they reward and punish students accordingly. Students, therefore, must balance their needs for avoiding the implications of failure with their desires to avoid punishment. Simultaneously, they must deal with the knowledge that failing with high effort suggests low ability, and that not trying often results in punishment and has its own negative implications for self-worth. Students who anticipate failure are in a no-win situation. If they try hard and fail, they look stupid; if they do not try, they are reprimanded by the teacher. The evidence is clear, however, that some students who have to choose between the teacher's wrath for not trying and the feelings of humiliation and incompetence associated with trying and failing will choose the former (Covington, Spratt, & Omelich, 1980).

Some students are clever enough to find a middle ground that allows them to avoid punishment for not trying. They exert just enough effort to stay out of trouble, but not so much that failure unambiguously implies lack of ability. They know that to maximize the desired image of a hard worker it is best to look eager, and then pray that the teacher calls on someone else. Extreme attention to note taking with head bowed so as not to catch the teacher's eye is a technique I used as a college student. Sitting in the back of the room, positioned out of view of the teacher, is another useful technique.

Covington and Beery (1976) gave examples of similar strategies that they referred to as *false effort*—feigning attention during a class discussion, asking a question even though the answer already is known, or giving the outer appearance of thinking by adopting a pensive quizzical expression. These behaviors do not reflect a real attempt to learn. Rather, they are designed to make the student look smart and attentive and to allow him to stay out of trouble.

Other ploys also are used to maintain a perception of ability while avoiding censure for not trying. *Excuses* are probably the most typically used strategy to avoid the negative sanctions associated with low effort, although clearly, to be effective, they must be used sparingly.[1]

Procrastination is another common strategy used to avoid the negative implications of failure. Creating a personal handicap by not studying until the very last minute provides the student with a ready, nonability-related explanation for subsequent failure. As mentioned previously, successful students occasionally use this technique to enhance their images of being highly competent. They are careful to announce before a test that they did not begin studying until midnight the night

---

[1]In my experience, college students are exasperated by a refusal to listen to their excuses. Allowing students to retake an examination or rewrite a paper seems to be less important to them than listening to the nonability-related reasons for their previous poor performance. An opportunity for success with the second round, apparently, is less effective in preserving a perception of competence and self-worth than the opportunity to make sure I attribute their previous failure to external causes (e.g., "My child was sick all weekend, and I wasn't able to study").

before and are concerned about their performance. Then, their good performance can be attributed to extremely high ability because effort has been ruled out as an explanation. This technique is also a useful safeguard for students who are uncertain about their levels of performance; if they do poorly they have a ready excuse that has ambiguous implications for their abilities.

Other strategies also are used by students to avoid the implications of failure for ability. One paradoxical strategy is to *set unattainable performance goals*. Failure is assured, but failure at an extremely difficult task usually does not imply low ability, whereas failure at a task that is considered to be very easy inescapably results in a judgment of low ability. Perhaps this is why Sears (1940) found that children who had a history of success in school set their academic goals at realistic levels, but students who had experienced considerable failures often overestimated, sometimes by extreme degrees, how well they would perform on various arithmetic and reading tasks. For some of the failure-prone students, the poorer their performance, the higher they set their aspirations. Sears suggested that the unrealistic goal setting might result also from the poor-performing students' unfulfilled desires for approval; the mere statement of a worthy goal, not its attainment, becomes the source of esteem.

If an individual is uncertain about her ability and wants to preserve an image of being a capable person, then tasks that provide the least information on ability should be attempted. Selecting very difficult tasks allows individuals who are uncertain about their abilities to avoid the danger of evidence suggesting incompetence. Even though failure may be ensured on a very difficult task, this failure provides little information on the individual's competency.

Evidence suggests that simply labeling a task as "highly difficult" can improve the performance of those who are concerned about performance and chronically worry about failure (Feather, 1961, 1963; Karabenick & Youssef, 1968). Presumably, the performance of these individuals is less debilitated by anxiety because if they fail, they can attribute the failure to the extreme difficulty of the task rather than to their own incompetencies.

Miller (1985) provided a compelling demonstration of how describing a task as being difficult can alleviate student anxiety and enhance effort. He gave sixth-grade children a series of matching tasks that were constructed in such a way as to ensure failure. Following this experience, the children were given an anagram task to work on while their behavior was monitored. Children who were told that the subsequent task was moderately difficult completed fewer anagrams than those who were told that the anagram task was very difficult. The concerns about competence that were created by experiencing failure on the matching tasks, and the performance deficits associated with such concerns, were alleviated by simply telling children that the next task was very difficult. Presumably, this message allowed children to try hard with no risk of demonstrating low competence on yet another task (see also Miller & Hom, 1990). The effect was especially prominent for boys, suggesting that boys may be more concerned about their public images than girls.

Success without Learning

Another approach to maintaining an image of ability is to *ensure success*. *Cheating* is perhaps the most common method of ensuring success without learning. Another method is to attempt only very easy tasks. Success is assured, but little learning results. This is Safe Sally's strategy (see Chapter 1). She avoids challenging tasks and, therefore, preserves her image of being a capable person. A related strategy is to have very low aspirations. A student may announce to friends before a test that he would be delighted just to be able to pass the test. Anything above a passing grade, therefore, can be construed as a success. In any new skill situation, it is useful to announce beforehand that "I'm not very good at this." This lowers the expectations of observers. Then, even mediocre performance is perceived as evidence that the person is "actually pretty good." (I do this every time I play tennis against a new opponent.)

A strategy to ensure success in a group question-and-answer period is to rehearse answers to the question that one is likely to be asked.[2] If teachers ask predictable questions, or if they question students in a predictable order, it is often possible to rehearse or plan a response to one's own question. Although this strategy precludes learning from other students' questions and answers, it maximizes the probability of giving a correct answer.

Related to these kinds of success-ensuring (but not necessarily learning-ensuring) tactics is what Covington and Beery (1976) referred to as *overstriving*. The overstriver is driven by an intense desire to succeed, but more important, to avoid failure. Again, Sally is a good example. Her schoolwork is characterized by overpreparedness and excessive attention to detail. Because of the tremendous effort exerted, successes naturally are attributed to effort. Thus, she continues to harbor doubts about her real abilities. Covington and Beery pointed out that overstrivers' uncertainties about their abilities make them extremely vulnerable when failure occurs. As a consequence, they develop a "loathing of failure far out of proportion to its importance" (p. 57).

Summary

These strategies can reduce anxiety or humiliation in the short run. However, all of them inhibit real learning and, in the long run, make real success impossible. Evidence suggesting that incompetence will mount, despite all efforts to avoid

---

[2] A few years ago I took a Spanish class in an adult evening program. The teacher frequently gave us a printed set of questions and proceeded around the table in order, asking students to answer the questions. I expertly avoided the public humiliation of giving a wrong answer by counting around the table to figure out which question I would be asked. I concentrated all my efforts on practicing my answer to that question. This classic technique effectively achieved my immediate goal—to be successful and therefore to avoid looking incompetent—but the positive consequences were short lived. By not attending to questions that other students answered, I minimized the amount that I learned. My strategy temporarily allowed me to preserve an image of competence, but I still cannot speak Spanish.

such a conclusion, and plausible self-serving explanations become more and more difficult to provide. Children who are uncertain about their competencies and, as a result, expend their energies on avoiding "looking dumb" rather than on learning, eventually become convinced of their incompetencies and stop trying altogether. Such children are transformed from failure-avoiding students (e.g., Dave) to failure-accepting students (e.g., Hannah). Dave's approach in achievement settings was hardly conducive to learning, but it did preserve some semblance of competence. Hannah had given up altogether and instead of attempting to give the impression that she knew what she was doing, she became resigned to her incompetence. Rather than searching for some external explanation for her failures, Hannah took responsibility for them. Thus, although Dave is able to maintain some, albeit fragile, sense of self-worth, at least for the present time, Hannah either must exclude academic ability as a factor related to self-worth, which is not easy in most schooling environments, or she must devalue her own worth, which is a tragedy.

GENDER DIFFERENCES IN SELF-PERCEPTIONS OF ABILITY

Although the evidence is inconsistent, many studies find that girls rate their competencies lower than boys, even when their performance is just as good (see Eccles, Wigfield, Harold, & Blumenfeld, 1993; Licht & Dweck, 1984; Meece & Courtney, 1992; Meece et al., 1982), especially in math and science (Betz & Hackett, 1983; Eccles, 1993; Entwisle & Baker, 1983; Fennema & Sherman, 1977; Hackett & Betz, 1992; Heller & Parsons, 1981; Kahle & Damnjanovic, 1994; Meece et al., 1990; Rennie, Parker, & Kahle, 1996; Stevenson & Newman, 1986; Stipek & Gralinski, 1991; Wigfield & Eccles, 1994). Gender differences are found even among gifted and high-achieving females (Eccles et al., in press). Girls' lower perceptions of their competencies are important because they may contribute to the underrepresentation of females in stereotypically male professions (Hackett & Betz, 1992; Meece & Courtney, 1992).

The reasons for gender differences, no doubt, are embedded deeply in cultural stereotypes and the messages teachers and parents subtly convey to boys and girls. There is some evidence that girls may be influenced more by parental evaluations than boys (Eccles et al., 1983), and Eccles (1993; Jacobs & Eccles, 1992) reported from her studies that the mothers who had stereotyped beliefs about math competency (i.e., boys are naturally more talented than girls), rated sons' competencies higher than daughters' competencies. Parents also claimed to spend less time working or playing on the computer with girls than with boys, and they reported that they encouraged girls less than boys to do math or science activities (Eccles, 1993). Whatever the roots of girls' tendencies to rate their competencies lower than boys, the challenge for teachers is to overcome such biases that could undermine girls' actual mastery in those domains in which their self-confidence is relatively low. Chapter 12 discusses strategies for conveying high expectations to both boys and girls.

AGE-RELATED CHANGES IN SELF-PERCEPTIONS OF ABILITY

Helpless Hannahs and Defensive Daves are more common in higher grades than in the first few grades of school. This is because children's concepts of ability change and because their judgments of their own abilities decline, on average, with age.

When asked about their academic abilities, most kindergarten-age children claim to be the smartest in their class. In many studies of self-perceptions of academic ability, children's ratings are near the top of the scale through the early elementary grades and decline, on average, thereafter (e.g., Eccles, Wigfield, Harold, & Blumenfeld, 1993; Wigfield & Eccles, 1994; see also Stipek & Mac Iver, 1989; Wigfield et al., 1996). Similar declines have been found for self-efficacy beliefs (Shell, Colvin, & Bruning, 1995). As they decline, self-perceptions of ability become more accurate because they correlate more strongly with external indices (e.g., teacher's ratings; see Marsh, 1993; Newman, 1984; Nicholls, 1978, 1979a; Wigfield, 1994).

The typically strong positive bias in young children and the ensuing decline in their perceived competencies can be explained, in part, by changes in children's conceptions of academic competence and the criteria they use to assess it. Children in preschool (and to some degree in the first year or two of elementary school) have a broad concept of ability that includes social behavior, conduct, work habits, and effort (Blumenfeld, Pintrich, Meece, & Wessels, 1982; Stipek & Daniels, 1990; Stipek & Tannatt, 1984; Yussen & Kane, 1985). During the elementary years, children's definitions of academic ability become narrower and more differentiated by subject matter (Marsh, Barnes, Cairns, & Tidman, 1984; see also Marsh & Hattie, 1996).

Systematic age differences also have been found in the type of information regarding competence that children attend to most, in how they process different types of information, and in their propensity to make judgments based on intraindividual versus interindividual comparisons. Interview studies suggest that preschool-age children and children in the first few grades of elementary school focus on effort expended (Harter & Pike, 1984), personal mastery (Blumenfeld, Pintrich, & Hamilton, 1986; Stipek, 1981), and social reinforcement (Lewis, Wall, & Aronfreed, 1963; Spear & Armstrong, 1978) in their ability assessments. Emphasis on these sources of information declines with age, and the way children interpret this kind of information changes.

Consider effort, for example. Young children assume that people who try hard are smart and that people who are smart try hard. Nicholls and Miller (1984b) described a study in which children were shown a videotape of two actors, one who obviously did not try and the other who tried hard. Both actors were shown to receive the same high score. Many of the younger children simply refused to believe that one of the actors succeeded without effort. Some claimed that this actor must have started earlier or "must have been thinking while fiddling" (p. 195). (See also Miller, 1985; Nicholls, 1978, 1983, 1989, 1990; Nicholls, Jagacinski, & Miller, 1986; Nicholls & Miller, 1984a, 1984b, 1984c.)

Not until about the ages of 11 or 12 do children fully differentiate among performance, effort, and ability—what Nicholls referred to as a differentiated or "mature" concept of ability. Only the adolescents in the study previously described showed evidence of perceiving an inverse relationship between effort and ability, claiming that the actor in the videotape who worked very hard was less smart than the actor who did not work hard but achieved the same level of performance.

While effort and mastery become less important indicators of academic competence and change in their implications, children pay increasing attention to grades (Blumenfeld et al., 1986; Nicholls, 1978, 1979a), and they become more sensitive to differential treatment by teachers (see the following paragraphs). However, the most important developmental changes in the ability-assessment process concerns the use of social comparative information.

Children as young as preschool age make social comparisons and competitive, "besting" verbal statements (Mosatche & Bragonier, 1981). By the age of 3 1/2, children also react differently to winning and losing a competition (Heckhausen, 1984). Evidence suggests, however, that although preschool-age children may make simple comparisons with one other individual, they do not use group normative information (i.e., their own performance compared to the performance of a group of peers) to assess their competence until later (Aboud, 1985; Boggiano & Ruble, 1979; Butler & Ruzany, 1993; Nicholls, 1978; Ruble, Boggiano, Feldman, & Loebl, 1980; Ruble, Grosovsky, Frey, & Cohen, 1992; Ruble, Parsons, & Ross, 1976).

The evidence on whether children use normative information to evaluate their competencies in the first few grades of school is inconsistent (Levine, Snyder, & Mendez-Caratini, 1982; Morris & Nemcek, 1982; Ruble & Frey, 1991; Ruble et al., 1980). It is clear, however, that dramatic changes occur between kindergarten and the second or third grade (Butler, 1989; Ruble et al., 1980; Ruble, Feldman, & Boggiano, 1976; Stipek & Tannatt, 1984). By the third or fourth grade, children's ability judgments are affected consistently by normative information, and they begin to explain these judgments in social–comparative terms. Older children are also more skilled than younger children at interpreting social comparative information (Aboud, 1985; Ruble, 1983). For example, in one study, fifth graders, when judging their performance relative to a peer, took into consideration the different amounts of time they and the peer were given to work on a test, while second graders did not (Aboud, 1985).

Students' attention to social comparison information increases even more on entry into junior high school (Feldlaufer, Midgley, & Eccles, 1988). Furthermore, during the junior and senior high school years, students place their achievements into an increasingly broader social context. Elementary school students compare themselves primarily to classmates. In junior high school, students begin to pay attention to track placement and grade point averages, which can be compared schoolwide. By the final years of high school, outcomes of scholarship competitions, college admissions, and other indicators of achievement relative to national norms figure into some students' judgments of their competencies. Analogous changes are likely to apply to athletic and other spheres of performance. Although younger children most likely compare their performance to teammates, older children begin to assess their own competencies in comparison to children on other teams, and eventually for some, to national records.

The shift toward using normative criteria to judge ability is undoubtedly a major reason for average decline from early grades to high school that is observed in children's ratings of their abilities. Children's own competencies, in an absolute sense, constantly are improving. Focusing on mastery and accepting praise at face value assures most young children that the judgments of their competencies will be positive. In contrast, social comparison inevitably leads to some negative judgments because half of the students in a class, by definition, must perform below average.

Classroom Practice Effects

Age-related changes in students' definitions of competence, self-ratings of ability, and predictions for success, to some degree, are a consequence of systematic shifts in the organizational, instructional, and evaluation practices that students are exposed to in school (see Anderman & Maehr, 1994; Eccles, 1993; Eccles & Midgley, 1990; Eccles et al., in press; Stipek & Mac Iver, 1989).

Preschool teachers usually accept a child's product as satisfactory as long as the child has worked on it for a reasonable amount of time, and most children receive positive feedback on tasks they complete (Apple & King, 1978; see also Blumenfeld et al., 1982). Tasks typically are performed individually or in small groups, and comparative information about classmates' performances is not readily available. Under these circumstances it is not surprising that preschool-age children rarely compare their performance with peers and are able to maintain positive perceptions of their competencies.

But children are not protected for very long from the potentially harsh effects of academic competition. The nature of tasks, competence feedback, and student–teacher relationships all change gradually during the early elementary school years, and sometimes dramatically when students enter junior high school.

Several changes in schoolwork and evaluation practices presumably contribute to a more differentiated concept of ability. Throughout the early elementary grades, teachers tend to emphasize effort and work habits, even in report card grades (Blumenfeld et al., 1983; Brophy & Evertson, 1978). Effort figures less prominently in report card grades as students move through elementary school (Entwisle & Hayduk, 1978), and by junior high, grades tend to be based more narrowly on test performance (Gullickson, 1985). Tasks also become more focused on intellectual skills as students advance in grade, and in junior high school teacher–student relationships become much more formal and centered on school performance (Eccles, Wigfield, Midgley, Reuman, MacIver, & Feldlaufer, 1993; Midgley, Anderman, & Hicks, 1995; Midgley et al., 1988, 1989b). Accordingly, children's concept of ability shifts from a poorly differentiated construct that includes effort, work habits, and social skills to a more narrowly defined construct that focuses more exclusively on performance of academic tasks.

Many changes in the nature of instruction and evaluation also foster student interest in social comparison. During the elementary school years, students increasingly are given tasks that involve a single right answer (Eccles, Midgley, & Adler, 1984; Higgins & Parsons, 1983). They also encounter ability grouping (Hallinan & Sorensen, 1983) and other public evidence (e.g., star charts) of their own and classmates' skills (Higgins & Parson, 1983). In time, assignments become more uniform among students (Eccles & Midgley, 1989), and older students experience more whole-group and less individualized and small-group instruction than younger students (Brophy & Evertson, 1978).

Social comparison is more salient as a result of these changes because uniform task structures reduce intraindividual variation in performance across time and make it easier to compare inequalities in performance across students. When tasks do not vary much from day to day, students perform more consistently than when the format and nature of tasks vary. When all students undertake the same task simultaneously, performance is more comparable, more salient, and more public than when tasks vary or are individualized (e.g., Blumenfeld et al., 1982; Marshall & Weinstein, 1984; Rosenholtz & Simpson, 1984b).

The amount of positive social reinforcement also declines as students advance in school (Pintrich & Blumenfeld, 1985) with grades being given more frequently and emphasized more (Harter, Whitesell, & Kowalski, 1992). Partly because grades are based increasingly on relative performance (i.e., a normal curve)—a criterion that requires some students to do poorly—they decline on average (Blumenfeld et al., 1983; Gullickson, 1985; Hill & Wigfield, 1984; Nottelmann, 1987). Because grades are compared easily, these changes in evaluation practices no doubt contribute to students' interest in social comparative information, as well as to the decline in average self-ratings.

In summary, as students progress through school, the nature and diversity of tasks, evaluation practices, and relations with teachers change in ways that increasingly emphasize individual differences in performance of academic tasks. These changes make it difficult for average and below-average students to maintain positive perceptions of competence. Changes in instructional and evaluation practices occur, however, in conjunction with changes in students' information processing abilities. We do not know, therefore, to what degree an increased emphasis on social comparison and to what degree declines in ability and judgments are an inevitable consequence of cognitive development, or primarily caused by changes in school practices.

A few motivation theorists have noted that students' perceptions of their competencies and general well-being in school are affected by an interaction between their own developmental levels and the environment, referred to as the "stage-environment fit" (Anderman & Maehr, 1994; Eccles & Midgley, 1989; Wigfield et al., 1996). They point out that the transition to middle school is accompanied by increased competition, more emphasis on evaluation, and more salient information on relative performance at a time when students are developing the cognitive capacity to process social comparative information and are unusually self-conscious and concerned about peer approval—when students are most vulnerable to the effects of social comparison information. They propose this stage-environment misfit as an explanation for the steep decline in self-perceptions of academic ability that sometimes has been found to accompany the transition to middle school (see Wigfield et al., 1996).

A common change students experience when they move from elementary to middle school is a shift from within-class ability grouping to between-class ability grouping—sometimes for individual courses (e.g., accelerated vs. regular English) and sometimes for all courses (e.g., honors vs. regular track). The next section discusses the implications of such groupings on students' perceptions of their abilities.

FRAME OF REFERENCE

A major concern in decisions about tracking and grouping practices is their effects on students' perceptions of their abilities. Teachers worry that students who are placed in the "low" group will develop low perceptions of their competencies and the accompanying feelings of shame and maladaptive behavior previously described. Research suggests that the effect of grouping practices depends to a considerable degree on who students compare themselves to (their frame of reference) when they judge their own abilities.

Marsh (1987) claimed that students primarily use their immediate social context for a standard—which he refers to as the "big fish, little pond effect." He found, for example, in one study that students' ratings of their academic competencies were relatively low in schools that enrolled relatively high-ability students (Marsh, 1984b; see also Bachman & O'Malley, 1986; Marsh & Parker, 1984; Meyer, 1970). In another study, the perceptions of competence of students in gifted and talented programs declined over time, whereas the self-ratings of equally high-achieving students in heterogeneously grouped classes did not (Marsh, Chessor, Cravn, & Roche, 1995; see also Fuligni, Eccles, & Barbar, 1995; Hoge & Renzulli, 1993). If students use the immediate social context as their frame of reference, relatively high-achieving students should have lower perceptions of their academic competencies in a high-achieving group, track, or school (because they compare themselves to high-achieving peers) than they would if they were grouped heterogeneously (giving them low- as well as high-achieving peers to compare themselves to); conversely, low-achieving students should have higher perceptions of their competencies in a low group, track, or school than in a heterogeneous group.

This analysis predicts that ability grouping should, on average, have a positive effect on relatively low-performing students' and a negative effect on relatively high-performing students' perceptions of competencies. Research indicating that self-ratings of ability also are based on group membership, however, suggests the opposite (Felson & Reed, 1986). To the degree that students base their perceptions of their abilities on their group membership, students placed in relatively high groups should rate their academic abilities higher than students placed in relatively low groups, regardless of their performance within the group.

Research indicates that students' self-perceptions are affected more by their group assignments when the ability groups are constituted within than when they are constituted between classrooms. Reuman (1989), for instance, found that high-achieving sixth graders had relatively higher achievement expectancies and low-achieving students had relatively lower achievement expectancies when grouped within their classrooms than when between-class grouping was used.

Eder (1983) provided ethnographic evidence that both frames of reference—one's own performance compared to members of the immediate group and the relative standing of one's group—are used by students as early as in the first grade. The effects of grouping and tracking, therefore, should vary according to how salient performance differences are within and between groups. To the degree that differences among students in the immediate social context are salient, students' performance relative to other students in their group should affect their perceptions of their own abilities. To the degree that differences among groups in a classroom or in a school are salient, students' group placements should affect their perceptions of competence. Variations in studies related to these variables may explain why research on the effects of ability group placement on students' perceptions of their competencies is inconsistent (see Fuligni et al., 1995; Goldberg, Passow, & Justman, 1966; Weinstein, 1976).

That students may not choose a frame of reference that will result in the most positive judgment was demonstrated in a study by Renick and Harter (1989). They found that most of the mainstreamed students with learning disabilities who they studied spontaneously compared their academic performance to the nondisabled students in their regular classroom. This was true even though they rated themselves higher when they specifically were asked to rate their competencies relative to students in the learning disabled class they attended for part of the day. The global self-worth ratings of these students also were predicted better by their perceptions of their competencies relative to nondisabled classmates than by their perceptions of their competencies relative to learning disabled peers.

In addition to comparing their performance to classmates, students use a personal frame of reference to judge their competencies; that is, they compare their own performance in different subject areas. Although the evidence is not entirely consistent, some studies suggest that judgments about competence in one domain are based partly on a person's perception of his performance in that domain relative to other domains (see Byrne, 1996; Marsh, 1986; Marsh, Byrne, & Shavelson, 1988; Skaalvik & Rankin, 1990). Thus, a student who is particularly good in math may rate herself lower in English than would be expected on the basis of her performance in English relative to classmates. An example of how a personal frame of reference can be used to judge competence is the straight "A" student who claims to be terrible at a subject in which she once received a "B."

Taken together, the research suggests that within-class ability grouping is likely to have the most negative effects on relatively low-achieving students' perceptions of competence. But the evidence is not overwhelming, and the effects of grouping practices need to be assessed in particular contexts. It is also important to understand the meaning that students give to their ability assessments. In some achievement contexts, a judgment of relatively low academic competence is devastating; in others, it is inconsequential. Chapter 7 provides specific suggestions for minimizing the negative emotional and behavioral effects of low-ability judgments.

ASSESSING ABILITY PERCEPTIONS

Most students reveal, through their behaviors, a fair amount of information about their confidence in their abilities. Behaviors such as those listed in Table 6-1 usually are associated with high and low self-confidence in ability. It is important to observe even high-achieving students because many, such as Sally, have very fragile confidence in their academic abilities (Kolb & Jussim, 1994; Phillips, 1984), and thus achieve less than they could (Miserandio, 1996).

Although observations are important, they usually are not sufficient for detecting low perceptions of ability. The same behavior can reflect different kinds of problems. A student might procrastinate because he is afraid of failing and needs a nonability-related explanation, or because he finds the work uninteresting. A child may say she "can't" do something because she genuinely believes she cannot, or when she just does not want to do an assignment. The claim that an assignment is "boring" sometimes is used to disguise a lack of confidence in being able to complete it, and is sometimes an honest appraisal of the work. It is, therefore, useful to supplement observations with other diagnostic methods.

Researchers have measured perceived academic competence both at a general level and for specific subject areas (see Byrne, 1996, and Keith & Bracken, 1996, for reviews of scales). Harter (1982) developed a measure for students above the second grade that has been used in many studies. Students are asked to identify which of two statements applies most to them (e.g., "Some kids often forget what they learn" vs. "Other kids can remember things easily"), and then to indi-

---

TABLE 6-1   Behaviors Reflecting Perceptions of Ability and Self-Efficacy

---

Students who are self-confident in their ability to succeed

◆ Approach tasks eagerly

◆ Persist in the face of failure

◆ Seek help only after they have tried on their own

◆ Enjoy and choose challenging work

◆ Volunteer to answer questions and provide answers when called on in class

◆ Help other students

◆ Show pride in their work

Students who lack self-confidence in their ability to succeed

◆ Say things like "I can't," and "It's too hard"

◆ Attribute success to external causes, such as help or luck

◆ Prefer easy work that can be done with little effort

◆ Are easily discouraged or distracted

◆ Give up easily

◆ Seek help without trying, or do not seek help even when they need it

◆ Do not volunteer answers to questions

◆ Volunteer to answer questions and then "forget" their answers

◆ Change assignments to something they can do

◆ Claim that the work is boring

◆ Make excuses for not completing work

◆ Procrastinate, then claim that they did not have adequate time to complete work

◆ "Overstrive" and repeatedly review and rewrite

◆ Obsess and have difficulty "letting go" of work

---

cate whether the selected statement is "really true for me" or "sort of true for me." The thirty-six-item scale includes three subscales that measure self-perceptions of cognitive, social, and physical competence, and a fourth general self-worth subscale. Harter and Pike (1984) created another version of this scale for children in preschool through the second grade that includes pictures and has four subscales: cognitive competence, physical competence, peer acceptance, and maternal acceptance. (See Fantuzzo, McDermott, Manz, Hampton, and Burdick, 1996, for a challenge to its validity for low-income children.)

Marsh and his colleagues (Marsh, Barnes, et al., 1984; Marsh & Gouvernet, 1989; Marsh & Holmes, 1990; Marsh, Smith, & Barnes, 1983) developed a measure of perceived competence that differentiates between subject areas. Their sixty-six-item Self-Description Questionnaire (SDQ) includes subscales for perceived competence in reading, mathematics, and all other school subjects, as well as subscales for four nonacademic areas: physical abilities, appearance, relations with peers, and relations with parents. Research using this measure suggests the importance of assessing perceptions of competence in specific domains, even for children in the early elementary grades (e.g., Byrne & Gavin, 1996; Eccles et al., 1993; Simpson, Licht, Wagner, & Stader, 1996; Wigfield et al., 1996).

Many researchers have asked a smaller set of questions to assess students' perceptions of academic competence in school in general or in particular subjects. Table 6-2 provides the questions Eccles (1980) and her colleagues asked, usually using a seven-point Likert scale. Even a three-item scale seems to work effectively for many research purposes.

Teachers as well as researchers can use these measures to identify students who have low perceptions of their academic abilities. Teachers often are surprised to find that some high-achieving students are less confident about their abilities than the teacher assumed on the basis of their objective performance. Students' answers to questions about their perceptions of their abilities to succeed at school tasks can help explain maladaptive (e.g., not trying, giving up easily) behavior and can help teachers to structure the curriculum and assignments in ways that maximize students' self-confidence.

Questions can be more specific than those in Table 6-2. For example, these questions could be used: "How good are you at multiplying fractions? Or writing a good paragraph? Or analyzing a poem?" It is also useful to ask students whether

---

TABLE 6-2 A Measure of Self-Perceptions of Academic Competence

1. How good are you at math?

          Not at all good   1 2 3 4 5 6 7   Very good

2. If you were to rank all the students in your math class from the worst to the best, where would you put yourself?

          The worst   1 2 3 4 5 6 7   The best

3. Compared to most of your other school subjects, how good are you at math?

          Much worse   1 2 3 4 5 6 7   Much better

Reprinted from Eccles, 1980.

Note that any subject area could be substituted for "math."

they see improvement in their skills, whether they expect to be able to complete tasks, and how difficult they find tasks. Again, questions can be as general or as specific as desired. Examples of questions that focus on specific tasks are given in Table 6-3.

It is also sometimes useful to know whether students view ability as something that they can improve through practice and effort or something that there is little they can do to change. The following questions can be used either in questionnaires or as "conversation starters" for discussions by small groups or an entire class.

♦ What does it mean to be smart? (In science? In math? In English?)

♦ Could a student who has a lot of trouble with math ever become really good at it?

♦ What would students who do not do well in math need to do if they wanted to do well?

TABLE 6-3 Sample Questions about Improvement, Expectations, and Task Difficulty

1. Are you better now than you were when you started doing this kind of work? (Circle one response.)

Not much better	A little bit better	Quite a bit better	A lot better

2. Do you feel confident that you could do harder problems, or do you need practice and help with these kinds of problems? (Circle one response.)

I will never be able to do this	I still need help with these	I need a little more practice with these	I can do harder problems now

3. Do you think you will be able to do this assignment well? (Circle one number.)

1	2	3	4	5	6	7
I definitely will not do it well			I will do OK			I definitely will do it well

4. Look at your math work for today. How hard do you think this work will be for you? (Circle one number.)

1	2	3	4	5	6	7
Really easy			Medium hard			Really hard

Adapted from MacGyvers & Stipek, *A teacher's guide to assessing and enhancing students' motivation*, unpublished manuscript, 1995.

♦ If a student did not think he is as smart in science as he would like to be, is there anything he could do to become smarter? If yes, what could he do? If no, why is there nothing he could do?

Time spent in such discussions or completing questionnaires is time away from the regular school curriculum, but identifying problems with self-confidence can provide much help in explaining behaviors that interfere with learning. In the long run, teachers who know and understand their students well will produce higher achievement levels in their students than teachers who do not devote time to trying to understand the source of maladaptive behavior.

CONCLUSION

No child or adult enjoys confronting tasks that engender feelings of incompetence. It is not surprising that individuals use a variety of tactics to avoid failure, or if failure is inevitable, to avoid looking stupid. The common tactics described by Covington and Beery (1976) may achieve the short-term goal of avoiding the implications of failure, but in the long term they undermine learning and performance. Yet this is the situation that many students face every day in school.

Being confident of success (high self-efficacy) is an essential ingredient for effective learning. Without this, students will not engage in productive learning behaviors. A general concept of oneself as being academically competent is extremely helpful, although the implications of low-competence judgments vary, depending on one's definition of ability—as a stable trait or something that can be improved through practice and effort—and depending on the social context of the classroom. Chapter 7 describes instructional strategies to maintain self-confidence in students.

TABLE 6-4 Summary of Terms

Term	Definition
Entity concept of ability	Belief that ability is a stable trait that individuals have a fixed amount of and that is affected only moderately by practice and effort
Instrumental–incremental concept of ability	Belief that ability, like a skill, can be increased through practice and effort
Self-worth	People's appraisal of their own value
Impression management	Making statements or engaging in behaviors with the explicit goal of influencing others' judgments of oneself

CHAPTER 7
Maintaining Positive Achievement-Related Beliefs

Students' beliefs affect their behaviors whether or not those beliefs are based on objective reality. Helpless Hannah (see Chapter 1) believes she is incompetent and expects to fail. She therefore avoids achievement situations whenever possible, and when she is required to perform a task—even one that she could do— she performs it halfheartedly and gives up easily. When Hannah inevitably fails, she attributes the failure to her lack of competence. Defensive Dave (see Chapter 1) is not convinced entirely that he is incompetent, but he also is not confident that he will succeed. He devotes his energies more to avoiding looking incompetent than to completing schoolwork. Safe Sally (see Chapter 1) does not know what she is really capable of learning because she never tests the limits of her skills. Hence, she continues to harbor doubts about her ability to succeed in challenging situations.

In contrast to these three students, students who believe that rewards are based on good performance and that they are able to perform well usually approach academic tasks eagerly, exert effort to increase mastery, focus their attention on strategies to solve the present problem or demonstrate their competencies, persist with tasks when they do not succeed immediately, and experience positive emotions in achievement contexts.

Previous chapters hint at the implications of research on achievement-related beliefs for practice. This chapter is devoted entirely to practical suggestions for fostering the positive beliefs that lead to productive learning behaviors and for minimizing the negative beliefs that inhibit learning.

First, however, it is important to clarify our goal. Certainly we do not want to try to dupe all students into thinking that they are the smartest in the class. By definition, half of the students in a class are below average with regard to any given skill. Regardless of what the teacher does, by second grade or earlier students become aware of differences between their own and their classmates' performance. Some students inevitably will perceive themselves as being less skillful than others in particular domains.

Despite their potential liabilities, these comparative assessments are not altogether harmful. Students need to know their strengths and weaknesses to make wise decisions about where to invest effort and about long-term educational and professional plans. And a realistic appraisal of one's competencies may not result in the maladaptive avoidance, defensive, and helpless behaviors that are described in Chapters 5 and 6. The consequences of such appraisals depend on their meaning to the student. Teachers may not be able to eliminate social comparison, but they have a considerable impact on the salience and meaning of students' judgments about their competencies and on their expectations for success with particular tasks.

One realistic and worthy goal, therefore, is for all students to believe that they are efficacious—that they have the competence to learn and to complete the tasks they encounter in school. A second, related set of goals is for all students to believe that they have personal control over their academic outcomes and to take pride in their accomplishments. A third goal, perhaps necessary for achieving the first two, is to foster an incremental concept of academic ability—the belief that ability is something that can be improved through practice and effort. Fortunately, achievement motivation researchers have provided many clues on how to accomplish these goals.

The first section of this chapter translates theory and research on achievement motivation into specific, concrete recommendations for classroom practice. Some of these recommendations are inferred from research findings on studies of achievement-related beliefs; others have been tested directly by teachers and researchers in real classrooms. This section is followed by a description of two comprehensive programs designed partly to address motivation problems related to maladaptive achievement-related beliefs—mastery learning and cooperative incentive structures. Appendix 7-A is designed to help teachers assess their own practices.

EFFECTIVE CLASSROOM PRACTICE

All aspects of classroom practice are interrelated. This section, nevertheless, is organized into different aspects of practices that researchers have examined in relation to achievement-related beliefs: tasks, goals, evaluation, giving help, direct statements, and classroom structure.

Tasks and Assignments

There are many qualities of tasks that teachers need to consider. The focus here is on qualities that are likely to affect students' beliefs about their competencies and their expectations for success.

1. **Give tasks that are challenging but achievable for all students.** Easy tasks do not produce feelings of competence because no improvement in skill level or understanding is required to achieve success. Attempts to complete very difficult tasks usually do not result in success; when they do, the amount of effort required can diminish the value of the accomplishment. Tasks of intermediate difficulty, those that allow students to experience improvement in their skills, are most effective in producing feelings of competence.

   a. **Vary the difficulty of tasks among students according to their skill levels.** A task that one student finds easy may be impossibly difficult for another. Thus, providing intermediate difficulty or more challenging tasks to a group of students varying in skill level requires varying the difficulty level of tasks. Teachers are sometimes reluctant to vary tasks because they are concerned that students will be embarrassed about doing assignments that are easier than those completed by many of their peers. But completing easier assignments and being able to take personal responsibility for success are far more likely to encourage self-confidence than repeatedly failing to do the more difficult tasks that other classmates are given. Moreover, all students can take pride in their successes if the teacher creates a climate in which hard work and success are rewarded at whatever level each student is working.

   b. **Provide tasks that can be completed at different levels.** Teachers can vary the difficulty partly by providing tasks that can be completed at different levels and by conveying different expectations. The same assignment—to write a book report, poem, or story—can be equally challenging for all students. It is important for students to understand that they are expected to complete the tasks at levels that require real effort and persistence, and that doing this will help them to develop their skills. Differential expectations can be conveyed by guiding choices (e.g., of the book selected to report on), and direct statements and evaluation (e.g., "This is technically correct, but you could have made a more compelling argument").

   Different skill levels often can be accommodated with the same task. Consider a math assignment in which all children are asked to graph data based on a student poll. The teacher might ask questions, either in a whole-group or a small-group format, that require analysis at different levels. Some students might be asked to report differences (e.g., between boys and girls), requiring them only to interpret the graph; others might be asked questions that require manipulations of the information, such as translating frequencies into percentages. The task, in this case, appears to be the same for all students, but the actual levels of mathematical problem solving with which students are involved are adjusted to their current mathematical skills.

The same math problem also can be approached differently by students who vary in skill level. For example, some students may be able to solve a problem using only one strategy; others will develop and compare the efficiency of several different strategies. The level of analysis of a poem or an historical event also may vary among students in a class. Thus, teachers can engage students at an appropriate level of challenge without having to create entirely different tasks for each student.

   c. **Make sure that the highest achievers are challenged.** Teachers usually worry more about motivating the relatively low-achieving students than about challenging the high-achieving ones. But a steady diet of success does not prepare students to deal with the initial difficulties in achieving success that high-achieving students inevitably will encounter in future educational contexts and throughout life. Many high-achieving students who enter a new academic arena—by taking an unusually difficult course, moving from the regular to the honors track in high school, or moving from high school to college, or college to graduate school—are ill-prepared for the challenges they will face. Because they always have succeeded, often without much effort, their self-confidence is fragile and collapses easily.

2. **Organize assignments to provide frequent opportunities for students to observe increases in their skills.** In addition to being moderately challenging, tasks need to provide opportunities for regular feedback, indicating improvement in skill or understanding. Initial failures in developing a skill are inevitable, but a long series of failures or of engagement without this feedback undermines feelings of competency.

   a. **Order problems and assignments by difficulty level.** This allows students to experience a sense of increasing mastery.

   b. **Break down difficult tasks into subunits.** This ensures that students receive positive competence feedback before they become discouraged or concerned about the direction in which they are headed.

Goals

Discouragement on a long-term task can be avoided by setting short-term goals; an appropriate level of challenge can be achieved by adjusting goals for students with varying skill levels.

3. **Create short-term (proximal) goals.** Although the long-range or **distal goals** are important for students to keep in mind, progress toward a long-term goal is sometimes difficult for students to gauge. **Proximal goals** can raise self-efficacy simply by making a task appear to be more manageable, and they can enhance perceptions of competence by giving continual feed-

back that conveys a sense of mastery (Bandura, 1981; Harackiewicz, Manderlink, & Sansone, 1992; Locke & Latham, 1990; Schunk, 1984a, 1990, 1991).

A study by Bandura and Schunk (1981) demonstrated the advantage of proximal goals. They gave elementary school-age children seven sets of subtraction problems to work on over seven sessions. Children were told either to complete one set each session (i.e., proximal goal), to complete all seven sets by the end of the seventh session (i.e., distal goal), or simply to work on the problems with no mention of goals. The proximal goal situation led to the highest self-efficacy and subtraction skill. Students in the distal goal condition performed no better than students who were given no specific goal (see also Schunk, 1983b, 1986; Schunk & Rice, 1989.)

4. **Vary goals among students.** Whereas it may be realistic for some students to aspire to filling in a multiplication grid in 2 minutes, a 4-minute goal may be equally challenging for others. Differential goal setting, however, will work only if appropriately challenging goals are valued and reinforced regardless of how they compare to other students' goals or achievements. Thus, completing the grid in 2 or 4 minutes needs to be reinforced in the same way if these two goals are to represent equal levels of challenge for the students who set them. Research has shown that goal setting has the best effect on performance when goals are specific (i.e., quantifiable or framed in terms of specific action as opposed to general terms, such as "I'll do my best") and when feedback provides information on performance relative to the goal (Locke & Latham, 1990, 1994).

5. **Engage students in personal goal setting.** Students sometimes undermine their own self-confidence by aspiring to unrealistic goals and failing to meet them, or they set goals that are reached too easily and do not produce any learning. Teaching students to set goals is important because they will need this skill when their achievement pursuits are not monitored on a day-to-day basis. Personal goal setting also has been shown to raise self-efficacy (Schunk, 1985a) and enhance performance (Hom & Murphy, 1985).

There is evidence that even young children can be taught to be realistic. Gaa (1973), for example, demonstrated that first and second graders can develop the necessary skills for setting appropriate goals for themselves—ones that are challenging but are likely to be achieved. Children who met weekly with an experimenter to set goals for the next week and discuss achievements relative to the previous week's goals set fewer and more appropriate goals at the end of the intervention and attained higher levels of reading achievement than children who did not have experience in setting and reviewing personal goals. Having students graph their goals and accomplishments can help them develop skills in setting appropriate goals (see also Gaa, 1979; Schunk, in press; Tollefson, Tracy, Johnsen, Farmer, & Buenning, 1984).

a. **Provide incentives for setting challenging goals.** That students sometimes will take the easy route when there is no disincentive to do so was shown in a study by Clifford (1988). She provided fourth, fifth, and sixth graders with items varying in difficulty from the Iowa Tests of Basic Skills in mathematics, spelling, and vocabulary. When students were told to select any six problems in each domain, they chose problems that were considerably below their ability levels. The low risk-taking tendency increased markedly with each grade level.

   Students can be offered incentives to set more challenging goals. For instance, more points can be given for more difficult math problems or spelling words. The student who is overly ambitious quickly learns that attempting words that are too difficult results in a lot of 0s and choosing words that are too easy results in a relatively low score. The number of points are maximized by selecting the most difficult words that the student is likely to spell correctly. The effects of such a system were documented by Clifford (1991) on her problem choice task previously described. When points were linked to the difficulty levels of problems (i.e., more points were given for more difficult problems), children were more willing to take risks.

Evaluation

External evaluation is often necessary for students to experience developing competence. Although they may be able to determine the correctness of their spelling words by consulting a master list, they usually need assistance in judging whether the imagery in their writing is more vivid, or their argument more persuasive, than it was previously. Teachers' feedback can direct future efforts, as well as point out newly developing competencies. Knowing what they need to do to improve their abilities gives students a perception of control over achievement outcomes, which, as research described in Chapter 5 indicates, enhances effort and learning. But some kinds of evaluation are more likely to accomplish these goals than others.

6. **Give students different ways to demonstrate what they know.** Giving students diverse opportunities to demonstrate their understanding gives a more complete picture of their skills, and it gives more students a chance to demonstrate competence. Understanding of mathematical concepts, for example, might be expressed by finding correct solutions, explaining an effective strategy for solving a problem either orally or in writing, depicting the problem and solution in a drawing, or assisting another student.

7. **Point out what is good, right, or shows improvement.** Students need external validation of the competencies they have developed, as well as information on how to improve. This is particularly true for assignments with which students are likely to have difficulty judging, such as a task that is new

for them (e.g., writing a book report or science laboratory report for the first time). Commending what is good (or shows improvement) lets students know that they are developing competencies. Recommendations also can be given to guide future efforts.

8. **Provide clear, specific, and informative feedback.**

   a. **Avoid global, uninformative praise.** "A nice job," "well done," or "good," on the cover of a paper does not tell a student that there were clear, well-defined standards that were met. Students also sometimes do not consider such global feedback as credible (Damon, 1995).

   b. **Provide written, substantive comments whenever possible.** Specific commendations (e.g., "The paper is well organized"; "The transitions are smooth"; "Your strategy is creative and shows that you really understand the math ideas"; "Your summary of the results of the experiment is clear and concise") provide clear, credible evidence of competence. Substantive and specific feedback also helps students develop criteria that they can use to assess their own skills and to identify their strengths and weaknesses.

9. **Base rewards (including high grades) on achieving a clearly defined standard or set of criteria or on personal improvement.** Whatever the form of rewards—good grades, stars, happy faces, privileges, or papers on the bulletin board—they should be based on a set of clearly defined criteria or standards. When they are based on a competitive standard they are not realistically available to many students. Some students never will receive feedback conveying competence, regardless of how hard they work or how much their skills improve.

   Ironically, a competitive standard for rewards may not even build self-confidence in the "winners." This is because some high-achieving students achieve at a high level, relative to classmates, with little effort and without developing their competencies. Thus, the external reward conflicts with their own observations and subjective experience. As mentioned previously, the high perceptions of competence developed by students who constantly are rewarded for their schoolwork regardless of their levels of effort are very fragile and fall apart in situations in which success or rewards do not come easily.[1]

10. **Give students multiple opportunities to achieve high grades.** Teachers can allow students to keep working (within some reasonable limit) until they have achieved satisfactory levels of mastery or performance. One teacher who I interviewed developed the simple but ingenious method of marking

---

[1]This "unraveling" of self-confidence is common among graduate students who were previously straight "A" students without having to work very hard. I have witnessed their self-confidence evaporate with the first critical feedback they received on their work.

incorrect responses on written assignments with a dot. Students continued to work on assignments until all answers were correct. The dots easily could be changed to check marks, which indicated correct answers, without leaving any evidence of the original errors. Thus, errors were treated as a natural step in mastering new material. Students also can be given opportunities to rewrite papers or redo assignments to achieve higher grades or demonstrate higher levels of mastery.

Providing substantive feedback en route to task completion is also helpful. This is a critical feature of the current popular approaches to teaching writing (e.g., Graves, 1983). Students write several drafts of their papers, concentrating on correcting different aspects of the writing (e.g., putting thoughts on paper, developing and organizing ideas, using correct mechanics) at different points in the process. Feedback along the way provides useful corrective information and gives students a feeling of control over their performance outcomes.

11. **Teach students to celebrate their classmates' successes, at whatever levels they occur.** The teacher is not the only evaluator in a classroom. Classmates' reactions to students' performance can be just as important, and peers can undermine the teacher's efforts. The values of the teacher, therefore, need to be internalized by every student in the classroom. This will occur, to some degree, by modeling desired responses. But students also can be instructed to support the teachers' goals. For example, they can be encouraged to applaud or congratulate their classmates for significant improvements, regardless of the students' relative skill levels. This conveys to students that improvement, which is genuinely available to all students, is valued, and it give students an example of how concrete behaviors are used to communicate this value to each other.

12. **Minimize public evaluations.** Wall charts and other public displays of students' performance may enhance the motivation of a very small group of top performers, but they can threaten and discourage other students, especially if evaluative criteria are uniform despite varying skill levels among students. And, for all students, these public displays orient attention to relative performance rather than personal improvement or mastery.[2]

   a. **If evaluation is public, it must be a "fair contest."** All students must have a realistic chance of "winning." This can occur by charting progress toward achieving goals that are adjusted to be realistically at-

---

[2]I experienced the negative effects of public displays of performance outcomes during my one-year stay at a French university, where it was customary to hand back papers and exams in the order of students' scores. The assumption, I am sure, was that the humiliation of being among the last to receive one's paper would foster greater effort to avoid future humiliation. What I observed in other students and experienced myself was withdrawal and discouragement. My solution, contrary to the instructor's intentions, was to miss class on the day that exams were returned.

tainable by all students. I observed an example of this in a classroom in which paper boats with students' names on them "raced" across a blue sheet of paper on the bulletin board. The position of each student's boat was determined by how much progress that student had made in mastering an increasingly difficult set of spelling words. All students began at the same point on the sheet of blue paper, even though their initial levels of mastery varied considerably. Consequently, the student who won the race would not have to be the one who attained the highest level of mastery. Rather, the winner would have made the most progress from his personal starting point.

b. **Have students keep personal progress records.** A better method than public displays for helping students monitor their progress is to have them keep records, including charts, in their desks. A personal chart, unlike a class chart, focuses students' attention on their own improvement and mastery, rather than on how they compare to classmates. It is also useful for communicating student goals and progress with parents.

c. **Give students an opportunity for private interactions with the teacher.** A classroom structure in which students' interactions with the teacher are either private or in small groups also can minimize the publicness of performance and evaluative feedback and therefore reduce the risk of embarrassment.

13. **Teach students to evaluate their own work.** An authority figure is not always available to give students feedback on how their competencies are developing. Students should be encouraged and taught to evaluate their own work and to monitor their own progress. This provides them with more opportunities to experience a sense of developing competencies and also to develop strategies to guide their own efforts for improvement.

a. **Encourage students to use their own judgments.** When students ask for feedback (e.g., "Is this good?"), encourage them to make judgments on their own (e.g., "What do you think? Does it look good to you?") and to consider strategies for making personal judgments (e.g., "Do you have any ideas about how you could figure out whether it is good, besides asking me?").

b. **Give students opportunities to check their own work.** Students can check their own solutions to math problems or check the accuracy of their spelling words, for example, against an answer sheet or by comparing them with those of a classmate. They can check facts by consulting an encyclopedia or using the Internet.

c. **Give students explicit instructions on how to evaluate their own work.** Students learn criteria for making independent judgments partly by receiving specific, substantive feedback on their work from teachers. They also need explicit instructions and reminders. Models are useful, although they need to be used carefully to minimize the potential for students developing an unnecessarily narrow view of a good product. Rubrics are often helpful, such as those used to assess writing samples in standardized tests.

d. **Link evaluation criteria directly to instruction.** Students will not be able to assess their own progress (and thus experience a sense of mastery) if the evaluation criteria they are given are not aligned with their instruction. If, for instance, math instruction is focused on providing clear and persuasive explanations for solutions, students should be given a set of criteria and strategies for determining whether an explanation is clear and persuasive. If writing instruction is focused on teaching students to use paragraphs, they should be given a set of criteria for writing a good paragraph. These criteria provide guidance as students construct explanations and paragraphs, and also give them a means for evaluating the quality of their work.

14. **Be clear and consistent.** Recall that perceptions of control require beliefs in contingency as well as competence (see Chapter 5). Clarity and consistency in the criteria for rewards are critical for students to maintain a sense of control over their learning outcomes. Even the most self-confident student can develop low perceptions of control and show evidence of helplessness if the criteria for evaluation or rewards are vague, inconsistent, and unpredictable.

Giving Help

When students work on challenging tasks they inevitably will encounter difficulties and will need help. Research suggests that the students who need help the most are typically the least likely to ask for it (Karabenick & Knapp, 1988; see also Newman, 1991; Newman & Schwager, 1992), and with increasing age, students become less likely to seek help. Good, Slavings, Harel, and Emerson (1987), for example, found that low-achieving students were fairly active participants in the classroom until the end of the third grade, but then became relatively passive. The decline most likely is explained by age-related increases in students' desires to avoid looking incompetent (see Chapter 6). There are, however, strategies for getting students to seek help when they need it.

15. **Encourage students to seek help.** Sometimes teachers need to remind students that having difficulty is not a reason for fear or embarrassment—that all students, even teachers, need to ask questions and seek assistance when they are developing new skills. Soliciting questions from students and checking for confusion and misunderstandings on a regular basis also helps.

a. **Model help seeking.** Having the teacher admit ignorance and use resources (including students in the class) to answer questions or obtain information is a powerful way to convey to students that it is okay not to know everything. This is an effective strategy for creating a classroom community of learners, which includes adults as well as children.

16. **Give no more assistance than is necessary.** Some kinds of help are more likely to foster feelings of mastery and competence than others. Nelson-Le Gall (1981, 1990, 1992, 1993) makes a useful distinction between "instrumental" or mastery-oriented help seeking, which enables students to complete tasks on their own, and "excessive" or dependency-oriented help seeking, which students use to get someone else to solve problems that they have not earnestly attempted to solve independently. Mastery-oriented help seeking allows students to take responsibility for their achievements and, thus, can contribute to students' perceptions of competence. Teachers need to recognize the difference between a real need for help and a failure to try, and when help is given, it should be limited to what is needed. The more that students can accomplish on their own, the better off they will be, both in terms of their learning and their perceptions of mastery.

a. **Teach students how to use classroom resources to answer their questions.** There are many resources in classrooms—dictionaries, encyclopedias, measuring instruments, newspapers, and now the Internet. Students may not think of using these resources, or they may not know how to use them. Encouraging and teaching students to use classroom resources reinforces the message that they should do what they can independently before asking for help.

17. **Encourage students to use peers for assistance.** Liberating teachers from serving as the sole source of information and assistance gives them more time to engage in instruction. Students also benefit from providing assistance to each other. It helps them to consolidate their own understanding and develop self-confidence, empathy, and teaching skills. It also creates a climate of collaboration and mutual support.

a. **Teach students how to give help.** Most students understand "giving help" to mean giving the right answer. I observed a first-grade classroom in which the children were generous with their help, but they had only one strategy—to give the answer. These first graders were so "helpful" that they often wrote the answers into their classmates' workbooks. Even older students need to be taught how to give instrumental help—help that fosters skills and independence rather than dependence on the one giving help. This can be done partly by modeling effective help-giving strategies, but it usually requires some explicit instructions and monitoring.

Direct Statements

Direct statements to students about their effort and competencies can affect their own interpretations of their performance and their perceptions of their competencies. In general, the goal is to make students believe that they are able to succeed if they try, and that when they fail it is because they were not trying hard enough, because they need more practice, or because they did not use appropriate strategies for approaching the task. Results of studies indicate the value of the following practices.

18. **Attribute "failure" to low effort or an ineffective strategy.** By explicitly attributing a failure to low effort (e.g., "I don't think you really were concentrating"), the teacher communicates a belief in the student's ability to succeed with some effort (Schunk, 1982, 1984a, 1984b). Any statement suggesting that a student who performed poorly exerted considerable effort (e.g., "Don't worry—you did the best you could do"), as sympathetic as it may appear, inadvertently can reinforce a student's doubts about her ability.

    Several researchers have encouraged strategy attributions over effort attributions (Borkowski, Carr, Rellinger, & Pressley, 1990; Clifford, 1984, 1991; Hattie, Biggs, & Purdie, 1996; Pressley, El-Dinary, Marks, Brown, & Stein, 1992; Reid & Borkowski, 1987). Students who do poorly despite considerable effort can become confused and discouraged if the teacher suggests that their poor performance is caused by poor effort. Focusing on the use of strategies provides recognition of their effort, and conveys a positive and sometimes constructive suggestion that the student needs to try an alternative approach to the problem. Schunk (1989a) pointed out that encouragement to use different strategies also can enhance feelings of self-efficacy by giving students a perception that they control their outcomes. Studies indicating that effective adult tutors are more likely to attribute outcomes to strategy than to effort illustrate the usefulness of strategy attributions (Lepper, Aspinwall, Mumme, & Chabay, 1990).

    Several researchers have demonstrated through **attribution retraining** programs that students' maladaptive beliefs can be changed into more adaptive ones by making the kinds of explicit statements previously suggested (see Forsterling, 1985, for a review). In perhaps the first attribution retraining study, Dweck (1975) showed that the belief that failure is caused by low ability can be changed into the belief that failure is caused by low effort or insufficient practice. She identified a number of extremely "helpless" elementary school-age children. These "helpless" children showed the attribution pattern associated with learned helplessness; that is, they took less personal responsibility for outcomes of their behavior and tended to place less emphasis on the role of effort than do nonhelpless children, and their performance following the occurrence of failure was impaired severely. During twenty-five daily training sessions, half of these children were given a heavy dose of success. The other half received attribution retraining; they had considerable success, but several failure trials were programmed each day. When failure occurred the experimenter explicitly commented to the children that the failure was due to a lack of effort. At the end of the training the children in the attribution retraining condition, but not the children in the success-only condition, attributed outcomes more to effort than they had prior to the training. The attribution retraining children also showed improvement in their responses to failure; rather than giving up, they persisted, using appropriate problem-solving strategies. Children who had been in the success-only treatment, in contrast, showed no improvement in their responses to failure. Some of these children even showed a tendency to react somewhat more adversely to failure than they had before the start of the treatment. This study suggests that success experiences may not be sufficient to encourage a student such as Hannah to try harder; instead, the teacher needs to change the students' perceptions of the cause of failure.

Teachers need to know their students' skills and monitor their behaviors well to make attributions that are fair, appropriate, and constructive. An effort attribution is unfair and can discourage a student who has been struggling, or even a student who does not try, because he knows that he really does lack the prerequisite skills to complete a task. Direct messages to students about the causes of their successes or failures, therefore, need to be based on close and careful observations of their behaviors and skills. When effort is still ineffective after a reasonable amount of time (which will vary depending on the age of the student and nature of the task), or when a student clearly lacks the skills required for more effective strategies, teachers need to acknowledge students' efforts and suggest adjusting the task or the students' goals so that effort will result in success.

a. **Model adaptive attributions.** Teacher modeling also can be used to influence students' attributions. For example, in a study designed to improve learning strategies among learning disabled students, the teacher purposefully made mistakes while giving instruction, and then made explicit attribution statements focusing on effort or strategy attributions: for instance, "I need to try and use the strategy" (Borkowski, Weyhing, & Carr, 1988).

19. **Attribute "successes" to effort and competence.** Schunk suggests that teachers also can enhance self-confidence by attributing success to ability. Attributing success to external causes (e.g., "You were lucky you solved that one") denies students an opportunity to take personal responsibility and experience pride in their successes, and will undermine their perceptions of their abilities.

Schunk cautioned against making effort attributions when success occurs because this actually can undermine feelings of competence. This was demonstrated in a study in which third graders, while working on subtraction problems, were told, "You're good at this," "You've been working hard," or both (Schunk, 1983a). The children who received only the ability attribution judged themselves to be the most efficacious and correctly solved the highest number of posttest problems (see also Schunk, 1984b). Schunk suggested that attributing success to effort reduces students' perceptions of their abilities because they believe that success requiring high effort indicates lower ability than success achieved without effort.

Despite Schunk's findings, teachers should not give successful students the impression that effort is unnecessary to achieve success. Optimal motivation on any task occurs when students assume that they possess the abilities to achieve success but that some effort also is required. No learning will result from success that is achieved without effort. Consequently, although teachers need to provide students with a learning context in which students feel competent, students must not perceive ability alone to be sufficient to achieve success.

Classroom Structure

In addition to feedback directed toward individual students, there are many aspects of the classroom environment that influence students' conceptions of ability and their evaluations of their own and their classmates' abilities. Classroom structure can affect students' judgments about their abilities by making relative performance more or less salient and by affecting the stability of performance over tasks and time.

20. **Differentiate tasks among students and over time.** Rosenholtz and Simpson (1984a, 1984b) demonstrated that the degree to which tasks are differentiated among students and over time affects students' judgments about their own abilities relative to classmates, and also affects the way that they conceptualize ability (see also Rosenholtz & Rosenholtz, 1981; Rosenholtz & Wilson, 1980; Simpson, 1981; Simpson & Rosenholtz, 1986). They claimed that an **undifferentiated academic task structure**—in which all students use the same materials to work on the same task that requires the same responses—promotes social comparison and causes students to perform consistently at the same relative level over time. Bossert (1979) further noted that teachers in classrooms with undifferentiated task structures, referred to as **unidimensional classrooms,** often face managerial problems with high achievers who finish their work earlier than others. Students who know they can finish regular assignments in less than the allotted time also sometimes fool around while they are working on the assignment, causing additional discipline problems.

In a **differentiated task structure,** different students may work on several different kinds of tasks on any day, and the types of tasks students are given varies from day to day. The differentiated task structure, used in **multidimensional classrooms,** makes social comparison less salient and results in less consistency in students' relative performance from task to task and from day to day.

Rosenholtz and Simpson (1984a) explained that task structure influences classroom processes in several mutually reinforcing ways. It influences (1) the distribution of actual performance, (2) the amount and salience of information available to students concerning their own and their classmates' performance, (3) the comparability of information about oneself and others, and (4) the consistency of information concerning any one type of performance for any one student. These consequences, in turn, affect the process of forming perceptions of ability.

Research findings generally support their analysis. Pepitone (1972) demonstrated experimentally that uniformity in curricular tasks results in greater social comparison behavior (e.g., "I made fewer mistakes than you") than differentiation in tasks. Studies also show that both teachers' evaluations of students and students' evaluations of themselves and their peers are stratified more (i.e., there is greater dispersion in judgments) in unidimensional than in multidimensional classrooms (Rosenholtz & Rosenholtz, 1981; Rosenholtz & Simpson, 1984b), and children's self-perceptions in unidimensional classrooms correspond more strongly to teacher evaluations (Rosenholtz & Rosenholtz, 1981; Simpson, 1981). Students also tend to agree with each other on their own and their classmates' relative abilities in unidimensional classrooms (Rosenholtz & Simpson, 1984a). In brief, compared to multidimensional classrooms, all participants in unidimensional classrooms agree more closely in their ratings of particular students. Thus, students develop a perception of ability as being stratified, measurable, and consensual—that is, as something that has an objective reality that can be perceived by others and oneself. This concept of ability is similar to IQ, and to what Dweck (1986) referred to as an "entity" theory (see Chapter 6).

21. **Point out "within-student" variation in skill levels.** When students' performance varies from task to task, teachers have the opportunity to convey to them the idea that skill development is incremental and domain specific. For example, they can point out to students who are having difficulty in one domain that they are doing well in another, and that with effort and persistence they eventually will do well in this domain.

22. **When instructing in a whole-class format, involve all students productively.** Whole-class instruction can make relative performance levels very salient. Bossert (1979) noted that in whole-class recitation, right and wrong answers automatically become both public and comparable. It is not unusual for a few self-confident students to dominate large-group instructional periods, while children lacking in self-confidence and fearing humiliation refuse to participate.

Group instruction, whether involving a small group or the whole class, does not need to have negative effects. Sensitive teachers who integrate wrong answers into their instruction, thus giving every student a feeling of having made a constructive contribution, can engage the participation of all children and avoid embarrassing them for giving wrong answers.

23. **Use "ability grouping" flexibly and temporarily to address specific skill needs.** Research on how skill-based grouping affects student learning as well as students' perceptions of their competencies is mixed (Fuligni et al., 1995; Mosteller, Light, & Sachs, 1996; Slavin, 1987b, 1990a, 1993), and it is likely that how it is implemented is at least as important as whether it is implemented. The following recommendations, in addition to those discussed in Chapter 12, should minimize potential negative effects.

    a. **Create temporary instructional groups.** These groups should be designed to help students develop and practice particular skills (Strein, 1993). If only a few students in the class have not understood the correct usage of quotation marks, bring them together for a few days to work specifically on that skill. Make sure that they have opportunities to practice the skill after they have been dispersed. The same strategy might be used for a group of students who have not learned their multiplication tables, who are having difficulty reading a map, or who have not learned how to access or scan information on the Internet.

        Temporary groupings also might be used to address the needs of students who are farther along in the curriculum than most of their classmates. For instance, students may be permitted to use technology to enrich the regular classroom curriculum, or they may be asked to read more broadly on a topic than other students and then share what they have read.

    b. **Allow students to volunteer for skill-based groups.** In a classroom in which students are unafraid to expose their ignorance and ask for help, skill-based groups can be voluntary. Teachers can announce that they will provide instruction related to a particular skill to all students who believe they need or would benefit from it. If the students who need the intervention do not volunteer, the teacher needs to consider whether the climate and expectations in the classroom make it risky for students to admit to having difficulty or needing extra help. All students should be allowed to volunteer for accelerated work. Teachers often are surprised to find that they have underestimated a student's capacity, and if the activity turns out to be too difficult for some students, they most likely will drop out on their own accord.

24. **Convey the value of many different kinds of skills.** Teachers also should give students opportunities to publicly demonstrate competence in many different domains, and they should express positive values for good performance in a variety of areas, including those that are not typically part of

school requirements (e.g., playing an instrument, athletics, rapping, drawing).

25. **Give relatively poor-performing students the role of "expert."** Research by Cohen showed that the status and participation of relatively low-performing students can be raised by calling other students' attention to their particular skills or talents, and recommending that other students use them as resources (Cohen & Lotan, 1995). Students whose skills are somewhat low relative to those of their classmates also can build self-confidence (and consolidate their skills) if given opportunities to tutor younger children (e.g., Cochran, Feng, Cartledge, & Hamilton, 1993).

COMPREHENSIVE PROGRAMS

Some educational researchers have developed and tested the effectiveness of comprehensive programs designed to foster positive achievement-related beliefs as well as maximize learning. **Mastery learning programs** and **cooperative incentive structures** have the most extensive research base and are described here as examples of integrated, "packaged" programs that teachers could choose to implement. Even a well-developed program, however, can be delivered in different ways. The previous principles, therefore, are important to keep in mind if such programs are implemented.

Mastery Learning Programs

Evaluation based on mastery is a central component of the various mastery-based educational programs inspired primarily by Bloom (1971, 1974, 1976, 1981). Bloom's own mastery learning model has been used in hundreds of classrooms throughout the United States and in as many as twenty other countries (Block, 1979). Consequently, many variations of the original model also exist. The fundamental assumption underlying mastery learning models is that all students can learn the basic school curriculum, but that some take longer than others. By providing slower-learning students with more time to master skills, all students will master the curriculum and all students will receive high grades.

Although mastery learning programs vary, they share several characteristics (see Guskey, 1987, 1990). Students are given regular feedback on their progress and corrective feedback to help them achieve mastery. Most programs also provide enrichment activities for students to extend and broaden their learning. Guskey (1990) emphasized the importance of congruence among the different instructional components—including what students are expected to learn, the instructional activities, feedback on learning progress, corrective activities, and procedures used to evaluate students' learning.

Mastery learning is a form of **outcome-based education (OBE),** which is currently promoted by many school reformers and policy makers (Evans & King, 1994; Varnon & King, 1993). Outcome-based education emphasizes setting clear objectives and giving students multiple and different kinds of opportunities to reach those objectives. It has been implemented at the district level (e.g., Johnson City, TN; New York) and in entire states (e.g., Utah, Missouri, Minnesota).

"Outcomes" in OBE are not always rooted in an academic content area. They also can include motivation orientations, such as self-directed learner, collaborative worker, or community contributor (Marzano, 1994). Outcome-based education is implemented in many different ways, and the effects of the general approach have not been evaluated systematically. Implementers and assessment experts are working on developing assessments of students' achievements related to identified outcomes, but much work remains to be done to develop reliable and valid performance-based assessments.

Our focus is on mastery learning programs rather than OBE because they are defined more clearly and have been assessed in many different educational contexts. The mastery learning program developed by Bloom, and another program developed by Keller, are described briefly in the proceeding paragraphs to illustrate different ways that mastery-based systems have been implemented in regular classrooms. Although guidelines and commercial materials for these programs are available, it is possible (and usually preferable) for teachers to design their own programs and to develop materials that are suited to their own styles of teaching and the particular characteristics and needs of their students (see Block, Efthim, & Burns, 1989, and Guskey, 1985, for practical suggestions).

Introducing the mastery learning model into a classroom does not necessarily affect the mode of instruction. Varying both the amount of time students spend on learning concepts or skills and the amount of time teachers spend evaluating them on their progress does not preclude, for example, whole-class instruction and lecturing, although more individualized instructional techniques may be easier to use.

Whatever the mode of instruction, however, mastery learning programs require clear instructional objectives. It is necessary to break a course or subject into small discrete units of learning to give students specific skills to work toward and to allow individualized evaluation of increments of mastery. In Bloom's Learning for Mastery (LFM) program, the teacher is instructed to develop brief, ungraded, student-scored, diagnostic progress tests used for formative evaluation of students' levels of understanding (Bloom, Hastings, & Madaus, 1971). These evaluations provide the teacher and student with feedback about the student's progress toward achieving the educational objectives. Students are given additional instructional material (i.e., "correctives") based on their specific levels of mastery. The correctives are used for further instruction and should differ from the teacher's group instruction. Students continue with the diagnostic test and corrective instruction cycle until they have achieved mastery. Students are supposed to do the additional studying on their own time, although class time often is set aside for this purpose (Block, 1974).

In the LFM program, grading is noncompetitive in that any student who has mastered the curriculum designated for that length of instructional time is given an "A." Ideally, all but a few students should achieve the predetermined level of mastery.

Keller (1968) developed an instructional model that is compatible with the basic assumptions of Bloom's model, but in practice works quite differently. In Keller's Personalized System of Instruction (PSI), students proceed through a set of written curriculum materials at their own pace. After initially attempting to complete the unit's material, a student takes the unit mastery test, given by a "proctor" (e.g., the teacher, a teacher's aide, or a more advanced student or classmate). If the student passes the test, she advances to the next unit. Otherwise, she uses the unit correctives to restudy the unmastered material. The cycle continues until the student demonstrates mastery on one form of the unit's test. Grading is noncompetitive, as it is in LFM programs.

The major difference between LFM and PSI programs is that in LFM classrooms students are expected to work on their own time to master material so that the entire class, together, can proceed to the next unit of study. In PSI classrooms, students continue to work at their own pace throughout the school year. This difference has two important implications. The LFM method theoretically should reduce the variability in achievement levels among students. Students who learn more slowly take more time to achieve mastery, but some of that additional time is their own. The PSI method actually could result in increased variability in mastery because the faster learners are not delayed in their progress by the slower learners, as they are to some degree in traditional, unidimensional classrooms. An advantage of the PSI method is that fast learners can create highly challenging and highly motivating educational programs, and they are spared the boredom that can result from having to go over material they already have mastered.

Mastery learning programs such as these two have been implemented in schools throughout the world and their effects on motivation and learning have been evaluated extensively. Evaluations indicate that mastery learning programs have positive effects on student attitudes and achievement, particularly for weaker students (Guskey & Pigott, 1988; Kulik, Kulik, & Bangert-Drowns, 1990a; Kulik, Kulik, & Cohen, 1979), although whether research has demonstrated positive effects on students' standardized test performance is disputed among reviewers (Anderson & Burns, 1987; Kulik, Kulik, & Bangert-Drowns, 1990b; Slavin, 1987b, 1990a).

Although most of the mastery learning programs that have been studied appear to have some positive effects on achievement, they are not entirely effective in achieving some motivation-related goals, such as focusing students' attention on improving their own skills as opposed to competing against classmates. Informal observations of mastery-based programs suggest that it is difficult to eliminate altogether students' interest in comparing their performance with that of classmates. Crockenberg and Bryant (1978) pointed out that booklets or units usually are organized hierarchically, and the level usually is indicated by a salient marker, such as color. Learners easily can determine who is more or less advanced in the curriculum, and some observers claim that many children are keenly aware of where they rank compared to their classmates. Buckholdt and Wodarski (1974) and Levine (1983) all noted children's tendencies to create a race to the end of the curriculum. Even when grading is noncompetitive, children sometimes themselves create a competitive situation. Despite this limitation, these well-tested programs provide teachers with evaluation models that are based on a mastery standard and that can be adapted to their own teaching styles and student needs.

Cooperative Incentive Structures

One way to use competitiveness constructively is to create group competition that rivals groups of students of equal ability levels against each other. Educational researchers have developed and tested instructional programs that involve cooperative group learning and team competition.

Johnson and Johnson (1985b, 1989) identified four basic elements that characterize cooperative group learning and distinguish it from traditional group learning. First, there is positive interdependence among group members—students need to be concerned about the performance of other students. Second, there is individual accountability—every student's mastery of the material is assessed and "counts." Third, there is face-to-face interaction among students, and fourth, students learn the social skills (e.g., communication, managing conflicts) needed to work collaboratively (see also Cohen, 1986; Slavin et al., 1985).

Slavin (1983a, 1987a) pointed out that cooperative learning programs vary in terms of two principle aspects of classroom organization: task structure and reward structure. All cooperative learning programs use cooperative task structures, in which students work collaboratively with classmates, usually in small groups. Not all programs reward students on the basis of their group (referred to as a cooperative incentive structure) as opposed to their individual performance. Slavin's (1983b, 1984) reviews of research on cooperative learning strongly suggested that the cooperative incentive structure results in the highest level of motivation and learning.

The defining feature of a cooperative incentive structure is that a group reward is contingent on the performance of all group members. By combining high- and low-performing students in groups and by making rewards contingent on the group's performance, cooperative incentive structures can equalize opportunities for rewards. A group reward structure, therefore, can relieve motivation problems that many low-ability students have in individual competition situations in which they have no hope of "winning."

Evidence suggests that when rewards are based on the sum of the group members' performance, simply being a member of a successful group provides all students with some of the advantages of success, such as high self-perceptions of ability, satisfaction, and peer esteem (Ames, 1981; Ames & Felker, 1979). Because cooperative incentive structures give all students an equal chance at being a member of the winning team, they also focus students' attention on effort as a cause of outcomes, rather than on ability (see Ames & Ames, 1984).

Johnson and Johnson (1985b) also stressed individual accountability, suggesting that positive interdependence can be achieved by dividing roles, materials, resources, or information among group members in a way that requires all students to contribute. Group size is an important consideration; as the size of the group increases, it becomes more difficult to identify individual members' contributions. They suggested using groups of two to six children. It is also important for all students to realize that their efforts are required for the group to succeed.

In a study of teachers endeavoring to implement reform-minded mathematics instruction, I observed many effective strategies for ensuring individual accountability. In several classes, for example, students knew that one member of their group would be asked to present and explain their group's strategy for solving a math problem to the class. Because they did not know which student would be chosen, they had to make sure that everyone in the group understood their strategy. In one class the teacher pulled names from a bowl to ensure that all students were called on an equal number of times.

By rewarding groups as well as individuals for their academic achievement, peer norms favor rather than oppose high achievement (see Johnson & Johnson, 1985b, and Sharan, 1990, for reviews). As in sports, where excellence in individual performance is encouraged by peers because it benefits the whole team, team competition in the classroom can result in greater student support of each other's achievements. Studies have found, for instance, that students in cooperative incentive structures are more likely than students in individual competitive situations to agree with such statements as, "Other children in my class want me to work hard" (e.g., Hulton & DeVries, 1976). Research also has shown that students in cooperative incentive structures are more likely to tutor, help, and encourage classmates than students in individualistic competitive structures (see Johnson & Johnson, 1985a, 1985b), and they are more likely to accept students with disabilities (Cosden & Haring, 1992).

Three programs using cooperative incentive structures are recognized for their amount of systematic development and research: Teams–Games–Tournaments, Student Teams and Achievement Divisions, and Jigsaw. These cooperative programs (described as follows) illustrate how cooperative incentive structures can be implemented in the classroom to make productive use of students' competitiveness and to maximize effort and performance.

In *Teams–Games–Tournaments* (TGT) students are assigned to four- or five-member teams. Each team is diverse in terms of its members' levels of achievement, race, gender, or other important variables. Teams should be matched equally on initial skill level. Students practice with teammates for game sessions in a tournament that is held once or twice a week. In the tournament each student is assigned to a tournament table where he competes individually against students from other teams. The students at each table have similar achievement levels. At each three-person game table students answer questions posed on card sets or game sheets to demonstrate mastery of specific skills. At the end of a game session, the top scorer at each table receives six points, the middle scorer four points, and the low scorer two points. Team scores are the sum of the points won by each team member. Team standings, based on the cumulative scores of each team for all the games in the tournament, are publicized in a weekly classroom newsletter.

In contrast to TGT, *Student Teams and Achievement Divisions* (STAD) programs do not include games and tournaments. With this program, students are assigned to four- or five-member teams that are heterogeneous in terms of past performance levels, gender, and ethnicity. Teammates usually are assigned adjacent seats and are encouraged to work together. The function of the team is to prepare its members to take individual quizzes twice a week. Students' scores on the quizzes are compared to the scores of others in their "division"—composed of students who are roughly equal in terms of past performance. The highest ranking score among that group of equals earns the maximum number of points regardless of the relative level of achievement for the division. Rewards, therefore, are contingent on performance within a group of students performing at about the same level, rather than on relative performance in a classroom of students achieving at very different levels. Thus, every student has an equal chance of attaining a high score.

The *Jigsaw* method originally was developed to foster peer cooperation and race relations by creating interdependence among students. A different portion of a learning task is assigned to each of five or six members on a team, and task completion requires contingent and mutual cooperation (Aronson, Stephan, Sikes, Blaney, & Snapp, 1978). The material to be learned is divided into as many parts as there are group members. All groups in the classroom study identical material that is subdivided identically among members. After receiving the task on cards, the jigsaw group disbands and new groups of students with the same task are formed. These new groups help each other learn the material and prepare presentations for the original jigsaw group. Students then return to their original jigsaw group and teach their parts to groupmates. All group members, therefore, are ultimately responsible for learning all the curriculum material. Teachers move among the groups, offering assistance, encouragement, or direction where it is needed. In the original Jigsaw model, students received individual grades based on their own test scores. In an adaptation, Jigsaw II (Slavin, 1980b), students' grades are based partly on their team scores.

The three cooperative learning programs reviewed here represent a vast number of cooperative learning experiments (see reviews by Johnson & Johnson, 1985a, Sharan, 1990, Slavin, 1977, 1980a, 1983a, 1984, 1990b, and Slavin et al., 1985). Practical guides exist to assist teachers in implementing cooperative learning and group evaluation structures (e.g., Burns, 1987; Cohen, 1986; Gibbs & Allen, 1978; Johnson, Johnson, Holubec, & Roy, 1984; Kagan, n.d.; Roy, 1982; Slavin, 1988, 1990b).

Although cooperative learning approaches have the potential to increase motivation and learning, this potential is not always realized. Cohen (1986) argued that students need careful preparation and training to engage in cooperative learning, and she provides many practical suggestions for such training. Webb (1984, 1985) conducted studies that demonstrate important differences in students' interactions (e.g., the nature of help sought and given) and learning as a function of the composition (e.g., gender, ability-level mix) of the group (see also Ross, 1995). Cosden and Haring (1992) pointed out that "free riders" (i.e., students who allow their groupmates to complete most of the work) are common, and some of the more capable students reduce their participation because they are exploited. Issues such as student training and group composition need to be considered carefully before a cooperative learning approach is implemented.

CONCLUSION

It is important for students to have a realistic understanding of their skills. Without this they are not likely to select tasks that will foster learning, and they will not make productive decisions about where to apply their efforts. To engage productively in school tasks, students need to feel efficacious—to believe that with some effort they will be able to complete the present tasks. And if they know they do not have the prerequisite skills to complete a task, they need to know that they can develop them. They also need to know that their efforts will be rewarded, regardless of their skill levels relative to those of classmates.

Teachers cannot and would not want to eliminate individual differences in students' academic achievements. But they can minimize maladaptive, face-saving behaviors that inhibit learning. These are worthy goals that lead to better learning and make school a more pleasant and rewarding place for students.

TABLE 7-1   Summary of Terms

Terms	Definition
Proximal goals	Short-term goals that can be achieved quickly
Distal goals	Long-term goals that may involve many steps
Attribution retraining	Making explicit statements to change a person's perceptions of the cause of failure (usually from ability to effort or strategy)
Undifferentiated academic task structure	A structure in which students work on the same tasks at the same time, and the nature of tasks varies little from day to day
Unidimensional classrooms	Classrooms with undifferentiated task structures in which valued performance outcomes are defined narrowly and social comparison information is salient
Differentiated task structure	A structure in which students work on different tasks at the same time and the nature of tasks varies from day to day
Multidimensional classrooms	Classrooms with differentiated task structures in which many different kinds of performance are valued and social comparison information is not salient
Mastery learning programs	Programs of instruction in which students move through the curriculum at their own pace, as a function of demonstrated mastery
Outcome-based education (OBE)	An instructional program that is guided by a set of well-defined objectives, frequent assessment, and multiple opportunities to achieve the objectives
Cooperative incentive structure	A structure in which students' rewards (e.g., grades) are based on their group's performance

Intrinsic
Motivation

A group of 4-year-olds sit at a table in a preschool. Two children are drawing a picture with markers; another carefully is gluing a cotton ball to a paper rabbit that she just cut. Two others explain that they are making a hotel out of blocks. The children work intensively and appear to enjoy these activities that, in addition to being fun, help them develop fine-motor and perceptual skills.

A strict reinforcement theorist would explain these children's efforts by their reinforcement histories: These or similar behaviors previously must have led to social approval or maybe even to tangible rewards. Or perhaps alternative behaviors (e.g., failing to engage in a teacher-sanctioned activity) were punished. A social cognitive theorist would add that the children may have observed other children being reinforced for these activities, and that they expected to be reinforced for their efforts in this situation or punished for alternative behaviors.

Intrinsic motivation theorists offer another explanation. They claim that humans are born with a disposition to develop skills and engage in learning-related activities; external reinforcement is not necessary because learning inherently is reinforcing. This chapter discusses three perspectives on intrinsic motivation, all based on the premise that humans have natural inclinations that render some tasks intrinsically motivating. According to these three views, humans innately are disposed to (1) seek opportunities to develop competencies, and (2) seek novelty—events and activities that are somewhat discrepant from their expectations; and they also (3) have an innate need to be autonomous and to engage in activities of their own volition.

These three perspectives on intrinsic motivation are not mutually exclusive. To the contrary, they are compatible and to some degree overlapping. Each is discussed in the following sections.

COMPETENCE MOTIVATION

In 1959, White published a now-classic paper presenting evidence that humans have an intrinsic need to feel competent and that such behaviors as exploration and mastery attempts are explained best by this innate motivation force. White claimed that the underlying need to feel competent explains behaviors as diverse as an infant examining an object visually, a 2-year-old building a tower of blocks, a 9-year-old playing a computer game, and an adolescent writing a story.

White's defense of an intrinsic **competence motive** rested partly on this motive's evolutionary adaptive value because it impels the organism to deal more effectively with the environment. He pointed out that humans, unlike lower animals, have few competencies that are provided innately, and they need to learn a great deal about how to deal with the environment. Thus, a drive or innate disposition to become competent has considerable adaptive value.

Piaget (1952) similarly claimed that, from the first day of life, humans naturally are inclined to practice newly developing competencies (what he called "schemes"), and that practicing new skills inherently is satisfying. For the very young infant, the "skill" may be as simple as grabbing an object; infants usually attempt to grasp nearly any object that is close to them and, as a consequence of practicing this skill in different contexts and with different objects, they become more adept at grasping differently shaped objects.

Piaget's theory provides an explanation for children's repetitive and occasionally annoying behaviors that appear to serve no purpose. For example, when children begin to learn to take off their own shoes, they repeatedly remove them, or they might turn doorknobs without any apparent desire to go through the doorway. Older children may make the same cookie recipe repeatedly until they have perfected it, listen to the same record until they have "mastered" every note and word, or play the same video game until they consistently "beat the machine."

As children develop they practice different and more varied skills, and consequently become more effective in their interactions with the environment. For instance, toddlers can develop their spatial abilities by doing increasingly difficult puzzles. Adolescents may become more adept at thinking hypothetically by playing chess or arguing politics.

Behaviors that children engage in to increase competence sometimes also result in tangible reinforcements. Most children enjoy eating the cookies they bake, but the feeling of competence that is derived from making a successful batch of cookies can be just as rewarding as the good taste. Infants and children also are encouraged to participate in some mastery activities and are praised for their successes (unless, for example, children remove their shoes just as the parents are leaving to take them outdoors). But children often practice newly developing skills without any reinforcement from the environment. Indeed, they engage in some activities that develop competence even when the activity results in some form of punishment. Consider the 1-year-old who frequently is "punished" by painful falls for practicing walking. I have yet to see a child stop trying to walk as a consequence of such punishment.

Principle of Optimal Challenge

Competence motivation explains children's efforts only on challenging tasks, on which their efforts will increase their competencies (Deci & Ryan, 1993). The motive to achieve competence does not explain participation in activities that are easy and will not lead to increased skills or understanding. Once children have mastered a skill, they no longer will practice it, except as a means to another end. Thus, once toddlers have mastered the skill of opening doors, they will not turn a doorknob unless they want to go into another room. The preschooler who fully comprehends the movie that she repeatedly has been watching suddenly becomes disinterested.

A study by Danner and Lonky (1981) demonstrated children's preference for tasks that allow them to practice newly developing skills. Children were given experience with three classification tasks of varying levels of difficulty and then were told that they could spend time working on any of the three tasks. Children spent the most time with and rated as most interesting the tasks that were one step ahead of their pretested level of classification skill. McMullin and Steffen (1982) found that when subjects worked on puzzles that became slightly more difficult with each trial, they displayed more subsequent intrinsic motivation than when the difficulty level remained constant.

Emotional Reactions to Mastery

According to White (1959) and Piaget (1952), the increasing competence that results from practicing newly developing skills and mastering challenging tasks engenders a positive emotional experience, which White referred to as a feeling of efficacy.[1] This feeling of efficacy (mastery or competence) is evident in children's smiles when they achieve some goal—completing a puzzle or drawing, or even doing a difficult arithmetic problem. It is this positive emotional experience that makes mastery behavior self-reinforcing.

Consistent with the principle of optimal challenge, several studies have confirmed that children's emotional responses (i.e., joy, pride) are most intense when they master moderately difficult tasks. Studies of infants as young as 8 weeks have shown that smiling is associated with processing novel visual stimuli (a form of mastering the environment for an infant) more than with processing familiar stimuli. As infants become older, they smile at increasingly complex stimuli, presumably because simple stimuli are no longer challenging (Shultz & Zigler, 1970).

Harter systematically studied positive emotion (smiling) in elementary school-age children's responses to mastery attempts. In several studies, she gave anagrams (i.e., letters that can be arranged into words) to children, and observers

---

[1]White's "feeling of efficacy" refers to the emotional consequences of mastery. It sometimes is referred to as a feeling of competence and is similar to pride, although unlike pride, it is not accompanied by the notion of an imagined or real audience. White's feeling of efficacy is different from Bandura's "self-efficacy," which is a cognitive judgment that a person's efforts are likely to lead to success.

rated the intensity of pleasure children expressed at the moment they solved each puzzle (Harter, 1974, 1978b). When the problems were extremely difficult and required an unusual amount of time and effort to solve, they expressed little pleasure and reported feelings of annoyance and frustration. Easily solved anagrams also did not produce very much smiling. Tasks that required some effort but were not extremely difficult resulted in the most positive expressions.

Competence motivation and the principle of challenge explain why adults derive little pleasure from beating someone who is much less skillful at tennis, or why people are compelled to try a steeper hill after mastering a ski run. Success at a challenging task, a situation that is most likely to lead to improved competence, results in the most positive emotional experience.

Effects of the Social Environment

Competence motivation has been presented as a biologically based "motive," compelling individuals to engage in activities that result in increased competency to deal with the environment. Although there is merit to this view, it is important to recognize the role of the social environment.

As children grow older, they increasingly require adult feedback to determine whether they have mastered tasks. Infants usually do not need an adult to tell them whether mastery has been achieved. Their mastery attempts, for the most part, are directed at affecting the environment in some way, and the feedback comes directly from the objects they manipulate; if the shoe comes off or the doorknob turns, they know they have been successful. Feedback is also intrinsic to some tasks for older children. A child who makes it around the ice rink for the first time without falling will experience efficacy regardless of whether an adult congratulates her. But an adult or older child often is needed to inform a child that his swimming stroke has improved, that the paper she wrote for her English class is well organized or vivid, or that his solutions to a set of arithmetic problems are correct. Thus, in some situations the feeling of competence requires social input.

Adults also influence standards of achievement by encouraging and praising particular outcomes. Thus, a parent who praises only certain kinds of drawings might influence a young child's artistic standards, and thus influence which drawings will engender feelings of competence. Differential reactions of adults to children's performance may explain, at least partly, why 85 percent correct answers or a grade of "B" will generate feelings of competence and pride in one child and incompetence and shame in another.

Classroom practices also can affect students' standards for achievement. Hanging only papers with 100 percent correct answers on the bulletin board may undermine feelings of competence in children who achieve lower, albeit respectable, scores. Grading competitively (i.e., based on a normal curve) can deny feelings of competence to children who cannot outperform classmates, even when their own performance has improved. Many children do not enjoy schoolwork because it fails to provide the feelings of competence and mastery they need to sustain intrinsic interest. Redefining what constitutes mastery can give these students opportunities to succeed and to find intrinsic value in school tasks (Stipek, 1997; see Chapter 10).

Self-Perceptions of Competence and Intrinsic Motivation

Just as feelings of efficacy and competence engendered by success at challenging tasks reinforce mastery efforts and enhance intrinsic motivation to engage in similar tasks, feelings of incompetence undermine intrinsic motivation. Working on a task without achieving success destroys enthusiasm for working on similar tasks.

This link between mastery and intrinsic motivation is seen in specific task situations, and it is evident, more generally, in associations between perceptions of academic competence and motivation to engage in academic tasks. Many studies have demonstrated that students who believe that they are academically competent are more intrinsically interested in school tasks than those who have low perceptions of their academic abilities (Boggiano, Main, & Katz, 1988; Gottfried, 1990; Harter, 1981a, 1992; Harter & Connell, 1984; Mac Iver, Stipek, & Daniels, 1991). People also are interested most in topics about which they have prior knowledge (see Tobias, 1994).

A study by Mac Iver, Stipek, and Daniels (1991) suggested a causal relationship between perceived competence and intrinsic motivation. These investigators assessed, at both the beginning and the end of the semester, junior and senior high school students' perceptions of their competencies and intrinsic interest in one subject they were studying. Analyses revealed that interest changed in the direction that perceived competence changed. That is, students whose perceptions of competence increased over the course of the semester rated the subject more interesting at the end of the semester than at the beginning, and those whose perceptions of competence decreased rated the subject as being less interesting at the end of the semester. Harter (1992) reviewed further evidence, based on path analyses, suggesting that perceptions of competence engender positive affective experiences, which in turn engender intrinsic motivation. She also described a study in which students' intrinsic motivation for academic work increased, remained the same, or decreased from elementary to junior high school, depending on whether their perceptions of their academic competencies increased, remained the same, or decreased (see also Harter, Whitesell, & Kowalski, 1992). Similar findings are reported for a group of gifted students who moved from a regular classroom to a program for gifted children (Harter, 1992).[2]

---

[2]For some children who experience incompetence, only a few success experiences can rekindle intrinsic interest. I observed this effect from my daughter's experience on a little league baseball team. At her first game she failed twice to make it to first base. Despite considerable praise for her efforts, she wanted to go home. Fearing that I never would get her back again (and believing that all she needed was to feel competent), I insisted that she stay. A subsequent hit and tour of the bases was all it took to create such enthusiasm that it was I who eventually had to beg her to leave.

In summary, it is believed that individuals naturally are inclined to seek opportunities to develop their competencies, and they derive pleasure from the experience of increased competence that these opportunities afford. Although the emphasis is different, the theoretical perspective on intrinsic motivation described next is related to the notion of competency motivation in the sense that novel situations require more effort to process than familiar or predictable ones. Therefore, they may produce similar feelings of efficacy.

NOVELTY

Theorists emphasizing the second perspective on intrinsic motivation portray humans as information processors. Berlyne (1966), Hunt (1965), and Kagan (1972) all claimed that humans are predisposed to derive pleasure from activities and events that provide some level of surprise, incongruity, complexity, or discrepancy from their expectations or beliefs. This theory may explain why an infant who is only a few months old looks longer at a novel stimulus than at a stimulus he has seen before (Hunter, Ames, & Koopman, 1983), why an 8-month-old likes to look at things upside down, or why a 2-year-old calls herself by a wrong name and then laughs hysterically. It also may explain why so many children like cartoons, science fiction, and video games.

According to information-processing theorists, pleasure is assumed to derive from creating, investigating, or processing stimuli that are moderately discrepant (Spielberger & Starr, 1994). Stimuli that are not discrepant or novel will not arouse interest, and stimuli that are too discrepant from the individual's expectations will be ignored, cause anxiety, or even provoke "terror and flight" (Berlyne, 1966, p. 30; see also Scheffler, 1991).

Thus, the information-processing approach is similar to Piaget's and White's competence motivation approaches, which assume that individuals seek tasks that are moderately challenging. A novel stimulus offers a challenge, just as a task might. Individuals must exert more effort to process or understand novel stimuli that are discrepant from their expectations or experiences than to process expected or familiar stimuli. Competence motivation and information-processing theorists also agree that once individuals encounter novel events or challenging tasks, they naturally are motivated to reduce the discrepancy—between their expectations and the novel stimuli or between their current skill levels and the skill levels required to complete the tasks. Deci (1975) described this as a perpetual process of seeking challenge and novelty and then "conquering" it. People seek novel situations and situations that challenge their current skill levels or understanding, and then they strive to achieve mastery—to conquer the challenge and experience feelings of competence or understanding.

SELF-DETERMINATION

A third perspective on intrinsic motivation stresses autonomy. deCharms, Deci, Ryan, and other achievement motivation theorists agree with White that individuals are motivated intrinsically to develop their competencies, and that feelings of competence enhance intrinsic interest in activities. They added, however, another innate need—the need to be self-determining. These theorists propose that individuals naturally are disposed to wanting to believe that they are engaging in activities by their own volition—because they want to rather than because they have to (deCharms, 1976, 1984; Deci, 1975; Deci & Ryan, 1985). They differentiate between situations in which individuals perceive themselves as being the cause of their own behaviors, which they refer to as an **internal locus of causality,** and situations in which individuals believe they are engaging in behavior to achieve rewards or please another person, or because of external constraints, referred to as an **external locus of causality.** These theorists claim that people are more likely to be motivated intrinsically to engage in an activity when their locus of causality is internal than when it is external.

According to the theory, the very same activity can be more motivating and pleasurable when one chooses to engage in it than when it is undertaken for some external purpose. Consider, for example, "pleasure reading." People use the phrase to refer to books or articles that they choose to read, not to class assignments. The phrase, therefore, implies that books read to meet course requirements do not engender pleasure. Ironically, if two roommates read the same book, the roommate who chooses to read it would enjoy it and the roommate who reads it for a class assignment would not enjoy it.

Many factors affect the perceived locus of causality, including the level of control exerted by others and the availability of rewards. Despite the important effects of these and other external variables, theorists stress that a person's perception of causality is more important than any objective measure of causality. Thus, two individuals in the same situation can have different ideas about their reasons for engaging in a particular behavior or activity.

Summary

Although White was the first to popularize the concept of competence motivation, the notion that individuals innately are disposed to strive for increasing competence and to take pleasure in its achievement is also critical to Deci and Ryan's theoretical formulation of intrinsic motivation (e.g., Deci, 1975; Deci & Ryan, 1985). They add that individuals also need to experience self-determination. Activities and situations that engender feelings of competence and self-determination, therefore, are the most intrinsically motivating. Information-processing theorists' claims fit neatly within this theoretical framework because novelty and complexity, in a sense, involve a perceptual and processing challenge.

ADVANTAGE OF INTRINSIC MOTIVATION

Theory and research suggest that there is considerable value to trying to maximize intrinsic motivation. The following sections discuss the advantages that have been demonstrated empirically.

Learning Activities Outside of School

Intrinsically motivated achievement behavior is desirable partly because external reinforcement is not always available. Students, such as Safe Sally (see Chapter 1), who become dependent on external rewards for learning, will not engage in intellectual activities outside of school where grades and other forms of recognition are less available. If learning is perceived as an activity that a person does only to obtain rewards and avoid punishment, there is no reason to do it when no rewards are available and punishment is not likely.

Preference for Challenge

Studies have shown that individuals are more likely to select challenging tasks when intrinsically motivated than when motivated to obtain an extrinsic reward (Boggiano, Pittman, & Ruble, 1982; Boggiano et al., 1988; Flink, Boggiano, Main, Barrett, & Katz, 1992; Pearlman, 1984; Pittman, Emery, & Boggiano, 1982; Shapira, 1976). Pearlman (1984), for example, found that when a reward (+3 points on the next test) or penalty (–3 points on the next test) was made contingent on whether students' solutions to a problem were correct or incorrect, they selected easier problems than when no reward or penalty was at stake. In a study by Pittman et al. (1982), the preference for simple versions of a task in a situation in which an extrinsic reward was offered carried over even to a situation in which the original reward contingencies were no longer in effect.

Conceptual Understanding

There is considerable evidence suggesting that individuals learn relatively more when they read material that they rate as being intrinsically interesting (see Shirey, 1992; Tobias, 1994; Wade, 1992). The enhanced learning occurs, at least partly, because people attend more to text that interests them and that this attention helps them process and remember what they have read (Anderson, 1982; Asher, 1980). Research further suggests that the conditions that produce interest and enjoyment (i.e., that foster intrinsic motivation) especially facilitate understanding and conceptual learning but not rote learning (e.g., Benware & Deci, 1984; Grolnick & Ryan, 1987; Ryan, Connell, & Plant, 1990).

Creativity

Studies have found that conditions supporting intrinsic motivation also foster greater creativity. In a study reported by Amabile (1983), female college students who expected to be graded produced artwork judged to be less creative than the work of those who did not expect to be evaluated. Butler and Nisan (1986) found that when evaluative feedback was given in the form of grades, students' performance on a quantitative task subsequently increased and their performance on a task assessing divergent (creative) thinking declined; written comments, in contrast, resulted in improved performance on both tasks. Studies by Amabile and Hennessey (1992) indicated that researchers were able to increase children's creativity by focusing their attention on their intrinsic interest and away from the extrinsic rewards related to tasks. In a study by McGraw and McCullers (1979), college students who were promised monetary rewards for solving a series of problems had more difficulty "breaking set" (i.e., solving problems that had different solutions from the previous problems) than students who did not expect monetary rewards.

The reasons for the negative effects of extrinsic motivation on conceptual and creative thinking in the studies previously described are unclear. Amabile (1983) suggested that extrinsic contingencies can create an instrumental focus that narrows attention and orients individuals to take the quickest and easiest solutions (see also Flink et al., 1992). It is also possible that students are used to being evaluated on rote learning more than on conceptual understanding; as a consequence, those who expected to be evaluated in the aforementioned studies focused their attention primarily on facts that could be memorized.

Pleasure and Involvement

Intrinsic interest or motivation also is associated with greater pleasure and more active involvement than extrinsic interest or motivation (Harter, 1992; see also Tobias, 1994). In addition, Miserandino (1996) found that students who reported engaging in schoolwork for intrinsic reasons also reported more involvement, persistence, participation, and curiosity and less boredom in school activities than students who claimed to be motivated extrinsically. Intrinsically motivated students also reported feeling less anxious and angry, and less likely to avoid schoolwork or fake diligence (see also Patrick et al., 1993).

In summary, because of these benefits of intrinsic motivation, it is important to take good advantage of this motivation system. Chapter 10 summarizes classroom practices that have been shown to maximize intrinsic motivation. The next section further details the links between intrinsic motivation and the extrinsic motivation system previously mentioned in Chapter 3.

INTRINSIC MOTIVATION AND EXTRINSIC REWARDS

Intrinsic motivation and motivation based on extrinsic rewards, to some degree, compete with each other. Research has shown that under certain circumstances, offering extrinsic rewards for engaging in tasks actually undermines intrinsic motivation. Two classic studies illustrated this effect of extrinsic reinforcement. Deci (1971) enlisted college students to participate in a problem-solving study over three sessions. In the first session, all students were asked to work on a series of interesting puzzles. In the second session, half of the students were told that they would be given an extrinsic reward (money) for correctly solving a second set of puzzles; no mention of a reward was made to the other half of the students. During the third session the experimenter left all of the students with the puzzles, telling them that they could work on them if they wanted, or they could look at current issues of *Time*, the *New Yorker*, and *Playboy*, which were placed near the students. In this last session, like the first, no students were offered extrinsic rewards.

Students were observed through a one-way mirror in order to assess the effect of rewards on the amount of time they chose to work on puzzles. In the second session, students who were offered rewards for working on the puzzles spent more time working on them than students who were not offered rewards. Thus, the extrinsic rewards had the immediate effect of increasing the amount of time subjects engaged in the task. In contrast, in the third session, when no rewards were offered to anyone, students who previously had been rewarded spent less time working on puzzles than students who never had been offered rewards. The rewarded students lost interest in the task when the rewards were withdrawn.

Lepper, Greene, and Nisbett (1973) conducted a similar study with preschool-age children, in which children who had been offered rewards for playing with Magic Markers subsequently spent less free time on the activity than children who never were given rewards. As many as one hundred studies have used paradigms that are similar to these two studies to examine the effects of rewards on subsequent engagement in various activities (see reviews by Bates, 1979; Cameron & Pierce, 1994; Deci & Ryan, 1985; Kohn, 1993; Lepper, 1983, 1996; Notz, 1975; Pittman, Boggiano, & Ruble, 1983; Ryan, Connell, & Deci, 1985; Tang & Hall, 1995). These studies suggest that external rewards can undermine intrinsic interest in a task, and the larger the reward, the more negative is its effect on intrinsic interest (Freedman, Cunningham, & Krismer, 1992).

This observed effect of extrinsic rewards contradicts reinforcement theory. According to reinforcement theory, a reward made contingent on a behavior increases the frequency of that behavior. When it is withdrawn the behavior should return to its baseline (i.e., its level of frequency before the reward had been given), but it should not dip below the baseline, as was found in these two and other studies.

Intrinsic motivation theorists assume that the negative effect the reward had on the target behavior after it was withdrawn can be explained only by cognitive or affective processes. "Self-attribution" theorists propose that when a reward is offered, individuals perceive the reward as being the reason for engaging in the activity, even though intrinsic interest might have been a sufficiently strong reason for them to perform the task. But because of their perception of the reason for performing the task, they cease the activity when the reward is withdrawn.

This effect of rewards on motivation is related to what theorists refer to as the **discounting principle.** According to the discounting principle, if one possible explanation for an individual's behavior is salient, all other explanations will be "discounted." An external reward for performing an activity is usually more salient than intrinsic reasons. Thus, an individual originally may perceive intrinsic interest as the reason for undertaking a task, but if a desired extrinsic reward for the behavior is offered, intrinsic interest is discounted and the more salient extrinsic reward is perceived to be the cause.

The discounting principle and the undermining effect of rewards are illustrated by an anecdote about an old man who was bothered by noisy boys playing in his neighborhood (Casady, 1975). The old man called the boys together and told them he was deaf; he then asked them to shout more loudly so he could enjoy their fun. In return he would pay each of them a quarter. The boys were delighted, and on the first day the old man was provided with a considerable amount of noise for his money. On the second day, he told the boys that he could afford to pay only twenty cents. The pay rate dwindled more each day, and eventually the boys became angry and told the old man that they certainly were not going to make noise for nothing!

Although self-attribution theorists focus on individuals' interpretations of events after they have occurred, cognitive evaluation theorists believe that the effect of rewards involves processes that occur at a deeper level than thoughts and occur prior to, during, and after task engagement. Deci and Ryan (1985) claim that rewards cause individuals to shift from internal to external locus of causality; rewards create feelings of being controlled and interfere with feelings of self-determination. Cognitive evaluation theorists conceptualize motivation on a continuum rather than in terms of an internal–external dichotomy. Thus, intrinsic motivation is proportional to the degree to which individuals perceive their behaviors as being self-determined or volitional rather than being controlled by others, by rewards, or by intrapsychic forces (e.g., guilt or a sense of obligation; Deci, Vallerand, Pelletier, & Ryan, 1991; Ryan & Connell, 1989; Ryan & Stiller, 1991).

Whether locus of causality is conceptualized as a dichotomy or as a continuous dimension, it is affected by the availability of rewards and other aspects of the social context. Rewards, however, can be used in different ways and for different purposes. The effects of rewards on locus of causality, and thus on intrinsic motivation, are determined by how they are used as much as by whether they are used.

Controlling versus Information Function of Rewards

Bandura (1982b), Deci (1975), and Lepper (1981), all distinguished between two uses of rewards in classrooms—(1) as incentives to engage in tasks (i.e., to control behavior) and (2) as information about mastery (see also Deci & Ryan, 1985; Ryan et al., 1985). Rewards used to control behavior as well as other instructional practices (e.g., close monitoring of performance) that shift students away from a perception of autonomy and personal causation and toward a perception of external causation undermine intrinsic motivation. Rewards used to provide information vary in their effect, depending primarily on whether the information is positive (i.e., suggesting competence) or negative (i.e., suggesting incompetence).

When the teacher makes recess (a reward) contingent on students finishing their math assignment, the reward contains no information about students' levels of mastery. In this situation the reward is used to control students' behaviors. Therefore, it will engender an external locus of causality, and ultimately students will complete their math assignments only as long as a reward is expected, even if they previously were interested in the task without any reward contingent on it. **Task-contingent rewards** (i.e., rewards based on engaging in the task), such as the preceding example, are experienced nearly always as controlling. Other practices that can create a feeling of being controlled and, thus, can undermine intrinsic interest include close monitoring (Lepper & Greene, 1975; Plant & Ryan, 1985), deadlines (Amabile, DeJong, & Lepper, 1976), evaluation (Hughes, Sullivan, & Mosley, 1985; Maehr & Stallings, 1972), imposing goals (Manderlink & Harackiewicz, 1984; Mossholder, 1980), and competition (Deci, Betley, Kahle, Abrams, & Porac, 1981; Fry & Coe, 1980; Vallerand, Gauvin, & Halliwell, 1986). Giving extrinsic rewards, therefore, constitutes one among many classroom practices that can foster the perception of an external locus of causality, which interferes with intrinsic motivation.

The effect of any of these practices on motivation, however, varies depending on the context and emphasis. Setting goals actually might enhance intrinsic motivation if students' own views are solicited and if the goals allow them to experience developing levels of mastery. Competition can make a task more exciting without undermining motivation if all students have equal chances of winning (and experiencing a feeling of competence), and if emphasis is placed on what is being learned rather than on who wins or loses.

Performance-contingent rewards, based on a specified level of performance, provide information about levels of mastery and are less likely than task-contingent rewards to undermine interest. They even may enhance it (Boggiano & Ruble, 1979; Karniol & Ross, 1977; Rosenfield, Folger, & Adelman, 1980; see also Deci & Ryan, 1992; Lepper, Keavney & Drake, 1996). The competence feedback implicit in social reinforcement is presumably why praise usually does not reduce intrinsic motivation even though it is external (Anderson, Manoogian, & Reznick, 1976; Blanck, Reis, & Jackson, 1984; Deci, 1971, 1972; Dollinger & Thelen, 1978; Swann & Pittman, 1977; see also Arkes, 1978, and Cameron & Pierce, 1994, for reviews).

Deci and Ryan (1985) cautioned, however, that even performance-contingent rewards can be perceived as controlling or informational, depending on the interpersonal context or the message that is conveyed. Praise, for example, can be worded so that it will be experienced as either informational (e.g., "Nice work—your argument is clear and compelling") or controlling (e.g., "Good job—you're doing it exactly they way I asked you to"). Research suggests that praise that is interpreted as informational supports intrinsic interest but praise that is interpreted as controlling does not (Pittman, Davey, Alafat, Wetherill, & Kramer, 1980; Ryan, 1982).

In summary, the evidence is clear that offering rewards for engaging in activities that individuals already find intrinsically motivating, or making them feel controlled in some other way, such as by monitoring their behaviors or focusing their attention on evaluation, will undermine their intrinsic interest. Essentially their attention shifts to external reasons for engaging in the activity, and when those extrinsic reasons are withdrawn, they are less intrinsically interested in it than they would have been if no reward had been offered.

The effects of rewards, however, vary substantially as a function of how they are given and how they are perceived by individuals. The distinction between task-contingent and performance-contingent rewards and related research illustrates the complexity of the teachers' job in monitoring the use of rewards in the classroom. Rewards are effective and advisable in many situations, but careful attention needs to be given to whether they are likely to be interpreted as controlling or informational. And even if they provide information, they support interest and motivation only if the information is positive—if it communicates mastery and competence.

INDIVIDUAL DIFFERENCES

If motivation to learn is innate, why do some students approach new tasks with enthusiasm and seem genuinely to enjoy learning, while others totally seem uninterested? The answer can be found directly in the theories previously discussed. Recall that individuals are assumed to be driven by needs for competence, novelty, and autonomy. Their intrinsic motivation, therefore, will vary according to the degree to which settings provide opportunities for them to meet these needs. A classroom that engenders feelings of incompetence or of being controlled, or in which activities are familiar and repetitive, will not engender intrinsic motivation.

Even within a classroom there will be individual differences in intrinsic interest in academic tasks because the same circumstances can be experienced differently by different students. A task that is optimally challenging (and therefore can engender feelings of mastery and competence) for some students may be too easy or impossibly difficult for others. Only those students who find the classroom's tasks moderately difficult will experience competence motivation. Teachers also sometimes treat students in a classroom differently—for instance, by granting more autonomy, and thus supporting intrinsic motivation, to some students (usually those who are already highly motivated) than to others.

Also, despite the innate origins of competence motivation, both how and how much it is manifested are influenced by the social environment. Relatively stable individual differences in mastery behavior can develop as a consequence of differences in the behavior of parents and other significant adults. Harter (1978a) speculated that some social reinforcement from early infancy is necessary to sustain a child's mastery attempts. She proposed that social reinforcement for attempting or mastering tasks enhances mastery behavior, whereas punishment for attempting or failing to master tasks inhibits intrinsic interest in achievement tasks. Children may develop a preference for easy work because their parents punished failure, and they will not want to risk the failure that sometimes occurs when initially attempting a moderately difficult task. Children who have overintrusive parents, and thus fail to develop self-confidence in their own abilities to complete tasks, may be overly dependent on the teacher for help. Previous experiences in achievement contexts can have enduring effects on students' behaviors that can be resistant to teachers' efforts to change.

Measures of Individual Differences in Motivation

In most experimental studies intrinsic motivation is measured by whether individuals voluntarily choose to engage or persist in an activity, or by their ratings of their interest in or enjoyment of a particular activity. Mitchell (1993) referred to such ratings as "situational interest." Several researchers have developed questionnaires to assess relatively stable individual differences in students' intrinsic motivation to engage in academic work. Harter (1981b), for example, developed a measure designed to assess five dimensions related to intrinsic motivation: (1) preference for challenging work versus preference for easy work; (2) learning that is motivated by curiosity versus learning that occurs to please the teacher; (3) desire to work independently versus dependency on the teacher for help; (4) independent judgment about selecting tasks versus reliance on the teacher's judgment; and (5) internal criteria for success or failure versus external criteria (e.g., grades, teacher feedback). For each dimension she pits responses that are presumed to reflect an intrinsic orientation toward academic work against responses presumed to reflect a more extrinsic orientation. Harter's measure has been tested on hundreds of elementary and junior high school students. Table 8-1 provides examples of statements students are asked to respond to when filling out the questionnaire.

Gottfried (1985, 1986, 1990) developed the Children's Academic Intrinsic Motivation Inventory (CAIMI), which assesses intrinsic interest in specific subject areas (reading, math, social studies, science), and in school in general. One version is for children in the lower elementary grades, and the other is for children above the third grade. Studies have revealed some stability in children's scores over a 2-year period.

TABLE 8-1 Sample Items from Harter's Intrinsic Motivation Scale

Really True for Me	Sort of True for Me			Really True for Me	Sort of True for Me
		Preference for Challenge	**Preference for Easy Work**		
4	3	Some kids like to go on to new work that's at a more difficult level	Other kids would rather stick to assignments that are pretty easy	2	1
		Pleasing Teacher/ Getting Grades	**Curiosity/ Interest**		
1	2	Some kids do extra projects so they can get better grades	Other kids do extra projects because they learn about things that interest them	3	4
		Dependence on Teacher	**Independent Mastery**		
1	2	When some kids get stuck on a problem they ask the teacher for help	Other kids keep trying to figure out the problem on their own	3	4
		Reliance on Teacher's Judgment	**Independent Judgment**		
1	2	Some kids think the teacher should decide what work to do	Other kids think they should have a say in what work they do	3	4
		Internal criteria	**External criteria**		
4	3	Some kids know whether or not they're doing well in school without grades	Other kids need to have grades to know how well they are doing in school	2	1

Reprinted from Harter, 1981b, p. 305. (A copy of the scale and a manual for scoring and interpreting results is available from Professor Susan Harter, Department of Psychology, University of Denver, 2155 S. Race, Denver, CO 80210.)

It is useful to assess intrinsic interest in different academic domains because there is considerable variation in students' interest in various school tasks. In addition to using the questionnaires previously discussed, teachers can assess students' intrinsic motivation for tasks by observing their behaviors in different task situations. Behaviors that are associated with high intrinsic interest are summarized in Table 8-2.

Perhaps the most straightforward and, ironically, least-used strategy is simply to ask students how interested they are in various school tasks. Teachers can create brief, anonymous questionnaires that ask students to rate their interest in some of the classwork they have been doing (see Table 8-3 for an example), or ask open-ended questions during a group discussion about what activities students enjoy and do not enjoy in school. Just asking these questions gives students the important message that their views are valued (although asking and ignoring their responses can engender cynicism).

Age-Related Changes

In addition to individual differences at any one age, there appear to be systematic differences in these dispositions associated with age. Harter (1981b, 1992) found that scores on her subscales measuring preference for challenge, curiosity and interest, and independent mastery all declined from the third to the ninth grades, while scores on the independent judgment and internal criteria subscales in-

---

TABLE 8-2 Behaviors Associated with Intrinsic Motivation

Students who are motivated intrinsically:

◆ Initiate learning activities on their own

◆ Prefer challenging tasks or pursue challenging aspects of tasks

◆ Spontaneously make connections between school learning and activities or interests outside of school

◆ Ask questions that go beyond the present task—to expand their knowledge beyond the immediate lesson

◆ Go beyond the requirements

◆ Are reluctant to stop working on tasks they have not completed

◆ Work on tasks whether or not extrinsic reasons (e.g., grades, close teacher supervision) are salient

◆ Smile and appear to enjoy working on tasks

◆ Express pride in their achievements

TABLE 8-3 An Example of a Teacher-Developed Measure of Intrinsic Motivation

Please rate how much you enjoy doing the following activities in this class.

	Not at All				A Lot
Doing problems in the arithmetic workbook	1	2	3	4	5
Doing arithmetic word problems on the board	1	2	3	4	5
Reading stories from reading books	1	2	3	4	5
Answering questions at the end of chapters in reading books	1	2	3	4	5
Working on science projects	1	2	3	4	5
Writing stories	1	2	3	4	5
Listening to the teacher read stories	1	2	3	4	5
Working on the class newspaper	1	2	3	4	5

creased with age and experience in school. Students apparently tend to become less motivated to engage in academic activities for their own pleasure, but become better able to judge the quality of their performance (see also Anderman & Maehr, 1994; Letter, Sethi, Dialdin, & Drake, 1995).

We can only speculate about the reasons for these shifts. Research on the undermining effect of external reinforcement on intrinsic motivation suggests that young students' interest in undertaking tasks for the sake of developing mastery may be replaced by an interest in obtaining external rewards, such as high grades. A second explanation concerns the consistent trend (discussed in Chapter 6) for students' perceptions of their competencies for mastering academic tasks to decline with age. Because low perceived competence dampens intrinsic motivation, it is not surprising that intrinsic interest in academic tasks declines along with perceptions of competence.

A third explanation is that the achievement context changes as a function of grade. For example, evaluation may be emphasized more in higher grades and failure may be tolerated less. Eccles and Midgley (1989) suggested that school becomes more formal, more evaluative, and more competitive, and that the focus shifts from the process of learning to evaluating products (see also Anderman & Maehr, 1994; Eccles, 1993; Midgley et al., 1995). A longitudinal study by Harter et al. (1992), of children making the transition to junior high school, confirmed that with each grade students perceived a greater emphasis on evaluation, performance, and social comparison. Moreover, those students who perceived a relatively greater emphasis on these variables scored higher on a scale of extrinsic motivation. These and other changes in educational practices, therefore, may contribute to the age-related declines observed on three of Harter's subscales of intrinsic motivation.

CONCLUSION

Although there is no doubt that external rewards can be powerful motivators of achievement-related behavior, individuals engage in many activities for which no tangible reinforcement is expected or likely. Intrinsic motivation theorists suggest that innate motives to develop competencies, experience novelty, and be self-determining also promote learning-related behavior. Educational contexts that provide students with opportunities to achieve these objectives are most likely to capitalize on these natural motives. Intrinsic motivation is worth promoting because it appears to foster creativity, conceptual learning, desires for challenge, and enjoyment.

It is possible for an individual to have both intrinsic and extrinsic motives for engaging in a particular activity, but many studies suggest that the availability of extrinsic rewards can undermine intrinsic interest in tasks—especially if individuals perceive the rewards as controlling rather than as providing information about their competencies. Individual differences in the degree to which intellectual tasks engender intrinsic interest are seen because students have different socialization histories and different perceptions of their academic competencies, and because they experience or perceive the same context differently.

This chapter described two motivation systems that teachers can use to engage students in the process of learning. Chapter 9 discusses a third motivation system that, similar to intrinsic motivation, is experienced as self-determining, but does not require intrinsically motivating tasks.

TABLE 8-4 Summary of Terms

Term	Definition
Intrinsic motivation	Motivation to engage in an activity in the absence of any extrinsic reward or purpose
Competence motive	Natural disposition to engage in tasks and activities that contribute to learning and development
Internal locus of causality	Perception of engaging in an activity by personal preference
External locus of causality	Perception of engaging in an activity for some external reward or for some reason other than personal preference
Discounting principle	Discounting a reason for engaging in an activity because another reason is more salient
Task-contingent rewards	Rewards based on engaging in an activity or completing a task
Performance-contingent rewards	Rewards based on achieving a specified level of performance

CHAPTER 9

Values, Goals, and Relationships

People rarely choose to do tasks that they expect to fail. But an affirmative answer to the question, "Can I do this?" is only one prerequisite to approaching and persisting with an activity. Another prerequisite is an affirmative answer to the question, "Do I want to do this?" Satisfied Santos (see Chapter 1) does not have a problem with self-confidence. His problem is that he does not value school tasks. He knows the way, but he lacks the will.

Santos might be willing to put more effort into his schoolwork, at least in the short run, if a highly desirable reward was made contingent on his effort. But as Chapter 3 indicates, salient extrinsic rewards have important limitations. Engaging students' intrinsic interest has advantages over extrinsic rewards, but it is not realistic to aspire to making every school task intrinsically interesting for every student.

Some students seem to work hard on assigned tasks that are not intrinsically interesting and for which no reinforcement is expected; they simply do what the teacher asks—even if the task is boring or unchallenging. What produces this behavior? Neither reinforcement theory nor intrinsic motivation theory seems to offer a satisfactory explanation.

This chapter proposes internalized values as an explanation for such achievement efforts. Two different theoretical frameworks for the study of values are discussed. One evolved from the self-determination branch of intrinsic motivation theory (see Chapter 8) and the other is based on Atkinson's expectancy x value theory (see Chapter 5).

Self-determination theorists (e.g., Ryan, Connell, Deci) claim that individuals internalize values that they are reinforced for and observe in their social surroundings. There is an element of choice and a feeling of self-determination when they engage in activities that are consistent with their values, but there is not necessarily any pleasure. Eccles and her colleagues study values in the context of an expanded expectancy x value theory. These researchers assume, along with

Atkinson, that individuals choose to engage in tasks that they expect to succeed with and that they value, but they conceptualize values more broadly than Atkinson and they make distinctions among types of values that are not made by self-determination theorists.

Related to the reasons for which individuals engage in activities are their goals—what they hope to accomplish. Goal theorists claim that individuals' goals have important implications for how they approach tasks and what they learn. The third section of this chapter examines research on these implications.

Relationships is the final topic of this chapter. Classrooms are very social places. Students form relationships with each other and with the teacher, and although researchers often study social relationships separately from academic activities, the two domains inextricably are related for the people in them. Thus, the last section of this chapter focuses on relationships, especially between teachers and students, and the implications of relationships for learning-related behavior.

SELF-DETERMINATION AND
INTERNALIZED MOTIVATION

According to self-determination theorists, some children learn from parents and other significant adults that achievement behaviors are valued in our society. They **internalize** these values as their own and behave in ways that are consistent with them.

The more individuals accept the values of their social surroundings as their own, the more they will experience socially sanctioned behavior as being self-determined. As mentioned in Chapter 8, Ryan, Deci, Connell, and their colleagues conceptualize motivation as a continuum from extrinsically controlled to self-determined. At one end of the continuum are externally controlled behaviors (e.g., those that are done to avoid punishment), and at the other end are intrinsically motivated behaviors (i.e., those that give pleasure). In the middle of the continuum are behaviors that originally were regulated by external contingencies (i.e., **extrinsically regulated**) but came to be experienced as self-determined or **self-regulated** behaviors; that is, they came to be adopted by the self as being valuable and worth doing (Connell & Wellborn, 1991; Ryan & Connell, 1989; Ryan et al., 1985; Ryan, Connell, & Grolnick, 1992; Ryan & Stiller, 1991).

Self-regulation of achievement behavior is believed to result from a process of internalization in the same way that all other behaviors valued in the child's social environment come under self-regulation, including moral behavior (e.g., not stealing) and social behavior (e.g., sharing) (Aronfreed, 1969; Bandura, 1991; Mussen & Eisenberg, in press). Children at first may need to be reinforced externally for certain behaviors that are not intrinsically interesting. Thus, a student at first may do homework assignments only to earn a star on a public chart or to avoid punishment. Gradually, as children learn to anticipate the reactions of others, they begin to internalize rules; they judge themselves for engaging or not engaging in behaviors in the same way that their parents or teachers previously judged them for engaging or not engaging. This internalization results in emotional reactions to compliance and noncompliance—referred to as **introjected regulation.** Thus, a student may finish her homework because she will experience anxiety or guilt if she does not, or she may spend time with her grandmother because it makes her feel good. Although external forces (promise of a reward or threat of punishment) are not present, introjected regulation is associated with feelings of being controlled or coerced more than with feelings of self-determination.

Ultimately, children accept as their own some of the values underlying the behaviors for which they previously were reinforced—a motivation level referred to as **identification.** At this point, behavioral regulation has been integrated into the self; the individual experiences volition without a sense of pressure or coercion. For example, a student might explain that he studies vocabulary words because he wants to be able to write and speak well—because he values these qualities. This student experiences self-determination, engaging in the activity because he wants to, even though he may not find it interesting or enjoyable and he is not reinforced externally for it. Thus, identified regulation is extrinsic in the sense that the individual is not intrinsically interested in the activity, but experiences it as being volitional. And research suggests that "identifying with" academic values has some of the same positive benefits as intrinsic motivation to engage in academic tasks, such as higher levels of engagement and more positive emotional experiences (e.g., Patrick et al., 1993).

The least coercive and salient forms of extrinsic reinforcement are most likely to facilitate identification with adults' values (as opposed to introjected regulation). Thus, children are more likely to integrate parents' and teachers' values if they are reinforced socially (e.g., praised) than if they are given tangible reinforcement (e.g., money, toys, candy). Both social and tangible reinforcements give the message that the activity is valued, but tangible reinforcement is more salient and gives children the additional message that they are not expected to engage in the activity unless they get something for it. This **minimal but sufficient principle** for rewards is derived in part from work comparing the effects of mild versus severe threats of punishment on children's abilities to inhibit themselves from engaging in prohibited activities (Lepper, 1973). Presumably salient rewards, like severe punishment, focus children's attention on the external reasons for a behavior more than less salient rewards.

This internalization process applies to any domain of activity. Thus, the student who internalizes his parents' value of athletic skills may demonstrate considerable effort on the football field, but little in the classroom. The student who learns to value the performing arts may practice an instrument every day, but put little effort into understanding the Civil War. Other students may put their effort into being tough, attractive, or funny. One student may not be motivated less than the other. Rather, they may value competency and success in different domains.

Students who have an internalized "schoolwork ethic" are undoubtedly the easiest to teach. For such students, teachers are not obliged to make tasks intrinsically interesting, to offer an external reward for effort, or to threaten punishment for not working. But such internalized values cannot be relied on alone. It is unlikely that valuing academic work can sustain effort in the absence of occasional rewards on a long series of tasks that are not intrinsically interesting and do not result in feelings of competence.

Measures of Internalized Motivation

Harter (1992, in press) developed a questionnaire containing a subscale that assesses internalized motivation. This questionnaire contains twenty-four items to assess three motivation orientations (i.e., extrinsic, intrinsic, internalized). The scale is introduced to children as a questionnaire asking them about their reasons for doing their schoolwork. An item assessing internalized motivation (e.g., "I do my schoolwork because I've learned for myself that it's important for me to do it") can be contrasted with an intrinsic reason (e.g., "I do my schoolwork because what we learn is really interesting") and an extrinsic reason (e.g., "I do my schoolwork because my teacher will be pleased with me if I do").

Ryan and Connell (1989) created the Self-Regulatory Style Questionnaire (SRQ), which assesses external, introjected, identified, and intrinsic motivations. In this questionnaire, respondents are asked to rate the degree to which various reasons explain their behaviors (see Table 9-1). Research has shown that external regulation measured by this scale is associated with perceptions of low support for autonomy in the classroom, anxiety, and less enjoyment of schoolwork. Identified and intrinsic motivations are associated with perceptions of high support for autonomy in the classroom and greater enjoyment.

Summary

According to self-determination theorists, individuals sometimes choose to engage in activities that they do not enjoy; the more they have internalized values related to the task or activity, the more they experience self-determination. Thus, many of the benefits of intrinsic motivation, previously described as activities that give pleasure, can be achieved by instilling values. Although conceptualized somewhat differently, internalized values are also critical to Eccles's theory of choice, described next.

EXPECTANCY x VALUES

Recall that Atkinson conceptualized incentive values as the expectation for pride or shame. Achievement situations expected to generate feelings of pride are presumed to have more value than those expected to produce feelings of shame. This is a very narrow conceptualization of values, and current theorists, most notably Eccles and her colleagues (1983), have offered broader conceptualizations. Eccles

TABLE 9-1 Sample Items from the Academic Self-Regulatory Style Questionnaire

All items are answered on a 1–4 scale (very true, sort of true, not very true, not at all true).

Why do I do my homework?

External *(Rule Following; Avoidance of Punishment)*

◆ Because I'll get in trouble if I don't

◆ Because that's what I'm supposed to do

◆ So that the teacher won't yell at me

◆ Because that's the rule

◆ So others won't get mad at me

Introjection *(Self- and Other-Approval; Avoidance of Disapproval)*

◆ Because I want the teacher to think I'm a good student

◆ Because I will feel bad about myself if I don't

◆ Because I'll feel ashamed of myself if I don't

◆ Because I want the other students to think I'm smart

◆ Because it bothers me when I don't

◆ Because I want people to like me

Identification *(Self-Valued Goal; Personal Importance)*

◆ Because I want to understand the subject

◆ Because I want to learn new things

◆ To find out if I'm right or wrong

◆ Because I think it's important to

Intrinsic *(Enjoyment, Fun)*

◆ Because it's fun

◆ Because I enjoy it

Reprinted from Ryan and Connell (1989). (The full scale is available from Richard Ryan, Department of Psychology, University of Rochester, Rochester, NY 14627.)

et al. (1983) proposed three kinds of values relevant to achievement (see also Wigfield, 1994b; Wigfield & Eccles, 1992).

Attainment value is the subjective importance of doing well on a task or in an achievement domain, and is determined by how the task or domain fulfills the individual's needs. Attainment value concerns the relevance of an activity to an individual's actual or ideal self-concept. Thus, individuals engage in activities and develop competencies that are consistent with their concepts of themselves (e.g., feminine, musically talented, socially deviant, hard working). Of the three kinds of values in Eccles's theory, attainment value is related most closely to internalized motivation in self-determination theory.

Utility value concerns the usefulness of a task as a means to achieve goals that might not be related to the task itself, such as career goals. For example, understanding chemistry and biology would have considerable utility value for a college student planning to attend medical school.

Intrinsic value is the immediate enjoyment one derives from performing a task. When a task has intrinsic value it is engaged in for its own sake, because it gives pleasure rather than for some other purpose.

Eccles and her colleagues point out that values need to be considered in the context of costs—in energy and the risks (e.g., of failure, humiliation), and in the options that are not available because of the choice a person makes (Wigfield & Eccles, 1992). For instance, college students who do not work hard in a particular class are not necessarily lazy or unmotivated. More likely they have chosen to exert their effort in other domains—some academic (e.g., other courses) and some not (e.g., athletics, social organizations, families, relationships). Students who face the difficult task of apportioning their time across different courses as final exams approach are painfully aware of the costs of achievement-related choices.

Effects of Values

Research indicates that values affect choices in activities as well as the level of effort and persistence. Eccles and her colleagues have shown that values also influence students' intentions and decisions about course enrollment, and even career choices (Eccles, 1984, 1994; Eccles, Adler, & Meece, 1984; Eccles, Midgley, & Adler, 1984; Feather, 1988; Meece & Courtney, 1992; Meece et al., 1990). For example, a path analysis conducted by Eccles (1984b) indicated that although elementary and high school students' expectancies for success predicted their subsequent performance in mathematics more strongly than did their achievement values, their math-related values predicted their intentions about whether to keep taking math courses. Moreover, Eccles (1984) and Eccles, Adler, & Meece (1984) found that eighth- and tenth-grade students' math-related values, not their self-concepts of ability in math, predicted actual enrollment decisions.

Values also mediate the effect of perceptions of competence on self-esteem (Harter, in press). In a study reported by Harter (1987), for example, low perceptions of competence had greater negative effects on self-esteem in domains children valued highly than in domains they valued less. Recall that according to self-worth theorists, individuals naturally are motivated to protect their self-esteem as much as possible. If doing poorly in valued domains threatens self-esteem, devaluing those domains in which one had low expectations for success would be an effective self-protective mechanism. This is a likely explanation for the devaluing of academic achievement that is common among adolescents who have a history of failure.

Pintrich and Schrauben (1992; see also Wigfield, 1994b) reported in their review of research that values also affect how students approach learning. The research suggests that when students are undertaking tasks in valued domains they are more likely to use active cognitive strategies, such as rehearsal, elaboration, and organization strategies, and they also are more likely to report that they were thinking critically about course material.

From Where Do Achievement Values Come?

As mentioned previously, self-determination theorists have described a process of internalization that begins with minimally sufficient external reinforcement for particular behaviors (e.g., effort on academic tasks), moves toward self-reinforcement or punishment (feeling good or bad about exerting or not exerting effort on schoolwork), and ends with total acceptance of a value (e.g., it is important to work hard in school).

Extrinsic reinforcement is not the only way adults can convey their own values regarding hard work and learning. They can model academic values by engaging in intellectual activities themselves (Eccles, 1993). They also can make direct statements, for example, "It's really important to be able to write well"; or "Don't worry about math; I was never good in it and I make a good living." In addition, adults subtly instill values, such as by what they pay attention to or their facial expressions in reaction to children's successful or failed mastery attempts. The father who ignores his son's recounting of the difficulties he is having with algebra but who becomes attentive when he mentions the field goal he missed at football practice makes a clear statement about what he thinks is more important.

Perceptions of competence may affect the attainment and even the utility value of academic work, just as they affect intrinsic value (see Chapter 8). Studies have found, for instance, that achievement values in mathematics are related positively to self-perceptions of competence in math (Eccles et al., 1983) and to the student's history of performance (Eccles, 1984); values are related inversely to anxiety about mathematics performance (e.g., Meece et al., 1990). Because the research is cross-sectional, we do not know whether children begin to value activities about which they are confident (as intrinsic motivation theory suggests), or whether they engage in activities they value and, as a consequence, develop competencies and self-confidence. Most likely, both are true.

Eccles et al. (1983) proposed that individuals' concepts of themselves—their self-schemas—also affect their values. For example, a student who considers herself to be a nonconformist, and perceives students who do everything the teacher tells them to do as being conformists, may devalue all schoolwork.

Most of the research on self-schema and values has focused on gender differences. The results of these studies suggest that with age, males increasingly value achievement in school, and females become more concerned about potential conflicts between academic and social goals (Sherman, 1979). Research generally supports the claim that gender typing certain domains as "masculine" or "feminine" influences the attainment value of performance in different domains for both males and females (see Eccles et al., 1983). Research suggests that science, in particular, is valued less by girls than by boys, and that gender differences increase with age (see Kahle & Meece, 1993). There is also some (albeit mixed) evidence to support the Eccles et al. (1983) proposal that the attainment value of mathematics achievement is relatively low for those females who perceive math courses to be masculine activities and who are compelled to avoid masculine activities to affirm their femininity (see also Eccles, 1984; Wigfield & Eccles, 1994; Wigfield et al., 1991).

The evidence is stronger for sex-stereotyping of math-related occupations than for math courses. Eccles points out, however, that if certain females are less likely to aspire to math-related professions because such professions are considered unfeminine, math courses will have less utility value for these females than they will for males. Sex stereotyping of careers, therefore, may be a more important mediator of sex difference in the perceived value of advanced math courses than is sex stereotyping of the courses themselves (see also Kahle & Meece, 1993; Stevenson & Newman, 1986).

Age-Related Changes

The developmental trajectory of academic values appears to parallel those of perceptions of competence and intrinsic motivation—that is, they decline with age. Several studies have shown that students tend to value academic tasks less as they get older, although the evidence is not as consistent as it is for perceived competence and varies by domain (see Eccles et al., 1983; Eccles & Midgley, 1989; Eccles, Midgley, & Adler, 1984; Eccles et al., 1989; Eccles, Wigfield, Harold, & Blumenfeld, 1993; Wigfield & Eccles, 1994; Wigfield, Eccles, Mac Iver, Reuman, & Midgley, 1991).

Young children may not differentiate among subjects or among the components of the Eccles model (i.e., attainment value, utility value, intrinsic value) as much as older children (Eccles & Wigfield, 1995; Wigfield & Eccles, 1992). Wigfield and Eccles (1992) proposed that for young children, the subjective value of a task is determined primarily by the amount of pleasure they derive from it. Perhaps as children become older and start to internalize social norms, values begin to figure more significantly into their assessment of tasks. One study, however, showed that even first-graders differentiated between their judgments of the usefulness and importance of different domains and their intrinsic interest in the domains (Wigfield & Eccles, 1994).

Measures of Values

Eccles and her colleagues have performed most of the research on achievement values. The measure they used in numerous studies, shown in Table 9-2, has good reliability and validity, and can be used with children as early as first grade.

Summary

There are, therefore, at least two reasons—in addition to obtaining rewards or pleasure—why students might choose to exert effort and persist with an academic activity. They may value the activity as something that is consistent with their

---

TABLE 9-2   Assessment of Achievement-Related Values

All items are answered on a 1–7 scale, with the anchors shown in parentheses. Any subject matter can be substituted for math.

Importance *(Attainment Value)*

◆ For me, being good in math is (not at all important, very important)

◆ Some kids find what they learn in one subject or activity more important than what they learn in another. Compared to most of your other activities, how important is it to you to be good at math?

Usefulness *(Utility Value)*

◆ Some things that you learn in school help you do things better outside of class— that is, they are useful. For example, learning about plants might help you grow a garden. In general, how useful is what you learn in math? (not at all useful, very useful)

◆ Some kids find what they learn in one subject or activity more useful than what they learn in another. Compared to most of your other activities, how useful is what you learn in math?

Interest *(Intrinsic Value)*

◆ In general, I find working on math assignments (very boring, very interesting [fun])

◆ How much do you like doing math? (not at all, very much)

◆ Some kids find that they like one subject or activity much more than another. Compared to most of your other activities, how much do you like math?

Reprinted from Eccles, Wigfield, Harold, and Blumenfeld (1993).

perceptions of themselves (e.g., artistic or feminine, a high-achiever or computer whiz), or they may believe that the activity or skill has some use in their lives outside of school (e.g., maintaining a budget, going to medical school).

Goal theorists believe that all reasons for doing schoolwork are not equal and that the reason for engaging in an activity has myriad implications for how individuals approach the task and what they learn. These implications are discussed next.

GOAL THEORY

Values and goals are related, but they involve different levels of analysis. Values pertain to general feelings or beliefs about domains of activities in relation to the self. Goals concern the reasons a person has for engaging in a particular activity. Although goal theorists measure general dispositions that are oriented toward one set of goals versus another, they primarily are concerned with people's immediate, subjective experiences in task situations.

Most goal theorists distinguish between **learning goals** (referred to by some researchers as "mastery" or "task" goals)—which concern mastery and developing understanding—and **performance goals**—which concern doing better than others, demonstrating more intelligence, and winning approval (Ames, 1992; Ames & Archer, 1988; Harackiewicz & Elliot, 1993; Nicholls, 1983; Maehr, 1984; Meece, 1991, 1994). Learning goals are most likely to be found in situations in which individuals undertake a task because they find it to be intrinsically interesting, because they have internalized values related to it, or because they see some utility in the skill that it is designed to teach. Performance goals reflect an extrinsic orientation—the individual is motivated more by obtaining extrinsic rewards (e.g., teacher praise, good grades) that are associated with outperforming peers or gaining social approval.

Implications of Task Goals

Dweck (1986) proposed that learning goals and performance goals have very different implications for how students behave in achievement settings and how they interpret performance outcomes (see also Dweck & Elliott, 1983; Dweck & Leggett, 1988; Elliott & Dweck, 1988; Lepper, 1988; Nicholls, Cobb, Yackel, Wood, & Wheatley, 1990). According to Dweck's theoretical analysis, students with learning goals seek challenging tasks that provide opportunities to develop new competencies, and they persist when they encounter difficulty. They base their judgments of competence on the amount of effort they expend and real learning, or mastery achieved. She predicted that students with performance goals, in contrast, want to look competent, such as Safe Sally (see Chapter 1), or avoid looking incompetent, such as Defensive Dave (see Chapter 1). They judge their competencies on how well they perform relative to others or to external feedback, not on their progress in understanding or mastery.

Dweck (1986) suggested that students with performance goals are most likely to accept entity theories of ability, and that performance goals are particularly debilitating for students who have low perceptions of their competencies. Those who are confident in their abilities should choose moderately difficult tasks to allow themselves to display their competencies. Because their goal is to look competent (as opposed to be competent), however, they may use shortcuts that achieve their immediate goals but do not actually foster learning (see also Nicholls, 1983). Students with performance goals who lack confidence in their abilities, such as Dave, should choose easy tasks to avoid displaying incompetence. When they encounter difficulty they either should engage in self-defeating strategies to avoid being seen as low in ability, or give up because they believe that they cannot demonstrate competence.

Only a few studies have differentiated between high- and low-self-confident individuals with performance goals. But most of Dweck's general claims about the effects of goal orientations are well supported by evidence, to which our discussion now turns.

Risk Taking and Challenge Seeking

Studies have shown that a task or mastery orientation is associated with moderate risk taking and willingness to engage in challenging tasks. In one study most task-oriented students selected tasks that were labeled "difficult," but that would promote skill development, whereas most performance-oriented students selected tasks that they were told would not teach them anything new, but would allow them to demonstrate their competencies (Elliott & Dweck, 1988). In another study students who perceived their classroom as being relatively mastery oriented claimed that they would prefer difficult science projects that would result in new learning rather than easy projects (Ames & Archer, 1988; see also Burhans & Dweck, 1995; Nicholls, 1984; Smiley & Dweck, 1994).

Focus of Attention

Research also suggests that learning versus performance goals has implications for students' attention while they work on tasks. When students are motivated to learn or master they focus more on the process of completing tasks (i.e., they are **task oriented**), but when they have performance goals they are more focused on the self, especially on external evaluations of the self (i.e., they are **ego oriented**) (Nicholls, 1979b, 1983; see also Butler, 1992, 1995).

An ego orientation is illustrated by a child in Peterson and Swing's (1982) study (mentioned in Chapter 2) who, when asked what she thought about during a math lesson, commented: "I was nervous, and I thought maybe I wouldn't know how to do things . . . I was mostly thinking . . . I was making a fool of myself" (p. 486). In contrast, a task-oriented child responded to the same question by describing in some detail the strategies she used to solve the problems.

Csikszentmihalyi (1975, 1988) refers to the intense involvement associated with a task orientation as **flow.** Individuals experiencing flow are so intensely attentive to the present tasks that they may lose awareness of time and space. Most great artists and scholars report that they experience flow when working in their fields. And people who are known for their creativity have commented that they were in a flow state when they did their best work (Nicholls, 1983).

Learning Behavior

Learning goals also are associated with the use of effective problem-solving strategies. In one study, for example, students scoring high on a measure of task orientation in science reported relatively greater use of active metacognitive strategies (e.g., reviewing material not understood, asking questions as they worked, making connections between current and past problems), and less use of "superficial engagement" (e.g., copying, guessing, skipping questions) than children who claimed to be relatively more performance oriented (Meece, Blumenfeld, & Hoyle, 1988). In other studies learning goals have been linked to the use of active learning strategies (e.g., planning, organizing material, setting goals) that are known to facilitate learning (Ames & Archer, 1988) and "deep" processing strategies (e.g., discriminating important information from unimportant information, trying to figure out how new information fits with what one already knows, monitoring comprehension) (Nolen, 1988; see also Meece, 1994; Pintrich & Schrauben, 1992).

The findings of at least one study support Dweck's (1986) proposal that performance goals undermine effective problem solving for children who have doubts about their competencies more than for self-confident children. Elliott and Dweck (1988) experimentally induced performance or learning goals by emphasizing either the benefits of learning or the importance of performance in their instructions. They also manipulated children's perceptions of skill on a task. When performance-oriented children who had low self-confidence encountered difficulty, their problem-solving strategies deteriorated. This was not true for performance-oriented children with high self-confidence. Learning or mastery-oriented children's strategies were not affected by whether they had high or low confidence in their abilities (see also Brockner, 1979; Smiley & Dweck, 1994).

Attributions

Learning goals also are associated with more constructive beliefs about what causes success or failure (Nicholls, 1992). In the study by Ames and Archer (1988), students who perceived their classroom to be mastery oriented tended to attribute success to high effort and effective learning strategies, and students who perceived their classroom to be more performance oriented tended to attribute failure to low ability. The latter students are disadvantaged because students who attribute failure to low ability have no reason to exert effort in the future (see Chapter 5; see also Nicholls, Cobb, Wood, Yackel, & Patashnick, 1990).

Studies also suggest that for students with mastery goals, more effort is associated with greater feelings of competence. Students with performance goals measure success using norms—that is, by measuring their performance relative to that of their classmates (Jagacinski & Nicholls, 1984; see Chapter 5)—and are interested particularly in obtaining normative information related to their performance (Butler, 1992).

Emotions

Individuals also have been found to experience greater pleasure and greater emotional involvement when they have mastery goals. In the Ames and Archer (1988) study, the more students perceived their classroom as supporting mastery goals, the more they liked the class. Elliott and Dweck (1988) reported that many of the children in a performance-oriented condition who had low perceptions of their abilities spontaneously expressed negative feelings about the task with comments such as, "After this [problem], then do I get to go?"; "This is boring"; or "My stomach hurts" (p. 10). Children who were task oriented rarely made such comments, regardless of whether they believed that they were competent at the task.

Ryan (1982; Ryan & Stiller, 1991) explains why performance goals might be unpleasant. He proposes that ego involvement is experienced as a kind of internal control or pressure that people apply to themselves. Being pressured by this internal constraint (i.e., a feeling that it is necessary to do well to prove one's self-worth) undermines intrinsic motivation and pleasure in the same way as external pressures (e.g., salient rewards, emphasis on evaluating, close monitoring).

Learning

Finally, goals affect what as well as how much students learn (see Jagacinski, 1992; Schunk, 1996; Utman, in press). One study, for example, manipulated whether fifth- and sixth-grade students were performance oriented (by claiming that performance on the task was diagnostic of problem-solving ability) or task oriented (by claiming that the task would be challenging and fun). Compared to subjects who were concerned primarily with mastering the task, subjects who were performance oriented showed poorer word recall at deep processing levels (i.e., having to do with meaning), but not at shallow processing levels (i.e., having to do with the sounds of words; Graham & Golan, 1991; see also Benware & Deci, 1984; Utman, in press).

Are Performance Goals All Bad?

In much of the achievement motivation literature, mastery goals and performance goals are described as though they compete with each other—as though students are either one or the other. Actually, studies often find either no correlation or a positive correlation between the levels of students' mastery and performance goals (Midgley et al., 1995; Nicholls, 1992; Stipek & Gralinski, 1996).

Although studies generally support the benefits of mastery goals when compared to performance goals, especially for students lacking self-confidence, not all studies find negative effects of performance goals. In the Stipek and Gralinski (1996) study, for instance, students who had relatively high performance goals claimed to employ both active and superficial learning strategies more than students who had low performance goals. In another study both performance and learning goals were associated positively with self-efficacy for middle school students (Midgley et al., 1995). And various other studies have shown that enjoyment actually is enhanced by performance-oriented instructions for individuals who have strong needs for achievement (as described in Chapter 5; Harackiewicz & Elliot, 1993). Perhaps the most accurate conclusion to draw from the research is that mastery goals are better than performance goals, but performance goals, if they are not excessive, are better than no goals at all.

Learning and mastery goals are the goals most often discussed opposite to performance goals in the achievement motivation literature, but Wentzel (1992, 1993a, 1993b, 1994, 1996) pointed out that students, particularly high-achieving students, have other goals that are unrelated to learning or mastery, but that have positive effects on learning. For example, students in her studies rate looking responsible, dependable, helpful, and compliant as being significant goals in their achievement contexts (see also Ainley, 1993; Meece & Holt, 1993; Urdan & Maehr, 1995). These **social responsibility goals** are extrinsic and are similar to performance goals in that they are unconnected to the learning purposes of schoolwork. Another goal that is not related directly to learning or mastery, and is more like a performance goal is the goal of bringing honor to the family. Social responsibility goals (referred to as social approval goals by Urdan and Maehr, 1995), if not excessive, may enhance productive achievement behaviors without negative consequences. Students who manifest these behaviors also are preferred by teachers (Wentzel, 1993a).

Therefore, some prudence is recommended in the rush to condemn performance goals or other goals that are not linked directly to learning and mastery. Learning goals do not preclude other goals, and although there are good reasons to minimize performance goals, the evidence is not convincing that students will benefit from their total demise.

Beyond Achievement

Goal theorists have focused on goals associated with completing academic tasks. This is a very narrow concern from the viewpoint of most students. Students may engage in tasks for reasons entirely unrelated to those studied by goal theorists (Urdan & Maehr, 1995). Making or maintaining friendships may be the primary goal for some students, particularly when they are engaging in tasks involving peer collaboration. Some students may work hard in school to maintain their social status in the high-achieving peer group. A high school boy may participate in a class discussion to attract attention from a girl in the class, or in an effort to convince his teacher that he should be allowed to leave class early on Fridays for football games. These nonachievement-related goals also should be considered in any effort to increase student engagement in academic tasks.

Teachers also need to be aware of goals that interfere with task engagement. Some adolescents, for instance, strive to maintain status in a peer group that devalues academic achievement. For these students, avoiding teacher approval is the primary goal. Because most parents and teachers value academic achievement, students whose peer group has different values and goals are caught in a conflict and may exert effort on schoolwork erratically.

Ethnicity, Culture, Values, and Goals

Goals need to be viewed through a broad cultural lens. And there is some evidence for systematic cultural variations within the United States in values and goals related to academic achievement.

For example, Ogbu (1992) proposed that some African-American students associate high academic achievement with "acting white" and denying their own culture. Their desire to maintain cultural connections engenders antiachievement goals. They do not exert effort on schoolwork, and even boast about this to ensure that they receive proper acknowledgment from their peers.

Studies of Latino families suggest other goals that, although constructive, might conflict with the goal structures of many schools. For instance, Delgado-Gaitan (1993) and Laosa (1982) proposed that goals of family cohesion and responsibility to the group, found to be particularly strong among many Latino families, may be inconsistent with the focus on individual effort and achievement found in most schools.

An understanding of cultural differences related to goals can help teachers interpret students' behaviors. A child who asks for help or gives help to a classmate on a test may not realize that he is cheating; he may not have fully understood that the purpose of the test is to assess his own understanding or skill, or this individualistic goal may not make sense to him. Some children may work poorly in competitive situations because they have been socialized to value collaboration, and thus are not comfortable with the goal of outperforming others.

It is important to avoid stereotyping students by ethnicity, given the considerable variation in goals, values, and cultural beliefs within ethnic groups. But understanding cultural differences in the goals students internalize in their family contexts can guide teachers' efforts to assist students' work in the classroom. As the final section in this chapter suggests, this needs to be done in a way that respects and supports the home culture of these students.

Assessing Students' Achievement-Related Goals

Several researchers have developed measures of students' goals. As is evident from the items on Ryan and Connell's (1989) measure (Table 9-1), their conceptualization of introjected and identified motivation overlaps substantially with what other researchers have referred to as performance goals and mastery goals, respectively. Thus, engaging in a task to achieve social approval (i.e., introjected regulation) is conceptualized as a performance goal, and engaging in a task to develop understanding or skills (i.e., identified motivation) is conceptualized as a learning or mastery goal.

Nicholls and his colleagues (1990) developed a measure to assess students' task versus ego orientation to schoolwork, and a third goal, which they referred to as "work avoidance." A series of statements are given, all with the stem, "I feel really pleased in school when. . . ." Children respond on a five-point scale, represented by YES, yes, ?, no, NO. The items are given in Table 9-3.

Ames and Archer (1988) developed a measure of students' perceptions of their classroom goals (see Table 9-4). Some of the questions refer to teacher or classroom practices that support mastery or learning goals (e.g., "In this class, making mistakes is a part of learning"). Other questions refer to practices that are more likely to foster performance goals (e.g., "In this class students compete to see who can do the best work"). Using this measure with students can reveal specific teacher behaviors and instructional strategies that inadvertently foster goals other than those teachers intended.

Students also reveal their goals through their behaviors. Table 9-5 includes behaviors that typically are associated with performance goals. Students who manifest these behaviors may be concerned more about doing well or looking good than they are about developing skills or mastering problems.

Summary

The work by goal theorists is important because it very clearly proves that the teacher's task is not only to "get students working." Different strategies for motivating students to work are likely to have different consequences, in part because the reasons students engage in academic tasks have so many implications for how and what they learn. Most studies suggest the value of a mastery or learning orientation, and several indicate that a concern about performance can be debilitating, especially for children who doubt their abilities.

A limitation of most of this research is the narrow focus on mastery and performance goals. Classrooms are social as well as academic contexts, and students have many other goals, some of which are only weakly linked to the instructional program and some of which work directly against academic performance.

Because classrooms and schools are social places, relationships are important and can influence students' learning. The implications of the social nature of education are discussed in the next and final section.

TABLE 9-3   Assessment of Students' Goals

Response scale is: YES   yes   ?   no   NO

I feel really pleased in school (math) when:

Task Orientation

◆ I solve a problem by working hard

◆ The problems make me think hard

◆ What the teacher says makes me think

◆ I keep busy

◆ I work hard all the time

◆ Something I learn makes me want to find out more

◆ I find a new way to solve a problem

◆ Something I figure out really makes sense

◆ Something I figure out makes me want to keep doing more problems

Ego Orientation

◆ I know more than the others

◆ I am the only one who can answer a question

◆ I finish before my friends

◆ I get more answers right than my friends

Work Avoidance

◆ I don't have to work hard

◆ All the work is easy

◆ The teacher doesn't ask hard questions

RELATIONSHIPS

Children who fare poorly in academics are burdened with more than the frustration and humiliation of their failures. Often they are not treated well by their

TABLE 9-4 Classroom Achievement Goals Questionnaire

In this class . . .

	Strongly Disagree		Neutral		Strongly Agree
Mastery-orientation items					
Making mistakes is a part of learning.	1	2	3	4	5
Students don't care about the grades other students get.	1	2	3	4	5
The teacher wants us to learn how to solve problems on our own.	1	2	3	4	5
It's important to keep trying even though you make mistakes.	1	2	3	4	5
Students are encouraged to find answers to their questions on their own.	1	2	3	4	5
The teacher tries to find out what each student wants to learn.	1	2	3	4	5
The teacher wants us to try new things.	1	2	3	4	5
Students are given a chance to correct their mistakes.	1	2	3	4	5
Performance-orientation items					
Students compete against each other to get high grades.	1	2	3	4	5
Only a few students can get top marks.	1	2	3	4	5
Students try hard to get the highest grade.	1	2	3	4	5
Students feel bad when they do not do as well as others.	1	2	3	4	5
Students compete to see who can do the best work.	1	2	3	4	5
The teacher favors some students more than others.	1	2	3	4	5
Students know if they're doing better or worse than the other students.	1	2	3	4	5
Students want to know how others score on assignments and tests.	1	2	3	4	5

Selected items used in Ames and Archer (1988).

TABLE 9-5   Student Behaviors Associated with Performance Goals

◆ Uses short cuts to complete tasks (tries to complete them without going through steps that would contribute to learning).

◆ Cheats.

◆ Seeks attention for good performance.

◆ Only works hard on graded assignments.

◆ Hides papers with low scores/grades.

◆ Compares scores/grades with those of classmates.

◆ Is upset by low scores/grades.

◆ Copies classmates' papers.

◆ Chooses tasks and courses that are most likely to result in positive evaluations.

◆ Is uncomfortable with assignments in which criteria for evaluation are not clear.

teachers and peers—not only as learners, but as people. Many children who fail in school have only negative interactions with their teachers. They are often in trouble—for not completing assignments or not paying attention, or for fooling around or misbehaving. Often they deserve to be sanctioned, but the classroom becomes a very unpleasant place for children who have mostly conflict- and discipline-related interactions with their teachers.

Contributing to some poor-achieving students' distress are peers, who can be very cruel, partly because the poor achievers often are also the troublemakers. Peers often exclude low achievers from play and birthday parties, resist being placed in work groups with them, and make fun of their academic problems. It is not surprising that many students' perceptions of themselves as being academically incompetent evolve into perceptions of themselves as being unworthy humans.

Only recently have researchers begun to examine the effect on motivation of students' relationships with teachers and their peers. Connell and Wellborn (1991) claim that **relatedness** is one of three basic human needs, along with feelings of competence and self-determination. Relatedness, in their framework, encompasses the need for feeling securely connected to individuals in the social context and "to experience oneself as worthy and capable of love and respect" (p. 51).

McCombs (1994) also acknowledges the importance of social relationships in educational contexts by including social support as one of three critical components in her model of motivation (along with "will" and "skill"). She describes social support as a "culture of trust, respect, caring, concern, and a sense of community with others" that provides opportunities for "individual choice, expression of self-determination and agency, and freedom to fail or take risks" (p. 54).

Theorists who have addressed the issue of social relationships all assert the fundamental importance of nourishing respect and worthiness in students. I concur with their view that relationships and the social climate of the classroom are at the heart of effective education. I have never seen a successful teacher who did not care about and respect his students as people, and who did not create a classroom "community of learners" in which students supported each other in their learning efforts. Research on social relationships in classrooms is only beginning, but what has been studied so far supports their importance.

Consequences of Relationships

Studies suggest that students who have positive, secure relationships with their teachers are engaged more highly in their academic work. A study by Skinner and Belmont (1993) is illustrative. They assessed teachers' perceptions of their involvement with their students using a measure that included items about their affection (i.e., how much they liked, appreciated, and enjoyed the student), attunement (i.e., understanding, sympathy, and knowledge about the student), and dependability (i.e., availability in case of need). Using similar items, students rated their own involvement with their teachers. Teachers' ratings of their involvement with students in the fall semester of the academic year strongly predicted students' self-perceptions (e.g., relatedness to the teacher, feelings of autonomy) assessed in the spring semester, which in turn predicted students' engagement in classroom activities.

The Skinner and Belmont (1993) study revealed an important reciprocal effect between teachers' and students' behaviors. Teachers' levels of involvement with students was enhanced by high levels of student engagement at the beginning of the year, which in turn enhanced students' feelings of relatedness to the teacher. The study demonstrates the bidirectional nature of student–teacher relationships, and the importance, for teachers, of recognizing the negative trajectories that can spiral into maladaptive interactions.

Research by Connell and Wellborn (1991) also showed that students' feelings of relatedness to their teachers and classmates are strong predictors of their cognitive, behavioral, and emotional engagement in classroom activities (see also Connell, 1991; Connell, Spencer, & Aber, 1994; Connell & Wellborn, 1991; Deci, Vallerand, Pelletier, & Ryan, 1991; Pianta & Nimetz, 1991; Pianta & Steinberg, 1992; Ryan & Powelson, 1991; Skinner & Wellborn, 1994). And Goodenow (1993) found that middle school students' feelings of being liked by their teachers and peers were associated with the belief that academics is intrinsically valuable; these feelings also were associated with high expectations for success, effort, and persistence.

Studies have shown that teachers' support even affects students' values. Eccles (1993) reports that the value of math increased for those students in her study who moved from an elementary school teacher who they perceived to be minimally supportive to a junior high school teacher who they perceived to be highly supportive; the value of math decreased for those students who moved from a highly supportive to a relatively unsupportive teacher.

A few people have speculated about why students are more engaged in classrooms in which they have developed positive, secure relationships with their teacher. A positive relationship may cause students to want to please their teacher by doing what she expects of them, or they may internalize (i.e., accept as their own) her values more readily if they like and respect her (Connell & Wellborn, 1991; Deci & Ryan, 1991; Ryan & Stiller, 1991). Harter (1987) suggested that the sense of self-worth fostered by belonging and being supported socially engenders a generally positive affective and motivation state. Certainly, it is difficult to become interested in activities while feeling anxious, humiliated, or ashamed, and students who believe that the teacher will continue to care about them, even if they perform poorly, should be more comfortable taking risks—for example, by volunteering answers, asking questions when they are having difficulty, or selecting challenging work.

Assessing Teacher–Student Relationships

All of the items from the measure used in the Skinner and Belmont (1993) study are provided in Table 9-6. Teachers can probe their own relationships with their students by completing these questions for some of the students in their class. The student items are parallel to the teacher items.

Pianta and Steinberg (1992) developed a measure for teachers of preschool and early elementary-age children, called the Student–Teacher Relationship Scale (STRS). The scale contains five subscales: (1) conflict and anger (e.g., "This child and I are always struggling"); (2) warmth and closeness (e.g., "I share a warm, affectionate relationship with this child"); (3) open communication (e.g., "This child shares information about him/herself with me"); (4) dependency (e.g., "This child is always seeking my help when it's not necessary"); (5) troubled feelings (e.g., "Despite my best efforts, I'm uncomfortable with how this child and I have gotten along"). Pianta and his colleagues have found that scores on this measure are fairly consistent over the early grades, and they predict future teachers' relationships with children, children's classroom behavior in future grades, teachers' retention decisions, and children's adjustment to kindergarten (e.g., Birch & Ladd, 1997; Pianta, 1994; Pianta & Steinberg, 1992; Pianta, Steinberg, & Rollins, 1995).

Age-Related Shifts

It is possible that the increase in alienation toward school and devaluing of school achievement that often is seen in adolescence (Anderman & Maehr, 1994) is in part due to the changing nature of relationships between teachers and students.

TABLE 9-6 Teachers' and Students' Ratings of Their Relationship

Response scale is *not at all true, not very true, sort of true, very true.*

Teacher Questions	**Student Questions**

Teacher Questions

Affection

This student is easy to like.

I enjoy the time I spend with this student.

Teaching this student isn't very enjoyable for me.

This student is difficult to like.

Attunement

I know a lot about what goes on for this student.

I know this student well.

I don't understand this student very well.

I don't know very much about what goes on for this student outside of school.

Dependability

When this student does not do as well as s/he can, I can make time to help him/her find ways to do better.

This student can count on me to be there for him/her.

Sometimes I feel like I can't be there for this student when s/he needs me.

I can't always be available to this student.

Student Questions

Affection

My teacher likes me.

My teacher really cares about me.

My teacher doesn't seem to enjoy having me in her class.

Attunement

My teacher spends time with me.

My teacher talks with me.

Dependability

My teacher is always there for me.

I can count on my teacher to be there for me.

I can rely on my teacher to be there when I need him/her.

I can't count on my teacher when I need him/her.

I can't depend on my teacher for the important things.

My teacher is never there for me.

Eccles (1993) summarizes studies in which middle school students reported having less positive relationships with their teachers after the transition to secondary school than before this transition occurred. Even outside observers have rated junior high school teachers as being less friendly, less supportive, and less caring than elementary school teachers (Feldlaufer, Midgley, & Eccles, 1988). The decrease in nurturing that has been observed at the transition to middle or junior high school may be related to an increased focus on performance (Midgley, Anderman, & Hicks, 1995).

Summary

Studying student–teacher relationships is a new area of research, but findings so far suggest the value of a social context that is accepting and supportive, in which each student is valued regardless of her academic skills or performance relative to others. Such an environment should go a long way toward diminishing the negative consequences of relatively poor performance; in a caring, supportive social context, being a slow learner or having difficulties with schoolwork should not be translated into feelings of being an unvalued or unworthy person.

CONCLUSION

Motivation theory and research have come a long way from the early, rather simplistic views of behavior that were based entirely on contingencies. Extrinsic reinforcement now plays a critical role in achievement-related behavior. But there are other motivation systems that teachers can exploit to engage students' interest and effort in academic work. In addition to obtaining rewards, individuals also engage in activities because they are fun, because their internalized values are associated with them, and because they serve purposes beyond the classroom.

The teacher's task is to create an environment that readily takes advantage of these other motivation systems that can enhance learning. As research on relationships suggest, this can be accomplished best within a social context in which all students are securely connected to and respected and valued by the teacher and peers.

TABLE 9-7 Summary of Terms

Term	Definition
	Self-Determination Theory
Internalized motivation	Motivation originally based on external figures (extrinsic regulation) that becomes self-regulated
Extrinsic regulation	Behavior is controlled by external consequences
Self-regulation	Controlling one's own behavior without external rewards or constraints
Introjected regulation	Behaving as the result of emotions (e.g., pride, guilt) associated with previously experienced parental responses (e.g., reward, punishment)
Identification	Caretakers' values are fully internalized
Minimal but sufficient principle	The less salient the extrinsic reward, the more likely the rewarded behavior will become valued (internalized) by the individual
	Eccles's Expectancy x Value Theory
Attainment value	The subjective importance of doing well on a task or in an achievement domain
Utility value	Perceived usefulness of a task as a means to achieve goals that might not be related to the task itself
Intrinsic value	The immediate enjoyment derived from doing a task
	Goal Theory
Learning/task mastery goals	Goals involving learning, mastery, or developing competencies
Performance goals	Goals are to demonstrate competence, to avoid demonstrating incompetence, or to gain social recognition or approval
Task-orientation	Attention is focused on strategies needed to complete a task or to develop understanding or skill
Ego-orientation	Attention is focused on the self, especially others' evaluation of the self
Flow	Intense task involvement
Social responsibility goals	Goals of looking responsible, dependable, helpful, or compliant
	Relationships
Relatedness	The need to be connected securely to individuals in the social context and to experience oneself as being worthy and capable of love and respect

Maximizing Intrinsic Motivation, Mastery Goals, and Belongingness

Teachers who want to enhance classroom learning have a variety of motivation systems to engage. The shortcomings of motivation for extrinsic rewards suggest the desirability of maximizing alternative systems of motivation. Chapters 8 and 9 promote intrinsic motivation to learn, fostering internalized academic values, and encouraging learning and mastery as goals. This chapter makes specific, practical suggestions for achieving these instructional objectives.

THE TEACHER'S TASKS

Often the teachers' first task is to reawaken a motivation system that may be barely operative when students enter their classrooms. After the first few grades in school, few students show the same determination and persistence with school-work that they demonstrated in infancy and early childhood or may still show outside of school. Being able to read, solve math problems, or write a good essay should engender the same feelings of competence in a school-age student that being able to walk, take off a shoe, or complete a puzzle engenders for the very young child. But the intrinsic motivation system, which has such a powerful effect on children before they enter school and in activities outside of school, seems to disappear when they enter the classroom. Still, teachers can exploit this powerful motivation force.

A second and related task for teachers is to refocus students' attention on understanding and developing their competencies and to diminish their concerns about external evaluation, especially grades. Grades are important; they have long-term implications for students' opportunities. But, as in Safe Sally's case (see Chapter 1), many students' concern with grades and social approval prevents them from taking advantage of offerings (e.g., advanced placement classes or higher level science and math courses) that might expand their future options.

Thus, with intrinsic motivation and mastery goals, the teacher's task usually is to rekindle or prevent deterioration of a motivation system that has atrophied. The nature of teachers' third task, to engender academic values, will vary according to the age and backgrounds of their students. The task for teachers of some young children, who are used to choosing their own activities, is to make them care somewhat about their performance—to convince them that they need to complete teacher-assigned work. Middle school teachers often need to convince students that academic success is as important as social success. In secondary school, some teachers have to work hard to overcome the effects of a peer culture that devalues academic work. In other contexts, teachers merely need to reinforce the values that children are exposed to at home.

In summary, the goal is to create an instructional program that capitalizes on students' intrinsic desires to learn, that focuses their attention on understanding and mastery, and that fosters academic values. This does not mean that extrinsic rewards have no place in the classroom. It is unrealistic to expect students to exert effort voluntarily and enthusiastically on all school tasks. Some extrinsic incentives for schoolwork are necessary, and students must be held accountable for their work, if not by grades then by some other means. The practical task, therefore, is how to create a context in which a focus on learning and understanding prevails, and in which extrinsic rewards and concerns about performance do not undermine intrinsic motivation and attention to understanding and mastery.

Critical to achieving this goal is engendering students' confidence in their academic competencies and high expectations for success with school tasks. Accordingly, every recommendation made in Chapter 7 is relevant to achieving these objectives. The practical recommendations in this chapter, which overlap somewhat with those made previously, are divided into four areas of classroom practice—tasks, evaluation and rewards, control, and climate. The recommendations reflect a mixture of general principles that should apply most if not all of the time (e.g., emphasis on effort and learning) and suggestions for specific practices that might be used occasionally (e.g., collaborative work).

TASKS

1. **Explain the purposes of tasks and the real-world significance of the skills they are designed to teach.** To maintain learning as a goal students need to be told the purposes of tasks, including what skills they are designed to teach and how those skills are important outside of school. The value of this is illustrated in a study in which students' beliefs about the real-world

significance of what they were learning in math was the second strongest predictor of how much they enjoyed and were interested in their math class (Mitchell, 1993).

Evidence from classroom research suggests that this principle is violated commonly. Anderson (1981, 1984) reported that the children he interviewed rarely knew why they were asked to complete particular assignments. Most explained simply, "It's just our work." The children's lack of understanding of the purposes of tasks was not surprising; the teachers he observed discussed the purpose of the content being taught for only 1.5 percent of the assignments they gave! In the 317 presentations of new tasks that Brophy (1983a) observed, none of the teachers commented that the tasks would help children develop skills that would bring them pleasure or enjoyment. Only a few (3 percent) expressed personal enthusiasm for a task, or tied it to the personal lives or interests of the students. Most comments would contribute little to students' motivation to work on the tasks. For example, some teachers indicated that students were not expected to like a task or do well on it (8 percent); others reminded students that their work would be checked or that they would be tested on it (6 percent), that there would be negative consequences for poor performance (4 percent), or that they had a limited amount of time (6 percent). Most teachers' remarks to students concerned procedural demands or evaluation (Brophy, Rohrkemper, Rashid, & Goldberger, 1983). And the most negative comments (e.g., "Get your nose in the book, otherwise I'll give out a writing assignment"; "This test is to see who the really smart ones are") were associated with relatively low student engagement in tasks (Brophy, 1987a, p. 204).

Real-world significance sometimes can be achieved by providing tasks that are similar to those encountered outside of school. Stigler and Stevenson (1991) noted that in American classrooms teachers typically teach rules for mathematical operations first and then, sometimes, they point out the real-world applications of them. Asian teachers, in contrast, often begin a lesson with a real-world problem from which students construct for themselves the mathematical rule. An example of this is a lesson in which a teacher begins by asking students how many liters of colored water are contained in a large beaker that she brought to class. Students generate the answer, and the concept of fractions, by pouring the water into smaller beakers and figuring out how many of these smaller beakers will fill the larger one. The lesson ends with a discussion of rules for writing fractions to represent the parts of a whole.

2. **Give challenging tasks.** Recall that intrinsic interest derives primarily from the feelings of competence that are associated with working on and completing tasks, and only moderately difficult tasks engender such feelings when they are completed. Information processing theorists claim, further, that optimal arousal and interest are generated by a moderate discrepancy be-

tween an external stimulus (or task) and an individual's representations (or skill level; see Chapter 8).

Consistent with these theories of intrinsic motivation is research on teaching and learning that has shown that engagement rates, as well as achievement gains, are enhanced when teachers give students assignments that they can complete successfully only if they invest reasonable effort. Assignments that are completed with little effort or that are confusing or frustrating result in low engagement (see Brophy & Alleman, 1991; Brophy & Good, 1986). Research also shows that individuals are motivated more to persist with tasks when there is an increasing standard of success than when the standard is constant (e.g., McMullin & Steffen, 1982), and they rate the classes that make them think hard, and tasks that challenge them to participate actively in thinking and learning, as the most interesting (Newmann, 1992; see also Boggiano et al., 1982; Danner & Lonky, 1981; Shapira, 1976).

Chapter 7 offers some suggestions for how teachers can provide challenging tasks for students with a broad range of skill levels. All of these practices directly should enhance interest in tasks by giving students opportunities to see their competencies developing. This chapter focuses especially on the needs of the relatively high-achieving students who, in many classrooms, finish assignments in less than the allotted time and with few mistakes. Because tasks are not challenging and do not offer good opportunities for them to improve their understanding and skills, these students are not intrinsically motivated to engage in schoolwork and usually focus more on right answers and grades than on learning and mastery. The following sections detail some strategies to engage these students' interest and focus on learning.

a. **Allow students to work at their own pace some of the time.** The general approach used in the mastery learning programs described in Chapter 7 can be integrated into many classroom structures. A middle school math program I observed is an example of a strategy that provides opportunities for fast learners to challenge themselves without pushing the slower learners too much. Each week students spent 2 days working in workbooks individually or in small groups at their own pace. The teacher walked around the classroom, assessing students' understanding and providing individualized and small-group instruction. During the other 3 days students worked together in heterogeneous groups on real-life projects to which they applied their math skills. The projects were sufficiently multidimensional (e.g., designing a library to scale) to allow students to contribute at their own levels of math understanding. These students thus benefited from both a mastery-based program and opportunities for collaborative peer learning.

b. **In whole-class instruction include problems and questions that challenge students with the highest levels of mastery.** Stigler and Stevenson (1991) observed that most math instruction in Asian classrooms uses a whole-class format, even though variation in student skill levels is as high as it is in American classrooms. Teachers give problems in the middle of the instructional period that can be solved at different levels of mathematical understanding. Students are encouraged to attempt different solution strategies, which subsequently are discussed and compared with those of the class.

c. **Include very challenging questions on assignments and tests.** Stevenson and Stigler (1992) also noted that in China assignments and tests usually include some very easy problems that every student in the class can solve, and some very difficult problems that no student in the class can solve. All students, therefore, begin a test expecting to solve some but not all of the problems. This is a clever method of challenging the fast learners and encouraging them to strive for higher levels of understanding without discouraging the slower learners from trying. (After all, no one in the class will get all of the problems right.)

d. **Provide enriching activities for students who have completed their work.** Give students opportunities to work on a class newspaper, write and put on a play, keep diaries, build a model of a bridge, communicate with a real scientist or a child in another city or country over the Internet, or engage in any number of other enriching activities that will allow them to challenge themselves. It is important that all children have opportunities to engage in these enriching activities, but some students who complete their regular work more quickly than others can take greater responsibility or spend more time on individual or small-group projects.

3. **Create tasks that allow students to engage in substantive, intellectual work.**

   a. **Give tasks that require higher-order or divergent thinking and active problem solving.** These are more intrinsically interesting than tasks that involve memorizing or applying simple rules or procedures. I observed a compelling demonstration of this principle in a fifth-grade class. The teacher allowed students who finished their math worksheets (i.e., one or two pages of calculations in their textbook) to work on a math puzzle—usually a fairly complicated word problem. Students rushed through their textbook problems for the opportunity to work on this more difficult problem. Seeing this occur daily provoked the question of what these students' motivation to do math and their math competencies would be if their math curriculum included more "puzzles" and fewer sets of repetitive calculations. Indeed, the problems given to students who completed their math assignments were precisely the kinds of authentic math-related work—requiring students to explore, conjecture, and reason logically—that the National Council of Teachers of Mathematics (1991) and other math reformers promote (e.g., Ball, 1993; Stein, Grover, & Henningsen, 1996).

Blumenfeld and Mergendoller (1992) described ways in which a science teacher provided opportunities for students to engage deeply in substantive scientific thinking. For example, the teacher built lessons so that the main idea was evident in presentations, demonstrations, discussions, and tasks; she posed high-level questions and pressed students to explain and justify their answers. (For descriptions of strategies that teachers can use to involve students in substantive mathematical thinking, see Ball, 1993; Fennema, 1993; Lampert, 1991; Peterson, 1991.)

b. **Give tasks that revolve around "big ideas" rather than focusing on small, fragmented skills or concepts.** A group of teachers interviewed by Zahorik (1996) gave examples of "big ideas" they used to engross students in various academic tasks, including reading, writing, and discussion: "One theory of why dinosaurs became extinct is that volcanic eruptions eliminated their food supply"; "No country exists that does not need another country for something"; "Plants and animals exist in a symbiotic relationship" (p. 559). Such broad issues force students to think about the connections between various concepts that they are learning and to analyze and reflect more deeply than they do when they are given simple, disconnected topics (e.g., the effect of volcanoes on vegetation, a particular economic policy of a specific country, the diet of a particular animal).

c. **Give open-ended tasks.** Usually open-ended tasks that require some creativity are more interesting than tasks that require simple right-or-wrong responses. Analyzing a story or comparing two poems, for instance, is usually more interesting than answering factual questions about a story or memorizing a poem.

4. **Give multidimensional tasks.** Multidimensional tasks that require sustained effort and result in a product are motivating particularly because they provide variability and an opportunity to experience pride in tangible accomplishments. Examples are math assignments that require problem solving, explanations of strategies, and visual representations of the solution; reports that require research and written summaries, and possibly some design or artwork; and experiments that require planning, manipulation of materials, observation, analysis, and summarizing.

Some assignments can be embedded in long-term projects. A class newspaper, for example, provides students with opportunities to do math (e.g., determining how much it will cost to produce the newspaper and how much they should charge per copy), social studies (e.g., writing on current political events), art (e.g., designing a logo), and tasks that develop other practical skills (e.g., using the computer to do word processing). Other examples of long-term projects include building a model city, creating a class book of poems, and drawing to scale a map of the school. (See Blumenfeld et al., in press, for a discussion of the motivating effect of project-based learning.)

5. **Provide tasks that require active student participation, exploration, and experimentation.** Tasks that involve high degrees of student participation and activity are more enjoyable than tasks that involve passive responses (Mitchell, 1993). Manipulation of materials and role playing also can generate a deeper understanding of the concepts and issues than more passive learning activities, such as listening or reading. Thus, learning measurement in the process of building a model is more interesting and more effective than doing a workbook page of measurement problems. A multiplication game with playing cards is more fun than reciting the multiplication tables. Acting out a real debate between loyalists and separatists in the New England colonial period is more enjoyable and develops a better appreciation of the issues than reading about the controversy in a textbook. Doing a science experiment is usually more engaging than watching a teacher perform it.

Even when a teacher uses a whole-class format, active participation can be achieved by encouraging students to ask questions, offer opinions, share personal observations and experiences, debate with each other, and engage in critical discussions. As Bruner (1966, p. 117) explained, "There are games not only with objects, but with ideas and questions" (see also Kuhn, 1992; Perkinson, 1993; Prawat, 1993).

a. **But make sure that "hands-on" activities involving exploration and experimentation also involve substantive learning.** Manipulation, exploration, and dramatization are highly motivating and can be extremely effective teaching tools if used effectively. Well-meaning teachers endeavoring to enhance their students' intrinsic interest often create tasks that are fun but do not teach anything. Zahorik (1996) found in his interviews of teachers that many treated "hands-on" activities more as ends than as means; they created activities that actually may have distracted attention from the concepts they were supposed to teach (see also Flick, 1993; Roth, 1992). To engender learning, hands-on activities need to be accompanied by some teaching. The best activities involve a focus on the concepts that they are designed to teach.

Instruction I observed in a fourth-grade classroom provides an example of what often occurs when hands-on activities are initiated in the absence of teaching. To introduce the concept of probability the teacher had children play a dice game in which they predicted and recorded outcomes of a series of throws. Student enthusiasm for the game was extremely high, but informal interviews with children after the game revealed that they had not extracted any mathematical principles from it. When the teacher began instruction on probability the next day, students made no connection between what they were learning and the "game" they had played the previous day. The activity might have been an effective strategy for giving students an intuitive notion of probability theory if students' attention had been called to particular patterns, and if individual results had been combined and discussed with the whole class. Unaccompanied by instruction the game had no value.

Dramatization designed to increase understanding of historical events is another common example of high motivation in the absence of learning. In the class plays that I have observed, more attention usually was given to costume and set than to the political or social issues that the teacher wanted students to understand. There surely are benefits (e.g., developing artistic talents or cooperation skills) derived from costume and set design, but more efficient productions and simulations might produce a better understanding of social history.

6. **Provide some tasks that are complex, novel, and have elements of surprise or fantasy.** Recall that one theoretical perspective on intrinsic motivation stresses novelty, incongruity, complexity, and surprise. Children usually like tasks that involve fantasy or simulation (e.g., role playing), incorporate game-like features, or include elements of uncertainty about the outcome, such as suspense or hidden information.

Suspense and curiosity can be induced by asking students a question before beginning a lesson (e.g., "What is 'glasnost'?"; "Why is blood blue under your skin and red outside?"; "What proportion of the U.S. mainland would Alaska cover?"; "Why do people in Mexico speak Spanish?"; "What happens when cabbage juice is mixed with water and vinegar?"). Instruction can begin with students' speculations and questions that force them to confront contradictions and errors in their thinking.

Studies using computer-assisted instruction (CAI) have demonstrated some of the positive effects on motivation of fantasy or other embellishments such as color, noise, or surprise outcomes (see Cordova & Lepper, 1996; Lepper, 1985; Lepper & Cordova, 1992; Lepper & Malone, 1987; Malone, 1981a, 1981b; Malone & Lepper, 1987; Parker & Lepper, 1992). Cordova and Lepper (1996) found that embedding fantasy into a CAI math task contributed to students' levels of involvement, complexity of problems attempted, learning, and enjoyment.

Some theorists warn, however, that such embellishments also can interfere with learning (see Blumenfeld, 1992; Lepper & Malone, 1987). Research on personalized anecdotes and vivid details shows that they can have detrimental effects if they are added to texts to create interest but are not related to main ideas (Garner, Alexander, Gillingham, Kulikowich, & Brown, 1991; Wade, 1992). Young children particularly have been found to have difficulty differentiating between nonessential and important elements of text (see Shirey, 1992). If embellishments such as color, fantasy, surprises, music, or anecdotes are used to increase intrinsic interest in schoolwork, they must be used carefully so that students' attention is not distracted from learning goals and so that whatever value they have for generating enthusiasm is not lost in actual learning.

7. **Give tasks that are linked to students' interests.** Students also are more motivated to engage in tasks that involve topics that are personally interesting. There is considerable evidence that reading materials that students find interesting are comprehended and remembered better (Anderson, Shirey, Wilson, & Fielding, 1987; Asher, Hymel, & Wigfield, 1978; Garner, Alexander, Gillingham, Kulikowich, & Brown, 1991; Garner, Gillingham, & White, 1989; Shirey & Reynolds, 1988). Adapting instruction to the personal interests of students is also a distinguishing feature of classrooms in which students report high levels of motivation to increase their knowledge of science (Meece, 1991).

   Personalizing tasks can have the added advantage of allowing students to explore issues that are emotionally troubling. Rueda and Moll (1994) described a teacher who asked students to write about recent violent incidents in their community. The teacher reported improved writing as well as exceedingly high levels of motivation to complete the task, with many students recounting personal experiences with great emotion.

   a. **Allow students some choice in topics.** For a social studies unit on Native Americans, for example, some students may prefer to research and write on agriculture or food, others on dress, and others on religion and ceremonies. Similarly, during silent reading periods a wide range of books can be offered so that all students may read books on topics that interest them.

   b. **Integrate students' interest and experiences into lessons and discussion.** When discussing examples or applications of concepts being learned, teachers can refer to people (e.g., TV characters, rock stars) or events that are likely to catch their students' attention. Abstract concepts or new material can be made meaningful by giving examples or analogies that refer to familiar concepts or events. Brophy (1987a) describes a history lesson on Roman society in which the teacher encouraged students to consider possible parallels between Roman gladiators and modern tolerance for violence in sports.

   c. **Invite students to express opinions or respond personally to the content.** I rarely have observed much enthusiasm for history and politics in classes that were taught in a matter-of-fact and unemotional way, with neither the teacher nor the students expressing opinions. Classes in which students openly debate controversial subjects are much livelier. Rather than avoiding controversial issues, teachers can encourage students to express and support their opinions, thus helping them to appreciate the complexity of the present issues and the diversity of perspectives.

Teachers also can incorporate students' questions and comments into instruction. I observed a good example of this in a kindergarten class where a child announced in the middle of a lesson on measurement that he was wearing new shoes. The teacher asked him and other students what size shoe they wore and launched into a lively discussion, with considerable student input, on size as a form of measurement.

d. **Connect new or abstract concepts to familiar or concrete ones.** Teachers also can use the kind of role playing and manipulations previously described to increase the meaningfulness of concepts or information that is distant from students' own experiences, or to make abstract concepts more concrete. Students who are learning about money can play store—taking turns playing the role of the buyer (who must decide how much to give the seller) and the seller (who must calculate change). High school students can explore economic principles by playing the stock market. Each member of the class might be given $1,000 in play money to buy stock, and then follow and chart their earnings. Class discussions could be devoted to the American economy, balance of trade, world events, and other factors that influence students' own stock prices. Stocks also could be bought and sold by small groups of students. This might engender some lively discussion of factors that affect the value of the stocks.

8. **Give students opportunities to collaborate.** Students tend to find cooperative learning groups more enjoyable than working independently (see Johnson & Johnson, 1985b; Mitchell, 1993). As discussed in Chapter 7, individual accountability is important, and cooperative learning activities need to be planned and implemented thoughtfully to ensure that all students actively participate in substantive intellectual work. Students can collaborate in pairs for a few minutes to solve a single math problem during whole-class instruction, as they often do in Japanese classrooms (Stigler & Stevenson, 1991), or they can collaborate for many weeks on a multidimensional task, such as developing a business—creating a marketing plan, maintaining spreadsheets, and calculating profit and loss.

9. **Vary tasks and format from day to day.** Avoid predictable, unvarying formats. A common practice for elementary-level math instruction, for instance, is to begin with 15–20 minutes of whole-class instruction, during which the teacher, and occasionally students, do a few problems on the board, and then allow students to do 25–30 minutes of seatwork—typically one page of problems from a textbook or workbook. Brophy (1986) described "a steady diet of routine and predictable lessons followed by routine and predictable assignments as 'the daily grind'" (p. 34; see also Brophy, 1987b), and some studies suggest that such a predictable routine undermines

motivation. Meece et al. (1989), for example, found that variability in tasks was one of the more salient features of the highly motivating science classrooms they studied (see also Blumenfeld & Mergendoller, 1992). Munk and Repp (1994) review studies suggesting that variation in tasks also reduces problem behavior.

Often the same skills can be promoted using alternative formats—such as integrating whole-class instruction and seatwork or breaking students into small groups or dyads to work on problems, as Japanese teachers do. Minor changes sometimes can have significant effects. A fifth-grade teacher once complained to me that students worked halfheartedly on their daily reading assignment—answering a series of questions at the end of a story they were asked to read. She changed the task one day by asking students to generate their own questions and exchange them with a friend in the class. This minor modification in the assignment sparked considerable enthusiasm that was sustained by other, equally modest modifications made thereafter.

Summary

The questions provided in Appendix 10–A can be used to help teachers assess the motivation value of their tasks. It is always important to ask oneself what students are likely to learn and whether the likely achievement gains are worth the amount of time and energy that the activity requires. Teachers always need to consider ways to increase the learning value of each activity they give students.

Even more important than these self-reflective exercises are careful observation and assessment of student learning. When students are working individually or in small groups, teachers can walk around the room, engaging students in conversation and asking questions to encourage their thinking and assess their developing understanding. Postactivity discussions are also useful for assessing the value of a task, and they increase the instructional value of the activity. It is useful for teachers to keep notebooks in which they make comments regarding student motivation and learning on particular activities—in part as a reference to consult later and in part to force assessment and reflection. Whatever the strategy, it is extremely important to assess how much students actually learn from tasks and adapt them when their learning goals are not realized.

EVALUATION AND REWARDS

The salience and nature of evaluation and use of rewards have profound effects on students' intrinsic interest in tasks and their goals while working on them. The most engaging activity can become oppressive if students focus their attention on external evaluation, particularly if the standards for evaluation are unclear or if a positive evaluation is perceived to be unattainable. The following sections offer

suggestions for using evaluation and extrinsic rewards to support rather than undermine motivation.

10. **De-emphasize external evaluation.** Stressing evaluation (e.g., by continually threatening bad grades or reminding students that they will be rewarded
with good grades if they engage in a particular behavior) focuses attention
on performance goals, engenders a feeling of being controlled, and destroys
whatever intrinsic interest students might have had in a task. Emphasizing
external evaluation has other negative effects on motivation and learning.
Research suggests, for instance, that students tend not to select challenging
tasks when they are concerned about external evaluation. This was illustrated in a study by Harter (1978b), in which elementary school children
were asked to solve anagrams at four difficulty levels. Half of the subjects
were instructed that the task was a game, and half were instructed that it was
an academic task for which they would receive letter grades. Under the game
condition, children chose and verbalized their preferences for optimally
challenging problems. Those children working for grades chose significantly easier anagrams to perform, expressed less pleasure (e.g., smiling)
when they solved problems, and verbalized more anxiety (see also Deci,
1992; Hughes et al., 1985; Maehr & Stallings, 1972; Salili, Maehr, Sorensen,
& Fyans, 1976).

Salient evaluation is a powerful strategy for undermining intrinsic interest in an activity. If teachers evaluated students' memory of the television
programs they watched the previous evening, even television viewing might
lose some of its intrinsic appeal.

11. **When you give grades or other forms of evaluation, base them as much
as possible on effort, improvement, and achieving a standard, rather
than on relative performance.** Because most schools require grades, teachers can try only to minimize the negative effects of grades on students' motivation. Research provides some clues about how this can be accomplished.

Ames and her colleagues (see Ames, 1984, 1986, and Ames & Ames,
1984, for reviews) found that the criteria for evaluation affect students' goals
(i.e., to perform versus to learn), their perceptions of the cause of success and
failure, and the kind of information they attend to when evaluating themselves. Research indicates that competition (i.e., focusing students' attention
on relative performance) tends to foster performance goals. For example, in
one study students working in a competitive goal structure were more likely
to claim that they were concerned with their abilities and less likely to claim
that they engaged in self-monitoring and self-instruction related to the task
than students who simply were asked to challenge themselves (i.e., an individualistic goal structure; Ames, 1986). Another study found that evaluation
reduced intrinsic interest in a task when it was based on social norms, but
actually increased intrinsic interest when it was based on achieving a predetermined score (Harackiewicz, Abrahams, & Wageman, 1987).

Researchers also have shown that in competitive contexts children emphasize ability (and sometimes luck) when interpreting their performance. In situations in which evaluation is based on group performance, personal improvement, or meeting a preestablished standard, children are more likely to attribute their performance to effort (Ames, 1978, 1981; Ames & Ames, 1978, 1981; Ames, Ames, & Felker, 1977; Rheinberg, 1983).

A study by Ames and Ames (1981) demonstrated that the criteria used for evaluation also affect the information children use to evaluate themselves. Children were given opportunities to establish personal performance histories for a task (i.e., success or failure) and then were introduced to either a competitive (i.e., with another child) or individualistic (i.e., challenging yourself) goal structure. When subsequently asked a series of questions, children's self-reward and feelings of satisfaction in the competitive situation were based on whether they won or lost, and not on the quality of their performance. Children in the individualistic goal structure focused on their personal histories with the task (i.e., whether they improved).

Evaluating students on personal improvement or in terms of a predetermined standard is preferable for both high- and low-achieving students. High-achieving students always have a higher standard of excellence to aspire to when the objective is to surpass their own previous levels of performance or to meet higher standards than they previously have achieved. Low-achieving students benefit because success defined in terms of improvement or achieving a standard is attainable, and effort always should have some payoff. By fostering the belief that effort leads to success, noncompetitive evaluation also engenders the perception that ability is something that improves with effort; it should increase low-achieving students' expectations for success, and it also may contribute to a perception of fairness.

Some of these benefits were demonstrated in a study by Covington and Omelich (1984b) with college students. They found that undergraduate psychology students who were graded using a mastery standard (i.e., grades were determined by what scores the students attained) perceived the grading system to be fairer and more responsive to effort than students who were graded using a competitive, norm-referenced standard (i.e., who were graded on a curve). The students in the mastery condition also aspired to higher grades and had more self-confidence about being able to achieve them.

12. **Emphasize the information contained in grades.** Rather than congratulate a student for getting an "A" on a test, as though the "A" itself was the goal, comment on the high level of competence the grade signifies. For some students a "B" or even a "C" might represent improvement. This, too, can be pointed out. Low grades, similarly, should not be presented as punishment, but as information—an indication that the student needs to exert more effort or needs some assistance.

Focus on the information purposes of tests as well. The effect of how tests are introduced has been recognized by researchers who want to manipulate subjects' goals in experiments; they typically induce performance goals or an ego orientation by introducing experimental tasks as measures of intelligence or competence (e.g., Ryan, 1982; Stipek & Kowalski, 1989). Explaining to students that a test will provide information about their levels of understanding or skill—information that can be used to guide individual students' subsequent efforts and the teacher's curriculum planning—engenders a task focus.

13. **Make grading criteria clear and fair.** Understanding the criteria used in grading contributes to students' feelings of having control over school outcomes. Involving students in discussions about grading criteria sometimes can foster better understanding and acceptance of the criteria and can inform teachers of perceptions of unfairness that need to be addressed, either by providing explanations or by changing the system.

14. **Provide substantive, informative feedback, rather than grades or scores, on assignments.** Give global evaluations, such as letter grades, infrequently because students typically attend only to the grades, even when they are accompanied by more useful information. Global performance feedback also fosters global self-evaluations (e.g., "I'm a 'C' student"), which serve no purpose. In contrast, specific and informative feedback on assignments helps students make specific and useful judgments about their strengths and weaknesses, and focuses their attention on what they need to do to improve.

Several studies have demonstrated the advantages of substantive evaluation. Butler and Nisan (1986) either wrote substantive positive and negative comments on sixth-grade students' papers that had no grades or they gave numerical (i.e., normatively distributed) grades with no comments. Students who received comments claimed to find the tasks more interesting. They also were more likely to attribute their effort on the task to their interest, and their success to their interest and effort, than children who received grades. The students who had received comments also performed better on a subsequent task requiring creativity. In a later study by Butler (1988), students who received written comments with substantive suggestions for improvement maintained a high interest in a task, whereas grades, with and without comments, undermined both interest and performance. In an experiment with fifth and sixth graders, evaluation in the form of global praise (e.g., "very good") and normatively distributed grades resulted in greater ego involvement, less task involvement, and lower interest and desire to engage further with the activity than did task-oriented evaluation involving comments containing both reinforcement and goal setting (e.g., "You thought of quite a few ideas; maybe it is possible to think of more unusual, original ideas"; Butler, 1987). Mac Iver (1990) found evidence that even retention and dropout rates can be improved by including written comments on report cards. He suggested that in addition to providing useful information, handwritten notes convey to low-achieving students that teachers are paying attention to them.

15. **Use tangible extrinsic rewards as little as possible.** Principles related to the use of tangible extrinsic rewards parallel those that apply to grades. Extrinsic rewards, like grades, focus students' attention on extrinsic reasons for engaging in a learning activity, undermine intrinsic interest, and discourage students from seeking challenging work (Boggiano, Pittman, & Ruble, 1982; Pearlman, 1984; Pittman, Emery, & Boggiano, 1982; Shapira, 1976). These effects of rewards are not limited to the particular context in which they are offered. In the Pittman et al. (1982) study, for instance, subjects' preference for a simple version of a task in extrinsic reward situations carried over to situations in which the original reward contingencies were no longer in effect.

Studies demonstrating that rewards undermine intrinsic interest have involved tasks that appealed to the subjects. Consequently, the reward was superfluous. In real classrooms rewards often are necessary to prod students into engaging in tasks in which they have little initial interest. Some students may not have been socialized to value a particular skill, may find a particular task uninteresting, or may not at first believe that they will be able to master a skill. Although they should be used as little as possible, in such circumstances rewards are appropriate, effective, and can be given in ways that do not have detrimental effects.

a. **Use rewards only when necessary and make them as "minimal" as possible.** Recall the "minimally sufficient" rule described in Chapter 9. A reward can be used to convey to students the cultural value of an activity. This value most likely will be internalized by students, however, if the reward is not so dramatic or salient that it becomes the sole focus of attention.[1]

b. **Make rewards contingent on the quality of work or a standard of performance, not simply on engaging in an activity.** Research indicates that rewards have the strongest undermining effects when they are expected, salient, and contingent on engaging in the task rather than on meeting a performance standard (see Deci & Ryan, 1987). Ames and Ames (1990) described an actual example of the effects of rewards contingent only on engaging in a task. Children in a classroom they observed received certificates for a special treat at a local restau-

---

[1]When I was a child my parents gave me 1 dollar for every "A" on my report card. Even in those days this was a modest reward for a semester of hard work. I do not know to what degree I can attribute my strong academic values to the dollar rewards, but I suspect that a much larger amount of money would have interfered with the internalization process described in Chapter 9.

rant for writing four book reports in 1 month; because quantity rather than quality was rewarded, the children chose short, easy, and often uninteresting books rather than longer or more challenging ones.

Rewards based only on engagement focus attention on their controlling function and thus undermine whatever intrinsic interest students may have had in the activity. They also convey the message that the activity is not worth doing without the reward. Rewards that are contingent on a particular level of performance focus students' attention on their information function. By conveying competence or mastery, rewards can increase intrinsic motivation.

c. **Withdraw external rewards as soon as possible.** When rewards are offered to initiate engagement in a task, an attempt should be made to shift students' attention to the intrinsic or utility value of the task, or to developing competence, as soon as possible. This, of course, can work only if the task is interesting and the skill useful, and if students experience success fairly soon after attempting it. If these conditions are met, the teacher may be able to maintain students' interest in completing tasks without continuing to offer external rewards.[2] Thus, just as students can turn their attention to extrinsic reasons for engaging in activities that previously they were motivated intrinsically to do, they can shift their attention from extrinsic to intrinsic reasons for engaging in an activity.

Summary

Students need to be held accountable, and they need evaluative feedback to give them information that they can use to guide future efforts. Evaluation and other rewards should not undermine students' motivation to engage in schoolwork, and even can increase it, if the information function is emphasized, if the process is viewed as being fair, and if positive evaluations and rewards are perceived as being genuinely achievable. Appendix 10–B can be used to help teachers evaluate their own evaluation practices.

CONTROL

Recall that a feeling of personal control or self-determination is considered by some motivation theorists to be a basic human need (see Chapter 8). People enjoy

---

[2]Occasionally students are "hooked" quickly and forget about the reward. In an attempt to get my daughter to try to learn to ice skate (after she had spent several sessions hugging the wall), I promised to give her an ice-skating outfit if she circled the rink without touching the wall. By the end of that session she accomplished the task. But she was so excited about her achievement and intrinsically motivated to continue to develop her skills, she forgot about the promised reward. It was at least a year later that she remembered.

more and are motivated more to engage in activities that they believe they are doing because they want to do them than activities that they believe they must do. Achieving a balance between giving appropriate limits and direction and allowing students some discretion and control is difficult, and implementing the following recommendations requires consideration of numerous variables, such as the age of the children and their experience and skill in making decisions. Efforts to implement these principles, however, should enhance students' motivation to engage in schoolwork.

16. **Give students as much discretion as they can handle productively.** Research has demonstrated several benefits of providing students with some control over their academic work. For example, many studies have demonstrated that students are more intrinsically motivated in classrooms in which teachers provide some opportunity for choice than in classrooms in which teachers are highly controlling (Deci, Nezlek, & Sheinman, 1981; Deci, Schwartz, Sheinman, & Ryan, 1981; Pascarella, Walberg, Junker, and Haertel, 1981; Rainey, 1965). Student choice was a particularly important feature of the science class referred to previously in which students were highly motivated (Meece et al., 1989). In small-group activities, for instance, students had some choice in their work partners, the materials they used, and how to complete the activities. Moreover, feedback was inherent in many of the small-group tasks, minimizing students' dependence on the teacher. In the classroom in which students expressed relatively low interest in learning science, the teacher determined the groups and specified all aspects of the materials and procedures. Choice even has been found to reduce disruptive behavior, presumably because it enhances students' interest in sanctioned activities (Munk & Repp, 1994).

A modest amount of choice may be all that is needed. Zuckerman, Porac, Lathin, Smith, and Deci (1978) increased intrinsic motivation by simply giving some of the subjects in their study an opportunity to select which three of six puzzles they worked on during an experiment (see also Cordova & Lepper, 1996; Swann & Pittman, 1977).

Increased student choice has been shown to enhance student learning as well as motivation. In Matheny and Edwards' (1974) study of twenty-five elementary school classrooms, teachers were trained to (1) give students some flexibility and responsibility for determining when they completed assignments; (2) allow students to score most of their own written work and to use individual conferences to evaluate their progress; (3) contract with students for long-range assignments; and (4) set up independent learning centers. Successful implementation of these strategies produced greater intrinsic motivation and greater gains in reading achievement. DeCharms (1976, 1984) reports that students who were trained to be "origins" rather than "pawns" (i.e., who were given more autonomy and responsibility for their learning) had better achievement scores and even better graduation rates than students in controlled classrooms (see also Wang, 1983; Wang & Stiles, 1976).

Corno and colleagues (1989; Corno & Rohrkemper, 1985) suggest another value of providing students with some control over their academic lives. They point out that students who always are told what to do, and how and when to do it, do not develop a sense of personal responsibility or strategies for regulating their own behaviors. They do not learn how to use internal resources to solve problems or engage in deliberate planning and monitoring.

This benefit of giving children some, but not too much, discretion in their activities is illustrated in a classic study by Lewin, Lippitt, and White (1939). In an examination of the effect of adult control on children's productivity, they compared three organizational climates on the behavior of 10-year-old boys who were members of after-school "hobby clubs." In the three different conditions, the adult either controlled virtually every activity (i.e., autocratic condition), allowed the children to do as they pleased (i.e., laissez-faire condition), or played an active role in the group's activities, but encouraged the children to participate in decision making (i.e., democratic condition). The autocratic and democratic groups were equally productive, and more productive than the laissez-faire group, when an adult was present. The difference between the two productive groups became apparent when the adult leader left the room. Children in the democratic group were affected little by the absence of the leader. They worked at the same level whether or not an adult was present. In contrast, productivity decreased markedly when the adult was absent from the autocratic group.

Providing students with some control may be particularly important as children enter adolescence. Ironically, research suggests that at this developmental stage, when children are concerned most with issues of autonomy, school and classroom structures typically become more structured and teacher controlled (Eccles & Midgley, 1989; Eccles, Wigfield, Midgley, et al., 1993).

There are many ways to provide some student choice without creating chaos in a classroom. And if students are not overconcerned about negative consequences of poor performance, the evidence suggests that they will choose challenging tasks that will promote learning. Strategies for increasing student autonomy and feelings of self-determination are given in the proceeding sections.

Note that the principles described in this section need to be applied to all students in a classroom. Ryan and Grolnick (1986) found that upper-elementary school-age students in the same classroom varied considerably in the degree to which they thought their classroom environment was one where they could be "origins" (i.e., responsible, instrumental, having an internal locus of causality), versus "pawns" (i.e., reactive, with little sense of personal causation), and that this variation in children's perceptions of control was associated significantly with their perceptions of competence and global self-worth. Sometimes the students who are disaffected the most from school and would benefit most from practices that enhance motivation are given the least amount of autonomy. Teachers need to be careful not to be satisfied with implementing practices that are motivating to only some students (usually those who need it least).

a. **Allow students to participate in the design of their academic tasks.** For example, rather than creating a list of vocabulary words to accompany a book students are reading, teachers can ask students to generate their own lists. In one class that I observed, each student contributed a word to a class list and became the "expert" on that word. This practice had the additional advantage of giving relatively low-achieving students an opportunity to be consulted by their peers for their expert knowledge.

b. **Give students choices in how tasks are completed.** After reading a story students might choose from among several assignments—to write a summary of the story, to write a sequel to the story, or to write about a similar experience of their own. The teacher's goal—for the students to practice writing—is accomplished regardless of their choices, and by having some freedom, they acquire more control and responsibility.

c. **Give students some choice in the difficulty levels of assignments or tasks that they complete.** This kind of choice has to be implemented cautiously because, as mentioned previously, students often select schoolwork that ensures a positive evaluation rather than work that challenges their current skill levels.

DeCharms (1976) describes an activity with a built-in incentive for selecting the appropriate difficulty level. Students play a spelling game that involves teams, as in a spelling bee. Each student is asked whether he wants to try an easy word (worth 1 point for the team), a moderately hard word (worth 2 points), or a hard word (worth 3 points). The difficulty level of the words is individualized as a function of each student's performance on the pretest. An easy word is one that the student previously spelled correctly. A moderately hard word is one that was spelled incorrectly, but could have been studied or learned in the 2 days between the pretest and the spelling bee. A hard word is from a new list that is tailored to the student's ability. When DeCharms tested this game, he found that the number of moderately hard words children chose increased over a 5-week period, indicating that students learned to set realistic but challenging goals for themselves. This technique could be adapted to many different kinds of tasks.

d. **Give students some discretion about when they complete particular tasks.** Some people like to do the most difficult or least appealing tasks first. Others prefer to do a few easier or more pleasant tasks to give them a feeling of accomplishment before they tackle the hard ones. Giving students the opportunity to order assignments according to their own preferences gives them a greater feeling of control and responsibility. Practices such as giving students a homework packet on Monday to be turned in on Friday, rather than giving homework on a daily basis, gives students more discretion and an opportunity to develop skills in managing and organizing their time.

e. **Allow students to evaluate some of their own assignments.** Students might check their solutions to math problems and their spelling words using answer sheets. Or they can be given rubrics or a set of questions to help them assess their work. They might, for instance, be asked to answer a series of questions after writing a paragraph (e.g., "Is there a topic sentence?"; "Are there at least three sentences that support or elaborate on the topic sentence?"; "Does the final sentence provide a transition to the next paragraph?"). Ultimately, students' mastery has to be assessed by the teacher, but on a day-to-day basis students benefit greatly from instruction and experience in evaluating their own work.

f. **Involve students in personal goal setting.** As suggested in Chapter 7, goals should be near (i.e., proximal), specific, and challenging. Students, for example, can set such goals as the number of words they will spell correctly on the next spelling test or the number of arithmetic problems they will solve each day, and record whether they meet their goals.

17. **Focus monitoring activities on learning and understanding rather than on student behavior.** Constant monitoring of student behavior and reminders of deadlines give students the impression that they are controlled rather than self-determined. Clearly, deadlines need to be given and enforced, and teachers need to monitor students closely to be able to provide assistance and instruction. But deadlines should not become the teacher's central focus, and teachers should avoid monitoring that has no instructional value and may be experienced as repressive. Looking over students' shoulders without engaging them in instructional conversations, walking around the room asking them how many problems they have completed, or telling them to get to work are practices experienced as controlling and unhelpful. Walking around the classroom checking students' understanding and engaging them individually in instructional conversations focuses their attention on understanding and mastery and facilitates motivation. It can serve the same purpose as getting distracted students to focus on tasks, but the

message the teacher gives by asking students about their understanding rather than admonishing them for not working is that the teacher is there to help students learn, not just to monitor and control their behaviors.

18. **Give help in a way that facilitates students' own accomplishments.** As mentioned in Chapter 7, unnecessary help can diminish feelings of competence that accompany success and therefore diminish intrinsic motivation. The negative effect of "overhelp" on intrinsic motivation has been demonstrated in studies of young children. Farnham-Diggory and Ramsey (1971), for instance, found that 5-year-old children who received frequent offers of help from an experimenter during a play session persisted half as long on a subsequent achievement task as children who had played uninterrupted for the same amount of time. Fagot (1973) and Hamilton and Gordon (1978) provide further evidence suggesting that children in classrooms in which teachers are directive and intrusive display relatively low task persistence. Students perceived by the teacher to have behavioral or learning problems are particularly vulnerable to being offered more help than they actually need.

19. **Hold students accountable.** Students need to understand that with personal control comes responsibility. They need to know what they will be held accountable for and when, and that there will be consequences for failing to meet their responsibilities. If their work is not completed when it is due, for example, they may need to lose some recess time or be required to complete it at home. I am not recommending severe punishment, but freedom without accountability can lead to chaos, which promotes neither motivation nor learning. If a substantial number of students are not using their freedom effectively, the teacher needs to reconsider the developmental appropriateness (e.g., based on age or experience) of the choices provided, or the need for instructing students in making wise choices.

Summary

Allowing some student choice fosters intrinsic interest in school tasks and has the added advantage of teaching self-management skills that are needed for success in higher grades and in the workplace. It is impossible for students to develop a sense of personal responsibility and the ability to regulate their own learning behaviors if they always are told what to do, and how and when to do it. A summary of the aforementioned strategies is found in Appendix 10–C.

As with most principles of good instruction, more is not necessarily better. As the Lewin et al. (1939) study demonstrated, there is such a thing as too much autonomy. Teachers need to experiment to find out how much autonomy students can handle, and they usually need to teach students strategies for taking productive advantage of the choices they are given.

CLASSROOM CLIMATE

Instructional settings can offer individuals opportunities to meet another fundamental human need—being socially connected. School provides a setting in which students can develop relationships that support their sense of well-being and feelings of belongingness, as well as their learning efforts. But not all schools and classrooms attain this goal. Some classrooms offer more opportunities for humiliation and social rejection than for social support and a feeling of being valued as humans. By implementing the following suggestions teachers can ensure that students' social needs are met and that social relationships support rather than undermine their ability to learn.

20. **Respect and value students as humans.** Rogers' (1951) recommendation that parents give their children "unconditional positive regard" applies equally to teachers. Students' intrinsic interest in academic work can flourish in classrooms in which the teacher makes students feel valued and secure, regardless of their skill levels. Defensive Dave (see Chapter 1) might not have to engage in such dysfunctional behavior if he believed that the teacher would accept and value him even if his performance was less than stellar. Students who believe that the teacher respects and supports them can take academic risks with impunity. Students who believe that their value in the teacher's eyes depends on their academic success risk more than a low grade; they risk humiliation and rejection.

    Respect may be the most important ingredient in supporting students' motivation to learn. It is conveyed in the most subtle ways—whether the teacher looks directly into the eyes of a student who is speaking; how long the teacher waits for a student to respond to a question; the teacher's facial expression when a student reveals poor understanding. Teachers' respect for students can affect students' respect for themselves, their motivation to engage in academic tasks, and even their attitudes and perceptions of the intrinsic value, perceived usefulness, and importance of academic subjects (Midgley, Feldlaufer, & Eccles, 1989). Although it can be described in behavioral terms it needs to come from the heart. Teachers who genuinely do not care about or like their students will have a difficult time convincing those students otherwise.

    a. **Show respect for students by being attentive and interested in them—as humans as well as students.** Solicit and be attentive to their ideas and opinions in class discussions. Show them that you take their ideas seriously by building on their comments or asking them follow-up questions.

        One of the best ways to show respect for students is to hold them to high expectations—by not accepting sloppy, thoughtless, or incomplete work, by pressing them to clarify vague comments, by encouraging them not to give up, and by not praising work that does not reflect genuine effort. Ironically, reactions that often are intended to protect students' self-esteem—such as accepting low-quality work—conveys a lack of interest, patience, or caring. "Tough love" can be given with support and compassion. Indeed, it shows students that you really care about their future.

Although the focus must remain on learning, it does not hurt to express interest in students' lives outside of school—to congratulate them for their efforts on the football field the night before, inquire how they are feeling after being out sick, or wish them a happy birthday. Teachers also can create a supportive climate by sharing their own feelings and values, and encouraging students to do the same. It is important that students are accepted and supported when they disclose their feelings.

b. **Avoid ridiculing or embarrassing students publicly or privately.** Engendering fear of ridicule or humiliation can control students' behaviors, but only at great cost. Fear of humiliation engenders avoidance, not approach. It makes students want to withdraw and play it safe, not to engage actively in learning tasks and take risks. Public humiliation may be worse than private interactions, but teachers are authority figures and need to be mindful that an offhand comment, even made in private, can have tremendous impact on a student's feelings of self-worth and respect.

c. **Avoid sarcasm.** Again, teachers need to recognize their importance— even for students who appear (most likely pretend) not to care. A sarcastic remark that might be considered humorous by another adult, or even by a child in another context, can be devastating in a context in which the adult has power and authority. Young children are particularly vulnerable because they are more likely to take teachers' comments at face value.

21. **Create a risk-free environment.** Students need to feel that they can take risks, make mistakes, and reveal a lack of understanding—without losing the positive regard of the teacher or classmates. There are many ways this can be achieved.

a. **Treat errors as a natural part of learning.** Outside of school, errors are considered to be a natural part of learning a skill. No one would expect to make perfect serves when learning how to play tennis or to bake a perfect soufflé on the first attempt. But in most classrooms errors are viewed negatively—as something to avoid. Red checks next to answers are reason for distress and "100%" at the top of a paper is cause for celebration. In school, students learn to devalue errors, even on assignments based on new material.

Displaying on the bulletin board papers with no errors or that have stars, smiling faces, and "As" on them can discourage the students who rarely achieve such recognition; it leads some high-achieving students, like Sally, to be distressed by anything less than 100 percent. Students deserve praise for attempting hard tasks, even if their efforts result in more errors than they would have made on an easier task. Sally might take more risks if she had teachers who praised effort on difficult tasks with a few or even many errors instead of teachers who praised perfect papers.

Classroom practices should resemble what research has shown to be used by expert tutors. Effective tutors rarely label a student's mistake as "incorrect" or as an "error," and they do not suggest answers (Lepper, Aspinwall, Mumme, & Chabay, 1990). Instead, they rely on indirect strategies; they direct children's attention to the source of the difficulty, offer hints, and give them a second chance. Thus, errors are treated as part of a process that occurs en route to achieving a correct solution.

b. **Emphasize the information value of errors.** In one fifth-grade classroom I observed the teacher asked children to try to identify the pattern of the errors they made on math problems, and then to devise and try to solve similar problems. In this way she stressed the information conveyed in errors and their use in directing future efforts to increase skills and understanding. Requiring students to correct errors on assignments forces them to try to remedy misunderstandings, and is preferable to having students simply take note of how many errors they made and move on to another assignment.

c. **Incorporate wrong answers as productive contributions.** In the American classrooms Stigler and Stevenson (1991) observed, teachers tended to look for the "right" answer, dismissing rather than taking advantage of errors. The Asian teachers they observed treated errors as topics for discussion from which all students can learn, thus turning every student's participation into a contribution. Meece, Blumenfeld, and Puro (1989) report that rather than turn to another student when one student failed to provide a satisfactory answer to a question (a common practice in American classrooms), the highly motivating science teacher they studied reworded the question or prompted students who responded incorrectly, or asked students to explain or justify their responses. Thus, they took advantage of, rather than dismissing, wrong answers.

22. **Create a community of learners that includes teachers as well as students.** Teachers instill academic values and engender interest in learning by modeling themselves as learners. They can share with students the ways in which their own learning activities help them understand and function in

real life. Specific examples are more persuasive than general comments. Teachers also should admit freely their own lack of knowledge and model the use of resources, including students, to address the gaps in their knowledge and skills.[3]

23. **Assist students in developing constructive relationships with each other.** Relationships among students affect their enjoyment and their ability to concentrate on academic tasks. Peers' respect and positive regard is just as important as those of teachers, especially as children approach adolescence.

   a. **Teach students to be respectful of each other.** To a considerable degree students take their cues from the teacher. A teacher who is abusive toward students will foster disrespect among students; a teacher who is accepting, supportive, and respectful will engender the same. Explicit discussion of what is acceptable and respectful classroom behavior and what is not also usually is needed. In one elementary school I worked in children were taught to differentiate between "put-ups" and "put-downs" from the first week of school, and they were reminded that only put-ups are acceptable. In the upper grades, students engaged in extended discussions of issues of respect and integrity, and the effects of their behaviors and remarks on others.

   b. **Help students develop positive relationships with each other.** Conflict among peers can interfere with students' motivation and ability to engage in academic work.[4] Although not usually seen as part of the "basic" curriculum, explicit instruction and discussion of social conflicts and problem-solving strategies are critical to a positive classroom climate, as well as to students' social–moral development.

CONCLUSION

Students are more intrinsically motivated and are focused more on learning and mastery when their tasks are moderately challenging, novel, and relevant to their own lives than when their tasks are too hard or too easy, repetitive, or perceived to

---

[3]I have begun to see more and more classrooms in which a few students become the technology experts, on whom the teacher and other students rely.

[4]My daughter's kindergarten teacher was an astute observer of the friendship networks and conflicts that developed among her students, and she organized instruction and activities to support positive relationships and minimize tension among children. When my daughter and two other girls developed a problematic triangle, she engaged the entire class in a discussion about the problems that arise when two children exclude another and reviewed some possible solutions. The teacher addressed the problem directly and sensitively, without referring to the particular children involved in the conflict, always showing respect for students' feelings. As a consequence, she contributed to a supportive classroom climate that fostered feelings of security while helping students develop social problem-solving skills.

be irrelevant. Students are intrinsically motivated to work when they feel self-determining rather than controlled, when the threat of negative external evaluation is not salient, and when their attention is not focused on extrinsic reasons for completing tasks. They also will feel more competence and pride, and thus more intrinsic interest in tasks, if they can take responsibility for their successes.

Extrinsic rewards are unavoidable. If used sparingly and thoughtfully, the promise of rewards can induce students to engage in learning activities that they otherwise may not attempt. Implementing the suggestions for effective use of extrinsic reinforcement and other methods for enhancing intrinsic motivation described in this chapter should, however, reduce the need for extrinsic rewards.

None of the recommendations made in this chapter will be effective if they are not implemented in a climate of support and respect that makes students feel secure and valued. Students will not be motivated to engage in the most intrinsically interesting tasks, even under optimal conditions of autonomy, if they fear humiliation or rejection from the teacher or their peers.

Achievement Anxiety

Anxiety is not all bad. A small amount of it does not undermine performance and may even facilitate it, especially if the task is not very difficult (Ball, 1995; Luthar, 1995; Sieber, O'Neil, & Tobias, 1977; Zeidner & Nevo, 1992). But for some students anxiety debilitates performance in achievement settings by interfering with learning and the retrieval of previously learned material. This chapter examines the measurement, effects, and origins of achievement anxiety and makes specific recommendations for minimizing its negative effects on learning and academic performance.

Most students who are highly anxious in achievement situations have low perceptions of their academic competencies (e.g., Bandalos et al., 1995; Benson, Bandalos, & Hutchinson, 1994; Harter, 1992; Zeidner, 1992; see also Hembree, 1988) and low self-efficacy (Bandura, 1988; Benson et al., 1994; Pintrich & De Groot, 1990); they become most anxious in situations that threaten their self-esteem (Schwarzer & Jerusalem, 1992). In the early work on test anxiety, Sarason, Davidson, Lighthall, Waite, and Ruebush (1960) described the test-anxious child as one who has "self-deprecatory attitudes, anticipates failure in the test situation in the sense that he will not meet the standards of performance of others or himself, and experiences the situation as unpleasant" (p. 20). Because high-anxious students fear failure, they avoid highly evaluative situations whenever possible and choose easy tasks on which success is fairly certain (Hill, 1972, 1980, 1984; Hill & Wigfield, 1984; Sarason & Sarason, 1990; Tobias, 1992). When they must perform in evaluative settings, they are overconcerned about evaluation of their performance, and these concerns interfere with their performance on the task.

A distinction usually is made between **trait anxiety,** a relatively stable personality characteristic, and **state anxiety,** a temporary emotional state (Hedl & Papay, 1982; Spielberger, 1972; Spielberger & Vagg, 1995). Individuals who generally are more prone than others to experiencing a state of anxiety in achievement contexts do not experience anxiety all of the time. Trait anxiety is believed to interfere with learning and performance only when the achievement conditions create a state of anxiety. Thus, even students who are prone to be anxious (i.e., who have high levels of trait anxiety) may be very relaxed in nonthreatening situations, such as when they are self-confident and expect to succeed, or when their performance will not be evaluated. Debilitating anxiety, therefore, can be minimized by creating conditions that do not engender a state of anxiety.

Anxiety in achievement contexts commonly is referred to as "test anxiety." "Test," however, is used broadly in this literature; the research usually is applicable to all situations in which a student's intellectual abilities are evaluated—ranging from formal testing situations to simply being asked a question by the teacher.

There are two components of achievement anxiety: a *cognitive* (i.e., worry) component and an *emotional* component (Liebert & Morris, 1967; Sarason & Sarason, 1990; Spielberger & Vagg, 1995). The cognitive or worry component of test anxiety (e.g., negative expectations for success, concerns about one's performance) is believed to interfere most directly with learning and task performance (see Deffenbacher, 1980, 1986; Hedl, 1987; Morris, Davis, & Hutchings, 1981; Sarason & Sarason, 1990; Tobias, 1992; Zeidner & Nevo, 1992). The emotional component refers to the autonomic (i.e., physiological) reactions that are evoked by evaluative stress, such as sweating and an accelerated heartbeat (Holroyd & Appel, 1980).

MEASURING ANXIETY

Several self-report instruments have been developed to measure students' propensity to experience anxiety in evaluative situations. (See Anderson and Sauser, 1995, for a summary and discussion of anxiety measures; see Bedell and Marlowe, 1995, for evidence on validity.) The original instrument used with children, the Test Anxiety Scale for Children (TASC), was developed by Sarason et al. (1960). Students respond to questions such as "Do you feel nervous while you are taking a test?" or "Do you think you worry more about school than other children?"

A positively worded revision of the TASC (called the TASC-Rx), was developed by Feld and Lewis (1969). "Do you feel relaxed while you are taking a test?" is an example of a question on this version of the scale. The authors found that students' responses to the questionnaire fell into four categories: (1) specific worrying about tests, (2) physiological reactions to evaluative pressure, (3) negative self-evaluation, and (4) worrying about school while at home. Children who ranked high in one category often did not rank high in other categories. Anxiety seems to be experienced by children in different ways and in different situations.

The results of this study have potential implications for the classroom. Remedies for high anxiety differ, depending on which "kind" of anxiety a student experiences. For example, the student who has unpleasant physiological reactions in test situations may need a different kind of intervention than a student who has a negative view of her ability to succeed. The first student may need instructions on test-taking strategies or simply more experience taking tests. The second student may need success experiences and other interventions, such as those described in Chapter 7, designed to build self-confidence.

Harnisch, Hill, and Fyans (1980) selected seven items from the TASC-Rx, primarily from the test-worry category, to create the Test Comfort Index (TCI). This scale, as well as the others, has been used extensively in classrooms for diagnostic and research purposes. Hill (1984) reports that school personnel prefer the TCI because it is quick and easy to administer and is worded positively. These seven questions are given in Table 11-1. The student responds with a "yes" or "no" to each question. According to research by Hill and his colleagues, it is highly likely that the test performance of students who answer "no" to these items does not provide an accurate assessment of their true competencies. Their anxiety probably interferes with their performance in the ways that are described in the proceeding sections.

A number of test anxiety scales have been developed for adults, including Sarason's (1978) Test Anxiety Scale and Spielberger's (1980) Test Anxiety Inventory. Sarason (1984) created the forty-item Reactions to Tests (RTT) measure, containing four subscales. Two subscales are associated with the emotional component of achievement anxiety—*tension* (e.g., "I feel distressed and uneasy before tests") and *bodily reactions* (e.g., "My heart beats faster when the test begins"); the other two are associated with the worry component—*worry* (e.g., "During tests, I wonder how the other people are doing") and *test-irrelevant thoughts* ("Irrelevant bits of information pop into my head during a test"; see also Zimmer, Hocevar, Bachelor, & Meinke, 1992).

It is useful to measure student anxiety directly because teacher observations are not always reliable. Sarason et al. (1960) found that when asked to rate student

TABLE 11-1 Test Comfort Index (TCI)

1. When the teacher says that she is going to give the class a test, do you feel relaxed and comfortable?
2. Do you feel relaxed before you take a test?
3. Do you feel relaxed while you are taking a test?
4. Do you feel relaxed when the teacher says that she is going to ask you questions to find out how much you know?
5. When the teacher says that she is going to give the class a test, do you usually feel that you will do good work?
6. While you are taking a test, do you usually think you are doing good work?
7. Do you like tests in school?

Reprinted from Harnisch, Hill, and Fyans (1980).

anxiety, teachers often underestimated the anxiety of high-performing students. They suggest that anxiety in bright, high-performing students is the most likely to be overlooked by teachers because their problems usually are not as obvious as those of hostile children who misbehave, or of extremely shy, withdrawn children.

Safe Sally (see Chapter 1) is an example of a high-performing student whose achievement anxiety is likely to be overlooked by the teacher. Although anxiety does not appear to interfere with her performance in the achievement situations that she limits herself to, it does inhibit her from achieving her full potential. Anxiety about performing poorly leads to obsessive studying and preparation, time that could be used for activities that would contribute more to her intellectual development, and it also underlies her avoidance of challenging achievement contexts.

ANXIETY AND ACHIEVEMENT

Considerable evidence indicates that students who have high levels of anxiety in achievement situations perform poorly compared to students who have relatively low levels of anxiety (e.g., Everson, Smodlaka, & Tobias, 1994; Pintrich & de Groot, 1990; see also Hembree, 1988). Demonstrating a link between achievement and anxiety, however, does not establish the causal direction of the association. Do students who have not mastered the material become anxious when they are evaluated? Do anxious students have difficulty learning new material? Or do anxious students have difficulty demonstrating what they know in evaluative situations?

Research suggests that the association between anxiety and achievement is extremely complex (Covington & Omelich, 1988; Everson et al., 1994), but certainly all of the previous questions, to some degree, can be answered with "yes." Anxiety interferes with learning and with the ability to demonstrate understanding. Students who are unprepared and who expect to fail are more likely to experience anxiety than students who are well prepared and self-confident. Anxiety is therefore a cause as well as a consequence of poor preparation.

Tobias (1977, 1980, 1986, 1992) suggests that anxiety interferes with learning and performance at three levels. First, anxiety inhibits the efficient *preprocessing* of new information—that is, of registering and internally representing instructional input. For instance, the student may have difficulty attending to and organizing the material presented. Second, anxiety interferes with *processing*—applying new understanding to generate solutions to problems. The student understands the new material, but when asked to apply it to a specific problem, he is unable to remember what he has learned or is unable to use effective problem-solving strategies. Third, Tobias suggests that anxiety interferes with the *output* of a response. The correct answer may be grasped and then lost before the student verbalizes or records it. Or the student may be able to demonstrate understanding immediately after the material is learned, but has difficulty reproducing it on a summative test given later. When someone claims that her mind "went blank," or that she is "blocking on a name," she is referring to the output level of a response.

Preprocessing and Processing

There is considerable evidence for the effect of anxiety on these three levels of learning and performance. Consider first the preprocessing and processing levels. Several researchers have found that high-anxious students have less effective study skills than students having lower levels of anxiety (Culler & Holahan, 1980; Desiderato & Koskinen, 1969; Naveh-Benjamin, McKeachie, & Lin, 1987; Topman, Kleijn, van der Ploeg, & Masset, 1992), and they also are more prone to using avoidance as a coping strategy (Blankstein, Flett, & Watson, 1992; Zeidner, 1994; see also Zeidner, 1995). In a study by Benjamin, McKeachie, Lin, and Holinger (1981), for example, high-anxious college students reported spending more time studying for exams than did low-anxious students, but the high-anxious students had more problems learning the material. High-anxious students also did more poorly on take-home exams, which presumably tested the students' abilities to analyze and organize information that was in front of them rather than their abilities to retrieve previously learned material.

Research evidence also suggests that high-anxious students are distracted easily when they are learning new material (Dusek, 1980; Dusek, Mergler, & Kermis, 1976; Eysenck, 1988, 1991; see also Hembree, 1988), but that they can be taught strategies that help focus their attention (Dusek, Kermis, & Mergler, 1975). In the Dusek et al. study, for instance, children were asked to memorize the positions of animal drawings in a stimulus array; the performance of high-anxious but not of low-anxious children improved considerably when they were asked to label the drawings as they were placed in the stimulus array. Presumably, the labeling helped the high-anxious children focus their attention on the central stimuli.

Output

Anxiety is believed to interfere in several ways with students' abilities to demonstrate their knowledge. Wine (1980) claims that attention in testing situations is divided between task-relevant and task-irrelevant thoughts. Individuals with high levels of anxiety devote significant amounts of attention to task-irrelevant thoughts, leaving only small amounts of attention for task-relevant responses.

Some task-irrelevant thoughts may not be related directly to concerns about inadequacies or performance. But most test anxiety theorists believe that people with high anxiety levels are preoccupied with "worrying" about their performance, and that this interferes with their abilities to retrieve and demonstrate skills and knowledge (e.g., Zatz & Chasin, 1985; see also Hembree, 1988; Sarason & Sarason, 1990; Schwarzer & Jerusalem, 1992; Tobias, 1986, 1992). Bandura (1988) proposed that individuals with low self-efficacy particularly dwell on their deficiencies and envision failure scenarios in threatening situations, diverting their attention away from their work. Both the thoughts themselves and their physiological effects (e.g., trembling) can interfere with performance.

Highly anxious students also may become obsessed with unimportant aspects of a task, such as their handwriting. Or, in severe cases, they may attend to entirely irrelevant aspects of a task. I once observed a child who was supposed to be answering a set of questions based on a paragraph. Rather than reading the paragraph, he busily counted and recounted the number of words it contained. This activity seemed to offer some relief; at least he was doing something. And by giving the teacher the impression that he was engaged in the task at hand, it delayed the inevitable negative teacher reaction to not completing the assignment. This is the kind of behavior that one might expect of Defensive Dave (see Chapter 1)—designed to promote, if only temporarily, a perception of competence.

Deficiencies in test-taking skills also are believed to account for poor performance (Bruch, Juster, & Kaflowitz, 1983). Students who are anxious in test situations seem to lack such abilities as interpreting instructions accurately, pacing themselves appropriately, and implementing other strategies (e.g., doing the easy questions first).

Summary

The research on anxiety and achievement provides strong evidence that anxiety interferes with both learning and performance. Thus, students who are highly anxious in achievement contexts have difficulty learning new material and often are unable to demonstrate what they have learned. Before discussing possible ways to minimize the debilitating effects of anxiety on learning and performance, our discussion considers some explanations that have been offered for the development of high achievement anxiety in some individuals.

ORIGINS OF ACHIEVEMENT ANXIETY

It already has been suggested that low confidence can cause anxiety in evaluative situations. Nevertheless, some individuals who usually perform well on tests experience severe anxiety, while some individuals who generally do poorly show little evidence of anxiety. Other factors must be involved.

Some theorists have suggested that anxiety has its roots in parent–child relationships. Sarason et al. (1960), for example, proposed that parents of highly anxious children hold unrealistically high expectations of them and are overly critical. The children internalize their parents' negative evaluations and consequently believe that they perform inadequately in achievement situations, regardless of their actual performance. The unconscious hostility toward the parent for being so critical is internalized in the form of anxiety, rather than externalized in overt aggressiveness.

Child-rearing explanations for the cause of achievement anxiety have not been well researched, although there is some evidence. One study found that high anxiety in children was associated with negative parental feedback (e.g., blame, punishment), inconsistency in child rearing, and parents' tendency to control and restrict their children (Krohne, 1992). Another study found that parents who expressed relatively more annoyance, anger, or disappointment and who tried to restrict their children's behaviors (e.g., urging the children to hurry up, giving instructions in a preemptory tone) while they completed homework assignments had more anxious children. Case studies of college students high in anxiety conducted by Anton and Lillibridge (1995), however, suggest that child rearing varies considerably among highly anxious students.

Early school experiences also may affect anxiety. The amount of success versus failure is undoubtedly important. Hill (1972) reported that although not all students who consistently fail become highly anxious, students with high achievement anxiety are more likely to have histories of failure than are students with low anxiety. It is possible that failure early in school affects later performance, partly because students who fail develop a propensity to experience anxiety in evaluative situations, which interferes with their future learning and performance. Given that perceptions of high academic ability decline with age, and that an understanding of ability as a stable capacity is not developed fully until early adolescence (see Chapter 6), it is not surprising that anxiety increases with age (Wigfield & Eccles, 1989, 1990).

But some students with histories of academic success still are highly anxious. The origins of anxiety may be different for high-achieving students. Wigfield and Eccles (1989) suggested that although low-achieving students develop anxiety as a result of repeated failures and low expectations for success, relatively high-performing students may become anxious because of unrealistic parental, peer, or self-imposed expectations that they should excel in all academic areas.

Classroom climate and other school-related factors also may be important. Zatz and Chassin (1985) found that high-anxious students performed more poorly on tests than did low- or medium-anxious students only in classes in which students perceived the threat of evaluation to be high. Helmke (1988) similarly showed that anxiety was especially debilitating in classrooms in which success and failure were very salient.

Wigfield and Eccles (1989) suggest that the transition to junior high school may engender anxiety because the uncertainty of a new school context, including a larger school and many teachers, is compounded with stricter grading, less autonomy, and more formal relationships with teachers. Standardized testing is another feature of school environments that can engender anxiety, especially if strongly emphasized. In high school, standardized tests, such as the Scholastic Aptitude Test (SAT), play a major role in students' long-term educational and occupational options, and are undoubtedly a major source of anxiety for some students.

Gender differences also are found commonly in studies of test anxiety (e.g., Everson, Millsap, & Rodriguez, 1991; Hembree, 1990; Hill & Sarason, 1966; Randhawa, 1994; Wigfield & Meece, 1988; Zeidner & Nevo, 1992; see Hembree, 1988, for a review). Females usually are found to have higher scores on measures of test anxiety than are males, and the difference increases with age and time at school. Sarason et al. (1960) suggest that boys may score lower than girls on measures of test anxiety because they are more reluctant to admit anxiety, not because they actually experience it less. Relatively higher anxiety among girls also could result from their lower perceptions of their abilities (see Chapter 6).

SUBJECT MATTER ANXIETIES

Some individuals develop anxiety about performance in specific subject areas or with regard to particular skills. They may be comfortable in most academic contexts, but have great difficulty performing in one particular domain. Two domains that have been studied are mathematics and writing.

Mathematics

Anxious Alma (see Chapter 1) is in good company. Mathematics anxiety, or "mathophobia," is widespread (Lazarus, 1975). College students report being much more anxious about math than English or social science (Everson, Tobias, Hartman, & Gourgey, 1993), or writing (Sapp, Farrell, & Durand, 1995). It is estimated that about one-third of college students suffer from some level of mathematics anxiety (Anton & Klisch, 1995).

Mathematics does not generate as much anxiety in young children as in older children and adults. In Goodlad's (1984) study of more than 17,000 young students, math was rated about the same as reading in a list of "liked" subjects (after art and physical education). In the National Assessment of Educational Progress, 9-year-olds ranked math as their best-liked subject; 13-year-olds ranked it second best; and in contrast to the younger children, 17-year-olds claimed that it was their least-liked subject (Carpenter et al., 1981). Significant declines in positive attitudes toward mathematics also have been shown during the adolescent years (Brush, 1979; Wigfield & Eccles, 1994; Wigfield, Eccles, Mac Iver, Reuman, & Midgley, 1991). Children are not born with mathematics anxiety. Instead, negative attitudes toward math develop over time, especially during adolescence.

Why does math, in particular, cause so much anxiety in many older students and adults? One only can speculate. Lazarus (1975) points out that mathematics anxiety has a "peculiar social acceptability. Persons otherwise proud of their educational attainments shamelessly confess to being 'no good at math'" (p. 281).

The way that math usually is taught also may explain why math anxiety is common. Lazarus (1975) proposes the cumulative nature of math curricula as one explanation; if you fail to understand one operation, you often are unable to learn anything taught beyond that operation.

From an observational study of math and social studies classes, Stodolsky (1985) proposed that math instruction fostered in students the belief that math is something that is learned from an authority, not figured out on one's own. She found that math classes were characterized by (1) a recitation and seatwork pattern of instruction, (2) a reliance on the teacher to present new concepts or procedures, (3) textbook-centered instruction, (4) textbooks that lacked developmental or instructional material for concept development, (5) a lack of manipulatives, and (6) a lack of social support or small-group work. The instructional format, the types of behavior expected from students, and the materials used also were more similar from day to day in math than in social studies classes. This lack of variety may contribute to anxiety because students who do not function well in the instructional format used in mathematics are not given opportunities to succeed under alternative formats.

Stodolsky (1985) also suggests that mathematics is an area in which ability, in the sense of being a stable trait, is believed to play a dominant role in performance—either one has the ability or one does not. And if one lacks ability in mathematics, nothing can be done about it. (This is what was defined as an "entity" theory of ability in Chapter 6.) In contrast, people generally believe that performance in other subjects, such as reading or social studies, can be improved with practice and effort (i.e., they hold an "incremental" theory of ability).

There is consistent evidence that females suffer more from mathematics anxiety than males (Hembree, 1990; Randhawa, 1994; Wigfield & Meece, 1988). Some researchers have proposed that mathematics anxiety contributes to observed gender differences in mathematics achievement and course enrollment (e.g., Tobias & Weissbrod, 1980), but the one study that actually assessed anxiety and enrollment plans found no association (Meece, Wigfield, & Eccles, 1990).

There is little agreement on the reasons for such gender differences. Ability differences, socialization differences, differences in the level of self-confidence, and the number of math courses taken all have been proposed as explanations (e.g., Parsons, Adler, & Kaczala, 1982). Whatever the reasons for the frequency and intensity of mathematics anxiety, particularly among women, it is a problem that warrants special attention by educational researchers and practitioners.

Writing

Perhaps everyone, at one time in their lives, experiences a certain amount of panic facing a blank piece of paper or computer screen, especially if the due date for a written product—a paper for a class, a report for work—is very near. "Writer's block" is so debilitating for some that they avoid courses and professions that require any amount of writing (see Daly & Miller, 1975b; Daly, Vangelisti, & Witte, 1988; Rose, 1985; Selfe, 1985).

Although psychoanalytic explanations have been suggested (Barwick, 1995; Grundy, 1993), the few studies that have been conducted suggest that writing anxiety reflects some of the same dynamics that explain general achievement anxiety. Writing anxiety, like achievement anxiety, is associated with relatively low expectations for success as well as lower writing quality (Daly, 1985). One study found, further, that high school students who had relatively high levels of writing anxiety reported that they experienced more criticism for their writing and less encouragement and support, and they also reported seeking help for writing problems less than students with low levels of writing anxiety (Daly, 1985). Rose's (1985) research on writer's block makes it very clear that the causes usually are multifaceted, and that although their roots may lie in early familial experiences, later and current experiences in writing contexts are also important.

Researchers have developed a measure of writing anxiety (Daly & Miller, 1975a) that has been shown to be associated more strongly with writing performance than a more general measure of achievement anxiety (Richmond & Dickson-Markman, 1985). Studies using this measure have found some gender differences, with females showing somewhat less writing anxiety than males. Individuals with high levels of writing anxiety also had high levels of reading anxiety and much anxiety about public speaking and interpersonal communication, but relatively low mathematics anxiety (Daly, 1985).

Writing anxiety afflicts teachers as well as students, and affects their behavior. Studies have found, for example, that high-apprehensive female teachers assign fewer writing assignments, and they are more likely to be concerned with issues of form and usage and less likely to emphasize personal or creative expression and effort than are low-apprehensive teachers (see Daly, 1985; Daly et al., 1988). Associations between teachers' own writing anxiety and their teaching methods were strongest in upper elementary school, when many important writing skills are supposed to be taught.

Studies of interventions find that simply taking writing courses decreases writing anxiety, at least temporarily (Basile, 1982; Fox, 1980). Zimmerman and Silverman (1982) report that the writing apprehension of fifth-grade students could be reduced by emphasizing prewriting activities, expressive writing, and positive evaluation (see Daly, 1985).

Although most research on writing anxiety, like most research on general achievement anxiety, has focused on the trait aspects, Daly (1985) points out that contextual variables influence anxiety in particular situations and, over time and collectively, contribute to trait anxiety. He proposes eight dimensions of writing situations that are important:

1. The degree of evaluation perceived to be present in the setting

2. The amount of perceived task ambiguity

3. The degree of conspicuousness experienced by writers

4. The perceived level of task difficulty

5. The amount of prior experience writers believe they have for a task

6. The personal salience or centrality of a task

7. The degree of novelty attached to both setting and task

8. The writers' perceptions of their audiences' likely reactions to and interest in the topic (adapted from Daly, 1985, pp. 43–82)

Teachers may be able to reduce writing anxiety by minimizing students' concerns about evaluation, making assignments and criteria for grading more clear, and making sure that students have the prior experience and familiarity they need to complete the writing task. Writing tasks, similar to all tasks, should be challenging but not so difficult or different from what students previously have experienced that they provoke a sense of incompetence or low expectations for success. A genuine and supportive audience (e.g., classmates, parents) also might help. Most of the strategies (discussed in the next section) that are designed to minimize all types of anxiety in achievement contexts also should reduce writing anxiety.

MINIMIZING THE NEGATIVE
EFFECTS OF ANXIETY

Different problems related to anxiety require different solutions, so it is important to analyze the nature of the problem before planning an intervention or changing classroom practices. Benjamin, McKeachie, and Lin (1987) distinguish, for example, between anxious students who have good study habits but cannot handle evaluative pressure (i.e., whose anxiety interferes with performance in the output phase) and students who do not master the material presented to them (i.e., whose anxiety interferes with the preprocessing and processing phases). More relaxed testing conditions and training in test-taking strategies would be appropriate for the former students, while study skills training would be more appropriate for the latter.

Teachers also need to be aware that the recommendations made for highly anxious students are not necessarily appropriate for students who have low anxiety levels. Indeed, occasionally conditions that maximize performance for highly anxious students undermine performance for students who have low anxiety levels. This is because for some students, a mild amount of anxiety actually facilitates performance.

Preprocessing

Interventions involving instruction on developing good study skills have success-fully reduced anxiety and increased performance among students who have diffi-culty learning new material (see Dendato & Diener, 1986; Naveh-Benjamin, 1991). Naveh-Benjamin (1991), for example, found that study skills training ben-efited highly anxious students with problems in processing information, whereas desensitization was more effective for high-test-anxious students who had prob-lems retrieving previously learned information (see also Algaze, 1995; Vagg & Papsdorf, 1995; Vagg & Spielberger, 1995).

There are other ways to assist students whose anxiety interferes with their abilities to process new information or material. To begin with, highly anxious students can be helped by having opportunities to reinspect material. If new infor-mation is presented in a lecture, it is important for the teacher to pause frequently and encourage questions, and to review the material (Helmke, 1988). If the mate-rial is presented in a film, highly anxious students can be allowed to review the film. If it is presented in written form, they can be encouraged to reread the mate-rial.

Clear, unambiguous instructions and a fair amount of structure also seem to facilitate the processing of new information for anxious students. Teachers also can give explicit instructions for strategies for learning material. In one fifth-grade class I observed the teacher gave students a list of written instructions de-signed to help them learn spelling words (e.g., "look at the word; say the letters to yourself; close your eyes and picture the word; write the word; check your accu-racy").

A self-paced curriculum can be helpful to highly anxious students, especially those who are achieving poorly. Having to keep up with the group can create anxiety. Knowing that new material and demands for performance will be regu-lated according to the student's own mastery should relieve some of this anxiety.

Processing and Output

Much of the research on alleviating anxiety in the output or production phase has involved **desensitization** and relaxation techniques (Algaze, 1995; Deffenbacher & Suinn, 1988; Dendato & Diener, 1986; Gonzalez, 1995; Naveh-Benjamin, 1991; see also Wigfield & Eccles, 1989). Students typically work through a desen-sitization hierarchy, usually in a group setting. For example, they begin by imag-ining that the teacher is announcing a test, and continue to imagine more threatening situations, such as taking home a test with a poor grade. The evidence suggests that desensitization can reduce anxiety, resulting in improvement of per-formance in some cases (see Hembree, 1988).

Cognitive therapies are designed to diminish the worry component of test anxiety—to alleviate preoccupation with performance, ability, or adequacy. Indi-viduals reflect on and analyze their anxiety-provoking and other task-irrelevant thoughts, and they develop coping strategies, such as concentrating on positive thoughts before a test and instructing themselves to attend to the task while studying or taking tests. The strategies are based on the cognitive behavioral modification approach described in Chapter 4 and have been shown to be effective, especially in combination with other treatments (Algaze, 1995; Fletcher & Spielberger, 1995; Vagg & Papsdorf, 1995; Vagg & Spielberger, 1995).

There are other things that teachers can do to alleviate the effects of anxiety at the processing and output stages that are integrated more easily into the classroom curriculum than desensitization or cognitive therapy. One approach is to introduce tasks in a nonthreatening way. I. Sarason (1973, 1975; Sarason & Sarason, 1990) reports that task-irrelevant, self-deprecatory thinking among high-test-anxious individuals is especially likely when tasks are introduced as a test of ability, or when attention is oriented to the evaluative aspect of tasks. In one study he gave a group of college students who were high and low in test anxiety a serial learning task of meaningless words (I. Sarason, 1961). Some students simply were given instructions necessary to respond to the task. Other students were told that the task was a measure of intelligence. High-anxious students who were told that the task measured intelligence performed significantly more poorly than high-anxious students who were given neutral instructions. The instructions had no effect on the low-anxious students' performance.

I. Sarason (1958) demonstrated in another study that instructions designed to allay concerns about ability can enhance the performance of high-anxious students. He eliminated performance differences between high- and low-anxious students by simply suggesting to the high-anxious students that they should relax, even if they do not learn the task immediately, because it is a very difficult task. The low-anxious students actually performed better without the reassuring introduction, presumably because their own motivation was heightened when they assumed that their performance provided information about their abilities.

This study illustrates how the same instructions can have different effects on different students, depending on the levels of anxiety they bring to the task. In general, Sarason and others have found that when preliminary instructions have an evaluative or achievement-orienting aspect, high-test-anxious subjects tend to perform at relatively low levels, whereas a modest evaluation or achievement orientation seems to have positive effects on the performance of low-test-anxious individuals.

Simply reminding students to focus their attention on a task or giving them reassuring directions (e.g., "Don't worry"; "You will do just fine") has been shown to improve the performance of individuals with high anxiety levels (Sarason & Sarason, 1990). Although, similar to the findings of the aforementioned study, the reassuring instructions seemed to undermine the performance of individuals who were low in anxiety—perhaps because they took them at face value and thus exerted less effort.

Giving students opportunities to correct errors also can alleviate anxiety. Students can be allowed to correct their own papers in some situations, and to redo incorrectly solved problems before their responses are turned in to the teacher. Permitting students to improve written assignments before a final grade is given also will alleviate anxiety.

Individualized interventions are also useful for students, such as Alma, who are debilitated severely by anxiety. In such extreme cases, a teacher may need to implement an individual anxiety-reduction plan, preferably one that is discussed and developed with the student. In Alma's case, for instance, the teacher might suggest a book on relaxation techniques. He privately may make arrangements to give her extra time on tests, or an opportunity to retake a test on which she believes she has not shown what she knows. The teacher also might help Alma build self-confidence by asking her to assist a student who is having difficulty with assignments. Whatever individual arrangements are made, they will be effective only if the classroom climate is generally positive and supportive.

Alleviating Test Anxiety

Several techniques have been developed to alleviate the debilitating effects of anxiety in testing situations. Tests should be presented as a means of assessing current understanding—to help students plan future efforts and to guide the teacher's instructional plans—not as the final assessment of students' competencies.

Having to rely entirely on memory in a testing context can create unnecessary anxiety, and memory supports have been shown to be helpful in alleviating anxiety (Gross & Mastenbrook, 1980; Sieber et al., 1977). Thus, a highly anxious student might perform better on a mathematics task if she is allowed to refer to a sample problem; she might do better on a set of questions related to a reading assignment if she is allowed to review the text on which the questions are based. Even when questions are constructed in such a way that having books and notes available is not very helpful, students often are more secure knowing that they have access to them.

Providing an opportunity to retake a test can enhance motivation and improve test scores, in part because it relieves anxiety. Covington and Omelich (1984b) found that undergraduate psychology students who were allowed to retake their midterm after several days of studying were more self-confident and ultimately received significantly higher scores than students who were not given this option.

Hill (1980, 1984) has conducted many studies on the effect of testing conditions on the performance of anxious children. In all of his studies the high-anxious students' performance improved considerably under optimal testing conditions. Three features of testing consistently have been shown to affect the performance of high-anxious students: (1) time limits; (2) difficulty of the test material; and (3) test instructions, question-and-answer formats, and other mechanics (e.g., computerized responses).

Hill and Eaton (1977) investigated the effects of time pressure on the performance of upper-elementary school students on an arithmetic computation test. When students were pressured for time, the high-anxious students took twice as long to do the problems and made three times as many errors as the low-anxious children. When there was no time pressure, high-anxious students worked almost as fast as low-anxious students and made only a few more errors. Several subsequent studies provide further evidence that relaxing time pressure improves the performance of high-anxious students (Plass & Hill, 1986; see Hill, 1984, for a review).

Because anxiety interferes with learning only on relatively difficult subject matter, the order of easy and difficult problems may affect performance. One study found that students who are prone to anxiety performed better on tasks that began with easy problems and became progressively more difficult than on tasks in which some difficult problems were placed early in the test (Lund, 1953, cited in Phillips, Pitcher, Worsham, & Miller, 1980). Zigler and Harter (1969) found that children's IQ test performance could be improved by simply adjusting the order of questions so that an easy question followed several consecutive incorrect responses.

Finally, test instructions and the test format can affect the performance of highly anxious students. Unfamiliar question formats, computerized answer sheets, and other unfamiliar aspects of standardized achievement tests can be intimidating, especially to students who are prone to anxiety. Hill's research (reviewed in Hill, 1984) suggested that many students perform below their capacity on standardized tests because they do not understand instructions or do not know how to use the answer sheets.

CONCLUSION

Not all anxiety is debilitating. For some students a modest amount of anxiety can motivate optimal performance. But anxiety also can interfere with learning and performance. One of the teacher's many tasks is to minimize the debilitating effects of anxiety. A general principle is to remove, as much as possible, the threat that failure can have on the student's ego. The strategies to diminish anxiety discussed in this chapter are summarized in Appendix 11–A.

TABLE 11-2 Summary of Terms

Term	Definition
Trait anxiety	Proneness to a state of anxiety in evaluative contexts—a relatively stable personality characteristic
State anxiety	A temporal state of anxiety in a particular evaluative context
Desensitization	Gradual introduction of increasingly threatening images and thoughts along with images and thoughts related to overcoming the threat

CHAPTER 12

Communicating Expectations

Teachers' expectations about students' learning can have profound implications for what students actually learn. Expectations affect the content and pace of the curriculum, the organization of instruction, evaluation, instructional interactions with individual students, and many subtle and not-so-subtle messages that affect students' own expectations for learning, and thus their behaviors.

The effect of teacher expectations on student learning was first demonstrated experimentally in a classic study by Rosenthal and Jacobson (1968). Elementary school teachers were told that some of the students in their class had shown on a written test that they had remarkable potential for academic growth. The designated students actually had been selected randomly, but 8 months later the students in the early grades for whom teachers were led to hold artificially high expectations showed greater gains in IQ than other students in the school. These students, in a sense, fulfilled their teachers' prophecies. This study has spawned virtually hundreds of studies on teachers' **self-fulfilling prophecies** (see Brophy, 1983b, Cooper & Tom, 1984, Dusek, 1975, 1985, Jussim, 1991, and Wigfield & Harold, 1992, for reviews).

Also providing evidence for the effects of teacher expectations on student learning are studies of naturally occurring variations in teachers' expectations. In some studies, for example, high teacher expectations at the beginning of the year predicted better performance at the end of the year than would have been predicted by prior performance and motivation (Jussim & Eccles, 1992; see also Jussim & Eccles, 1995; Jussim, Madon, & Chatman, 1994). Such findings suggest that teachers' expectations somehow affected how much students learned. Studies of effective schools also find that expectations for student learning is one of the strongest predictors of student achievement. Students attending schools in which teachers expect all students to learn achieve at higher levels than students attending schools in which teachers do not hold uniformly high expectations (Edmonds,

1979; Madaus, Airasian, & Kellaghan, 1980; Marks, Doane, & Secada, in press; Rutter, Maughan, Mortimore, Ouston, & Smith, 1979).

Expecting all students to learn does not mean expecting the exact same pace and style of learning, or the same level of achievement for all students. Good teachers make fine-tuned, well-informed judgments, which vary among their students, about the appropriate content and pace of instruction. But good teachers do expect all students to master the curriculum.

This chapter summarizes research on the bases and stability of teachers' expectations, how expectations affect teacher behavior, and how students perceive differential teacher behavior. It also suggests strategies for ensuring that appropriate and well-informed judgments, rather than erroneous expectations based on stereotypes or inaccurate information, are used to plan instruction.

WHAT ARE TEACHERS' EXPECTATIONS BASED ON?

Teachers' expectations about individual students are based primarily on students' past academic performance (Brophy, 1983b; Jussim & Eccles, 1992; Jussim, Eccles, & Madon, 1996; Parsons, Kaczala, & Meece, 1982; West & Anderson, 1976). Previous performance is usually the least biased and most appropriate information available. Its value in guiding instructional decisions, however, is limited. Many of the approaches to assessing students' competencies that are used in schools (e.g., multiple choice tests) do not give students sufficient or appropriate opportunities to demonstrate what they know, and thus underestimate their skills. Even when performance assessments provide an accurate picture, for students who have received poor instruction in the past, assessments may lead teachers to underestimate the pace of instruction or the difficulty level of the material they could handle in a more effective instructional program. This is why teachers continually need to create opportunities for students to disprove their assumptions about what and how quickly they can learn.

Irrelevant factors, such as sibling's performance (Thurlow, Christensen, & Ysseldyke, 1983), physical attractiveness (Dusek & Joseph, 1983), and stereotypes also have been shown to play a role in teachers' expectations about student learning (see Jussim et al., 1994, for a review). There is evidence, for instance, that teachers tend to perceive boys to have more talent in mathematics than girls, and girls to exert more effort (e.g., Jussim & Eccles, 1992). Most studies on gender examine differential teacher behavior directly, rather than teacher expectations as a mediator. These studies are summarized later in the chapter.

More research has been conducted on the effects of racial stereotypes on teacher expectations than on gender bias. One methodology that has been used is to give teachers written descriptions of students. The race of the student is manipulated by using a photograph, videotape, or audiotape varying the dialect of the speaker. Most of these studies find that teachers express higher expectations for the white child, despite all relevant information being equivalent (Baron, Tom, & Cooper, 1985; Dusek & Joseph, 1983; McCombs & Gay, 1988). Survey research assessing teachers' expectations for their own students report similar disparities in teachers' judgments of African American and Caucasian students, although the differences are similar to differences in objective measures of performance (e.g., Jussim, Eccles, & Madon, 1996).

African American males may be particularly vulnerable to low teacher expectations. Black males were the least likely to be praised by most of the first-grade teachers in a study by Grant (1985), and they engaged in a lower proportion of interactions with teachers relative to peers. Irvine (1990) found that teachers' initial impressions of black males were also more persistent than were their initial impressions of other students. Findings of a study by Garibaldi (1993) suggested that teachers may underestimate what African American males can and want to achieve academically. Half of the African American high school students in his New Orleans study claimed that their teachers did not set high enough goals for them and they wished their teachers would push them harder.

Studies also suggest that teachers have relatively low expectations for children from low-income families (Comer, 1993; Williams, 1976; Winfield, 1986). Winfield (1986), for example, described teachers who did not believe that their high-risk inner-city students could learn at all; they gave up altogether, or they tried to shift responsibility away from themselves by referring students for psychological testing or special education.

Because race and social class are associated strongly, it is difficult to identify the variable most affecting teachers' expectations. In a meta-analysis of studies assessing the role of stereotypes in teachers' expectations, Dusek and Joseph (1983), however, concluded that social class was more powerful than ethnicity, and also more powerful than gender and physical attractiveness.

There is considerable variation in the degree to which teachers have differential expectations based on gender, race, or class stereotypes, and to a considerable degree, the size of differences based on race and social class in teacher judgments correspond closely to the size of differences found in objective measures of performance (Jussim et al., 1996). To a significant degree, teacher judgments reflect a reality that exists for other reasons. When actual effects of teacher expectations are demonstrated, they are usually modest.

Modest effects, nevertheless, can be important. Initially, there is some evidence that girls, African Americans, and low-income students may be more susceptible to teacher expectation influences than boys, Caucasians, and higher-income students (Jussim et al., 1996). Also, modest effects may become large if they accumulate over time. And classroom teacher expectancy effects often are supplemented by the effects of larger institutional practices, such as the distribution of resources among schools and opportunities within schools created by such practices as tracking. Teachers, therefore, need to be vigilant about stereotypes and other irrelevant information affecting their judgments about students.

Teachers' Self-Efficacy

Another factor that affects teachers' expectations for their students' learning is their belief about their own competencies and control over how much their students learn. New teachers who are overwhelmed and not well prepared sometimes believe that teachers (in general) can teach children effectively, but they themselves lack the skills, patience, or other qualities required to help students master the curriculum. Some teachers have low expectations for students' learning because they perceive parents as unable or unwilling to support students' academic efforts (Ashton, 1985; Ashton & Webb, 1986; Gibson & Dembo, 1984; Guskey & Passaro, 1994). Many of the teachers in an intervention study by Weinstein, Madison, and Kuklinski (1995) did not believe that changes in their own practices would be sufficient to overcome parent and student factors outside of their control. In their intervention designed to raise teachers' expectations for student learning, a major task was getting teachers to shift the locus of blame and responsibility from low-achieving students and families to an analysis of their own teaching practices.

Teachers also may have low expectations because they believe school resources (e.g., assisting personnel, curriculum materials, space, administrative support for their own professional development) are not sufficient for them to teach students effectively, or that class size is too large (Marks et al., in press). The broader community context, including the availability of health and other services, also can affect teachers' self-efficacy and expectations for students' learning. Regularly confronting students who are on drugs; who are victims, witnesses, or perpetrators of violence; who are emotionally distraught or hungry; or who have chronic health problems can challenge the self-confidence, resolve, and expectations for success of the most competent teacher.

Teachers' beliefs about the malleability of students' abilities also can affect their self-efficacy as well as their expectations about their students' achievement potential. Teachers, like students, vary in the degree to which they see ability as being a fixed, inherited trait that students (and teachers) cannot do much about (i.e., an "entity" theory) versus being a set of skills that can be developed by good teaching and practice (i.e., an "incremental" theory). Teachers who believe that students' native abilities limit their potential for mastering the curriculum may not believe they can do much to help some students learn.

Teachers' self-efficacy is important because it affects their behaviors. Ashton (1985; Ashton & Webb, 1986), for instance, found that teacher self-efficacy was associated with teachers' choice of instructional activities, amount of effort expended in teaching, student encouragement, and the degree of persistence maintained when confronted with difficulties in the classroom. Teachers with high self-efficacy have been observed in other studies to be less overtly controlling of student behavior in the classroom (Woolfolk & Hoy, 1990) and more effective in leading students to correct responses in classroom discussions (Gibson & Dembo, 1984). There is also evidence that differential treatment of high and low achievers may occur more in teachers with relatively low self-efficacy. In the Ashton and

Webb (1986) study, for example, teachers with low self-efficacy called on low-achieving students less often, assigned more busy work to low-achieving students, and in general interacted and gave more appropriate praise and feedback to high-achieving than low-achieving students.

In summary, teachers' expectations for student learning come from many sources that vary substantially in their validity. The problem is not that teachers have expectations; it is that expectations sometimes are based on erroneous or incomplete information, that instructional decisions and other teacher behaviors are based on these invalid judgments, and, as the next section shows, that expectations are resistant to change.

STABILITY OF EXPECTATIONS

Inaccurate expectations often are not corrected because teachers create situations in which only confirming evidence is possible. For instance, teachers sometimes develop strong "theories" about students and structure the learning environment in a way that does not allow information that is contrary to their theory to emerge. Thus, for example, students assigned to the lowest reading group never may have an opportunity to demonstrate that they could manage more difficult text and tasks.

Students' opportunities can be limited severely by teachers' unchallenged assumptions. I once observed a first grader who had made no progress in 6 months of reading instruction. The teacher knew that the child had been exposed prenatally to drugs; she was convinced that the drugs caused brain damage and that the child's extremely poor reading skills were inevitable. She consequently made no effort to experiment with alternative approaches to reading instruction with him and, therefore, denied him any opportunity to disconfirm her theory. The school psychologist eventually intervened and gave the child a sixth-grade student tutor. In 2 months he was reading at the same level as his classmates in the lowest reading group. He did not excel, but he did learn to read and might not have if the teacher had continued to base curriculum decisions on her original theory.

Expectations also bias what teachers see and how they interpret what they see. Consequently, teachers might not notice information contrary to their theories, even if it is present. Classrooms are busy places. Jackson (1968) claimed that a single elementary school teacher may engage in more than 1,000 interpersonal exchanges a day with students. Under such conditions, certain biases are likely to affect what the teacher notices. For instance, teachers are more likely to monitor closely students who they expect to fool around than students who they expect to be on task. They are, therefore, more likely to notice the off-task behavior of the former than of the latter group, and thus maintain their perceptions of the former as being easily distracted.

Expectations also can bias interpretations of students' behaviors. For example, researchers have shown that outside observers tend to interpret people's behaviors in terms of a stable disposition (e.g., "She is misbehaving because she is a difficult or poorly adjusted child"), whereas actors are more likely to focus on the specific aspects of the situation as causes (e.g., "I pulled my classmate's hair because she took my favorite pencil"). They refer to this bias as the **actor–observer effect** (Ross, 1977; Ross & Nisbett, 1991).

Given the tendency to assume stable traits, teachers can be expected to interpret behavior in ways that are consistent with their prior beliefs. Thus, if a student whom the teacher believes is very bright gives a wrong answer, the teacher is likely to attribute the wrong answer to a nonability-related cause, such as inattention. The same answer from a student perceived to be less intelligent may be interpreted as confirmation of the student's limited ability. Biases in how teachers interpret student behavior, just like biases in what teachers notice, contribute to the stability of teachers' judgments about students.

In addition to being fairly stable, teachers' judgments affect their own behaviors toward students—sometimes in appropriate ways that enhance learning, sometimes in ways that inhibit students' academic growth. The next section summarizes research on teacher behavior that is associated with their expectations and is likely to affect student learning.

HOW DO TEACHERS' EXPECTATIONS AFFECT STUDENT LEARNING?

The term "self-fulfilling prophecy" is apt because once an expectation develops, even if it is wrong, people behave as if the belief was true. In so behaving they actually can cause their expectancies to be fulfilled. Self-fulfilling prophecies occur only if the original expectation was erroneous and a change was brought about in the student's behavior as a consequence of the expectation.

Researchers have studied the ways in which teachers' beliefs about students affect their behaviors toward students. Some kinds of differential behavior toward students who vary in their mastery of the curriculum are appropriate and productive. Giving some students more advanced material than others is clearly necessary when there is variability in student skill level, and students need different amounts and kinds of teacher assistance and attention. Nevertheless, most of the teacher behaviors described later, which have been shown to be associated with high versus low expectations, cannot be defended as appropriate individualization.

Teacher Behavior Toward High- and Low-Expectancy Students

Rosenthal (1974) divided teacher behavior associated with high or low expectations into four categories: socioemotional climate, inputs, outputs, and affective feedback. Examples of each of the four categories are described as follows (see also Good, 1987).

Socioemotional Climate

◆ Smiling and nodding

◆ Friendliness

Inputs

◆ Distance of seat from teacher

◆ Amount of teacher interaction

◆ Amount of information given to learn or number of problems to complete

◆ Difficulty and variability of assignments

Outputs

◆ Calling on during class discussions

◆ Providing clues, and repeating or rephrasing questions

◆ Time waited for student to respond to teacher question

◆ Level of detail and accuracy of feedback

Affective Feedback

◆ Amount of criticism

◆ Amount (and basis) of praise

◆ Pity or anger expressed for low performance

Some of these differential behaviors have direct effects on learning, and consequently widen the gap between relatively low- and high-achieving students. For example, students who are given more clues and more opportunities to learn, and who are called on more frequently, should learn more than students who are given fewer opportunities to learn. Other teacher behaviors, such as those affecting the socioemotional climate or affective feedback, influence learning indirectly by affecting students' own beliefs about their competencies, their expectations for success, and consequently their effort and other achievement behaviors.

Teachers vary greatly in the degree to which they treat low- and high-expectancy students differently, and also in the nature of their differential treatment. The teachers in some studies paid more attention to high-expectancy students, and in other studies teachers evidenced "compensatory" behaviors, focusing more on low-expectancy students (see Babad, 1992).

Even behaviors designed to provide extra support for low-expectancy students, however, can undermine learning. First, such compensatory behavior sometimes is accompanied by subtle negative behaviors or expressions. Babad (1992), for example, observed that teachers often displayed negative emotions (e.g., hostility, tenseness, anxiety, condescension) while they invested greater time and attention to relatively low-achieving students. Second, low-performing students can interpret teacher behavior that is meant to protect their feelings or help them learn as evidence of their low competencies, and this in turn lowers their own expectations and effort. Behavior reflecting the best intentions, ironically, can do the most harm.

Well-Meaning But Counterproductive Teacher Behaviors

Consider, for example, the research on pity and anger mentioned in Chapter 5. Recall that children as young as 6 years understand that anger is aroused when another's failure is attributed to controllable factors, such as lack of effort, and that by about the age of 9 years children understand that pity is aroused when another's failure is perceived to be caused by uncontrollable causes (Weiner et al., 1982; see also Graham, 1990, 1994; Graham & Weiner, 1993). Graham (1984a) demonstrated in an experiment that pity, which usually is meant to protect students' positive feelings about themselves, actually can have the opposite effect. An experimenter expressed either mild anger or pity to children who had experienced failure. Children who had the sympathetic experimenter were more likely to attribute their failure to a lack of ability than children who had an angry experimenter. The latter were more likely to attribute their failure to a lack of effort. Children who received pity also had lower expectations for success in the future than children who received an angry response from the experimenter. By simply expressing an emotion, the experimenter affected children's perceptions of the cause of their failure and consequently their expectations regarding future outcomes. The sympathetic emotion had the more negative effects.

This process can be illustrated by a teacher's likely responses to Satisfied Santos and Helpless Hannah (see Chapter 1) for turning in a math assignment that is only half completed. The teacher, believing that Santos is capable of finishing the task, attributes the incomplete paper to his typical halfhearted effort. With exasperation in her voice, the teacher threatens Santos with punishment: "If you don't finish your assignment tomorrow, you'll stay after school until it is finished." Santos knows that the teacher is angry because she thinks that he did not exert much effort and could have finished the assignment if he had tried. The teacher's emotional response, therefore, serves to reinforce Santos's own confidence in his ability.

A different reaction might occur in Hannah's case. The teacher is likely to believe that Hannah is unable to do any better, and might tell her sympathetically not to worry about not being able to complete the task. Hannah interprets the teacher's sympathy as evidence of the teacher's low perceptions of her competence, thus reinforcing her own doubts about her ability to do the assigned work.

A related counterintuitive finding concerns the effect of praise. In some circumstances there appear to be negative side effects of praise, at least for older children and adults. As mentioned in Chapter 3, praise for successful performance on an easy task can be interpreted by a student as evidence that the teacher has a low perception of his ability. As a consequence, it actually can lower rather than enhance self-confidence. Criticism following a poor performance, under some circumstances, can be interpreted as an indication of the teacher's high perception of the student's ability.

Praise and criticism can have these paradoxical effects because of their link with effort attributions, and because, as mentioned in Chapter 6, individuals perceive effort and ability to be related inversely. Recall that if two students achieve the same outcome, the one who tried harder is judged by children over about the age of 11 as being lower in ability (Nicholls & Miller, 1984a). Research has shown, accordingly, that children older than about 11 (but not younger) rate a child who was praised by the teacher as being lower in ability than a child who was not praised, and they rate a child who was criticized as being higher in ability than a child the teacher did not criticize (Barker & Graham, 1987).

The potential for negative effects of praise and positive effects of criticism on children's self-confidence also was shown in a naturalistic study by Parsons, Kaczala, & Meece (1982). They found in the twenty fifth- to ninth-grade mathematics classrooms they observed that the amount of criticism of the quality of students' work was related positively to students' self-perceptions of their math abilities and future expectations, unless the criticism was in reaction to a student-initiated question. Praise related to work was associated positively with mathematical self-concept for boys but not for girls. The researchers concluded that teachers who believe that they should avoid criticism and give praise freely overlook the power of the context and of students' interpretations of the meaning of the message. They suggest that well-chosen criticism can convey as much positive information as praise.

Helping behavior also can give students a message that they are perceived as being low in ability, and it can undermine the positive achievement-related emotions associated with success. Meyer (1982) describes a study by Conty in which the experimenter offered unsolicited help either to the subject or to another individual in the room working on the same task. Subjects who were offered help claimed to experience negative emotions (e.g., incompetence, anger, worry, disappointment, distress, anxiety) more, and positive emotions (e.g., confidence, joy, pride, superiority, satisfaction) less, than subjects who observed another person being helped. Graham and Barker (1990) report that children as young as 6 years rated a student they observed being offered help to be lower in ability than another student who was not offered help.

Again, an attributional analysis explains the effect of help on ability judgments and emotional reactions. Research has shown that in various contexts individuals are more likely to help others when their need is perceived to be caused by uncontrollable factors, such as low ability, than when their need is attributed to controllable factors, such as insufficient effort (see Weiner, 1986, 1992). This was shown in a classroom study by Brophy and Rohrkemper (1981). They reported, for instance, that teachers expressed a greater commitment to helping "problem" students when the causes of need were presumed to be uncontrollable, such as low ability or shyness, than when the problems were attributed to controllable factors, such as lack of effort.

There are many other ways that teachers unintentionally can communicate low expectations. Good and Brophy (1978) describe the behavior of a physics professor who believed that females have difficulty with physics. To avoid embarrassing them, he never called on them to answer a mathematical question or to explain difficult concepts. He also showed his concern by looking at one of the girls after he introduced a new point and asking, "Do you understand?" (p. 75). Such "helpful" behavior undoubtedly gave the females in the class a clear negative message about the teacher's perception of their competencies.

Ability Grouping and Tracking

Although ability grouping can help teachers differentiate instruction, simply assigning a student to a group can create a self-fulfilling prophecy. Even though teachers are usually responsible for students' reading group placement, there is evidence that by the end of the year the placement itself predicts teachers' as well as parents' perceptions of students' competencies, over and above the effect of students' initial skills (Pallas, Entwisle, Alexander, & Stluka, 1994; see also Alexander, Dauber, & Entwisle, 1993; Pallas, Entwisle, Alexander, & Stluka, 1994). Weinstein (1976) found that the reading group to which students were assigned contributed 25 percent to the prediction of midyear achievement over and above the students' initial readiness scores. That ability grouping is used more frequently for reading than for math instruction may explain why some studies find that teacher expectations have a stronger impact on reading achievement than on math achievement (Smith, 1980).

Ability group placement affects learning in part because teachers often perceive all members of a group to be equivalent, despite the considerable variation that usually exists within groups. Because teachers' expectations are influenced by group placement itself, they often do not monitor individual progress as much as they should, and they do not adjust instruction or move a student to another group when the student would benefit from different instructional input.

Another problem with ability grouping is that teachers often vary the nature and pace of instruction between groups more than is necessary or appropriate. In general, studies find that students in high reading groups receive more effective instruction than students in low reading groups. Reading lessons for high compared to low groups have been observed to be structured more loosely, to involve more meaningful questions and opportunities to connect reading to personal experiences, and to be more fun. Decoding skills, rather than meaning, often are stressed more with the "low" group (Borko & Eisenhart, 1986; Dreeben & Barr, 1988; Hiebert, 1983; McDermott, 1987).

There is similar evidence indicating that students in low-ability tracks are taught differently than students in high-ability tracks. Again, some differences, such as the pace of the curriculum, may reflect appropriate accommodations to students' learning needs. But many differences in teacher behavior toward students are unnecessary and constrain the achievement of students in the low-ability track.

Consider, for instance, Oakes' (1990) analysis of survey data from 6,000 math and science classes in 1,200 U.S. elementary, junior high, and senior high schools. Teachers of low-ability math and science classes claimed to emphasize students' own interests less than other teachers. They also placed less emphasis on developing inquiry skills and problem solving, developing skills for communicating math and science ideas, and preparing students for further study in math and science. She reported, furthermore, that in secondary schools, students in low-ability track science and math classes spent more time than students in high-ability track classes engaging in solitary seatwork, doing worksheets, and taking tests or quizzes. In science classes, they spent less time engaging in hands-on activities and more time reading. In a previous study she found that teachers of high-track classes more often included competence and autonomous thinking among the most important curricular goals for students (Oakes, 1985).

Research further suggests that students in different tracks experience differences in teachers' behaviors. Vanfossen, Jones, and Spade (1987), for example, report from national survey data that college-track students were more likely than other students to describe their teachers as patient, respectful, clear in their presentations, and enjoying their work. These differential behaviors are not necessary and they undoubtedly exacerbate the existing differences between high and low achievers.

DO TEACHERS TREAT GIRLS AND BOYS DIFFERENTLY?

Differences in teachers' expectations may underlie the differences in teacher behavior toward boys and girls that have been observed in some studies. Differential teacher behavior may, in turn, explain girls' lower perceptions of their competencies and lower expectations for success, especially in math and science (see Chapter 6), as well as their substantially lower participation rates in higher-level mathematics and science courses and careers (Kahle, 1996a).

Classroom observation studies suggest that differential treatment of girls and boys in math and science is common. Researchers have found in some observation studies that teachers talk to, call on, engage in longer interactions, praise, and give more corrective feedback to boys than to girls (e.g., Jones & Wheatley, 1990; Kahle, 1990; Leinhardt, Seewald, & Engel, 1979; Morse & Handley, 1985; Stallings, 1985; Tobin, Kahle, & Fraser, 1990). Becker (1981) observed, for example, that although there were no differences in student-initiated interactions with teachers in a sample of geometry classes, 63 percent of the teacher-initiated academic contacts were with boys. Girls received 30 percent of the encouraging comments and 84 percent of the discouraging comments. Morse and Hadley reported that female student-initiated interactions with science teachers declined from 41 percent to 30 percent of the total from the seventh to the eighth grades (see Kahle & Meece, 1993, and Kimball, 1989, for reviews). Some differential teacher behavior can be very subtle. Ethnographies describe teachers leaning forward, looking into eyes, and nodding and smiling to boys more than to girls in science classes (see Kahle, 1996a).

Parsons, Kaczala, & Meece (1982) found that student gender was related only modestly to student–teacher interaction patterns they studied in mathematics classrooms for the fifth to ninth grades, but differences in teacher treatment and in math self-concept were more prominent among the students for whom teachers held relatively high expectations. Among the relatively high-achieving students, girls were praised less and had lower perceptions of their math competencies than boys. These may be the very girls who otherwise would have aspired to a career involving mathematics or science.

Brophy (1985) points out that some differential behavior toward boys and girls may reflect teacher reactions to differences in boys' and girls' behaviors (e.g., volunteering to answer questions). Researchers have reported that a major source of gender differences in classroom interaction was boys' domination of discussion (see Kahle, 1996b).

Eccles and Blumenfeld (1985) suggest that gender differences in the subjective meaning of teacher behavior may be as important as gender differences in teacher behavior per se. They found, for example, that girls tended to be more reactive to criticism and less reactive to praise than boys. Equal amounts of praise and criticism, therefore, could cause gender differences in performance expectations.

The same instructional approach also may have different effects on girls and boys. Eccles and Blumenfeld (1985) report that in classrooms in which there were considerable differences between girls' and boys' own expectations, teachers were unusually critical, often using sarcasm to "put a student in his or her place" (p. 108). In classrooms in which gender differences in expectations were not found, teachers engaged in more private, conference-like interactions, and in public question-and-answer sessions they called on all students rather than relying on volunteers.

There is also more direct evidence that teachers' beliefs about gender differences affect student learning, and that boys are not always the beneficiaries of gender-related expectations. Palardy (1969), for instance, studied five first-grade teachers who thought that boys could learn to read just as successfully as girls, and five who expected girls to be more successful. Although students were comparable on reading readiness scores taken in September, by March boys in classrooms in which teachers expected girls to read better actually performed more poorly on a reading achievement test than did girls; in the other classrooms no difference was found in boys' and girls' reading achievement scores.

In summary, there is evidence that some teachers behave differently toward girls and boys, but it is not clear to what degree their differential behaviors are a result of differences in boys' and girls' behaviors in class. It is also possible that the same behavior and instructional practices can have different effects on boys and girls so that equal treatment leads to different outcomes.

STUDENTS' PERCEPTIONS OF TEACHERS' EXPECTATIONS

"I can basically do whatever I want because they just figure I'm doing something for the school," claims a high-status high school student in an ethnography by Eckert (1989, p. 115). The student was clearly aware that he was given favorable treatment as the result of teachers' positive expectations. Presumably other students were equally convinced that they would not be given the benefit of the doubt.

Research has shown that students are aware of teachers' differential behavior toward high and low achievers, and that their perceptions of their teachers' behaviors affect their own expectations (Weinstein, 1985, 1989, 1993; see also Babad, 1990, 1992). The following are examples of some of the differential treatment students in one study claimed to observe in their own class (Weinstein & Middlestadt, 1979):[1]

- ◆ High achievers are granted special privileges.

- ◆ High achievers are allowed to make up their own projects.

- ◆ The teacher is concerned more that low achievers learn something than enjoy themselves.

- ◆ The teacher asks high achievers to suggest or direct activities.

- ◆ The teacher allows high achievers to do as they like as long as they complete the assigned work.

- ◆ High achievers spend more time discussing outside student activities than class-related materials.

---

[1] A copy of the questionnaire can be obtained from Professor Rhona Weinstein, Psychology Department, University of California, Berkeley, CA 94720.

- The teacher gives high achievers enough opportunity to respond before calling on someone else.

- The teacher trusts high achievers.

- The teacher collects work before low achievers have had a chance to finish.

- Low achievers are not expected to complete their work.

Teachers are not necessarily aware of such differential treatment. Babad (1992) found in the classrooms she studied that students and teachers usually agreed that low-expectancy students received more learning support and less pressure than high-expectancy students. But although teachers claimed that they provided more emotional support for high-expectancy students, students perceived the opposite.

The classrooms Weinstein (1985, 1988) has studied varied greatly in the degree to which students perceived the teacher as behaving differently toward high and low achievers. The more teachers were perceived as treating high and low achievers differently, the closer students' expectations for themselves were aligned with their teacher's expectations for them (Brattesani, Weinstein, & Marshall, 1984). Perceived differences in teacher treatment, therefore, appeared to affect students' self-perceptions.

The kinds of differential behavior students perceive toward relatively high- and low-achieving students certainly have the potential for widening performance gaps. Consider, for example, differences in autonomy and respect. The evidence in Chapter 11 points to the importance of these two variables in students' motivation. If the classrooms Weinstein and her colleagues have studied are typical, then high-achieving students are provided an instructional context that is more supportive of motivation than the instructional context provided for low-achieving students. Added to the aforementioned evidence suggesting different instructional input, it is not surprising that high- and low-achieving students' achievement difference increase with time in school.

Can the negative effects of teachers' expectations be avoided? Good and Brophy (1986) described three types of teachers with regard to expectations. The first group is *proactive*. Such teachers do not allow expectations to undermine effective interactions with children and appropriate instructional activities. The second group is *reactive*. They allow existing differences between high and low achievers to influence their own behaviors in ways that can undermine the learning of relatively low-achieving students. For instance, high achievers have more response opportunities simply because they raise their hands more often than low achievers. In the third group, *overreactive* teachers provide qualitatively and quantitatively different instruction as a function of their expectations. The proceeding section offers a few suggestions to help teachers become proactive and avoid negative consequences of teacher expectations.

AVOIDING THE NEGATIVE
EFFECTS OF EXPECTATIONS

1. **Communicate high expectations.** Teachers should communicate positive beliefs, expectations, and attributions in their interactions with students. They can do this explicitly, by telling students that they know they will be able to achieve a particular outcome, or implicitly, by providing opportunities to work on challenging tasks, by encouraging them to persist when they encounter difficulty, by calling on all students, not just those who can be depended on for the right answer, by praising only performance that truly deserves praise, and in countless other subtle ways by conveying confidence in students' ability to succeed at classroom tasks.

2. **Maintain high standards.** Teachers often set low standards to ensure that they protect the self-esteem of their students. My view is that self-esteem is an American obsession that seriously undermines rather than contributes to self-confidence in students. Too many teachers, in my opinion, request and accept performance below what students are capable of achieving, asserting that more challenging work will threaten their self-confidence.

   As a result of these well-intentioned but misguided practices, students adopt low standards for themselves, and the fragile self-confidence they develop is shattered in the first situation in which they are held to higher standards. Students take their cues regarding acceptable performance primarily from their teacher, and at best will work to (and not above) whatever standards are set.

   Genuine and robust self-confidence comes from encountering, persisting with, and ultimately meeting challenges. This requires instruction, tasks, and standards that students can achieve, but only with genuine effort and persistence. To ensure that students realistically can achieve classroom standards, the teacher must monitor carefully students' efforts, understanding, and task completion.

3. **Base judgments of children's skill levels on valid and reliable information.** Some educational specialists recommend that teachers purposefully remain ignorant of all past information on students' academic performance to avoid self-fulfilling prophecies. I would not make that recommendation because such information can be useful. Comments from previous teachers can help a new teacher initially structure an appropriate instructional program for a student. Test scores and other information in students' records also can be informative. But the new teacher should assess carefully the reliability of all existing information. And this information should not be seen as the "truth," but rather as hypotheses about the student that the student is given ample opportunities to disprove.

Information suggesting poor past performance should be interpreted as a problem to be solved, not as a prediction for the future. As mentioned previously, low achievement may be the result of poor teaching or inadequate opportunities to demonstrate competencies. Students who previously have performed poorly may flourish in a new educational context, if given a chance.

Teachers also must guard against allowing irrelevant information, such as race, social class, or gender, from influencing their expectations for a student. The basis for expectations of students must be examined carefully. It is useful for teachers to reflect on their own gender, racial and social class stereotypes to make them conscious, and then to consider, for specific children, whether stereotypes might be influencing their perceptions.

4. **Continually reexamine judgments about students.** Even judgments about students based on teachers' own observations should be thought of as hypotheses that continually need to be reevaluated. It is natural for expectations to bias what teachers see as well as their interpretation of what they see. Teachers, therefore, need to seek disconfirming evidence, in case their "working theory" is no longer accurate. This requires careful observation and some experimentation. For example, the teacher may give a student more autonomy or more difficult material than she previously has had.

Goldenberg (1989, 1992) illustrates the importance of such experimentation in his ethnography of a teacher whose high expectations were not adjusted in time to provide a student with the instruction she needed. Despite positive indicators at the beginning of first grade, including reading-readiness scores, Sylvia had some difficulty in completing her assignments and fell behind. Making excuses for Sylvia's poor performance, the teacher maintained high expectations for her reading achievement and did not make needed changes. When an observer forced her to attend to Sylvia's difficulties in reading, the teacher adjusted Sylvia's reading instruction. Her reading improved at a much faster rate, but the intervention came too late. By the end of the year Sylvia was among the poorest readers in the class.

Goldenberg (1989) compares Sylvia to Marta, who began first grade with a poor prognosis. The first-grade teacher originally predicted that Marta's reading achievement would be among the lowest in the class, partly because of her attitude and behavioral problems. But after the first few months of school she noticed some improvement in Marta's behavior, and tried including her in a higher reading group. From the moment Marta was placed in the higher group her reading skills began to improve much more rapidly than they had previously. The contrast between Sylvia and Marta clearly demonstrates the value of careful teacher observation, of altering expectations as a function of those observations, and of adjusting educational interventions accordingly.

Sometimes teachers are not fully aware of the assumptions they make about students. It is helpful for teachers to review explicitly the assumptions about individual students that are guiding their curriculum decisions. One method is to write down beliefs about a particular student and evaluate their validity. How good is the evidence for each assumption? Have alternative assumptions or explanations for the student's behavior been tested? What experiments might be tried to test the validity of the assumption?

5. **Do not differentiate behavior toward low- and high-performing students unless there are good reasons for doing so.** Teachers constantly should monitor their own behaviors and assess the degree to which they may be behaving differently toward different children. Good and Brophy (1986) suggest asking questions such as those in Appendix 12–A to help monitor behavior toward students varying in skill levels. It is important to monitor subtle as well as more obvious differential behavior—such as emotional reactions to students' performance, the conditions under which help is provided, the degree to which warmth and humor is directed toward students, or in the amount of responsibility given to students for self-evaluation.

It is not easy to manage a classroom, teach, and monitor one's own assumptions and subtle behavior simultaneously. Being aware of the potential ways in which one may communicate low expectations is an important first step. There are many strategies teachers can use to become more aware of their behaviors. For instance, it is sometimes useful to make a diagram of the seating in the classroom to check whether the high-expectancy students are more likely than the low-expectancy students to be toward the front of the classroom. It is also helpful to have another individual—an aide, student teacher, or fellow teacher—observe and point out differential behavior that a teacher may not realize he is exhibiting.

Another method of evaluating teacher behavior toward high- and low-expectancy students is to assess directly the students' perceptions of differential behavior. Weinstein and her colleagues have developed a questionnaire that can be used for this purpose (see footnote 1, page 215).

There are other strategies that can be employed to ensure equitable treatment of students. In one classroom I observed, for example, the teacher pulled students' names from a fish bowl to call on them, ensuring an opportunity for everyone without having to keep track mentally of whom she had called on already. Alternating gender (i.e., boy, girl, boy, girl) when calling on students helps avoid gender bias and is a simple system to implement.

6. **Never give up on a student.** Finally, although there are tremendous differences in the rate at which students learn, all students who have not been identified as learning handicapped can master the basic curriculum. Some students do not, but it is not due to lack of ability. Most students' failure to learn is caused by problems such as poor motivation or inappropriate instruction. The teacher who continues to expect each and every student in a class to learn invariably will be more successful in achieving that goal than the teacher who designates certain students as "impossible to teach."

CONCLUSION

Teachers' expectations for students' academic performance are based primarily on their own experience with their students' behaviors and performance. But they also are influenced by group stereotypes and various beliefs—(e.g., about the importance of innate ability and parent behavior, about their competencies as teachers). Erroneous expectations are difficult to change because they affect the opportunities teachers give students to demonstrate their competencies, and they bias teachers' perceptions and interpretations of student behavior.

Teacher expectations are important because they influence teacher behavior in ways that can undermine student learning. Teachers need to evaluate carefully and continually the assumptions they make about students and reflect critically on how these assumptions affect their behaviors and instructional strategies. They need to give students opportunities to disconfirm their theories, and to adjust their instruction and tasks accordingly. And they need to ensure that the kinds of accommodations they make are appropriate and necessary, and that they do not give subtle cues that convey low expectations that could undermine students' own confidence in their ability to learn.

TABLE 12-1 Summary of Terms

Term	Definition
Self-fulfilling prophecy	Initial erroneous expectations cause targets to act in a way consistent with those expectations, which in turn causes the expectations to be realized
Actor–observer effect	Observers' tendency to interpret behavior in terms of a stable disposition, and actors' to attribute behavior to situational factors

CHAPTER 13

Real Students, Real Teachers, Real Schools

This book divides students into many psychological pieces by discussing independently the many factors that influence their behaviors in achievement settings. But teachers deal with whole children. So now, like all the King's horses and all the King's men, we will try to put the pieces back together (hopefully with greater success).

To do this, possible strategies are considered for addressing the problems posed by the five children introduced in Chapter 1. This is followed by a discussion of some of the difficulties teachers often encounter in their efforts to increase students' motivation. The next sections move beyond the classroom to the broader school and community context to discuss additional variables that affect students' motivation directly and indirectly by supporting or undermining teachers' efforts.

OUR FIVE CHILDREN

Dave

Defensive Dave does everything a student might do to avoid looking stupid. He relies substantially on classmates for answers to assignments, and he pretends that he cannot find his assignments when he believes his answers might be wrong. Dave has elaborate excuses for unfinished work or poor performance. He also pays little attention to directions and sometimes flaunts his low level of effort.

Dave is a classic example of Covington's "failure-avoiding" student (see Chapter 6). He is not confident that he actually could achieve success by legitimate methods, such as learning the material and completing tasks on his own. Consequently, he devotes his effort to avoiding failure rather than to trying to succeed. Dave's behavior is logical in the sense that it achieves his short-term goal of not looking stupid. He completes, more or less, many of the tasks, but by not trying too hard, he persuades others to attribute his poor performance to his lack of effort rather than to a lack of ability. Despite its internal logic, his behavior is, in the long term, highly maladaptive. Poor performance will become increasingly inevitable and difficult to rationalize.

What does a teacher do with a student such as Dave? Two changes are essential. First, Dave must begin to believe that he can achieve real success on his own. Second, negative consequences of failure must be removed so that Dave can focus on achieving success rather than on avoiding failure.

Making Dave believe that success is a realistic goal may require changing the definition of success. Dave never will expect to succeed if success is based on normative criteria. Success must be redefined in terms of personal improvement or in terms of achieving some predetermined, realistically achievable standard of excellence. Making success achievable also may require adapting the difficulty level of tasks. For example, if the standard for a "B" on a spelling test is 80 percent correct, the difficulty of the spelling words will need to be adjusted so that this is a realistic goal. Dave's confidence in his ability to achieve success can be reinforced by explicitly attributing his successes to effort and ability, pointing out that other students who he most likely perceives to be like him have achieved particular goals, and using some of the other strategies for maintaining self-confidence that are described in Chapter 7.

To alleviate Dave's concerns about failure, the teacher must accept initial poor performance, as long as he makes an effort. The teacher needs to convince him that it is all right to make mistakes, while encouraging him to keep trying (i.e., to convey the message that he is expected to improve). If Dave gives a wrong answer in a public context (e.g., in a group or class discussion), the teacher should find something valuable in the answer, and continue to engage him in conversation until he has demonstrated to himself, and to the class, that he is able to reach some meaningful level of understanding. He also might be given several opportunities to obtain a reasonably good grade. Thus, if Dave misses too many problems on a mathematics test, he could be given a "preliminary" grade and an opportunity to study and retake the test until his performance is acceptable—to both him and the teacher.

Such practices should reduce Dave's need to avoid failure, and thus his maladaptive avoidance behavior. Indeed, in some sense they should eliminate the notion of "failure" altogether, replacing it with something more like "nonsuccess."[1]

---

[1] I give three grades on graduate students' papers: "not there yet," "OK," and "really good." They cannot have any "not-there-yet" grades and still receive an "A" in the course, but they can rewrite papers as many times as there is time for me to review them before the end of the course.

Hannah

It is not easy to increase the effort of a student such as Dave, but finding solutions to the motivation problems presented by Helpless Hannah is even more challenging. Though Dave has not given up totally on trying to look competent, Hannah steadfastly is convinced that she lacks ability and inevitably will fail. She has conceded defeat.

Many of the Hannahs that I have seen are substantially behind their classmates academically, and they often are out of the mainstream socially. Although some students who are discouraged very easily perform adequately, albeit less well than they could, students such as Hannah, who have given up altogether, consistently perform poorly.

Hannah needs considerable individual attention, which is extremely difficult for a teacher who attends to twenty-five to thirty-five students. Creative use of older children, high school students, and retired individuals from the community can help students such as Hannah. If parents or older siblings are willing and able, they also may be enlisted to help Hannah at home. These "tutors" must be instructed on how to be accepting and encouraging, and they need to be taught specific strategies for helping Hannah develop her skills. Close teacher supervision of tutors is essential.

Tasks must be developed carefully so that they are appropriate for Hannah's skill level. Initially, the material may need to be easy, even for her, to provide her with the success experiences she needs to build her self-confidence. Increases in difficulty should be very gradual because she is likely to become discouraged easily.

Obviously, 1 or 2 hours each day of individual tutoring is the most that realistically can be expected. Consequently, Hannah's teacher also must find ways to incorporate Hannah into the classroom. All of the previous suggestions for helping Dave also would be appropriate for Hannah, although it may take even greater efforts to involve her in classroom activities. Hannah also could be given responsibilities (e.g., leading the line to recess, taking the lunch money to the principal's office) to give her some social prestige and to publicize the teacher's faith in her ability to perform a task. The strategy that Cohen and Lotan (1995) developed—finding something that a student is good at, remarking on it publicly, and placing the student in an expert role for that or a related activity—could be particularly useful to enhance Hannah's status in her own as well as her classmates' eyes (see Chapter 7).

Such superficial demonstrations of valuing Hannah, however, will not be effective unless she also experiences real improvement in her own skills. The best way to help a student such as Hannah is to ensure that she learns—to increase her skill level and allow her to enjoy the same motivating feelings of developing competencies that the other students experience.

Sally

In contrast to Dave and Hannah, most teachers enjoy having students like Safe Sally in their classrooms. Sally's elementary school teachers probably praised her for her work, which she completed precisely according to their instructions, put her many papers with 100 percent correct answers on the bulletin board, and gave her special privileges. Sally became hooked on these social rewards and is afraid to try anything that may cause her to lose them. Her self-worth has become dependent on others' approval and symbols (e.g., grades) associated with that approval.

In the long run, an appropriate goal for Sally would be to develop more independent standards for judging her work. But in the short term, her teachers can capitalize on her responsiveness to external contingencies and make their approval contingent on a new set of behaviors. Thus, for example, her teachers can make good grades contingent, at least in part, on her doing work that challenges her current competency level. They can praise her for attempting tasks that require considerable effort and persistence, regardless of how well she performs. Her teachers also might refrain from congratulating her for getting the highest grade in the class or completing exams with no errors. There are also more subtle ways that her teachers can convey that they value risk taking. For example, they can make smiles and sustained interactions contingent on risk taking rather than on "good" or correct performance.

If the long-term goal is to reduce Sally's dependency on extrinsic approval and rewards, another motivation system must be developed instead. This will not be easy because the present motivation system has served her well for many years. Her teachers must try to awaken her interest and curiosity. This can be accomplished partly by modeling their own intrinsic interest in the subjects they teach. Students know early in the semester which teachers really love their subjects, and to some degree, their own views are affected by their teachers' views.

Sally's teachers also can encourage her to engage in learning activities outside of the class requirements. Time could be set aside in an English class for Sally and other students to discuss books they have read "for fun" or plays they have seen. Teachers can provide opportunities for students to share their own journals, short stories, or poems with their classmates. Newspaper articles read at home can be discussed in social studies classes. In science classes students could share their own observations of scientific phenomena.

Changes in the way tests and grades are discussed may reduce Sally's excessive need to do well on tests and her obsession with grades. Focusing on the information tests provide might diminish Sally's view of test performance as an index of her self-worth as a human. Being clear about the criteria for good grades but not continually calling students' attention to grades might reduce Sally's focus on external evaluation as the reason for working.

The goal is not to eliminate altogether Sally's concerns about performance, but to reduce them so that they do not interfere with her enjoyment of learning and willingness to approach challenging learning situations in which high performance is not guaranteed. Implementing the aforementioned suggestions might help Sally begin to relax and allow herself to enjoy learning for its own sake, rather than seeing it only as a means to a high grade and teacher admiration.

Santos

Satisfied Santos is, in nearly every respect, the opposite of Sally. He eagerly seeks out intellectual challenges and enjoys developing his skills. The problem is that the challenges he seeks and the skills he develops rarely coincide with the school curriculum. Indeed, nearly all of his intellectual activities (e.g., computer or science projects) occur outside of the classroom.

Santos is motivated to stay out of trouble and therefore to obtain minimally respectable grades, but not to excel in school subjects. His threshold for acceptable grades is about a "C+." But he easily could be a straight "A" student if he exerted some effort on school tasks.

Despite Santos's many intellectual achievements, he is not mastering material that wise adults believe is important to know in our society. Santos's teachers have a difficult task. They need to get Santos to attend to the school curriculum without dampening his curiosity and enthusiasm for intellectual challenge.

The first step is to gain some knowledge of Santos's own intellectual interests. The second step is to try to take advantage of these interests and to incorporate them into his school assignments. For instance, if his English teacher is teaching students about biographies, the teacher might encourage Santos to read a biography of a scientist. His geometry teacher might ask him to build a miniature city from another planet in which all buildings have to be built to scale and conform to certain unusual shapes. His interest in space and the pleasure he derives from building things might make the mastery of geometry and measurement more meaningful and fun. It is unrealistic to expect Santos's teachers to find creative ways to engage his interest in all schoolwork, but occasional attempts, such as these examples, might help convince Santos of the practical value of mastering the school curriculum.

In general, there are two principles that need to be kept in mind for students such as Santos. First, teachers should give such students as much choice as possible. The more choices students have in selecting the specific tasks they do, the more likely they are to find something that interests and engages them. Why assign the same biography to every student in the class, for example, when there are many excellent biographies that would appeal to students' diverse interests?

Second, an effort must be made to demonstrate the usefulness of "school knowledge." If students are learning composition skills, why not have them write personal journals, letters to the President, or stories for a school newsletter? Certainly these approaches to engaging the enthusiasm of a bright but uninterested student such as Santos will be more effective than repeatedly warning him that he will receive a bad grade.

Santos's teacher also might capitalize on his "threshold," requiring greater effort and task completion than he currently is exerting to achieve the "C+" he seems to need. This clearly has to be done carefully, to avoid an appearance of unfairness that could alienate Santos altogether. But certainly if grades, to some degree, are based on effort and improvement, the teacher has license to penalize Santos for performing below his capacity.

Alma

Finally, we come to Anxious Alma. Alma can learn the mathematical concepts that are taught, but has difficulty demonstrating her knowledge and is extremely uncomfortable in mathematical learning contexts. Alma's mathematics teacher needs to help Alma develop strategies for reducing her anxiety in evaluative situations, and she needs to eliminate the risk that Alma believes failure might bring.

Given the severity and uniqueness of the problem, Alma's teacher might begin by discussing these observations directly with Alma, expressing concern that her anxiety in evaluative situations interferes with her enjoyment of math and will make her unwilling to take challenging math courses in the future. Although Alma at first may be reluctant to talk about her anxiety, she ultimately might be convinced to begin a personalized program to try to alleviate it. A program might have the following components:

♦ Alma reads a book from the library on relaxation techniques and shares with the teacher a few techniques that she found useful.

♦ Alma commits to volunteering once each day to contribute to class discussion; in exchange, the teacher promises not to call on her when she does not volunteer.

♦ To build Alma's self-confidence, the teacher assigns her to assist another student having difficulty with the homework.

There are strategies that also could be used to make tests less frightening. Alma, for instance, could be given more time to finish tests. It also might be helpful to give her a few sample problems to refer to, or to allow her to refer to her textbook during a test. The problems in the test should require understanding of the mathematical concepts involved, but she may be reassured by having access to examples. In addition, she might be told that she can retake a test if she believes that anxiety interfered with her performance. This alone might relieve anxiety enough to make it unnecessary to fulfill the promise.

Special accommodations for students who suffer from debilitating anxiety can be made in particular classes, but teachers also need to address the underlying problems, to prepare students to function effectively in classes in which the teacher may be less accommodating, or in situations (e.g., standardized tests) in which accommodations are not possible. Self-confidence is usually at the root of anxiety. Thus, any strategies a teacher might use to build self-confidence, such as those suggested for Dave and Hannah, apply also to students such as Alma.

IT IS HARDER THAN IT SOUNDS

Successfully implementing the aforementioned suggestions, and others made in previous chapters, is not easy for numerous reasons. Students sometimes can be their own worst enemies, slow to respond to or even reject practices that are different from those that they are used to. The same practice also often affects students in the same class differently. Many of the practices that have been recommended require shifting substantial control from teachers to students, which is difficult for many teachers. The practices described also require enormous skill and commitment; teachers need to be very knowledgeable of their students' competencies and interests and to be attentive to their own behaviors toward students. Finally, the recommended practices usually cannot stand alone; they work only if they are embedded in a complex set of mutually reinforcing practices. This section elaborates on these challenges.

The Undermining Effects of Students

Teachers' efforts to increase student motivation can fail miserably if they do not take into account the dispositions and expectations of their own students. The following are examples of problems that can arise with teachers' initial attempts to apply a few of the principles of motivation discussed in this book.

- ◆ *Minimize extrinsic rewards.* Students accustomed to working for grades and other rewards may cease working altogether if extrinsic rewards are diminished. Students need to be weaned slowly from their dependence on external rewards, and this extrinsic motivation system must be replaced with an alternative system that will motivate them to engage in schoolwork.

- ◆ *Provide challenging tasks.* If tasks suddenly become much more challenging than what students are used to, they may become discouraged rather than more intrinsically interested. The level of challenge needs to be increased gradually, and students need to feel comfortable and safe experiencing initial difficulties.

- u *Give open-ended tasks.* Students who mostly have dealt with closed-ended tasks with one right answer are accustomed to clear, unambiguous feedback. Open-ended tasks that provide opportunity for creative, substantive problem solving involve more risk because the standards for evaluation are more difficult to understand and there is greater uncertainty about what constitutes a "good" performance. To deal with the anxiety about performance that such tasks sometimes provoke, students often try to turn open-ended assignments that have considerable potential for creativity into more prescribed and boring procedural tasks.[2]

♦ *Maximize student autonomy.* Giving more responsibility for selecting and completing tasks to students who have not had experience assessing their own competencies or working independently initially can be counterproductive. Most students need help in developing strategies for assessing their own understanding and mastery level, and they need guidance in how to select and plan what needs to be done to complete tasks and further their understanding.

♦ *Provide opportunities for collaboration.* Giving students who are used to working alone an opportunity to collaborate with classmates is initially just as likely to result in dependency (i.e., one or two children completing the task while others fool around) or conflict (i.e., disagreements among students) as it is to promote productive collaboration. Most students need to be given explicit instruction in using effective strategies for help seeking, help giving, and collaboration.

As ineffective as some traditional instructional approaches are, they are predictable, and students sometimes will resist change. Even if students welcome change, they often lack the skills they need to make good use of it. If the kinds of changes recommended in this book, however, are implemented gradually and with careful planning, students eventually should thrive on them. However carefully changes are implemented, teachers must nevertheless be prepared for some false starts and slippage. Sometimes the current system needs to fall apart a little before it comes back together in a new, improved form.

Different Students, Different Needs

To complicate matters further, an educational environment that is good for one student is not necessarily good for another. The principles discussed in this book need to be adjusted somewhat to students' individual needs.

For example, although it is true that challenging tasks are generally more intrinsically interesting, students who have a long history of failure, such as Hannah, or who lack self-confidence, such as Dave, initially may need tasks that they can complete easily, with a heavy dose of praise for their efforts. Slowly, more difficult problems or tasks can be interspersed among ones that they can do fairly easily. Sally, however, though she may complain at first, should be able to

[2]When I assign a paper in my graduate courses, students invariably ask many questions to decrease the ambiguity: "How many pages?"; "Double-spaced or single-spaced?"; "Do we need to use sources outside of class readings?"; "How many references should we have?"; "Is it all right to use quotations?" I find myself making up answers to relieve students' anxiety, even though my answers end up limiting students' options in ways that I did not intend, thus reducing the intrinsic motivation value of the task.

rise quickly to the challenge of more demanding tasks. Santos, too, immediately should thrive on challenge, if the tasks are related to his interests.

Students also vary in their goals, so that the same goal structure will affect some students positively and others negatively. A student such as Santos, who primarily is motivated intrinsically, will not work hard in a classroom in which the teacher stresses extrinsic consequences, but may thrive in a classroom in which the teacher emphasizes the intrinsic value of schoolwork. Students such as Sally, in contrast, initially may not work hard in a class in which the teacher stresses learning and mastery.[3] Teachers need not capitulate to students' goal orientations, but they should be aware of them and of possible conflicts between their classroom practices and their students' orientations. They also may need to individualize somewhat the messages they convey to different students.

Giving Up Control

Giving up some control to provide students with more autonomy is difficult for most teachers. And the more teachers are held accountable for student learning, the harder it is to share control with students. The effect of accountability on teachers' behaviors was demonstrated in a study by Deci, Spiegel, Ryan, Koestner, and Kauffman (1982). They asked psychology students to train other students in an experiment. Student trainers who were told that they were responsible for how well the other student performed talked more, were more critical of the student, gave more commands, and allowed less choice and autonomy than student teachers who were instructed simply to teach the task (see also Flink, Boggiano, & Barrett, in press.)

Even without these external pressures, many teachers fear that increasing student discretion will lead to confusion and chaos rather than constructive student-initiated learning. Their fears are not without cause for two reasons. First, more skill and planning is required on the teacher's part to maintain order in a classroom in which students are given choices and discretion than in a classroom in which students always are told exactly what to do and how and when to do it. Teachers often lack the skills and the time for such planning. Second, most students are unaccustomed to much freedom, and they sometimes do not use it responsibly.

There are several things teachers can do to minimize the likelihood that their fears of chaos will hold true and to ensure that students exercise their choice and responsibility effectively. First, teachers should increase student autonomy gradually, giving students an opportunity to show that they can use it productively. Second, teachers need to ensure that directions are clear and not too com-

---

[3] I found this to be true when I first began teaching college students. In an effort to orient students' attention toward the joy of learning about child psychology, I did not give grades for class participation or papers. I found very quickly that my own goal orientation was initially incompatible with the goal orientation of most of the students. Rather than studying to understand child development, they studied to get good grades in their other classes and came to my class unprepared.

plicated. Written instructions, summarizing the steps of a task, are often helpful and reduce dependency on the teacher for reminding them of next steps. Third, explicit instructions and discussion related to managing time and tasks are helpful. Giving up control can be frightening, but if done carefully and thoughtfully, it can be liberating for the teacher as well as motivating for students.

Knowing Students

Many of the principles of motivation described in this book require a great deal of knowledge of students' skills (e.g., to create optimally challenging tasks), interests, values, and motivation (e.g., self-confidence, anxieties). Knowing each student well and continually assessing each student's knowledge and interests to provide appropriate tasks requires an enormous amount of effort. To the degree that teachers are successful in promoting independence and engaging students more enthusiastically in schoolwork, time spent in management activities decreases. This gives teachers more time to engage in assessment activities, such as interacting with students individually and in small groups, and examining their written work.

Self-Monitoring

Teachers must be aware of their own biases, beliefs, expectations, and behaviors toward students and ask themselves questions (e.g., "Am I smiling more at girls? Sustaining instructional conversations longer with boys? Giving students who are relatively slow to catch on too little time to answer questions?"). Monitoring one's own behavior to avoid differential or ineffective behavior towards students is extremely difficult to do while teaching, assessing students, and managing a classroom. It is useful to have an aide, a colleague, or even a trusted parent observe the classroom. Students' own perceptions also can be elicited. Self-monitoring will become easier and more automatic with practice and time.

Everything Is Related to Everything Else

Although most instructional practices have been treated independently in this book, all of the practices recommended depend substantially on each other for their effectiveness.

Consider, for example, providing students with more choice in tasks. If choice is given in a classroom in which performance outcomes and external evaluation are stressed, students are likely to select easy tasks that will not help them develop new skills. Habitual concerns about performance most likely explain why Clifford (1991) found that, when given a choice, students tended to select tasks that offered very little risk of failure. The older the students in their studies, the less willing they were to take academic risks. Only in a context in which errors and initial failures are considered a natural part of learning and in which evaluation is based primarily on effort and personal improvement will students choose tasks that challenge their current skill levels.

Collaborative learning also will work, but only in some contexts. If it is not implemented in a classroom in which students respect and support each other's learning (i.e., a "community of learners"), it can result in conflict and many hurt feelings rather than collaboration. Collaborative learning will work effectively only if the teacher models, and demands from students, respect for students as humans, a sense of responsibility for each other's learning, and a value on inclusion and full participation of all students.

Another example of the interconnections among the aforementioned motivation principles concerns evaluation. A teacher who reduces the emphasis on external evaluation but continues to give boring, too easy, or too difficult tasks, will not see increased effort on assignments or the use of effective problem-solving strategies. Indeed, if tasks are repetitive, irrelevant, and boring, none of the principles that are discussed in this book will improve students' motivation.

Although the links between various practices, in some respects, make the task of increasing student motivation more difficult, in other respects they make the task easier because they also reinforce each other. For example, giving students choices usually results in students' engagement in activities that are more personally interesting, and thus doubly supports their intrinsic motivation. Thus, as teachers gradually try to change their classroom practices, they will find that it becomes easier with time.

BEYOND THE CLASSROOM

No teacher, however good or committed, can meet the previously described challenges alone or in a school context that is not supportive of her efforts to improve. Teachers can motivate students only if they themselves are motivated. They can make students feel valued and secure only if they feel valued and secure; they can foster enthusiasm for learning in students only if they are enthusiastic about teaching. The school culture can make or break a teacher in the same way that the classroom culture can support or undermine students' efforts to learn. Fortunately, the principles of motivation discussed in this book apply to teachers as well as students.

Support for Risk Taking

It is not easy to be self-critical—to examine one's own practices and be able to admit that they are lacking. Teachers need to be confident that they can share, with impunity, the problems they discover in this self-evaluative process and that they have the support they need to help them address the problems they find. They need to be able to reveal to administrators and colleagues areas in which they do not believe they are being successful without fearing reprisal or humiliation. The respectful and supportive social context that is required for students to be comfortable and take risks is just as critical for teachers.

Cooperation and Collaboration

Teachers must have access to resources at the school level to help them evaluate and improve their practices. They need others to observe their classrooms, and they need to observe other teachers' classrooms. Teachers also need to be able to share problems and receive ideas from other teachers and experts. A school climate that provides opportunities for such teacher collaboration is critical to maximizing student learning. The evidence is clear that students achieve most in schools where teachers develop a strong professional community, and where there is a shared sense of purpose, a collective focus on student learning, collaborative instructional creativity, and reflective professional dialogue (Marks et al., in press).

Time

The kinds of tasks and activities that engage students' interest and enthusiasm and the kind of qualitative evaluative feedback needed to focus their attention on learning and mastery take much more time than assigning pages from a textbook and checking the correctness of students' answers. Considerable time also is required for the teacher collaboration and professional development described.

As schools and instruction currently are organized, teachers simply do not have the time they need to provide effective, motivating instruction. At the elementary level most teachers have virtually no time built into their workday to plan instruction or even to evaluate students' work. Either teacher schedules need to be changed, to include noninstructional time during the day, or the teacher's day has to be lengthened (with appropriate compensation) to include time for these activities.

Autonomy

The principle of maximum autonomy applies to both teachers and students. Teachers need a free hand to experiment with strategies that are compatible with their skills and personality as well as those of their students, and they need to make some of their own choices. Coherence in a school's curriculum and some articulation across grades is important. But teachers can be involved in school curriculum decisions, and even after they are made, some flexibility should remain for personalizing instruction.

DeCharms (1976) recognized the importance of this broader school context in the program he developed to foster feelings of personal causation in students. He argued that if teachers become pawns (i.e., passive, controlled), their students cannot become origins (i.e., active, responsible agents in their education). In his program, teachers were given more responsibility over their school program, and opportunities to set their own goals and make decisions about how to reach those goals. They were encouraged to do the same for students. The program was unusually successful in improving student achievement. DeCharms (1976, 1984) also found that predominantly poor, African American students who had been in the nine experimental "origins" classrooms in the sixth and seventh grades made greater achievement gains than students in the control group. The advantage of the origin group persisted through the eighth grade, even though neither group continued training that year. The origin group even had a higher high school completion rate than the control group. These are extraordinary results for a relatively modest intervention, perhaps because the classroom intervention was embedded in an intervention that gave essentially the same treatment to teachers.

School Policies

Teachers' efforts in individual classrooms easily can be undermined by school policies that are incompatible with teachers' motivation goals. Recognizing this, some motivation researchers have developed interventions to change practices in the broader school context to those that will support teachers' efforts to change the culture of their classrooms (Anderman & Maehr, 1994; Maehr & Anderman, 1993; Midgley, 1993; Midgley, Anderman, & Hicks, in press; Urdan, Midgley, & Wood, 1995; Weinstein et al., 1991).

There are various school level policies that are relevant to the motivation issues discussed in this book. For instance, inequitable allocation of resources among students—with high-achieving students receiving the most experienced and most qualified teachers or receiving additional opportunities (e.g., access to technology, opportunities to work on the school newspaper or yearbook)—gives a clear message about what (and who) is valued. Such inequities also affect the quality of instruction and educational experiences students receive, which in turn affects their motivation to engage in academic activities.

Schoolwide decisions about textbooks, curriculum, and even field trips significantly affect the nature of tasks and the real-world relevance of the educational experiences that teachers can provide. Whether teachers are allowed or encouraged to collaborate and whether there is some flexibility in class scheduling will affect opportunities for multidisciplinary and project-based learning activities. Maehr and Anderman (1993) pointed out that even janitorial policies can inhibit project-based learning, which, although messy, can be very intrinsically motivating and productive.

What schools recognize publicly through such practices as honor rolls and certificates is important. It is difficult for teachers to focus students' attention on mastery and learning in a school that recognizes only excellence in outcome for high performers. The emphasis on effort or improvement in the classroom needs to be matched, at least to some degree, at the school level.

Ability grouping and tracking are perhaps the most powerful ways to emphasize differences in skill levels and to foster an entity concept of ability. The more pervasive and rigid grouping is, the more it will undermine the motivation goals discussed in this book.

Schoolwide testing practices also influence the instructional program and thus student motivation. If teachers are evaluated on the basis of their students' scores on tests of basic, rote skills, it will be difficult for them to emphasize, in their teaching, the kind of problem solving and understanding that engages students' intrinsic interest in schoolwork.

The amount of real choice that students have in selecting classes and other activities at the school level will influence their sense of self-determination and, hence, their motivation within classes. In some schools the most desirable courses and opportunities are not available to the students who are in greatest need of increased motivation.

The most important school level variable affecting student motivation is the least tangible. The same climate of positive regard and trust recommended for classrooms also must be present at the school level. School counselors, specialists, athletic coaches, and administrators need to treat students with respect. They need to maintain and convey the same level of high expectations for students to learn, and the same level of concern for them as humans that teachers need to show.

CAN IT BE DONE?

Most children arrive at school self-confident, eager to learn, and enthusiastic about schoolwork. This book is about maintaining this high level of motivation, stemming, and sometimes reversing, the common shift toward focusing on extrinsic rewards, being concerned about performance, and losing interest in schoolwork. The task is challenging.

Is it impossible? I do not think so. I have seen many classrooms—from kindergarten to twelfth grade—in which students enthusiastically and self-confidently are engaged in learning activities. There is convincing evidence that a high level of student motivation and pleasure in learning can be achieved in any classroom.

Each of the many excellent teachers I have observed has a unique approach. Strategies that work effectively for one teacher and one group of students can fail in another classroom with another teacher and a different group of students. The principles of effective teaching and the suggestions made in this book, therefore, need to be adapted to each teacher's style and skills and to the specific characteristics of each group of students.

Because students need time to adjust, and because teachers need time to experiment and test new instructional practices, it is important not to be too ambitious, not to try too much too fast. A more effective strategy for teachers, and for students as well, is to create proximal goals. Initial goals might be as modest as trying to persuade a particular student to exert some effort or to take a risk, to create tasks that are linked more closely to students' personal interests and lives outside of school, or to give more informative evaluative feedback.

As changes are made, their effects need to be observed carefully. Is the student exerting more effort or taking more risks? Do students seem more interested in the tasks? Do they use the substantive evaluative feedback to guide their efforts? This book provides many examples of specific student behaviors that teachers can observe to give them information about their students' beliefs and dispositions related to motivation. Direct, open conversations are also useful. They contribute to a classroom climate of trust, convey the teachers' genuine interest in students' views, and provide valuable information on students' perspectives on particular instructional practices.

This process of reflection and self-evaluation, modification, and observation of effects is repeated continually. Whether a teacher's purpose is to improve classroom management, increase motivation, or enhance learning, good teachers continually evaluate, fine-tune, and reevaluate their practices.

This process of development and reform cannot be implemented without support. Teachers are at the front lines. But without a broad, societal commitment to making schools places where teachers and students can thrive, the status quo will prevail. Substantial changes in student motivation and learning require substantial changes in the way schools are organized, for both students and teachers. It also will require community support for innovation and a broad social commitment to making education a top moral and fiscal priority. It is a big job, and all of us have to do our part.

Appendix 2–A: Identifying Motivation Problems

INSTRUCTIONS

1. Observe students for a few days before recording which behaviors typically are seen. To make some of these judgments you may need to try new teaching practices (e.g., give choices in assignments with different difficulty levels, give some ungraded assignments, provide some time and opportunities to work on unassigned tasks).

2. Select students who appear to have relatively serious motivation problems and rate their behaviors in different subject areas or for different types of tasks or learning contexts.

3. If there are two adults in the classroom (e.g., a teacher and an aide), it is instructive for both to fill out the form for the same student. Differences can reveal biases in the teacher's or the aide's perceptions of a student, or context effects on behavior (because the teacher and aide see the student in different contexts).

Note: The first twelve behaviors are important for performing adequately on basic school tasks. Students who do not demonstrate these behaviors are most likely not mastering the school curriculum as well as they could. The remaining items are highly desirable behaviors that reflect maximum motivation for intellectual pursuits.

Child's Name: _____

1. _____ Pays attention to the teacher

2. _____ Begins working on tasks immediately

3. _____ Follows directions on tasks

4. _____ Maintains attention until tasks are completed

5. _____ Completes work

6. _____ Turns assignments in on time

7. _____ Persists rather than gives up when problems appear difficult

8. _____ Works autonomously

9. _____ Volunteers answers in class

10. _____ Has test performance that reflects the skill level demonstrated on assignments

11. _____ Seeks help when it is needed

12. _____ Is not upset by initial errors or difficulties

13. _____ Enjoys challenging work

14. _____ Works intensely

15. _____ Asks questions to expand knowledge beyond immediate lesson

16. _____ Engages in learning activities that are not required

17. _____ Is reluctant to stop working on tasks when highly engaged

18. _____ Engages in learning activities after assignments are completed

19. _____ Appears happy, proud, enthusiastic, and eager

20. _____ Strives to improve skills, even when already performing well relative to classmates

21. _____ Initiates challenging learning activities on his or her own

22. _____ Works hard on ungraded tasks

Appendix 3–A:
External Reinforcement:
Teacher Self-Reports

INSTRUCTIONS

This form is designed to help you reflect on your use of external rewards and punishment. After completing the form, examine your responses for inconsistencies between your values and goals and your behaviors.

1. *What reinforcements do you use?*

	never	occasionally	often
◆ Social reinforcement (praise)	_____	_____	_____
◆ Symbolic rewards (e.g., stickers)	_____	_____	_____
◆ Good grades	_____	_____	_____
◆ Material rewards (e.g., food, prizes, trinkets)	_____	_____	_____
◆ Public recognition (e.g., putting paper on bulletin board)	_____	_____	_____
◆ Privileges (e.g., playing with special materials)	_____	_____	_____
◆ Responsibilities (e.g., taking roll, running errands to the office)	_____	_____	_____
◆ Other: _____	_____	_____	_____

2. *What punishments do you use?*

	never	occasionally	often
◆ Private criticism or reprimands	_____	_____	_____
◆ Public criticism or reprimands	_____	_____	_____
◆ Bad grades	_____	_____	_____
◆ "Time out" (i.e., social isolation)	_____	_____	_____
◆ Loss of privileges (e.g., no recess)	_____	_____	_____
◆ Other: _____	_____	_____	_____

3. *On what behaviors or outcomes is reinforcement contingent?*

	never	occasionally	often
◆ High effort or attention	_____	_____	_____
◆ Absolute performance (e.g., few errors)	_____	_____	_____
◆ Relative performance (e.g., fewer errors than most other students)	_____	_____	_____
◆ Improved performance	_____	_____	_____
◆ Following directions	_____	_____	_____
◆ Finishing	_____	_____	_____
◆ Creativity	_____	_____	_____
◆ Personal initiative	_____	_____	_____
◆ Helpfulness (e.g., to another child)	_____	_____	_____
◆ Other: _____	_____	_____	_____

4. *On what behaviors or outcomes is punishment contingent?*

	never	occasionally	often
◆ Low effort or inattention	_____	_____	_____
◆ Absolute performance (e.g., many errors)	_____	_____	_____
◆ Relative performance (e.g., more errors than most other students)	_____	_____	_____
◆ No improvement	_____	_____	_____

	never	occasionally	often
◆ Not following directions	_____	_____	_____
◆ Not finishing	_____	_____	_____
◆ Lack of personal initiative	_____	_____	_____
◆ Dependency (i.e., asking for help needlessly)	_____	_____	_____
◆ Refusal to help others	_____	_____	_____
◆ Misbehavior	_____	_____	_____
◆ Other: _____	_____	_____	_____

5. *Are there any students in your class who frequently are rewarded (e.g., with good grades, praise, recognition) for outcomes that did not require much effort (i.e., were achieved fairly easily)?*

6. *Are there any students in your class who are not rewarded (e.g., with good grades, praise, or recognition), even when they try?*

7. *Are the rewards in your classroom realistically available to all students?*

Appendix 3–B: Observations of Teachers' Uses of Praise

INSTRUCTIONS

Each time the teacher uses verbal praise, an observer indicates whether the praise was "effective" or "ineffective" according to a set of criteria. Effective praise is described to the left of the slash; ineffective praise either is described to the right of the slash or is the absence of the effective criterion. Put a plus ("+") if the praise was effective according to a particular criterion, a minus ("−") if the praise was ineffective according to the criterion, or nothing if you are unsure or if the criterion is not applicable. Observers should fill out this form in various situations in which the teacher is likely to praise students (e.g., during reading groups, during whole-class or small-group question-and-answer periods). Teachers should examine criteria in which there are a large number of minuses. These provide specific information regarding ways in which praise might be used more effectively.

Observations of Teachers' Use of Praise

	1	2	3	4	5	6	7	8
(+) contingent on behavior or outcome/(−) random, unsystematic								
(+) specifies particulars of accomplishment/(−) global								
(+) spontaneous, credible/(−) bland, perfunctory								
(+) specifies performance (or effort) criteria/(−)								
(+) provides information about competence/(−)								
(+) stresses students' own behaviors/ (−) stresses social comparison								
(+) focuses on improvement/(−) focuses on relative performance								
(+) focuses on effort or personal meaning of accomplishment/(−)								
(+) attributes success to effort and ability/(−) attributes success to ability or external factors								
(+) fosters endogenous attributions/ (−) fosters exogenous attributions								
(+) focuses on student's task behaviors/(−) focuses on teacher's authority								
(+) focuses on task behavior/ (−) distracts attention from task behavior								

Based on Brophy (1981).

Appendix 7–A: Evaluating Your Practices

INSTRUCTIONS

Reflect on the degree to which you implement each of the following principles for maintaining positive achievement-related beliefs.

Tasks and Assignments

1. Are they challenging (i.e., achievable, but require some effort and persistence) for all students?

2. Are they organized to provide frequent opportunities for students to observe increases in their skills?

Goals

3. Are goals likely to be achieved before students become discouraged?

4. Are goals appropriately adjusted to students' individual skill levels?

5. Are students involved in setting their own goals?

Evaluation

6. Do students have diverse opportunities to demonstrate what they know or understand?

7. Have you pointed out what is good, right, or shows improvement?

8. Is feedback clear, specific, and informative?

9. Are rewards based on achieving a clearly defined standard or set of criteria, or on personal improvement?

10. Do students have multiple opportunities to achieve high grades?

11. Do students celebrate each other's achievements, regardless of their relative levels?

12. Are public evaluations minimized?

13. Can students evaluate their own work?

14. Are criteria for evaluation clear and consistent?

Help Seeking

15. Do students seek help when they need it?

16. Is assistance limited to what is necessary?

17. Do students seek help from their classmates?

Direct Statements

18. Do you attribute failure to low effort or ineffective strategies?

19. Do you attribute success to effort and competence?

Classroom Structure

20. Are tasks differentiated among students and over time?

21. Do you point out variation in skill levels (within students)?

22. Are all students productively involved in whole-class discussions?

23. Is ability grouping used flexibly and temporarily to address specific skill needs?

24. Do you convey to students the value of many different kinds of skills?

25. Do you give relatively poor-performing students the role of expert?

Appendix 10–A:
Evaluating Your Tasks

1. Do students understand the purpose of tasks (i.e., what they will learn from them) and exactly what they are expected to do to complete them?

2. Are tasks challenging for all students who are expected to complete them (i.e., will all students be able to complete them, but only with some genuine effort)? Do you:

   ◆ Allow students to move at their own pace?

   ◆ Include challenging questions in whole-class discussions and tests?

   ◆ Provide enriching activities for students to do if they finish their regular work?

3. Do tasks provide students with an opportunity to do substantive intellectual work that will contribute to some learning goal? For example, do they engage students in

   ◆ Higher-order thinking?

   ◆ Active problem solving?

   ◆ Thinking about "big ideas"?

   ◆ Addressing open-ended questions?

4. Do tasks vary from day to day? Are they often:

   ◆ Multidimensional?

   ◆ Complex or novel, or containing an element of surprise (e.g., by revealing contradiction in students' thinking)?

   ◆ Actively involving student participation, exploration, or experimentation?

   ◆ Personally meaningful?

   ◆ Collaborative?

Appendix 10–B:
Evaluating Your Evaluation

1. Do you emphasize learning, mastery, and understanding more than external evaluation?

2. Do you provide substantive feedback that can be used to guide future efforts?

3. Is the information value of evaluation emphasized more than the reward or punishment value?

When grades are given

4. Are they based on effort, improvement, and achieving a standard, rather than on relative performance?

5. Are grading criteria clear and fair?

When tangible extrinsic rewards are promised

6. Are they necessary?

7. Are they contingent on the quality of work or a standard of performance, not simply on engaging in an activity?

8. Are they withdrawn as soon as possible?

Appendix 10–C: Evaluating Control

1. Are students given the maximum amount of autonomy that they can handle, for example, by giving them choices in

   ◆ Designing tasks?

   ◆ Determining how tasks are completed?

   ◆ Selecting the difficulty levels of tasks?

   ◆ Deciding when to undertake tasks?

   Or by allowing them to

   ◆ Correct their own work?

   ◆ Set personal goals?

2. Is monitoring performed in a way that focuses on students' understanding and skill development rather than on controlling their behaviors?

3. Are students given help in a way that facilitates their own accomplishments?

Appendix 11–A: Strategies for Reducing Anxiety

Preprocessing Problems

◆ Provide opportunities to reinspect material.

◆ Encourage questions and check for understanding.

◆ Review material frequently.

◆ Give clear, unambiguous instructions.

◆ Provide a fair amount of structure for learning.

◆ Allow variability in pacing of instruction.

Processing and Output Problems

◆ Instruct students in relaxation techniques.

◆ Introduce tasks and tests in a nonthreatening way (e.g., to provide information about which skills need further work).

◆ Give opportunities to improve written assignments (e.g., correct errors, rewrite papers) and allow students to retake tests.

◆ Provide memory supports during a test (e.g., a sample problem, original text, lecture notes).

◆ Eliminate time pressure.

◆ Order questions so that those in the beginning are easier.

◆ Familiarize students with test format ahead of time.

Appendix 12–A: Questions for Teachers to Ask to Help Them Monitor Behavior Toward High and Low Achievers

1. Am I as friendly with low-achieving students as I am with high-achieving students?
2. Do I praise or encourage "lows" when they initiate comments?
3. Do I stay with "lows" in failure situations?
4. Do I praise "lows" only for performance that is truly deserving of praise (i.e., that required real effort)?
5. Do I call on "lows" in public situations?
6. How often do "lows" have positive success experiences in public situations?
7. Are "lows" needlessly criticized for wrong answers or failure to respond?
8. Are "lows" placed in a "low group" and treated as group members rather than as individuals?
9. Do I ignore the minor inappropriate behavior of "lows," or do mild violations of classroom rules bring on strong reprimands?
10. Do I make assignments variable, interesting, and challenging for "lows"?
11. How frequently do "lows" have a chance to evaluate their own work and to make important decisions?
12. What are the work preferences of individual students—do they like to work in pairs—and how often are those work preferences honored?
13. Do I intervene with "highs" when they are having difficulty?
14. Do I praise "highs" regardless of their effort or the quality of their performance?

From Good, T., & Brophy, J. (1986). *Educational psychology* (3rd ed.). White Plains, NY: Longman. Reprinted by permission of Addison-Wesley Educational Publishers Inc.

References

Aboud, F. (1985). The development of a social comparison process in children. *Child Development, 56,* 682–688.

Abramowitz, A., & O'Leary, S. (1991). Behavioral interventions for the classroom: Implications for students with ADHD. *School Psychology Review, 20,* 220–234.

Ainley, M. (1993). Styles of engagement with learning: Multidimensional assessment of their relationship with strategy use and school achievement. *Journal of Educational Psychology, 85,* 395–405.

Alexander, K., Dauber, S., & Entwisle, D. (1993). First-grade classroom behavior: Its short- and long-term consequences for school performance. *Child Development, 64,* 801–803.

Algaze, B. (1995). Cognitive therapy, study counseling, and systematic desensitization in the treatment of test anxiety. In C. Spielberger & P. Vagg (Eds.), *Test anxiety: Theory, assessment, and treatment* (pp. 133–152). Washington, DC: Taylor & Francis.

Alschuler, A. (1968). *How to increase motivation through climate and structure* (Working Paper No. 8-313). Cambridge, MA: Harvard University, Graduate School of Education, Achievement Motivation Development Project.

Amabile, T. (1983). *The social psychology of creativity.* New York: Springer-Verlag.

Amabile, T., DeJong, W., & Lepper, M. (1976). Effects of externally imposed deadlines on subsequent intrinsic motivation. *Journal of Personality and Social Psychology, 34,* 92–98.

Amabile, T., & Hennessey, B. (1992). The motivation for creativity in children. In A. Boggiano & T. Pittman (Eds.), *Achievement and motivation: A social-developmental perspective* (pp. 54–74). New York: Cambridge University Press.

Ames, C. (1978). Children's achievement attributions and self-reinforcement: Effects of self-concept and competitive reward structure. *Journal of Educational Psychology, 70,* 345–355.

Ames, C. (1981). Competitive versus cooperative reward structure: The influence of individual and group performance factors on achievement attributions and affect. *American Educational Research Journal, 18,* 273–288.

Ames, C. (1984). Competitive, cooperative and individualistic goal structures: A cognitive-motivational analysis. In R. Ames & C. Ames (Eds.), *Research on motivation in education: Vol. 1. Student motivation* (pp. 177–207). New York: Academic Press.

Ames, C. (1986). Conceptions of motivation within competitive and noncompetitive goal structures. In R. Schwarzer (Ed.), *Self-related cognitions in anxiety and motivation* (pp. 229–245). Hillsdale, NJ: Lawrence Erlbaum Associates.

Ames, C. (1992). Classrooms: Goals, structures, and student motivation. *Journal of Educational Psychology, 84,* 261–271.

Ames, C., & Ames, R. (1978). Thrill of victory and agony of defeat: Children's self and interpersonal evaluations in competitive and non-competitive learning environments. *Journal of Research and Development in Education, 12,* 79–81.

Ames, C., & Ames, R. (1981). Competitive versus individualistic goal structures: The salience of past performance information for causal attributions and affect. *Journal of Educational Psychology, 73,* 411–418.

Ames, C., & Ames, R. (1984). Goal structures and motivation. *Elementary School Journal, 85,* 39–52.

Ames, C., & Ames, R. (1990). Motivation and effective teaching. In L. Idol & B. Jones (Eds.), *Educational values and cognitive instruction: Implications for reform* (pp. 247–271). Hillsdale, NJ: Lawrence Erlbaum Associates.

Ames, C., Ames, R., & Felker, D. (1977). Effects of competitive reward structure and valence outcome on children's achievement attributions. *Journal of Educational Psychology, 69,* 1–8.

Ames, C., & Archer, J. (1988). Achievement goals in the classroom: Students' learning strategies and motivation processes. *Journal of Educational Psychology, 80,* 260–267.

Ames, C., & Felker, D. (1979). An examination of children's attribution and achievement-related evaluations in competitive, cooperative, and individualistic reward structures. *Journal of Educational Psychology, 71,* 413–420.

Anderman, E., & Maehr, M. (1994). Motivation and schooling in the middle grades. *Review of Educational Research, 65,* 287–309.

Anderson, L. (1981). Short-term students' responses to classroom instruction. *Elementary School Journal, 82,* 97–108.

Anderson, L. (1984). The environment of instruction: The function of seatwork in a commercially developed curriculum. In G. Duffy, L. Roehler, & J. Mason (Eds.), *Comprehensive instruction: Perspectives and suggestions* (pp. 93–103). New York: Longman.

Anderson, L., & Burns, R. (1987). Values, evidence, and mastery learning. *Review of Educational Research, 57,* 215–223.

Anderson, L., Evertson, C., & Brophy, J. (1979). An experimental study of effective teaching in first-grade reading groups. *Elementary School Journal, 79,* 193–223.

Anderson, R. (1982). Allocation of attention during reading. In A. Flammer & W. Kintsch (Eds.), *Discourse processing* (pp. 292–305). New York: North-Holland.

Anderson, R., Manoogian, S., & Reznick, J. (1976). The undermining and enhancing of intrinsic motivation in preschool children. *Journal of Personality and Social Psychology, 34,* 915–922.

Anderson, R., Shirey, L., Wilson, P., & Fielding, L. (1987). Interestingness of children's reading material. In R. Snow & M. Farr (Eds.), *Aptitude, learning, and instruction: III. Conative and affective process analyses* (pp. 287–299). Hillsdale, NJ: Lawrence Erlbaum Associates.

Anderson, S., & Sauser, W. (1995). Measurement of test anxiety: An overview. In C. Spielberger & P. Vagg (Eds.), *Test anxiety: Theory, assessment, and treatment* (pp. 15–33). Washington, DC: Taylor & Francis.

Anton, W., & Klisch, M. (1995). Perspectives on mathematics anxiety and test anxiety. In C. Spielberger & P. Vagg (Eds.), *Test anxiety: Theory, assessment, and treatment* (pp. 93–106). Washington, DC: Taylor & Francis.

Anton, W., & Lillibridge, E. M. (1995). Case studies of test-anxious students. In C. Spielberger & P. Vagg (Eds.), *Test anxiety: Theory, assessment, and treatment* (pp. 61–78). Washington, DC: Taylor & Francis.

Apple, M., & King, N. (1978). What do schools teach? In G. Willis (Ed.), *Qualitative evaluation: Concepts and cases in curriculum criticism* (pp. 444–465). Berkeley, CA: McCutchan.

Arkes, H. (1978). Competence and the maintenance of behavior. *Motivation and Emotion, 2,* 201–211.

Aronfreed, J. (1969). The concept of internalization. In D. Goslin (Ed.), *Handbook of socialization theory and research* (pp. 263–323). New York: Rand-McNally.

Aronson, E., Stephan, C., Sikes, J., Blaney, N., & Snapp, M. (1978). *The jigsaw classroom.* Beverly Hills: Sage Publications.

Asher, S. (1980). Topic interest and children's reading comprehension. In R. Spiro, B. Bruce, & W. Brewer (Eds.), *Theoretical issues in reading comprehension* (pp. 525–534). Hillsdale, NJ: Lawrence Erlbaum Associates.

Asher, S., Hymel, S., & Wigfield, A. (1978). Influence of topic interest on children's reading comprehension. *Journal of Reading Behavior, 10,* 35–47.

Ashton, P. (1985). Motivation and teachers' sense

of efficacy. In C. Ames & R. Ames (Eds.), *Research on motivation in education: Vol. 2. The classroom milieu* (pp. 141–174). Orlando, FL: Academic Press.

Ashton, P., & Webb, R. (1986). *Making a difference: Teachers' sense of efficacy and student achievement*. New York: Longman.

Atkinson, J. (1964). *An introduction to motivation*. Princeton, NJ: Van Nostrand.

Babad, E. (1990). Measuring and changing teachers' differential behavior as perceived by students and teachers. *Journal of Educational Psychology, 82*, 683–690.

Babad, E. (1992). Teacher expectancies and nonverbal behavior. In R. Feldman (Ed.), *Applications of nonverbal behavioral theories and research* (pp. 167–190). Hillsdale, NJ: Lawrence Erlbaum Associates.

Bachman, J., & O'Malley, P. (1986). Self-concepts, self-esteem and education experiences: The frog pond revisited (again). *Journal of Personality and Social Psychology. 50*, 35–46.

Ball, D. (1993). With an eye on the mathematical horizon: Dilemmas of teaching elementary school mathematics. *The Elementary School Journal, 93*, 373–397.

Ball, S. (1995). Anxiety and test performance. In C. Spielberger & P. Vagg (Eds.), *Test anxiety: Theory, assessment, and treatment* (pp. 107–113). Washington, DC: Taylor & Francis.

Bandalos, D., Yates, K., & Thorndike-Christ, T. (1995). Effects of math self-concept, perceived self-efficacy, and attributions for failure and success on test anxiety. *Journal of Educational Psychology, 87*, 611–623.

Bandura, A. (1965). Influence of models' reinforcement contingencies on the acquisition of imitative responses. *Journal of Personality and Social Psychology, 1*, 589–595.

Bandura, A. (1977a). Self-efficacy: Toward a unifying theory of behavioral change. *Psychological Review, 84*, 191–215.

Bandura, A. (1977b). *Social learning theory*. Englewood Cliffs, NJ: Prentice Hall.

Bandura, A. (1981). Self-referent thought: A developmental analysis of self-efficacy. In J. Flavell & L. Ross (Eds.), *Social cognitive development: Frontiers and possible futures* (pp. 200–239). New York: Cambridge University Press.

Bandura, A. (1982a). The self and mechanisms of agency. In J. Suls (Ed.), *Psychological perspec-tives on the self* (Vol. 1, pp. 3–39). Hillsdale, NJ: Lawrence Erlbaum Associates.

Bandura, A. (1982b). Self-efficacy mechanism in human agency. *American Psychologist, 37*, 122–147.

Bandura, A. (1986). *Social foundations of thought and action: Social cognitive theory*. Englewood Cliffs, NJ: Prentice Hall.

Bandura, A. (1988). Self efficacy conception of anxiety. *Anxiety Research. An International Journal, 1*, 77–98.

Bandura, A. (1991a). Self-regulation of motivation through anticipatory and self-regulatory mechanisms. In R. Dienstbier (Ed.), *Perspectives on motivation: Nebraska Symposium on Motivation* (Vol. 38, pp. 237–288). Lincoln: University of Nebraska Press.

Bandura, A. (1991b). *Self-regulation of motivation through anticipatory and self-reactive mechanisms and motivation: Nebraska Symposium on Motivation* (Vol. 38, pp. 69–164). Lincoln: University of Nebraska Press.

Bandura, A. (1992a). Exercise of personal agency through the self-efficacy mechanism. In R. Schwarzer (Ed.), *Self-efficacy: Thought control of action* (pp. 3–64). Washington, DC: Hemisphere Publishing.

Bandura, A. (1992b). Social cognitive theory of social referencing. In S. Feinman (Eds.), *Social referencing and the social construction of reality in infancy* (pp. 175–208). New York: Plenum.

Bandura, A. (1993). Perceived self-efficacy in cognitive development and functioning. *Educational Psychologist, 28*, 117–148.

Bandura, A. (1995). Exercise of personal and collective efficacy in changing societies. In A. Bandura (Ed.), *Self-efficacy in changing societies* (pp. 1–45). New York: Cambridge University Press.

Bandura, A. (1997). *Self-efficacy: The exercise of control*. New York: Freeman.

Bandura, A., Barbaranelli, C., Caprara, G., & Pastorelli, C. (1996). Multifaceted impact of self-efficacy beliefs on academic functioning. *Child Development, 67*, 1206–1222.

Bandura, A., & Schunk, D. (1981). Cultivating competence, self-efficacy, and intrinsic interests through proximal self-motivation. *Journal of Personality and Social Psychology, 41*, 586–598.

Bandura, A., & Walters, R. (1963). *Social learning and personality development*. New York: Holt, Rinehart, & Winston.

Barker, G., & Graham, S. (1987). Developmental study of praise and blame as attributional cues. *Journal of Educational Psychology*, *79*, 62–66.

Barwick, N. (1995). Pandora's box: An investigation of essay anxiety in adolescents. *Psychodynamic Counselling*, *1*, 560–575.

Baron, R., Tom, D., & Cooper, H. (1985). Social class, race, and teacher expectations. In J. Dusek (Ed.), *Teacher Expectations* (pp. 251–269). Hillsdale, NJ: Lawrence Erlbaum Associates.

Basile, D. (1982). Do attitudes about writing change as composition skills improve? *Community College Review*, *9*, 22–27

Bates, J. (1979). Extrinsic reward and intrinsic motivation: A review with implications for the classroom. *Review of Educational Research*, *49*, 557–576.

Becker, J. (1981). Differential treatment of females and males in mathematics classes. *Journal for Research in Mathematics Education*, *12*, 40–53.

Bedell, J., & Marlowe, H. (1995). An evaluation of test anxiety scales: Convergent, divergent, and predictive validity. In C. Spielberger & P. Vagg (Eds.), *Test anxiety: Theory, assessment, and treatment* (pp. 35–45). Washington, DC: Taylor & Francis.

Benjamin, M., McKeachie, W., & Lin, Y-G. (1987). Two types of test anxious students: Support for an information processing model. *Journal of Educational Psychology*, *59*, 128–132.

Benjamin, M., McKeachie, W., Lin, Y-G., & Holinger, D. (1981). Test anxiety: Deficits in information processing. *Journal of Educational Psychology*, *73*, 816–824.

Benson, J., Bandalos, D., & Hutchinson, S. (1994). Modeling test anxiety among males and females. *Anxiety, stress, and coping*, *7*, 131–148.

Benware, C., & Deci, E. (1984). Quality of learning with an active versus passive motivational set. *American Educational Research Journal*, *21*, 755–765.

Berlyne, D. (1966). Curiosity and exploration. *Science*, *153*, 25–33.

Berry, J., & West, R. (1993). Cognitive self-efficacy in relation to personal mastery and goal setting across the life-span. *International Journal of Behavioral Development*, *16*, 351–379.

Betz, N., & Hackett, G. (1983). The relationship of mathematics self-efficacy expectations to the selection of science-based college majors. *Journal of Vocational Behavior*, *23*, 329–345

Birch, S., & Ladd, G. (1997). The teacher–child relationship and children's early school adjustment. *Journal of School Psychology*, *35*, 61–79.

Blanck, P., Reis, H., & Jackson, L. (1984). The effects of verbal reinforcements on intrinsic motivation for sex-linked tasks. *Sex Roles*, *10*, 369–387.

Blankstein, K., Flett, G., & Watson, M. (1992). Coping and academic problem-solving ability in test anxiety. *Journal of Clinical Psychology*, *48*, 37–46.

Block, J. (Ed.). (1974). *Schools, society, and mastery learning*. New York: Holt, Rinehart & Winston.

Block, J. (1979). Mastery learning: The current state of the craft. *Educational Leadership*, *37*, 114–117.

Block, J., Efthim, H., & Burns, R. (1989). *Building effective mastery learning schools*. New York: Longman.

Bloom, B. (1971). Mastery learning and its implications for curriculum development. In E. W. Eisner (Ed.), *Confronting curriculum reform* (pp. 17–55). Boston: Little, Brown.

Bloom, B. (1974). An introduction to mastery learning theory. In J. H. Block (Ed.), *Schools, society, and mastery learning* (pp. 3–14). New York: Holt, Rinehart & Winston.

Bloom, B. (1976). *Human characteristics and school learning*. New York: McGraw-Hill.

Bloom, B. (1981). *All our children learning*. New York: McGraw-Hill.

Bloom, B., Hastings, J., & Madaus, G. (1971). *Handbook on formative and summative evaluation of student learning*. New York: McGraw-Hill.

Blue, S., Madsen, C., & Heimberg, R. (1981). Increasing coping behavior in children with aggressive behavior: Evaluation of the relative efficacy of the components of a treatment package. *Child Behavior Therapy*, *3*, 51–60.

Blumenfeld, P. (1992). Classroom learning and motivation: Clarifying and expanding goal theory. *Journal of Educational Psychology*, *84*, 272–281.

Blumenfeld, P., Hamilton, V., Bossert, S.,

Wessels, K., & Meece, J. (1983). Teacher talk and student thought: Socialization into the student role. In J. M. Levine & M. C. Wang (Eds.), *Teacher and student perceptions: Implications for learning* (pp. 143–192). Hillsdale, NJ: Lawrence Erlbaum Associates.

Blumenfeld, P., & Mergendoller, J. (1992). Translating motivation into thoughtfulness. In H. Marshall (Ed.), *Redefining student learning: Roots of educational change* (pp. 207–239). Norwood, NJ: Ablex.

Blumenfeld, P., Pintrich, P., & Hamilton, V. (1986). Children's concepts of ability, effort, and conduct. *American Educational Research Journal, 23,* 95–104.

Blumenfeld, P., Pintrich, P., Meece, J., & Wessels, K. (1982). The formation and role of self-perceptions of ability in elementary classrooms. *Elementary School Journal, 82,* 401–420.

Blumenfeld, P., Soloway, E., Marx, R., Krajcik, J., Guzdial, M., & Palincsar, A. (in press). Motivating project-based learning: Sustaining the doing, supporting the learning. *Educational Psychologist.*

Boggiano, A., Main, D., & Katz, P. (1988). Children's preference for challenge: The role of perceived competence and control. *Journal of Personality and Social Psychology, 54,* 134–141.

Boggiano, A., Pittman, T., & Ruble, D. (1982). The mastery hypothesis and the over-justification effect. *Social Cognition, 1,* 38–49.

Boggiano, A., & Ruble, D. (1979). Competence and the overjustification effect: A developmental study. *Journal of Personality and Social Psychology, 37,* 1462–1468.

Borko, H., & Eisenhart, M. (1986). Students' conceptions of reading and their experiences in school. *Elementary School Journal, 86,* 589–611.

Borkowski, J., Carr, M., Rellinger, E., & Pressley, M. (1990). Self-regulated strategy use: Interdependence of metacognition, attributions, and self-esteem. In B. Jones (Ed.), *Dimensions of thinking: Review of research* (pp. 53–92). Hillsdale, NJ: Lawrence Erlbaum Associates.

Borkowski, J., & Thorpe, P. (1994). Self-regulation and motivation: A life-span perspective on underachievement. In D. Schunk & B. Zimmerman (Eds.), *Self-regulation of learning and performance* (pp. 45–73). Hillsdale, NJ: Lawrence Erlbaum Associates.

Borkowski, J., Weyhing, R., & Carr, M. (1988). Effects of attributional retraining on strategy-based reading comprehension in learning-disabled students. *Journal of Educational Psychology, 80,* 46–53.

Bornstein, P., & Quevillon, R. (1976). The effects of a self-instructional package on overactive preschool boys. *Journal of Applied Behavior Analysis, 9,* 179–188.

Bossert, S. (1979). *Tasks and social relationships in classrooms.* (The Arnold and Caroline Rose Monograph Series of the American Sociological Association). New York: Cambridge University Press.

Bouffard-Bouchard, T. (1990). Influence of self-efficacy on performance in a cognitive task. *Journal of Social Psychology, 139,* 353–363.

Bouffard-Bouchard, T., Parent, S., & Larivee, S. (1991). Influence of self-efficacy on self-regulation and performance among junior and senior high-school age students. *International Journal of Behavioral Development, 14,* 153–164.

Brattesani, K., Weinstein, R., & Marshall, H. (1984). Student perceptions of differential teacher treatment as moderators of teacher expectation effects. *Journal of Educational Psychology, 76,* 236–247.

Brockner, J. (1979). Self-esteem, self-consciousness, and task performance: Replications, extensions, and possible explanations. *Journal of Personality and Social Psychology, 37,* 447–461.

Brooks-Gunn, J., Guo, G., & Furstenberg, F. (1993). Who drops out of and who continues beyond high school? A 20-year follow-up of Black urban youth. *Journal of Research on Adolescence, 30,* 271–294.

Brophy, J. (1981). Teacher praise: A functional analysis. *Review of Educational Research, 51,* 5–32.

Brophy, J. (1983a). Fostering student learning and motivation in the elementary school classroom. In S. Paris, G. Olson, & H. Stevenson (Eds.), *Learning and motivation in the classroom* (pp. 283–305). Hillsdale, NJ: Lawrence Erlbaum Associates.

Brophy, J. (1983b). Research on the self-fulfilling prophecy and teacher expectations. *Journal of Educational Psychology, 75,* 631–661.

Brophy, J. (1985). Interactions of male and female

students with male and female teachers. In L. Wilkinson & C. Marrett (Eds.), *Gender influences in classroom interaction* (pp. 115–142). Hillsdale, NJ: Lawrence Erlbaum Associates.

Brophy, J. (1986). *Socializing student motivation to learn*. (Teaching Research Series No. 169). East Lansing: Michigan State University, Institute for Research.

Brophy, J. (1987a). On motivating students. In D. Berliner & B. Rosenshine (Eds.), *Talks to teachers* (pp. 201–245). New York: Random House.

Brophy, J. (1987b). Socializing students' motivation to learn. In M. Maehr & D. Kleiber (Eds.), *Advances in motivation and achievement: Vol. 5. Enhancing motivation* (pp. 181–210). Greenwich, CT: JAI Press.

Brophy, J., & Alleman, J. (1991). A caveat: Curriculum integration isn't always a good idea. *Educational Leadership, 49,* 66.

Brophy, J., & Evertson, C. (1978). Context variables in teaching. *Educational Psychologist, 12,* 310–316.

Brophy, J., Evertson, C., Anderson, L., Baum, M., & Crawford, J. (1976). *Student personality and teaching: Final report of the Student Attribute Study*. Educational Resources Information Center. (ERIC Document Reproduction Service No. ED 121 799)

Brophy, J., & Rohrkemper, M. (1981). The influence of problem ownership on teachers' perceptions of and strategies for coping with problem students. *Journal of Educational Psychology, 73,* 295–311.

Brophy, J., Rohrkemper, M., Rashid, H., & Goldberger, M. (1983). Relationships between teachers' presentations of classroom tasks and students' engagements in those tasks. *Journal of Educational Psychology, 75,* 544–552.

Brown, R., & Pressley, M. (1994). Self-regulated reading and getting meaning from text: The transactional strategies instruction model and its ongoing validation. In D. Schunk & B. Zimmerman (Eds.), *Self-regulation of learning and performance* (pp. 101–124). Hillsdale, NJ: Lawrence Erlbaum Associates.

Bruch, M., Juster, H., & Kaflowitz, N. (1983). Relationships of cognitive components of test anxiety to test performance: Implications for assessment and treatment. *Journal of*

Counseling Psychology, 30, 527–536.

Bruner, J. (1966). *Toward a theory of instruction*. Cambridge, MA: Harvard University Press.

Brush, L. (1979). *Why women avoid the study of mathematics: A longitudinal study*. Cambridge, MA: Abt Associates.

Buckholdt, D., & Wodarski, J. (1974, August). *The effects of different reinforcement systems on cooperative behaviors exhibited by children in classroom contexts*. Paper presented at the annual meeting of the American Psychological Association, New Orleans, LA.

Burhans, K., & Dweck, C. (1995). Helplessness in early childhood: The role of contingent worth. *Child Development, 66,* 1719–1738.

Burns, M. (1987). *A collection of math lessons: From grades 3 through 6*. New York: Cuisennaire.

Butkowsky, I., & Willows, D. (1980). Cognitive-motivational characteristics of children varying in reading ability: Evidence for learned helplessness in poor readers. *Journal of Educational Psychology, 72,* 408–422.

Butler, R. (1987). Task-involving and ego-involving properties of evaluation: Effects of different feedback conditions on motivational perceptions, interest, and performance. *Journal of Educational Psychology, 79,* 474–482.

Butler, R. (1988). Enhancing and undermining intrinsic motivation: The effects of task-involving and ego-involving evaluation on interest and performance. *British Journal of Educational Psychology, 58,* 1–14.

Butler, R. (1989). Mastery versus ability appraisal: A developmental study of children's observations of peers' work. *Child Development, 60,* 1350–1361.

Butler, R. (1992). What young people want to know when: Effects of mastery and ability goals on interest in different kinds of social comparisons. *Journal of Personality and Social Psychology, 62,* 934–943.

Butler, R. (1994). Teacher communications and student interpretations: Effects of teacher responses to failing students on attributional inferences in two age groups. *British Journal of Educational Psychology, 64,* 277–294.

Butler, R. (1995). Motivational and informational functions and consequences of children's attention to peers' work. *Journal of Educational Psychology, 87,* 347–360.

Butler, R., & Nisan, M. (1986). Effects of no feedback, task-related comments, and grades on intrinsic motivation and performance. *Journal of Educational Psychology, 78,* 210–216.

Butler, R., & Ruzany, N. (1993). Age and socialization effects on the development of social comparison motives and normative ability assessment in kibbutz and urban children. *Child Development, 64,* 532–543.

Byrne, B. (1996). Academic self-concept: Its structure, measurement, and relation to academic achievement. In B. Bracken (Ed.), *Handbook of self-concept: Developmental, social, and clinical considerations* (pp. 287–316). New York: John Wiley & Sons.

Byrne, B., & Gavin, D. (1996). The Shavelson model revisited: Testing for the structure of academic self-concept across pre-, early, and late adolescents. *Journal of Educational Psychology, 88,* 215–228.

Cain, K., & Dweck, C. (1989). The development of children's conceptions of intelligence: A theoretical framework. In R. Sternberg (Ed.), *Advances in the psychology of human intelligence* (Vol. 5, pp. 47–82). Hillsdale, NJ: Lawrence Erlbaum Associates.

Cameron, J., & Pierce, W. (1994). Reinforcement, reward, and intrinsic motivation: A meta-analysis. *Review of Educational Research, 64,* 363–423.

Carpenter, T., Corbitt, M., Kepner, H., Lindquist, M., & Reys, R. (1981). *Results from the second mathematics assessment of the National Assessment of Educational Progress.* Reston, VA: National Council of Teachers of Mathematics.

Casady, M. (1975). The tricky business of giving rewards. *Psychology Today, 8,* 52.

Chapman, M., Skinner, E., & Baltes, P. (1990). Interpreting correlations between children's perceived control and cognitive performance: Control, agency, or means-ends beliefs? *Developmental Psychology, 26,* 246–253.

Chen, C., & Stevenson, H. (1995). Motivation and mathematics achievement: A comparative study of Asian-American, Caucasian-American, and East Asian high school students. *Child Development, 66,* 1215–1234.

Chen, C., & Uttal, D. (1988). Cultural values, parents' beliefs, and children's achievement in the United States and China. *Human Development, 31,* 351–358.

Clifford, M. (1984). Thoughts on a theory of constructive failure. *Educational Psychologist, 19,* 108–120.

Clifford, M. (1988). Failure tolerance and academic risk-taking in ten to twelve-year-old students. *British Journal of Educational Psychology, 58,* 15–27.

Clifford, M. (1991). Risk taking: Theoretical, empirical, and educational considerations. *Educational Psychologist, 26,* 263–297.

Cochran, L., Feng, H., Cartledge, G., & Hamilton, S. (1993). *Behavioral Disorders, 18,* 292–302.

Cohen, E. (1986). *Designing groupwork.* New York: Teachers College Press.

Cohen, E., & Lotan, R. (1995). Producing equal-status interaction in the heterogeneous classroom. *American Educational Research Journal, 32,* 99–120.

Cohen, H. (1973). Behavior modification in socially deviant youth. In C. Thoresen (Ed.), *Behavior modification in education: Seventy-second yearbook of the National Society for the Study of Education, 72, Part I* (pp. 291–314). Chicago: University of Chicago Press.

Collins, J. (1982, March). *Self-efficacy and ability in achievement behavior.* Paper presented at the annual meeting of the American Educational Research Association, New York.

Comer, J. (1993). *School power: Implications of an intervention project.* New York: Free Press.

Connell, J. (1985). A new multidimensional measure of children's perceptions of control. *Child Development, 56,* 1018–1041.

Connell, J. (1991). Context, self, and action: A motivational analysis of self-system processes across the life span. In D. Cicchetti & M. Beeghly (Eds.), *The self in transition: Infancy to childhood* (pp. 61–97). Chicago: University of Chicago Press.

Connell, J., & Ryan, R. (1984). A developmental theory of motivation in the classroom. *Teacher Education Quarterly, 11,* 64–77.

Connell, J., Spencer, M., & Aber, L. (1994). Educational risk and resilience in African-American youth: Context, self, action, and outcomes in school. *Child Development, 65,* 493–506.

Connell, J., & Wellborn, J. (1991). Competence, autonomy, and relatedness: A motivational analysis of self-system processes. In M. Gunnar & L. Sroufe (Eds.), *Self processes in development: Minnesota Symposium on Child Psychology* (Vol. 23, pp. 43–77). Hillsdale,

NJ: Lawrence Erlbaum Associates.

Cooper, H., & Tom, D. (1984). Teacher expectations research: A review with implications for classroom instruction. *Elementary School Journal, 85,* 77–89.

Cordova, D., & Lepper, M. (1996). Intrinsic motivation and the process of learning: Beneficial effects of contextualization, personalization, and choice. *Journal of Educational Psychology, 88,* 715–730.

Corno, L. (1989). Self-regulated learning: A volitional analysis. In B. Zimmerman & D. Schunk (Eds.), *Self-regulated learning and academic achievement: Theory, research, and practice* (pp. 111–141). New York: Springer-Verlag.

Corno, L., & Rohrkemper, M. (1985). The intrinsic motivation to learn in classrooms. In C. Ames & R. Ames (Eds.), *Research on motivation in education, Vol 2: The classroom milieu* (pp. 53–90). Orlando, FL: Academic Press.

Cosden, M., & Haring, T. (1992). Cooperative learning in the classroom: Contingencies, group interactions, and students with special needs. *Journal of Behavioral Education, 2,* 53–71.

Covington, M. (1984). The self-worth theory of achievement motivation: Findings and implications. *The Elementary School Journal, 85,* 5–20.

Covington, M. (1985). Strategic thinking and the fear of failure. In J. Segal, S. Chipman, & R. Glaser (Eds.), *Thinking and learning skills, Vol 1: Relating instruction to research.* Hillsdale, NJ: Lawrence Erlbaum Associates.

Covington, M. (1992). *Making the grade: A self-worth perspective on motivation and school reform.* New York: Cambridge University Press.

Covington, M., & Beery, R. (1976). *Self-worth and school learning.* New York: Holt, Rinehart and Winston.

Covington, M., & Omelich, C. (1979a). Effort: The double-edged sword in school achievement. *Journal of Educational Psychology, 71,* 169–182.

Covington, M., & Omelich, C. (1979b). It's best to be able and virtuous too: Student and teacher evaluative responses to successful effort. *Journal of Educational Psychology, 71,* 688–700.

Covington, M., & Omelich, C. (1981). As failures

mount: Affective and cognitive consequences of ability demotion in the classroom. *Journal of Educational Psychology, 73,* 796–808.

Covington, M., & Omelich, C. (1984a). An empirical examination of Weiner's critique of attribution research. *Journal of Educational Psychology, 76,* 1214–1225.

Covington, M., & Omelich, C. (1984b). Task-oriented versus competitive learning structures: Motivational and performance consequences. *Journal of Educational Psychology, 7,* 1038–1050.

Covington, M., & Omelich, C. (1988). Achievement dynamics: The interaction of motives, cognitions, and emotions over time. *Anxiety Research, 1,* 165–183.

Covington, M., Spratt, M., & Omelich, C. (1980). Is effort enough or does diligence count too? Student and teacher reactions to effort stability in failure. *Journal of Educational Psychology, 72,* 717–729.

Cramer, J., & Oshima, T. (1992). Do gifted females attribute their math performance differently than other students? *Journal for the Education of the Gifted, 16,* 18–35.

Crandall, V. J. (1963). Achievement. In H. Stevenson (Ed.), *Child psychology: Sixty-second yearbook of the National Society for the Study of Education* (pp. 416–459). Chicago: University of Chicago Press.

Crandall, V. C. (1967). Achievement behavior in young children. In W. W. Hartup & N. L. Smothergill (Eds.), *The young child* (pp. 165–185). Washington, DC: National Association for the Education of Young Children.

Crandall, V., Katkovsky, W., & Crandall, V. (1965). Children's beliefs in their own control of reinforcement in intellectual-academic achievement situations. *Child Development, 36,* 91–109.

Crandall, V., Katkovsky, W., & Preston, A. (1962). Motivational and ability determinants of young children's intellectual achievement behaviors. *Child Development, 33,* 643–661.

Crockenberg, S., & Bryant, B. (1978). Socialization: The "implicit curriculum" of learning environments. *Journal of Research Development in Education, 12,* 69–78.

Csikszentmihalyi, M. (1975). *Beyond boredom and anxiety.* San Francisco: Jossey-Bass.

Csikszentmihalyi, M. (1988). The flow experience

and its significance for human psychology. In M. Csikszentmihalyi & I. Csikszentmihalyi (Eds.), *Optimal experience* (pp. 15–35). Cambridge, MA: Cambridge University Press.

Culler, R., & Holahan, C. (1980). Test anxiety and academic performance: The effects of study-related behaviors. *Journal of Educational Psychology, 72,* 16–20.

Daly, J. (1985). Writing apprehension. In M. Rose (Ed.), *When a writer can't write* (pp. 43–82). New York: Guilford Press.

Daly, J., & Miller, M. (1975a). The empirical development of an instrument to measure writing apprehension. *Research in the Teaching of English, 9,* 242–249.

Daly, J., & Miller, M. (1975b). Further studies in writing apprehension: SAT scores, success expectations, willingness to take advanced courses and sex differences. *Research in the Teaching of English, 9,* 250–256.

Daly, J., Vangelisti, A., & Witte, S. (1988). Writing apprehension in the classroom context. In B. Rafoth & D. Rubin (Eds.), *The social construction of written communication* (pp. 147–171). Norwood, NJ: Ablex.

Damon, W. (1995). *Greater expectations: Overcoming the culture of indulgence in America's homes and schools.* New York: Free Press.

Danner, F., & Lonky, E. (1981). A cognitive-developmental approach to the effects of rewards on intrinsic motivation. *Child Development, 52,* 1043–1052.

Deaux, K. (1976). Sex: A perspective on the attributional process. In J. Harvey, W. Ickes, & R. Kidd (Eds.), *New directions in attribution research* (Vol. 1, pp. 335–352). Hillsdale, NJ: Lawrence Erlbaum Associates.

deCharms, R. (1976). *Enhancing motivation.* New York: Irvington Publishers.

deCharms, R. (1983). Intrinsic motivation, peer tutoring, and cooperative learning: Practical maxims. In J. Levine & M. Wang (Eds.), *Teacher and student perceptions: Implications for learning* (pp. 391–398). Hillsdale, NJ: Lawrence Erlbaum Associates.

deCharms, R. (1984). Motivating enhancement in educational settings. In R. Ames & C. Ames (Eds.), *Research on motivation in education. Vol. 1: Student motivation* (pp. 275–310). New York: Academic Press.

Deci, E. (1971). The effects of externally mediated

rewards on intrinsic motivation. *Journal of Personality and Social Psychology, 18,* 105–115.

Deci, E. (1972). Intrinsic motivation, extrinsic reinforcement, and inequity. *Journal of Personality and Social Psychology, 22,* 113–120.

Deci, E. (1975). *Intrinsic motivation.* New York: Plenum.

Deci, E. (1992). The relation of interest to the motivation of behavior: A self-determination theory perspective. In K. Renninger, S. Hidi, & A. Krapp (Eds.), *The role of interest in learning and development* (pp. 43–70). Hillsdale, NJ: Lawrence Erlbaum Associates.

Deci, E., Betley, G., Kahle, J., Abrams, L., & Porac, J. (1981). When trying to win: Competition and intrinsic motivation. *Personality and Social Psychology, 7,* 79–83.

Deci, E., Nezlek, J., & Sheinman, L. (1981). Characteristics of the rewarder and intrinsic motivation of the rewardee. *Journal of Personality and Social Psychology, 40,* 1–10.

Deci, E., & Ryan, R. (1985). *Intrinsic motivation and self-determination in human behavior.* New York: Plenum.

Deci, E., & Ryan, R. (1987). The support of autonomy and the control of behavior. *Journal of Personality and Social Psychology, 53,* 1024–1037.

Deci, E., & Ryan, R. (1991). A motivational approach to self: Integration in personality. In R. Dienstbier (Ed.), *Nebraska Symposium on motivation, 1990: Perspectives on motivation. (Current theory and research in motivation)* (Vol. 38, pp. 237–288). Lincoln: University of Nebraska Press.

Deci, E., & Ryan, R. (1992). The initiation and regulation of intrinsically motivated learning and achievement. In A. Boggiano & T. Pittman (Eds.), *Achievement and motivation: A social-developmental perspective* (pp. 9–36). New York: Cambridge University Press.

Deci, E., Schwartz, A., Sheinman, L., & Ryan, R. (1981). An instrument to assess adults' orientations toward control versus autonomy with children: Reflections on intrinsic motivation and perceived competence. *Journal of Educational Psychology, 73,* 642–650.

Deci, E., Spiegel, N., Ryan, R., Koestner, R., & Kauffman, M. (1982). Effects of performance standards on teaching styles: Behavior of controlling teachers. *Journal of*

Educational Psychology, 74, 852–859.

Deci, E., Vallerand, R., Pelletier, L., & Ryan, R. (1991). Motivation and education: The self-determination perspective. *The Educational Psychologist, 26,* 325–346.

Deffenbacher, J. (1980). Worry and emotionality in test anxiety. In I. Sarason (Ed.), *Test anxiety: Theory, research and applications* (pp. 111–128). Hillsdale, NJ: Lawrence Erlbaum Associates.

Deffenbacher, J., & Suinn, R. (1988). Systematic desensitization and the reduction of anxiety. *Counseling Psychologist, 16,* 9–30.

Deffenbacher, T. L. (1986). Cognitive and physiological components of test anxiety in real-life exams. *Cognitive Therapy & Research, 10,* 636–644.

Delgado-Gaitan, C. (1993). Parenting in two generations of Mexican American families. *International Journal of Behavior Development, 16,* 409–427.

Dendato, K., & Diener, D. (1986). Effectiveness of cognitive/relaxation therapy and study-skills training in reducing self-reported anxiety and improving the academic performance of test-anxious students. *Journal of Counseling Psychology, 33,* 131–135.

Desiderato, O., & Koskinen, P. (1969). Anxiety, study habits, and academic achievement. *Journal of Counseling Psychology, 16,* 162–165.

Diener, C., & Dweck, C. (1978). An analysis of learned helplessness: Continuous changes in performance, strategy, and achievement cognitions following failure. *Journal of Personality and Social Psychology, 36,* 451–462.

Diener, C., & Dweck, C. (1980). An analysis of learned helplessness: II. The processing of success. *Journal of Personality and Social Psychology, 39,* 940–952.

Dollinger, S., & Thelen, M. (1978). Over-justification and children's intrinsic motivation: Comparative effects of four rewards. *Journal of Personality and Social Psychology, 36,* 1259–1269.

Dulany, D. (1968). Awareness, rules, and propositional control: A confrontation with S–R behavior theory. In T. Dixon & D. Horton (Eds.), *Verbal behavior and general behavior theory* (pp. 340–387). Englewood Cliffs, NJ: Prentice Hall.

Dusek, J. (1975). Do teachers bias children's learning? *Review of Educational Research, 45,* 661–684.

Dusek, J. (1980). The development of test anxiety in children. In I. Sarason (Ed.), *Test anxiety: Theory, research, and applications* (pp. 87–110). Hillsdale, NJ: Lawrence Erlbaum Associates.

Dusek, J. (Ed.). (1985). *Teacher expectancies.* Hillsdale, NJ: Lawrence Erlbaum Associates.

Dusek, J., & Joseph, G. (1983). The bases of teacher expectancies: A meta-analysis. *Journal of Educational Psychology, 75,* 327–346.

Dusek, J., Kermis, M., & Mergler, N. (1975). Information processing in low- and high-test-anxious children as a function of grade level and verbal labeling. *Developmental Psychology, 11,* 651–652.

Dusek, J., Mergler, N., & Kermis, M. (1976). Attention, encoding, and information processing in low- and high-test-anxious children. *Child Development, 47,* 201–207.

Dweck, C. (1975). The role of expectations and attributions in the alleviation of learned helplessness. *Journal of Personality and Social Psychology, 31,* 674–685.

Dweck, C. (1986). Motivational processes affecting learning. *American Psychologist, 41,* 1040–1048.

Dweck, C., & Bempechat, J. (1983). Children's theories of intelligence: Consequences for learning. In S. Paris, G. Olson, & H. Stevenson (Eds.). *Learning and motivation in the classroom* (pp. 239–255). Hillsdale, NJ: Lawrence Erlbaum Associates.

Dweck, C., & Elliott, E. (1983). Achievement motivation. In P. Mussen (Ed.), *Handbook of child psychology. Vol. IV: Socialization, personality, and social development* (pp. 643–691). New York: John Wiley & Sons.

Dweck, C., & Goetz, T. (1978). Attributions and learned helplessness. In W. Harvey & R. Kidd (Eds.), *New directions in attribution research* (Vol. 2, pp. 157–179). Hillsdale, NJ: Lawrence Erlbaum Associates.

Dweck, C., & Leggett, E. (1988). A social-cognitive approach to motivation and personality. *Psychological Review, 95,* 256–273.

Dweck, C., & Reppucci, N. (1973). Learned helplessness and reinforcement responsibility in children. *Journal of Personality and Social Psychology, 25,* 109–116.

Earley, P., & Lituchy, T. (1991). Delineating goal and efficacy effects: A test of three models. *Journal of Applied Psychology, 76,* 71–98.

Eccles, J. (1980). *Self-perceptions, task perceptions and academic choice: Origins and change.* Final

Report to National Institute of Education. Washington, DC.

Eccles, J. (1984). Sex differences in achievement patterns. In T. Sonderegger (Ed.), *Nebraska Symposium on Motivation* (Vol. 32, pp. 97–132). Lincoln: University of Nebraska Press.

Eccles, J. (1993). School and family effects on the ontogeny of children's interests, self-perceptions, and activity choices. In J. Jacobs (Ed.), *Developmental perspectives on motivation, Vol. 40 of the Nebraska Symposium on Motivation* (pp. 145–208). Lincoln: University of Nebraska Press.

Eccles, J. (1994). Understanding women's educational and occupational choices: Applying the Eccles et al. model of achievement-related choices. *Psychology of Women Quarterly, 18*, 585–609.

Eccles, J., Adler, T., Futterman, R., Goff, S., Kaczala, C., Meece, J., & Midgley, C. (1983). Expectancies, values, and academic behavior. In J. T. Spence (Ed.), *Achievement and achievement motives: Psychological and sociological approaches* (pp. 75–146). San Francisco: W. H. Freeman.

Eccles, J., Adler, T., & Meece, J. (1984). Sex differences in achievement: A test of alternative theories. *Journal of Personality and Social Psychology, 46*, 26–43.

Eccles, J., & Blumenfeld, P. (1985). Classroom experiences and student gender: Are there differences and do they matter? In L. Wilkinson & C. Marrett (Eds.), *Gender influences in classroom interaction* (pp. 79–114). Hillsdale, NJ: Lawrence Erlbaum Associates.

Eccles, J., & Midgley, C. (1989). Stage environment fit: Developmentally appropriate classrooms for early adolescents. In R. Ames & C. Ames (Eds.), *Research on motivation in education. Vol. 3: Goals and cognitions* (pp. 139–186). New York: Academic Press.

Eccles, J., & Midgley, C. (1990). Changes in academic motivation and self-perception during early adolescence. In R. Montemayor (Ed.), *Early adolescence as a time of transition* (pp. 1–29). Beverly Hills, CA: Sage.

Eccles, J., Midgley, C., & Adler, T. (1984). Grade-related changes in the school environment: Effects on achievement motivation. In J. Nicholls (Ed.), *Advances in motivation and achievement. Vol. 3: The development of achievement motivation* (pp. 283–331).

Greenwich, CT: JAI Press.

Eccles, J., & Wigfield, A. (1993). Age and gender differences in children's self- and task perceptions during elementary school. *Child Development, 64*, 830–847.

Eccles, J., & Wigfield, A. (1995). In the mind of the actor: The structure of adolescents' achievement task values and expectancy-related beliefs. *Personality and Social Psychology Bulletin, 21*, 215–225.

Eccles, J., Wigfield, A., Flanagan, C., Miller, C., Reuman, D., & Yee, D. (1989). Self-concepts, domain values, and self-esteem: Relations and changes at early adolescence. *Journal of Personality, 57*, 283–310.

Eccles, J., Wigfield, A., Harold, R., & Blumenfeld, P. (1993). Age and gender differences in children's self- and task perceptions during elementary school. *Child Development, 64*, 830–847.

Eccles, J., Wigfield, A., Midgley, C., Reuman, D., Mac Iver, D., & Feldlaufer, H. (1993). Negative effects of traditional middle schools on students' motivation. *The Elementary School Journal, 93*, 553–574.

Eccles, J., Wigfield, A., & Schiefele, U. (in press). Motivation to succeed. In B. Damon (Ed.), *Handbook of child psychology* (5th ed., Vol. IV). New York: John Wiley & Sons.

Eckert, P. (1989). *Jocks and burnouts: Social categories and identity in the high school.* New York: Teachers College Press.

Eder, D. (1983). Ability grouping and students' academic self-concepts: A case study. *The Elementary School Journal, 84*, 149–161.

Edmonds, R. (1979). Effective schools for the urban poor. *Educational Leadership, 37*, 15–18.

Eisenberger, R. (1992). Learned industriousness. *Psychological Review, 99*, 248–267.

Elliott, E., & Dweck, C. (1988). Goals: An approach to motivation and achievement. *Journal of Personality and Social Psychology, 54*, 5–12.

Ensminger, M., & Slusarcick, A. (1992). Paths to high school graduation or dropout: A longitudinal study of a first grade cohort. *Sociology of Education, 65*, 95–113.

Entwisle, D., & Baker, D. (1983). Gender and young children's expectations for performance in arithmetic. *Developmental Psychology, 19*, 200–209.

Entwisle, D., & Hayduk, L. (1978). *Too great expectations: Young children's academic outlook.* Baltimore: Johns Hopkins University Press.

Estes, W. (1972). Reinforcement in human behavior. *American Scientist, 60,* 723–729.

Eswara, H. (1972). Administration of reward and punishment in relation to ability, effort, and performance. *Journal of Social Psychology, 87,* 137–140.

Evans, K., & King, J. (1994). Research on OBE: What we know and don't know. *Educational Leadership, 51*(6), 1217.

Everson, H., Millsap, R., & Rodriguez, C. (1991). Isolating gender differences in test anxiety: A confirmatory factor analysis of the Test Anxiety Inventory. *Educational & Psychological Measurement, 51,* 243–251.

Everson, H., Smodlaka, I., & Tobias, S. (1994). Exploring the relationship of test anxiety and metacognition on reading test performance: A cognitive analysis. *Anxiety, Stress & Coping: An International Journal, 7,* 85–96.

Everson, H., Tobias, S., Hartman, H., & Gourgey, A. (1993). Test anxiety and the curriculum: The subject matters. *Anxiety, Stress & Coping: An International Journal, 6,* 1–8.

Eysenck, M. (1988). Anxiety and attention. *Anxiety Research: An International Journal, 1,* 9–15.

Eysenck, M. (1991). Anxiety and attention. In R. Schwarzer & R. A. Wicklund (Eds.), *Anxiety and self-focused attention* (pp. 125–131). New York: Harwood Academic.

Fagot, B. (1973). Influence of teacher behavior in the preschool. *Developmental Psychology, 9,* 196–206.

Fantuzzo, J., McDermott, P., Manz, P., Hampton, V., & Burdick, N. (1996). The pictorial scale of perceived competence and social acceptance: Does it work with low-income urban children? *Child Development, 67,* 1071–1084.

Fantuzzo, J., & Polite, K. (1990). School-based, behavioral self-management: A review and analysis. *School Psychology Quarterly, 5,* 180–198.

Farnham-Diggory, S., & Ramsey, B. (1971). Play persistence: Some effects of interruptions, social reinforcement, and defective toys. *Developmental Psychology, 4,* 297–298.

Feather, N. (1961). The relationship of persistence at a task to expectations for success and achievement-related motives. *Journal of Abnormal and Social Psychology, 63,* 552–561.

Feather, N. (1963). Persistence at a difficult task with an alternative task of intermediate difficulty. *Journal of Abnormal and Social Psychology, 66,* 604–609.

Feather, N. (1988). Values, valences, and course enrollment: Testing the role of personal values within an expectancy-valence framework. *Journal of Educational Psychology, 80,* 381–391.

Feld, S., & Lewis, J. (1969). The assessment of achievement anxieties in children. In C. P. Smith (Ed.), *Achievement-related motives in children* (pp. 151–199). New York: Russell Sage Foundation.

Feldlaufer, H., Midgley, C., & Eccles, J. (1988). Student, teacher, and observer perceptions of the classroom environment before and after the transition to junior high school. *Journal of Early Adolescence, 8,* 133–156.

Felson, R., & Reed, M. (1986). Reference groups and self-appraisals of academic ability and performance. *Social Psychology Quarterly, 49,* 103–109.

Fennema, E., & Sherman, J. (1977). Sex-related differences in mathematics achievement, spatial visualization, and affective factors. *American Educational Research Journal, 14,* 51–71.

Fincham, F., Hokoda, A., & Sanders, R. (1989). Learned helplessness, test anxiety, and academic achievement: A longitudinal analysis. *Child Development, 60,* 138–145.

Finn, J. (1989). Withdrawing from school. *Review of Educational Research, 59,* 117–142.

Fletcher, T., & Spielberger, C. (1995). Comparison of cognitive therapy and rational-emotive therapy in the treatment of test anxiety. In C. Spielberger & P. Vagg (Eds.), *Test anxiety: Theory, assessment, and treatment* (pp. 153–169). Washington, DC: Taylor & Francis.

Flick, L. (1993). The meanings of hands-on science. *Journal of Science Teacher Education, 4,* 1–8.

Flink, C., Boggiano, A., & Barrett, M. (1990). Controlling teaching strategies: Undermining children's self-determination and performance. *Journal of Personality and Social Psychology, 59,* 916–924.

Flink, C., Boggiano, A., Main, D., Barrett, M., & Katz, P. (1992). Children's achievement-related behaviors: The role of extrinsic motivational orientations. In A. Boggiano & T. Pittman (Eds.), *Achievement and motivation: A social-developmental perspective* (pp. 189–

214). New York: Cambridge University Press.

Forsterling, F. (1985). Attributional retraining: A review. *Psychological Bulletin, 98,* 495–512.

Fox, K. (1980). Treatment of writing apprehension and its effects on composition. *Research in the Teaching of English, 14,* 39–49.

Freedman, J., Cunningham, J., & Krismer, K. (1992). Inferred values and the reverse-incentive effect in induced compliance. *Journal of Personality and Social Psychology, 62,* 357–368.

Frieze, I. (1975). Women's expectations for and causal attributions of success and failure. In M. Mednick, S. Tangri, & L. Hoffman (Eds.), *Women and achievement* (pp. 158–171). New York: John Wiley & Sons.

Fry, P., & Coe, K. (1980). Interaction among dimensions of academic motivation and classroom social climate: A study of the perceptions of junior high and high school pupils. *British Journal of Educational Psychology, 50,* 33–42.

Fuligni, A., Eccles, J., & Barbar, B. (1995). The long-term effects of seventh-grade ability grouping in mathematics. *Journal of Early Adolescence, 15,* 58–89.

Gaa, J. (1973). Effects of individual goal-setting conferences on achievement, attitudes, and goal-setting behavior. *Journal of Experimental Education, 42,* 22–28.

Gaa, J. (1979). The effects of individual goal-setting conferences on academic achievement and modification of locus of control orientation. *Psychology in the Schools, 16,* 591–597.

Garbarino, J. (1975). The impact of anticipated rewards on cross-age tutoring. *Journal of Personality and Social Psychology, 32,* 421–428.

Garibaldi, A. (1993). Creating prescriptions for success in urban schools: Turning the corner on pathological explanations for academic failure. In T. Tomlinson (Ed.), *Motivating students to learn: Overcoming barriers to high achievement* (pp. 125–138). Berkeley, CA: McCutchan.

Garner, R., Alexander, P., Gillingham, M., Kulikowich, J., & Brown, R. (1991). Interest and learning from text. *American Educational Research Journal, 28,* 643–659.

Garner, R., Gillingham, M., & White, C. (1989). Effects of "seductive details" on macroprocessing and microprocessing in adults and children. *Cognition and Instruction, 6,* 41–57.

Gibbs, J., & Allen, A. (1978). *Tribes: A process for peer involvement.* Oakland, CA: CenterSource Publications.

Gibson, S., & Dembo, M. (1984). Teacher efficacy: A construct validation. *Journal of Educational Psychology, 76,* 569–582.

Gitelson, I., Petersen, A., & Tobin-Richards, M. (1982). Adolescents' expectancies of success, self-evaluations, and attributions about performance on spatial and verbal tasks. *Sex Roles, 8,* 411–419.

Goldberg, M., Passow, A., & Justman, J. (1966). *The effects of ability grouping.* New York: Teachers College Press.

Goldenberg, C. (1989). Making success a more common occurrence for children at risk for failure: Lessons from Hispanic first-graders learning to read. In J. Allen & J. Mason (Eds.), *Risk makers, risk takers, risk breakers: Reducing the risk for young literacy learners* (pp. 48–78). Portsmouth, NJ: Heinemann.

Goldenberg, C. (1992). The limits of expectations: A case for case knowledge about teacher expectancy effects. *American Educational Research Journal, 29,* 517–544.

Gonzalez, H. (1995). Systematic desensitization, study skills counseling, and anxiety-coping training in the treatment of test anxiety. In C. Spielberger & P. Vagg (Eds.), *Test anxiety: Theory, assessment, and treatment* (pp. 117–132). Washington, DC: Taylor & Francis.

Good, T. (1987). Teacher expectations. In D. Berliner & B. Rosenshine (Eds.), *Talks to teachers* (pp. 159–200). New York: Random House.

Good, T., & Brophy, J. (1978). *Looking in classrooms* (2nd ed.). New York: Harper & Row.

Good, T., & Brophy, J. (1986). *Educational psychology* (3rd ed.) New York: Longman.

Good, T., Slavings, R., Harel, K., & Emerson, H. (1987). Student passivity: A study of question asking in K–12 classrooms. *Sociology of Education, 60,* 181–199.

Goodenow, C. (1993). Classroom belonging among early adolescent students: Relationships to motivation and achievement. *Journal of Early Adolescence, 13,* 21–43.

Goodlad, J. (1984). *A place called school.* New York: McGraw-Hill.

Gottfried, A. (1985). Academic intrinsic motivation in elementary and junior high school students. *Journal of Educational Psychology,* 77, 631–645.

Gottfried, A. (1986). *Children's academic intrinsic motivation inventory.* Odessa, FL: Psychological Assessment Resources.

Gottfried, A. (1990). Academic intrinsic motivation in young elementary school children. *Journal of Educational Psychology,* 82, 525–538.

Graham, L., & Wong, B. (1993). Comparing two modes of teaching a question-answering strategy for enhancing reading comprehension: Didactic and self-instructional training. *Journal of Learning Disabilities,* 26, 270–279.

Graham, S. (1984a). Communicating sympathy and anger to Black and White children: The cognitive (attributional) consequences of affective cues. *The Journal of Personality and Social Psychology,* 47, 14–28.

Graham, S. (1984b). Teacher feelings and student thoughts: An attributional approach to affect in the classroom. *Elementary School Journal,* 85, 91–104.

Graham, S. (1990). Communicating low ability in the classroom: Bad things good teachers sometimes do. In S. Graham & V. Folkes (Eds.), *Attribution theory: Applications to achievement, mental health, and interpersonal conflict* (pp. 17–36). Hillsdale, NJ: Lawrence Erlbaum Associates.

Graham, S. (1991). A review of attribution theory in achievement contexts. *Educational Psychology Review,* 3, 5–39.

Graham, S. (1994). Classroom motivation from an attributional perspective. In M. Drillings (Ed.), *Motivation: Theory and research* (pp. 31–48). Hillsdale, NJ: Lawrence Erlbaum Associates.

Graham, S., & Barker, G. (1990). The downside of help: An attributional-developmental analysis of helping behavior as a low ability cue. *Journal of Educational Psychology,* 82, 7–14.

Graham, S., Doubleday, C., & Guarino, P. (1984). The development of relations between perceived controllability and the emotions of pity, anger, and guilt. *Child Development,* 55, 561–565.

Graham, S., & Golan, S. (1991). Motivational influences on cognition: Task involvement,

ego involvement, and depth of information processing. *Journal of Educational Psychology,* 83, 187–194.

Graham, S., & Harris, K. (1994). The role and development of self-regulation in the writing process. In D. Schunk & B. Zimmerman (Eds.), *Self-regulation of learning and performance* (pp. 203–228). Hillsdale, NJ: Lawrence Erlbaum Associates.

Graham, S., & Weiner, B. (1993). Attributional applications in the classroom. In T. Tomlinson (Ed.), *Motivating students to learn: Overcoming barriers to high achievement* (pp. 179–195). Berkeley, CA: McCutchan.

Graham, S., & Weiner, B. (1996). Theories and principles of motivation. In D. Berliner & R. Calfee (Eds.), *Handbook of educational psychology* (pp. 63–84). New York: Macmillan.

Grant, L. (1985). Race-gender status, classroom interaction, and children's socialization in elementary school. In L. Wilkinson & C. Marrett (Eds.), *Gender influences in classroom interaction* (pp. 57–78). Orlando, FL: Academic Press.

Graves, D. (1983). *Writing: Teachers and children at work.* Portsmouth, NH: Heinemann.

Greene, J. C. (1985). Relationships among learning and attribution theory motivation variables. *American Educational Research Journal,* 22, 65–78.

Grolnick, W., & Ryan, R. (1987). Autonomy in children's learning: An experimental and individual difference investigation. *Journal of Personality and Social Psychology,* 52, 890–898.

Gross, T., & Mastenbrook, M. (1980). Examination of the effects of state anxiety on problem-solving efficiency under high and low memory conditions. *Journal of Educational Psychology,* 72, 605–609.

Grundy, D. (1993). Parricide postponed: A discussion of some writing problems. *Contemporary Psychoanalysis,* 29, 693–710.

Gullickson, A. (1985). Student evaluation techniques and their relationship to grade and curriculum. *Journal of Educational Research,* 79, 96–100.

Guskey, T. (1985). *Implementing mastery learning.* Belmont, CA: Wadsworth.

Guskey, T. (1987). The essential elements of mastery learning. *Journal of Classroom Interaction,* 22, 19–22.

Guskey, T. (1990). Cooperative mastery learning strategies. *The Elementary School Journal, 91,* 33–42.

Guskey, T., & Passaro, P. (1994). Teacher efficacy: A study of construct dimensions. *American Educational Reearch Journal, 31,* 627–643.

Guskey, T., & Pigott, T. (1988). Research on group-based mastery learning programs: A meta-analysis. *Journal of Educational Research, 8,* 197–216.

Hackett, G. (1995). Self-efficacy in career choice and development. In A. Bandura (Ed.), *Self-efficacy in changing societies* (pp. 232–258). New York: Cambridge University Press.

Hackett, G., & Betz, N. (1992). Self-efficacy preceptions and the career-related choices of college students. In D. Schunk & J. Meece (Eds.), *Student perceptions in the classroom* (pp. 229–246). Hillsdale, NJ: Lawrence Erlbaum Associates.

Hallahan, D., & Sapona, R. (1983). Self-monitoring of attention with learning-disabled children: Past research and current issues. *Journal of Learning Disabilities, 16,* 616–620.

Hallinan, M., & Sorensen, A. (1983). The formation and stability of instructional groups. *American Sociological Review, 48,* 838–851.

Hamilton, H., & Gordon, D. (1978). Teacher-child interactions in preschool and task persistence. *American Educational Research Journal, 15,* 459–466.

Harackiewicz, J., Abrahams, S., & Wageman, R. (1987). Performance evaluation and intrinsic motivation: The effects of evaluative focus, rewards, and achievement orientation. *Journal of Personality and Social Psychology, 53,* 1015–1023.

Harackiewicz, J., & Elliot, A. (1993). Achievement goals and intrinsic motivation. *Journal of Personality and Social Psychology, 65,* 904–915.

Harackiewicz, J., Manderlink, G., & Sansone, C. (1992). Competence processes and achievement motivation: Implications for intrinsic motivation. In A. Boggiano & T. Pittman (Eds.), *Achievement and motivation: A social-developmental perspective* (pp. 115–137). New York: Cambridge University Press.

Harnisch, D., Hill, K., & Fyans, L. (1980, April). *Development of a shorter, more reliable and more valid measure of test motivation.* Paper presented at the annual meeting of the National Council on Measurement in Education, Boston.

Harter, S. (1974). Pleasure derived from cognitive challenge and mastery. *Child Development, 45,* 661–669.

Harter, S. (1978a). Effectance motivation reconsidered: Toward a developmental model. *Human Development, 21,* 34–64.

Harter, S. (1978b). Pleasure derived from challenge and the effects of receiving grades on children's difficulty level choices. *Child Development, 49,* 788–799.

Harter, S. (1981a). A model of mastery motivation in children: Individual differences and developmental change. In W. Collins (Ed.), *Minnesota symposia on child psychology* (Vol. 14, pp. 215–255). Hillsdale, NJ: Lawrence Erlbaum Associates.

Harter, S. (1981b). A new self-report scale of intrinsic versus extrinsic orientation in the classroom: Motivational and informational components. *Developmental Psychology, 17,* 300–312.

Harter, S. (1982). The perceived competence scale for children. *Child Development, 53,* 87–97.

Harter, S. (1987). The determinants and mediational role of global self-worth in children. In N. Eisenberg (Ed.), *Contemporary topics in developmental psychology* (pp. 219–241). New York: John Wiley & Sons.

Harter, S. (1992). The relationship between perceived competence, affect, and motivational orientation within the classroom: Process and patterns of change. In A. Boggiano & T. Pittman (Eds.), *Achievement and motivation: A social-developmental perspective* (pp. 77–114). New York: Cambridge University Press.

Harter, S. (in press). The development of self-representations. In W. Damon (Series Ed.) & N. Eisenberg (Vol. Ed.), *Handbook of child psychology. Vol. 3: Social, emotional, and personality development* (5th ed.). New York: John Wiley & Sons.

Harter, S., & Connell, J. (1984). A comparison of alternative models of the relationships between academic achievement and children's perceptions of competence, control, and motivational orientation. In J. Nicholls (Ed.), *The development of achievement-related conditions and behavior* (pp. 219–250). Greenwich, CT: JAI Press.

Harter, S., & Pike, R. (1984). The pictorial scale of perceived competence and social acceptance for young children. *Child Development, 55,* 1969–1982.

Harter, S., Whitesell, N., & Kowalski, P. (1992). Individual differences in the effects of educational transitions on young adolescent's perceptions of competence and motivational orientation. *American Educational Research Journal, 29,* 777–807.

Hattie, J. (1992). *Self-concept.* Hillsdale, NJ: Lawrence Erlbaum Associates

Hattie, J., Biggs, J., & Purdie, N. (1996). Effects of learning skills interventions on student learning: A meta-analysis. *Review of Educational Research, 66,* 99–136.

Hayes, S., Rosenfarb, I., Wolfert, E., Munt, E., Korn, Z., & Zettle, R. (1985). Self-reinforcement effects: An artifact of social standing setting? *Journal of Applied Behavior Analysis, 18,* 201–204.

Heckhausen, H. (1984). Emergent achievement behavior: Some early developments. In J. Nicholls (Ed.), *Advances in motivation and achievement. Vol. 3: The development of achievement motivation* (pp. 1–32). Greenwich, CT: JAI Press.

Hedl, J. (1987). Explorations in test anxiety and attribution theory. In R. Schwarzer, H. Van der Ploeg, & C. Spielberger (Eds.), *Advances in test anxiety research* (Vol. 5, pp. 55–65). Berwyn, PA: Swets North America.

Hedl, J., & Papay, J. (1982). The factor structure of the State-Trait Anxiety Inventory for Children: Kindergarten through the fourth grades. *Personality and Individual Difference, 3,* 439–446.

Heller, K., & Parsons, J. (1981). Sex differences in teachers' evaluative feedback and students' expectations for success in mathematics. *Child Development, 52,* 1015–1019.

Helmke, A. (1988). The role of classroom context factors for the achievement-impairing effect of test anxiety. *Anxiety Research, 1,* 37–52.

Hembree, R. (1988). Correlates, causes, effects, and treatment of test anxiety. *Review of Educational Research, 58,* 47–77.

Hembree, R. (1990). The nature, effects, and relief of mathematics anxiety. *Journal for Research in Mathematics Education, 21,* 33–46.

Hiebert, E. (1983). An examination of ability grouping in reading instruction. *Reading Research Quarterly, 18,* 231–255.

Higgins, E., & Parsons, J. (1983). Social cognition and the social life of the child. Stages as subcultures. In E. T. Higgins, D. N. Ruble, & W. W. Hartup (Eds.), *Social cognition and social development: A sociocultural perspective* (pp. 15–62). New York: Cambridge University Press.

Hill, K. (1972). Anxiety in the evaluative context. In W. W. Hartup (Ed.), *The young child* (Vol. 2, pp. 225–283). Washington, DC: National Association for the Education of Young Children.

Hill, K. (1980). Motivation, evaluation and educational testing policy. In L. J. Fyans (Ed.), *Achievement motivation: Recent trends in theory and research* (pp. 34–95). New York: Plenum.

Hill, K. (1984). Debilitating motivation and testing: A major educational problem, possible solutions, and policy applications. In R. Ames & C. Ames (Eds.), *Research on motivation in education. Vol. 1: Student motivation* (pp. 245–272). New York: Academic Press.

Hill, K., & Eaton, W. (1977). The interaction of test anxiety and success/failure experiences in determining children's arithmetic performance. *Developmental Psychology, 13,* 205–211.

Hill, K., & Sarason, S. (1966). The relation of test anxiety and defensiveness to test and school performance over the elementary-school years: A further longitudinal study. *Monographs of the Society for Research in Child Development, 104* (31, Whole 2).

Hill, K., & Wigfield, A. (1984). Test anxiety: A major educational problem and what can be done about it. *The Elementary School Journal, 85,* 105–126.

Hoge, R., & Renzulli, J. (1993). Exploring the link between giftedness and self-concept. *Review of Educational Research, 63,* 449–465.

Holloway, S. (1988). Concepts of ability and effort in Japan and the United States. *Review of Educational Research, 58,* 327–345.

Holloway, S., Kashiwagi, K., Hess, R. D., & Azuma, H. (1986). Causal attributions by Japanese and American mothers and children about performance in mathematics. *International Journal of Psychology, 21,* 269–286.

Holroyd, K., & Appel, M. (1980). Test anxiety and physiological responding. In I. Sarason (Ed.), *Test anxiety: Theory, research, and applications* (pp. 129–151). Hillsdale, NJ: Lawrence Erlbaum Associates.

Holt, J. (1964). *How children fail.* New York: Pitman.

Hom, H., & Murphy, M. (1985). Low need achievers' performance: The positive impact of a self-determined goal. *Personality and Social Psychology Bulletin, 11,* 275–285.

Hughes, B., Sullivan, H., & Mosley, M. (1985). External evaluation, task difficulty, and continuing motivation. *Journal of Educational Research, 78,* 210–215.

Hughes, C., Korinek, L., & Gorman, J. (1991). Self-management for students with mental retardation in public school settings: A research review. *Education and Training in Mental Retardation, 26,* 271–291.

Hull, C. (1943). *Principles of behavior.* New York: Appleton-Century-Crofts.

Hull, C. (1951). *Essentials of behavior.* New Haven: Yale University Press.

Hulton, R., & DeVries, D. (1976). *Team competition and group practice: Effects on student achievement and attitudes* (Report No. 212). Baltimore: Johns Hopkins University, Center for Social Organization of Schools.

Hunt, J. McV. (1965). Intrinsic motivation and its role in psychological development. In D. Levine (Ed.), *Nebraska symposium on motivation* (Vol. 13, pp. 189–282). Lincoln: University of Nebraska Press.

Hunter, M., Ames, D., & Koopman, R. (1983). Effects of stimulus complexity and familiarization time on infant preferences for novel and familiar stimuli. *Developmental Psychology, 19,* 338–352.

Irvine, J. (1990). *Black students and school failure.* Westport, CT: Greenwood Press.

Jackson, P. (1968). *Life in classrooms.* New York: Holt, Rinehart & Winston.

Jacobs, J., & Eccles, J. (1992). The impact of mothers' gender-role stereotypic beliefs on mothers' and children's ability perceptions. *Journal of Personality and Social Psychology, 63,* 932–944.

Jagacinski, C. (1992). The effects of task involvement and ego involvement on achievement-related cognitions and behaviors. In D. Schunk & J. Meece (Eds.), *Student perceptions in the classroom* (pp. 307–326). Hillsdale, NJ: Lawrence Erlbaum Associates.

Jagacinski, C., & Nicholls, J. (1990). Reducing effort to protect perceived ability: "They'd do it but I wouldn't." *Journal of Educational Psychology, 82,* 15–21.

Johnson, D., & Johnson, R. (1985a). The internal dynamics of cooperative learning groups. In R. Slavin, S. Sharan, S. Kagan, R. Hertz, Lazarowitz, N. Webb, & R. Schmuck (Eds.), *Learning to cooperate, cooperating to learn* (pp. 103–124). New York: Plenum.

Johnson, D., & Johnson, R. (1985b). Motivational processes in cooperative, competitive, and individualistic learning situations. In C. Ames & R. Ames (Eds.), *Research on motivation in education. Vol. 2: The classroom milieu* (pp. 249–286). Orlando, FL: Academic Press.

Johnson, D., & Johnson, R. (1989). Toward a cooperative effort. *Educational Leadership, 46,* 80–81.

Johnson, D., Johnson, R., Holubec, E., & Roy, P. (1984). *Circles of learning: Cooperation in the classroom.* Alexandria, VA: Association for Supervision and Curriculum Development.

Jones, G., & Wheatley, J. (1990). Gender differences in teacher–student interactions in science classrooms. *Journal of Research in Science Teaching, 27,* 861–874.

Jussim, L. (1991). Social perception and social reality: A reflection-construction model. *Psychological Review, 98,* 54–73.

Jussim, L., & Eccles, J. (1992). Teacher expectations II: Construction and reflection of student achievement. *Journal of Personality and Social Psychology, 63,* 947–961.

Jussim, L., & Eccles, J. (1995). Naturally occurring interpersonal expectancies. In N. Eisenberg (Ed.), *Social development: Review of personality and social psychology, 15* (pp. 74–108). Thousand Oaks, CA: Sage Publications.

Jussim, L., Eccles, J., & Madon, S. (1996). Social perception, social stereotypes, and teacher expectations: Accuracy and the quest for the powerful self-fulfilling prophecy. In M. Zanna (Ed.), *Advances in experimental social psychology* (Vol. 28, pp. 281–388). New York: Academic Press.

Jussim, L., Madon, S., & Chatman, C. (1994). Teacher expectations and student achievement: Self-fulfilling prophecies, biases, and accuracy. In L. Heath, R. Tindale, J.

Edwards, E. Posavac, F. Bryant, E. Henderson-King, Y. Suarez-Balcazar, & J. Myers (Eds.), *Applications of heuristics and biases to social issues* (pp. 303–334). New York: Plenum Press.

Kagan, J. (1972). Motives and development. *Journal of Personality and Social Psychology, 22,* 51–66.

Kagan, S. (undated). *Cooperative learning resources for teachers.* Riverside: University of California.

Kahle, J. (1990). Real students take chemistry and physics: Gender issues. In K. Tobin, J. Kahle, & B. Fraser (Eds.), *Windows into science classrooms: Problems associated with higher-level cognitive learning* (pp. 92–134). New York: Falmer.

Kahle, J. (1996a). Equitable science education: A discrepancy model. In L. Parker, L. Rennie, & B. Fraser (Eds.), *Gender, science and mathematics* (pp. 129–139). Dordrecht, Netherlands: Kluwer Academic Publishers.

Kahle, J. (1996b). Opportunities and obstacles: Science education in the schools. In C. Davis, A. Ginorio, C. Hollenshead, B. Lazarus, & P. Rayman (Eds.), *The equity equation: Fostering the advancement of women in the sciences, mathematics, and engineering* (pp. 57–95). San Francisco: Jossey-Bass.

Kahle, J., & Damnjanovic, A. (1994). The effect of inquiry activities on elementary students' enjoyment, ease, and confidence in doing science: An analysis by sex and race. *Journal of Women and Minorities in Science and Engineering, 1,* 17–28.

Kahle, J., & Meece, J. (1993). Research on gender issues in the classroom. In D. Gabel (Ed.), *Handbook of research on science teaching and learning.* New York: Macmillan.

Kamann, M., & Wong, B. (1993). Inducing adaptive coping self-statements in children with learning disabilities through self-instruction training. *Journal of Learning Disabilities, 26,* 630–638.

Kamii, C. (1984). Viewpoint: Obedience is not enough. *Young Children, 39,* 11–14.

Karabenick, S., & Knapp, J. (1988). Help seeking and the need for academic assistance. *Journal of Educational Psychology, 80,* 406–408.

Karabenick, S., & Youssef, Z. (1968). Performance as a function of achievement motive level and perceived difficulty. *Journal of Personality and Social Psychology, 10,* 414–419.

Karniol, R., & Ross, M. (1977). The effect of performance-relevant and performance-irrelevant rewards on children's intrinsic motivation. *Child Development, 48,* 482–487.

Kazdin, A. (1974). Self-monitoring and behavior change. In M. Mahoney & C. Thoresen (Eds.), *Self-control: Power to the person* (pp. 218–246). Monterey, CA: Brooks-Cole.

Kazdin, A. (1975). Recent advances in token economy research. In M. Hersen, R. Eisler, & P. Miller (Eds.), *Progress in behavior modification.* (Vol. 1, pp. 233–274). New York: Academic Press.

Kazdin, A. (1988). The token economy: A decade later. In G. Davey & C. Cullen (Eds.), *Human operant conditioning and behavior modification* (pp. 119–137). New York: John Wiley & Sons.

Kazdin, A., & Bootzin, R. (1972). The token economy: An evaluative review. *Journal of Applied Behavior Analysis, 5,* 343–372.

Keith, L., & Bracken, B. (1996). Self-concept instrumentation: A historical and evaluative review. In B. Bracken (Ed.), *Handbook of self-concept: Developmental, social, & clinical considerations* (pp. 91–170). New York: John Wiley & Sons.

Keller, F. (1968). Goodbye, teacher. . . . *Journal of Applied Behavior Analysis, 1,* 79–89.

Kelly, H. (1967). Attribution theory in social psychology. In D. Levine (Ed.), *Nebraska symposium on motivation* (pp. 192–238). Lincoln: University of Nebraska Press.

Kern, L., Dunlap, G., Childs, K., & Clarke, S. (1994). Use of a classwide self-management program to improve the behavior of students with emotional and behavioral disorders. *Education and Treatment of Children, 17,* 445–458.

Kimball, M. M. (1989). A new perspective on women's math achievement. *Psychological Bulletin, 105,* 198–214.

Kirby, K., Fowler, S., & Baer, D. (1991). Reactivity in self-recording: Obtrusiveness of recording procedure and peer comments. *Journal of Applied Behavior Analysis, 24,* 487–498.

Kohn, A. (1993). *Punished by rewards: The trouble with gold stars, incentive plans, A's, praise, and other bribes.* Boston: Houghton Mifflin.

Kolb, K., & Jussim, L. (1994). Teacher expectations and underachieving gifted children. *Roeper Review, 17,* 26–30.

Krohne, H. (1992). Developmental conditions of

anxiety and coping: A two-process model of child-rearing effects. In K. Hagtvet & T. Johnsen (Ed.), *Advances in test anxiety research* (Vol. 7, pp. 143–155). Amsterdam: Swets & Zeitlinger.

Kuhn, D. (1992). Thinking as argument. *Harvard Educational Review, 46,* 155–178.

Kulik, C-L., Kulik, J., & Bangert-Drowns, R. (1990a). Effectiveness of mastery learning programs: A meta-analysis. *Review of Educational Research, 60,* 265–299.

Kulik, J., Kulik, C-L., & Bangert-Drowns, R. (1990b). Is there better evidence on mastery learning? A response to Slavin. *Review of Educational Research, 60,* 303–307.

Kulik, J., Kulik, C-L., & Cohen, P. (1979). A meta-analysis of outcome studies of Keller's Personalized System of Instruction. *American Psychologist, 34,* 307–318.

Lalli, E., & Shapiro, E. (1990). The effects of self-monitoring and contingent reward on sight word acquisition. *Education and Treatment of Children, 12,* 129–141.

Lampert, M. (1991). Connecting mathematical teaching and learning. In E. Fennema, T. P. Carpenter, & S. J. Lamon (Eds.), *Integrating research on teaching and learning mathematics* (pp. 121–152). Albany: State University of New York Press.

Laosa, L. (1982). School, occupation, culture and family: The impact of parental schooling on the parent-child relationship. *Journal of Educational Psychology, 74,* 791–827.

Lazarus, M. (1975, June 28). Rx for mathophobia. *Saturday Review, 2,* pp. 46–48.

Lee, S., Ichikawa, V., & Stevenson, H. W. (1987). Beliefs and achievement in mathematics and reading: A cross-national study of Chinese, Japanese, and American children and their mothers. In M. Maehr & D. Kleiber (Eds.), *Advances in motivation and achievement. Vol. 5: Enhancing motivation* (pp. 149–179). Greenwich, CT: JAI Press.

Lefcourt, H. (1976). *Locus of control: Current trends in theory and research.* Hillsdale, NJ: Lawrence Erlbaum Associates.

Lefcourt, H. (1992). Durability and impact of the locus of control construct. *Psychological Bulletin, 112,* 411–414.

Leinhardt, G., Seewald, A., & Engel, M. (1979). Learning what's taught: Sex differences in instruction. *Journal of Educational Psychology, 71,* 432–439.

Lenz, R. (1992). Self-managed learning strategy systems for children and youth. *School Psychology Review, 21,* 211–228.

Leonard, J., Reyes, O., Danner, K., & de la Torre, G. (1994). Academic achievement as a buffer to peer rejection for transfer children. *Journal of Instructional Psychology, 21,* 351–352.

Lepper, M. (1973). Dissonance, self-perception, and honesty in children. *Journal of Personality and Social Psychology, 25,* 65–74.

Lepper, M. (1981). Intrinsic and extrinsic motivation in children: Detrimental effects of superfluous social controls. In A. Collins (Ed.), *Aspects of the development of competence: The Minnesota Symposia on Child Psychology* (Vol. 14, pp. 155–214). Hillsdale, NJ: Lawrence Erlbaum Associates.

Lepper, M. (1983). Extrinsic reward and intrinsic motivation: Implications for the classroom. In J. Levine & M. Wang (Eds.), *Teacher and student perceptions: Implications for learning* (pp. 281–317). Hillsdale, NJ: Lawrence Erlbaum Associates.

Lepper, M. (1985). Microcomputers in education. *American Psychologist, 40,* 1–18.

Lepper, M. (1988). Motivational considerations in the study of instruction. *Cognition and Instruction, 5,* 289–309.

Lepper, M. (1996). Intrinsic motivation and extrinsic rewards: A commentary on Cameron and Pierce's meta-analysis. *Review of Educational Research, 66,* 5–32.

Lepper, M., Aspinwall, L., Mumme, D., & Chabay, R. (1990). Self-perception and social-perception processes in tutoring: Subtle social control strategies of expert tutors. In J. Olson & M. Zanna (Eds.), *Self-inference processes: The Ontario Symposium* (Vol. 6, pp. 217–237). Hillsdale, NJ: Lawrence Erlbaum Associates.

Lepper, M., & Cordova, D. (1992). A desire to be taught: Instructional consequences of intrinsic motivation. *Motivation and Emotion, 3,* 187–209.

Lepper, M., & Greene, D. (1975). Turning play into work: Effects of adult surveillance and extrinsic rewards on children's intrinsic motivation. *Journal of Personality and Social Psychology, 31,* 479–486.

Lepper, M., Greene, D., & Nisbett, R. (1973). Undermining children's intrinsic interest with intrinsic rewards: A test of the overjustification hypothesis. *Journal of Personality and Social Psychology, 28,* 129–137.

Lepper, M., Keavney, M., & Drake, M. (1996). Intrinsic motivation and extrinsic rewards: A commentary on Cameron and Pierce's meta-analysis. *Review of Educational Research, 66,* 5–32.

Lepper, M., & Malone, T. (1987). Intrinsic motivation and instructional effectiveness in computer-based education. In R. Snow & M. Farr (Eds.), *Aptitude, learning, and instruction: III. Cognitive and affective process analysis* (pp. 255–286). Hillsdale, NJ: Lawrence Erlbaum Associates.

Lepper, M., Sethi, S., Dialdin, D., & Drake, M. (1997). Intrinsic and extrinsic motivation: A developmental perspective. In S. Luthar, J. Barach, D. Cichetti, & J. Weisz (Eds.), *Developmental psychopathology: Perspectives on adjustment, risk, and disorder* (pp. 23–50). New York: Cambridge University Press.

Levine, J. (1983). Social comparison and education. In J. Levine & M. Wang (Eds.), *Teacher and student perceptions: Implications for learning* (pp. 29–55). Hillsdale, NJ: Lawrence Erlbaum Associates.

Levine, J., Snyder, H., & Mendez-Caratini, G. (1982). Task performance and interpersonal attraction in children. *Child Development, 53,* 359–371.

Lewin, K., Lippitt, R., & White, R. (1939). Pattern of aggressive behavior in experimentally created "social climates." *Journal of Social Psychology, 10,* 271–299.

Lewis, M., Alessandr, S., & Sullivan, M. (1992). Differences in shame and pride as a function of children's gender and task difficulty. *Child Development, 63,* 630–638.

Lewis, M., Wall, M., & Aronfreed, J. (1963). Developmental change in the relative values of social and nonsocial reinforcement. *Journal of Experimental Psychology, 66,* 133–137.

Licht, B. (1992). The achievement-related perceptions of children with learning problems. In D. Schunk & J. Meece (Eds.), *Student perceptions in the classroom* (pp. 247–264). Hillsdale, NJ: Lawrence Erlbaum Associates.

Licht, B. (1993). Learning disabled children's achievement related beliefs: Impact on their motivation and strategic learning. In L. Meltzer (Ed.), *Strategy assessment and instruction for students with learning disabilities: From theory to practice* (pp. 195–220). Austin, TX: PROED.

Licht, B., & Dweck, C. (1984). Determinants of academic achievement: The interaction of children's achievement orientations with skill area. *Developmental Psychology, 20,* 628–636.

Liebert, R., & Morris, L. (1967). Cognitive and emotional components of test anxiety: A distinction and some initial data. *Psychological Reports, 20,* 975–978.

Lipinski, D., Black, J., Nelson, R., & Ciminero, A. (1974). Influence of motivational variables on the reactivity and reliability of self-recording. *Journal of Consulting and Clinical Psychology, 42,* 118–123.

Litrownik, A., & Freitas, J. (1980). Self-monitoring in moderately retarded adolescents: Reactivity and accuracy as a function of valence. *Behavior Therapy, 11,* 245–255.

Little, T., Oettingen, G., Stetsenko, A., & Baltes, P. (1995). Children's action-control beliefs about school performance: How do American children compare with German and Russian children? *Journal of Personality and Social Psychology, 69,* 686–700.

Locke, E., Frederick, E., Lee, C., & Bobko, P. (1984). Effect of self-efficacy, goals and task strategies on task performance. *Journal of Applied Psychology, 69,* 241–251.

Locke, E., & Latham, G. (1990). *A theory of goal setting and task performance.* Englewood Cliffs, NJ: Prentice Hall.

Locke, E., & Latham, G. (1994). Goal setting theory. In H. O'Neil & M. Drillings (Eds.), *Motivation: Theory and research* (pp.13–29). Hillsdale, NJ: Lawrence Erlbaum Associates.

Luria, A. (1961). *The role of speech in the regulation of normal and abnormal behaviors.* New York: Liveright.

Luster, T., & McAdoo, H. (1996). Family and child influences on educational attainment: A secondary analysis of the High/Scope Perry Preschool data. *Developmental Psychology, 32,* 26–39.

Luthar, S. (1995). Social competence in the school setting: Prospective cross-domain associations among inner-city teens. *Child Development, 66,* 416–429.

Maag, J., Rutherford, R., & DiGangi, S. (1992). Effects of self-monitoring and contingent reinforcement on on-task behavior and academic productivity of learning-disabled students: A social validation study. *Psychology in the Schools, 29,* 157–172.

Mace, F., Belfiore, P., & Shea, M. (1989). Operant

theory and research on self-regulation. In B. Zimmerman & D. Schunk (Eds.), *Self-regulated learning and academic achievement: Theory, research, and practice* (pp. 27–50). New York: Springer-Verlag.

Mace, F., & Kratochwill, T. (1988). Self-monitoring. In J. Will, S. Elliott, & F. Gresham (Eds.), *Handbook of behavior therapy in education* (pp. 489–522). New York: Plenum.

Mac Iver, D. (1990). *A national description of report card entries in the middle grades* (Report No. 9). Baltimore: Johns Hopkins University, Center for Research on Effective Schooling for Disadvantaged Students.

Mac Iver, D., Stipek, D., & Daniels, D. (1991). Explaining within-semester changes in student effort in junior high school and senior high school courses. *Journal of Educational Psychology, 83,* 201–211.

Madaus, G., Airasian, P., & Kellaghan, T. (1980). *School effectiveness: A reassessment of the evidence.* New York: McGraw Hill.

Maehr, M. (1984). Meaning and motivation: Toward a theory of personal investment. In R. Ames & C. Ames (Eds.), *Research on motivation in education. Vol. 1: Student motivation* (pp. 115–144). Orlando, FL: Academic Press.

Maehr, M., & Anderman, E. (1993). Reinventing schools for early adolescents: Emphasizing task goals. *Elementary School Journal, 93,* 593–610.

Maehr, M., & Stallings, W. (1972). Freedom from external evaluation. *Child Development, 43,* 117–185.

Mahn, C. S., & Greenwood, G. E. (1990). Cognitive behavior modification: Use of self-instruction strategies by first-graders on academic tasks. *Journal of Educational Research, 83,* 158–161.

Malone, T. (1981a). Toward a theory of intrinsically motivating instruction. *Cognitive Science, 4,* 333–369.

Malone, T. (1981b). What makes computer games fun? *Byte, 6,* 258–277.

Malone, T., & Lepper, M. (1987). Making learning fun: A taxonomy of intrinsic motivation for learning. In R. Snow & M. Farr (Eds.), *Aptitude, learning, and instruction: III. Cognitive and affective process analysis* (pp. 223–253). Hillsdale, NJ: Lawrence Erlbaum Associates.

Manderlink, G., & Harackiewicz, J. (1984). Proximal vs. distal goal setting and intrinsic motivation. *Journal of Personality and Social Psychology, 47,* 918–928.

Marks, H., Doane, K., & Secada, W. (in press). Support for student achievement. In F. Newmann and Associates, *Restructuring for student achievement: The impact of structure and culture in 24 schools.* San Francisco: Jossey-Bass.

Marsh, H. (1984a). Relations among dimensions of self-attribution, dimensions of self-concept, and academic achievement. *Journal of Educational Psychology, 76,* 3–32.

Marsh, H. (1984b). Self-concept, social comparison, and ability grouping: A reply to Kulik and Kulik. *American Educational Research Journal, 2,* 799–806.

Marsh, H. (1986). Verbal and math self-concepts: An internal/external frame of reference model. *American Educational Research Journal, 23,* 129–149.

Marsh, H. (1987). The big-fish-little-pond effect on academic self-concept. *Journal of Educational Psychology, 79,* 280–295.

Marsh, H. (1990). Causal ordering of academic self-concept and academic achievement: A multivariate, longitudinal panel analysis. *Journal of Educational Psychology, 82,* 646–656.

Marsh, H. (1993). Physical fitness self-concept: Relations of physical fitness to field and technical indicators for boys and girls aged 9–15. *Journal of Sport and Exercise Psychology, 15,* 184–206.

Marsh, H., Barnes, J., Cairns, L., & Tidman, M. (1984). Self-description questionnaire: Age and sex effects in the structure and level of self-concept for preadolescent children. *Journal of Educational Psychology, 76,* 940–956.

Marsh, H., Byrne, B., & Shavelson, R. (1988). A multifaceted academic self-concept: Its hierarchical structure and its relation to academic achievement. *Journal of Educational Psychology, 80,* 366–380.

Marsh, H., Cairns, L., Relich, J., Barnes, J., & Debus, R. (1984). The relationship between dimensions of self-attribution and dimensions of self-concept. *Journal of Educational Psychology, 76,* 3–32.

Marsh, H., Chessor, D., Cravn, R., & Roche, L. (1995). The effects of gifted and talented programs on academic self-concept: The big fish strikes again. *American Educational Research Journal, 32,* 285–319.

Marsh, H., & Gouvernet, P. (1989). Multidimensional self-concepts and perceptions of control: Construct validation of responses by children. *Journal of Educational Psychology, 81*, 57–69.

Marsh, H., & Hattie, J. (1996). Theoretical perspectives on the structure of self-concept. In B. Bracken (Ed.), *Handbook of self-concept: Developmental, social, & clinical considerations* (pp. 38–90). New York: John Wiley & Sons.

Marsh, H., & Holmes, I. (1990). Multidimensional self-concepts: Construct validation of responses by children. *American Educational Research Journal, 27*, 89–117.

Marsh, H., & Parker, J. (1984). Determinants of student self-concept: Is it better to be a relatively large fish in a small pond even if you don't learn to swim as well. *Journal of Personality and Social Psychology, 47*, 213–231.

Marsh, H., Smith, I., & Barnes, J. (1983). Multitrait-multimethod analyses of the self-description questionnaire: Student-teacher agreement on multidimensional ratings of student self-concept. *American Educational Research Journal, 26*, 333–357.

Marshall, H., & Weinstein, R. (1984). Classroom factors affecting students' self-evaluation: An interactional model. *Review of Educational Research, 54*, 301–325.

Marshall, H., & Weinstein, R. (1986). Classroom context of student-perceived differential teacher treatment. *Journal of Educational Psychology, 78*, 441–453.

Marzano, R. (1994). Lessons from the field about outcome-based performance assessments. *Educational Leadership, 51*(6), 44–50.

Masters, J., Furman, W., & Barden, R. (1977). Effects of achievement standards, tangible rewards, and self-dispensed achievement evaluations on children's task mastery. *Child Development, 48*, 217–224.

Matheny, K., & Edwards, C. (1974). Academic improvement through an experimental classroom management system. *Journal of School Psychology, 12*, 222–232.

McClelland, D. (1961). *The achieving society*. New York: The Free Press.

McClelland, D. (1971). *Motivational trends in society*. New York: General Learning Press.

McCombs, B. (1994). Strategies for assessing and enhancing motivation: Keys to promoting self-regulated learning and performance. In H. O'Neil & M. Drillings (Eds.), *Motivation: Theory and research* (pp. 49–69). Hillsdale, NJ: Lawrence Erlbaum Associates.

McDermott, R. (1987). The explanation of minority school failure, again. *Anthropology and Education Quarterly, 18*, 361–364.

McGraw, K., & McCullers, J. (1979). Evidence of a detrimental effect of extrinsic incentives on breaking a mental set. *Journal of Experimental Social Psychology, 15*, 285–294.

McMullin, D., & Steffen, J. (1982). Intrinsic motivation and performance standards. *Social Behavior and Personality, 10*, 47–56.

Meece, J. (1991). The classroom context and students' motivational goals. In M. Maehr & P. Pintrich (Eds.), *Advances in motivation and achievement* (Vol. 7, pp. 261–285). Greenwich, CT: JAI Press.

Meece, J. (1994). The role of motivation in self-regulated learning. In D. Schunk & B. Zimmerman (Eds.), *Self-regulation of learning and performance* (pp. 25–44). Hillsdale, NJ: Lawrence Erlbaum Associates.

Meece, J., Blumenfeld, P., & Hoyle, R. (1988). Students' goal orientations and cognitive engagement in classroom activities. *Journal of Educational Psychology, 80*, 514–523.

Meece, J., Blumenfeld, P., & Puro, P. (1989). A motivational analysis of elementary science learning environments. In M. Matyas, K. Tobin, & B. Fraser (Eds.), *Looking into windows: Qualitative research in science education* (pp. 13–23). Washington, DC: American Association for the Advancement of Science.

Meece, J., & Courtney, D. (1992). Gender differences in students' perceptions: Consequences for achievement-related choices. In D. Schunk & J. Meece (Eds.), *Student perceptions in the classroom* (pp. 209–228). Hillsdale, NJ: Lawrence Erlbaum Associates.

Meece, J., & Holt, K. (1993). A pattern analysis of students' achievement goals. *Journal of Educational Psychology, 85*, 582–590.

Meece, J., Parsons, J., Kaczala, C., Goff, S., & Futterman, R. (1982). Sex differences in math achievement: Towards a model of academic choice. *Psychological Bulletin, 91*, 324–348.

Meece, J., Wigfield, A., & Eccles, J. (1990). Predictors of math anxiety and its influence on young adolescents' course enrollment intentions and performance in mathematics.

Journal of Educational Psychology, 82, 60–70.

Meichenbaum, D. (1977). *Cognitive behavior modification*. New York: Plenum.

Meichenbaum, D., & Asarnow, J. (1979). Cognitive-behavioral modification and metacognitive development: Implications for the classroom. In P. Kendall & S. Hollon (Eds.), *Cognitive-behavioral interventions: Theory, research, and procedures* (pp. 11–35). New York: Academic Press.

Meid, E. (1971). *The effects of two types of success and failure on children's discrimination learning and evaluation of performance.* (Doctoral dissertation, Yale University, 1971). *Dissertation Abstracts International, 32*, 7347–7348.

Meyer, J. (1970). High school effects on college intentions. *American Journal of Sociology, 76*, 59–70.

Meyer, W. (1982). Indirect communications about perceived ability estimates. *Journal of Educational Psychology, 74*, 888–897.

Meyer, W. (1987). Perceived ability and achievement-related behavior. In F. Halisch and J. Kuhl (Eds.), *Motivation, intention, and volition* (pp. 73–85). New York: Springer-Verlag.

Meyer, W. (1992). Paradoxical effects of praise and criticism on perceived ability. In W. Stroebe & M. Hewstone (Eds.), *European review of social psychology* (Vol. 3, pp. 259–283). Chichester, England: John Wiley & Sons.

Meyer, W., Bachmann, M., Biermann, V., Hempelmann, P., Ploger, F., & Spiller, H. (1979). The informational value of evaluative behavior: Influence of praise and blame on perceptions of ability. *Journal of Educational Psychology, 71*, 259–268.

Midgley, C. (1993). Motivation and middle level schools. In P. Pintrich & M. Maehr (Eds.), *Advances in motivation and achievement: Motivation and adolescent development* (Vol. 8, pp. 217–274). Greenwich, CT: JAI Press.

Midgley, C., Anderman, E., & Hicks, L. (1995). Differences between elementary and middle school teachers and students: A goal theory approach. *Journal of Early Adolescence, 15*, 90–113.

Midgley, C., Arunkumar, R., & Urdan, T. (1996). "If I don't do well tomorrow, there's a reason": Predictors of adolescents' use of academic self-handicapping strategies. *Journal of Educational Psychology, 88*, 423–434.

Midgley, C., Feldlaufer, H., & Eccles, J. (1988).

The transition to junior high school: Beliefs of pre- and posttransition teachers. *Journal of Youth and Adolescence, 17*, 543–562.

Midgley, C., Feldlaufer, H., & Eccles, J. (1989). Student/teacher relations and attitudes toward mathematics before and after the transition to junior high school. *Child Development, 60*, 981–992.

Midgley, C., & Urdan, T. (1995). Predictors of middle school students' use of self-handicapping strategies. *Journal of Early Adolescence, 15*, 389–411.

Miller, A. (1985). A developmental study of the cognitive basis of performance impairment after failure. *Journal of Personality and Social Psychology, 49*, 529–538.

Miller, A. (1986). Performance impairment after failure: Mechanism and sex differences. *Journal of Educational Psychology, 78*, 486–491.

Miller, D., & Hom, H. (1990). Influence of extrinsic and ego incentive value on persistence after failure and continuing motivation. *Journal of Educational Psychology, 82*, 539–545.

Miller, D., & Ross, M. (1975). Self-serving bias in the attribution of causality: Fact or fiction? *Psychological Bulletin, 82*, 213–235.

Miserandino, M. (1996). Children who do well in school: Individual differences in perceived competence and autonomy in above-average children. *Journal of Educational Psychology, 88*, 203–214.

Mitchell, M. (1993). Situational interest: Its multifaceted structure in the secondary school mathematics classroom. *Journal of Educational Psychology, 85*, 424–436.

Mone, M., & Baker, D. (1992). A social-cognitive, attributional model of personal goals: An empirical evaluation. *Motivation & Emotions, 16*, 297–321.

Montessori, M. (1964). *The Montessori method*. New York: Schocken.

Morris, L., Davis, M., & Hutchings, C. (1981). Cognitive and emotional components of anxiety: Literature review and a revised worry-emotionality scale. *Journal of Educational Psychology, 73*, 541–555.

Morris, W., & Nemcek, D. (1982). The development of social comparison motivation among preschoolers: Evidence of a stepwise progression. *Merrill-Palmer Quarterly, 28*, 413–425.

Morse, L., & Handley, H. (1985). Listening to

adolescents: Gender differences in science classroom interaction. In L. Wilkinson & C. Marrett (Eds.), *Gender influences in classroom interaction* (pp. 37–56). Orlando, FL: Academic Press.

Mosatche, H., & Bragonier, P. (1981). An observational study of social comparison in preschoolers. *Child Development, 52*, 376–378.

Mossholder, K. (1980). Effects of externally mediated goal setting on intrinsic motivation: A laboratory experiment. *Journal of Applied Psychology, 65*, 202–210.

Mosteller, F., Light, R., & Sachs, J. (1996). Sustained inquiry in education: Lessons from skill grouping and class size. *Harvard Educational Review, 66*, 797–842.

Multon, K., Brown, S., & Lent, R. (1991). Relation of self-efficacy beliefs to academic outcomes: A meta-analytic investigation. *Journal of Counseling Psychology, 38*, 30–38.

Munk, D., & Repp, A. (1994). The relationship between instructional variables and problem behavior: A review. *Exceptional Children, 60*, 390–401.

Mussen, P., & Eisenberg, N. (in press). Child-rearing and pro-social behavior. In D. Stipek & A. Bohart (Eds.), *Constructive and destructive behavior: Implications for family, school, and society*.

National Council of Teachers of Mathematics. (1989). *Curriculum and evaluation standards for school mathematics*. Reston, VA: Author.

Naveh-Benjamin, M. (1991). A comparison of training programs intended for different types of test-anxious students: Further support for an information processing model. *Journal of Educational Psychology, 83*, 134–139.

Naveh-Benjamin, M., McKeachie, W., & Lin, Y-G. (1987). Two types of test-anxious students: Support for an information processing model. *Journal of Educational Psychology, 79*, 131–136.

Nelson-Le Gall, S. (1981). Help-seeking: An understudied problem-solving skill in children. *Developmental Review, 1*, 224–246.

Nelson-Le Gall, S. (1990). Classroom help-seeking behavior of African-American children. *Education and Urban Society, 24*, 27–40.

Nelson-Le Gall, S. (1992). Children's instrumental help seeking: Its role in the social acquisition of knowledge and skill. In R. Hertz-Lazarowitz & N. Miller (Eds.), *Interaction in cooperative groups: The theoretical anatomy of group learning* (pp. 49–68). New York: Cambridge University Press.

Nelson-Le Gall, S. (1993). Perceiving and displaying effort in achievement settings. In T. Tomlinson (Ed.), *Motivating students to learn: Overcoming barriers to high achievement* (pp. 225–244). Berkeley, CA: McCutchan.

Newman, R. (1984). Children's achievement and self-evaluations in mathematics: A longitudinal study. *Journal of Educational Psychology, 76*, 857–873.

Newman, R. (1991). Goals and self-regulated learning: What motivates children to seek academic help? In M. Maehr & P. Pintrich (Eds.), *Advances in motivation and achievement* (Vol. 7, pp. 151–183). Greenwich, CT: JAI Press.

Newman, R., & Schwager, M. (1992). Student perceptions and academic help-seeking. In D. Schunk & J. Meece (Eds.), *Student perceptions in the classroom* (pp. 123–146). Hillsdale, NJ: Lawrence Erlbaum Associates.

Newmann, F. (1992). Higher order thinking and prospects for classroom thoughtfulness. In F. Newmann (Ed.), *Student engagement and achievement in American secondary schools* (pp. 62–91). New York: Teachers College Press.

Nicholls, J. (1975). Causal attributions and other achievement-related cognitions: Effects of task outcome, attainment value, and sex. *Journal of Educational Psychology, 31*, 379–389.

Nicholls, J. (1978). The development of the concepts of effort and ability, perception of own attainment, and the understanding that difficult tasks require more ability. *Child Development, 49*, 800–814.

Nicholls, J. (1979a). Development of perception of own attainment and causal attributions for success and failure in reading. *Journal of Educational Psychology, 71*, 94–99.

Nicholls, J. (1979b). Quality and equality in intellectual development: The role of motivation in education. *American Psychologist, 34*, 1071–1083.

Nicholls, J. (1980). A re-examination of boys' and girls' causal attributions for success and failure based on New Zealand data. In L. Fyans

(Ed.), *Achievement motivation: Recent trends in theory and research* (pp. 266–288). New York: Plenum.

Nicholls, J. (1983). Conception of ability and achievement motivation: A theory and its implications for education. In S. Paris, G. Olson, & H. Stevenson (Eds.), *Learning and motivation in the classroom* (pp. 211–237). Hillsdale, NJ: Lawrence Erlbaum Associates.

Nicholls, J. (1984). Achievement motivation: Conceptions of ability, subjective experience, task choice, and performance. *Psychological Review, 91,* 328–346.

Nicholls, J. (1989). *The competitive ethos and democratic education.* Cambridge, MA: Harvard University Press.

Nicholls, J. (1990). What is ability and why are we mindful of it? A developmental perspective. In R. Sternberg & J. Kolligian, Jr. (Eds.), *Competence considered* (pp. 11–40). New Haven, CT: Yale University Press.

Nicholls, J. (1992). Students as educational theorists. In D. Schunk & J. Meece (Eds.), *Student perceptions in the classroom* (pp. 267–286). Hillsdale, NJ: Lawrence Erlbaum Associates.

Nicholls, J., Cobb, P., Wood, T., Yackel, E., & Patashnick, M. (1990). Assessing students' theories of success in mathematics: Individual and classroom differences. *Journal for Research in Mathematics Education, 21,* 109–122.

Nicholls, J., Cobb, P., Yackel, E., Wood, T., & Wheatley, G. (1990). Students' theories about mathematics and their mathematical knowledge: Multiple dimensions of assessment. In G. Kulm (Ed.), *Assessing higher order thinking in mathematics* (pp. 137–154). Washington, DC: American Association for the Advancement of Science.

Nicholls, J., Jagacinski, C., & Miller, A. (1986). Conceptions of ability in children and adults. In R. Schwarzer (Ed.), *Self-related cognitions in anxiety and motivation* (pp. 265–284). Hillsdale, NJ: Lawrence Erlbaum Associates.

Nicholls, J., & Miller, A. (1984a). Conceptions of ability and achievement motivation. In R. Ames & C. Ames (Eds.), *Research on motivation in education. Vol. 1: Student motivation* (pp. 39–73). New York: Academic Press

Nicholls, J., & Miller, A. (1984b). Development and its discontents: The differentiation of the concept of ability. In J. Nicholls (Ed.), *Advances in motivation and achievement. Vol. 3: The development of achievement motivation* (pp. 185–218). Greenwich, CT: JAI Press.

Nicholls, J., & Miller, A. (1984c). Reasoning about the ability of self and others: A developmental study. *Child Development, 55,* 1990–1999.

Niedenthal, P., Tangney, J., & Gavanski, I. (1994). "If only I weren't" versus "If only I hadn't": Distinguishing shame and guilt in counterfactual thinking. *Journal of Personality & Social Psychology, 67,* 585–595.

Nottelmann, E., & Hill, K. (1977). Test anxiety and off-task behavior in evaluative situations. *Child Development, 48,* 225–231.

Nolen, S. (1988). Reasons for studying: Motivational orientations and study strategies. *Cognition and Instruction, 5,* 269–287.

Notz, W. (1975). Work motivation and the negative effects of extrinsic rewards: A review with implications for theory and practice. *American Psychologist, 30,* 804–891.

Numi, J. (1991). The effect of others' influence, effort, and ability attributions on emotions in achievement and affiliative situations. *Journal of Social Psychology, 131,* 703–715.

Oakes, J. (1985). *Keeping track: How schools structure inequality.* New Haven, CT: Yale University Press.

Oakes, J. (1990). *Multiplying inequalities: The effects of race, social class, and tracking on opportunities to learn math and science.* Santa Monica, CA: Rand.

Ogbu, J. (1992). Understanding cultural diversity and learning. *Educational Researcher, 21,* 5–14.

O'Leary, K. (1978). The operant and social psychology of token systems. In A. Catania & T. Brigham (Eds.), *Handbook of applied behavior analysis: Social and instructional processes* (pp. 179–207). New York: Irvington.

O'Leary, K., & Drabman, R. (1971). Token reinforcement programs in the classroom: A review. *Psychological Bulletin, 75,* 379–398.

O'Leary, S., & Dubey, D. (1979). Applications of self-control procedures by children: A review. *Journal of Applied Behavior Analysis, 12,* 449–465.

Pajares, F. (1996). Self-efficacy beliefs in academic

settings. *Review of Educational Research, 66,* 543–578.

Pajares, F., & Miller, M. (1994). Role of self-efficacy and self-concept beliefs in mathematical problem solving: A path analysis. *Journal of Educational Psychology, 86,* 193–203.

Palardy, J. (1969). What teachers believe—what children achieve. *Elementary School Journal, 69,* 370–374.

Palincsar, A., & Brown, A. (1984). Reciprocal teaching of comprehension-fostering and comprehension-monitoring activities. *Cognition and Instruction, 1,* 117–175.

Palincsar, A., & Brown, A. (1987). Advances in improving the cognitive performance of handicapped students. In M. Wang, M. Reynolds, & H. Walberg (Eds.). *Handbook of special education: Research and practice. Vol. 1: Learner characteristics and adaptive education* (pp. 93–112). Oxford: Pergamo.

Pallas, A., Entwisle, D., Alexander, K., & Stluka, M. (1994). Ability-group effects: Instructional, social, or institutional? *Sociology of Education, 67,* 27–46.

Paris, S., Cross, D., & Lipson, M. (1984). Informed strategies for learning: A program to improve children's reading awareness and comprehension. *Journal of Educational Psychology, 76,* 1239–1252.

Paris, S., & Oka, E. (1986). Children's reading strategies, metacognition and motivation. *Developmental Review, 6,* 25–86.

Parker, L., & Lepper, M. (1992). The effects of fantasy contexts on children's learning and motivation: Making learning more fun. *Journal of Personality and Social Psychology, 62,* 625–633.

Parsons, J., Adler, T., & Kaczala, C. (1982). Socialization of achievement attitudes and beliefs: Parental influences. *Child Development, 53,* 310–339.

Parsons, J., Kaczala, C., & Meece, J. (1982). Socialization of achievement attitudes and beliefs: Classroom influences. *Child Development, 53,* 322–339.

Parsons, J., Meece, J., Adler, T., & Kaczala, C. (1982). Sex differences in attributions and learned helplessness. *Sex Roles, 8,* 431–432.

Pascarella, E., Walberg, H., Junker, L., & Haertel, G. (1981). Continuing motivation in science for early and late adolescents. *American Educational Research Journal, 18,* 439–452.

Patrick, B., Skinner, E., & Connell, J. (1993). What motivates children's behavior and emotion? Joint effects of perceived control and autonomy in the academic domain. *Journal of Personality and Social Psychology, 65,* 781–791.

Pearlman, C. (1984). The effects of level of effectance motivation, IQ, and a penalty/reward contingency on the choice of problem difficulty. *Child Development, 55,* 537–542.

Pepitone, E. (1972). Comparison behavior in elementary school children. *American Educational Research Journal, 9,* 43–63.

Perkinson, H. (1993). *Teachers without goals, students without purposes.* New York: McGraw-Hill.

Peterson, P., & Swing, S. (1982). Beyond time on task: Students' reports of their thought processes during classroom instruction. *The Elementary School Journal, 21,* 487–515.

Phillips, B., Pitcher, G., Worsham, M., & Miller, S. (1980). Test anxiety and the school environment. In I. Sarason (Ed.), *Test anxiety: Theory, research, and applications* (pp. 327–346). Hillsdale, NJ: Lawrence Erlbaum Associates.

Phillips, D. (1984). The illusion of incompetence among academically competent children. *Child Development, 55,* 2000–2016.

Phillips, D., & Zimmerman, M. (1990). The developmental course of perceived competence and incompetence among competent children. In J. Kolligian & R. Sternberg (Eds.), *Competence considered* (pp. 41–66). New Haven, CT: Yale University Press.

Piaget, J. (1952). *The origins of intelligence in children.* New York: W. W. Norton.

Pianta, R. (1994). Patterns of relationships between children and kindergarten teachers. *Journal of School Psychology, 32,* 15–31.

Pianta, R., & Nimetz, S. (1991). Relationships between children and teachers: Associations with classroom and home behavior. *Journal of Applied Developmental Psychology, 12,* 379–393.

Pianta, R., & Steinberg, M. (1992). Teacher–child relationships and the process of adjusting to school. In R. Pianta (Ed.), *Beyond the parent: The role of other adults in children's lives* (pp. 61–80). San Francisco: Jossey-Bass.

Pianta, R., Steinberg, M., & Rollins, K. (1995). The first two years of school: Teacher–child relationships and deflections in children's classroom adjustment. *Development and Psychopathology, 7,* 295–312.

Pintrich, P., & Blumenfeld, P. (1985). Classroom experience and children's self-perceptions of ability, effort, and conduct. *Journal of Educational Psychology, 77,* 646–657.

Pintrich, P., & De Groot, E. (1990). Motivational and self-regulated learning components of classroom academic performance. *Journal of Educational Psychology, 82,* 33–40.

Pintrich, P., Roeser, R., & De Groot, E. (1994). Classroom and individual differences in early adolescents' motivation and self-regulated learning. *Journal of Early Adolescents, 14,* 139–161.

Pintrich, P., & Schrauben, B. (1992). Students' motivational beliefs and their cognitive engagement in classroom academic tasks. In D. Schunk & J. Meece (Eds.), *Student perceptions in the classroom: Causes and consequences* (pp. 149–183). Hillsdale, NJ: Lawrence Erlbaum Associates.

Pittman, T., Boggiano, A., & Ruble, D. (1983). Intrinsic and extrinsic motivational orientations: Limiting conditions on the undermining and enhancing effects of reward on intrinsic motivation. In J. Levine & M. Wang (Eds.), *Teacher and student perceptions: Implications for learning* (pp. 319–340). Hillsdale, NJ: Lawrence Erlbaum Associates.

Pittman, T., Davey, M., Alafat, K., Wetherill, K., & Kramer, N. (1980). Informational versus controlling verbal rewards. *Personality and Social Psychology Bulletin, 6,* 228–233.

Pittman, T., Emery, J., & Boggiano, A. (1982). Intrinsic and extrinsic motivational orientations: Reward-induced changes in preference for complexity. *Journal of Personality and Social Psychology, 42,* 789–797.

Plant, R., & Ryan, R. (1985). Intrinsic motivation and the effects of self-consciousness, self-awareness, and ego-involvement: An investigation of internally-controlling styles. *Journal of Personality, 53,* 435–449.

Plass, J., & Hill, K. (1986). Children's achievement strategies and test performance: The role of time pressure, evaluation anxiety, and sex. *Developmental Psychology, 22,* 31–36.

Prawat, R. (1993). The value of ideas: Problems versus possibilities in learning. *Educational Researcher, 22,* 5–16.

Pressley, M., El-Dinary, P., Marks, M., Brown, R., & Stein, S. (1992). Good strategy instruction is motivating and interesting. In K. Renninger, S. Hidi, & A. Krapp (Eds.), *The role of interest in learning and development* (pp. 333–358). Hillsdale, NJ: Lawrence Erlbaum Associates.

Rainey, R. (1965). The effects of directed vs. nondirected laboratory work on high school chemistry achievement. *Journal of Research in Science Teaching, 3,* 286–292.

Randhawa, B. (1994). Self-efficacy in mathematics, attitudes, and achievement of boys and girls from restricted samples in two countries. *Perceptual & Motor Skills, 79,* 1011–1018.

Randhawa, B., Beamer, J., & Lundberg, I. (1993). Role of mathematics self-efficacy in the structural model of mathematics achievement. *Journal of Educational Psychology, 85,* 41–48.

Reid, M., & Borkowski, J. (1987). Causal attributions of hyperactive children: Implications for teaching strategies and self-control. *Journal of Educational Psychology, 79,* 296–307.

Renick, J., & Harter, S. (1989). Impact of social comparisons on the developing self-perceptions of learning disabled students. *Journal of Educational Psychology, 81,* 631–638.

Rennie, L., Parker, L., & Kahle, J. (1996). Informing teaching and research in science education through gender equity initiatives. In L. Parker, L. Rennie, & B. Fraser (Eds.), *Gender, science and mathematics* (pp. 203–221). Dordrecht, Netherlands: Kluwer Academic Publishers.

Rest, S., Nierenberg, R., Weiner, B., & Heckhausen, H. (1973). Further evidence concerning the effects of perceptions of effort and ability on achievement evaluation. *Journal of Personality and Social Psychology, 28,* 187–191.

Reuman, D. (1989). How social comparison mediates the relation between ability-grouping practices and students' achievement expectancies in mathematics. *Journal of Educational Psychology, 81,* 178–189.

Rheinberg, F. (1983). Achievement evaluation: A fundamental difference and its motivational consequences. *Studies in Educational Evaluation, 9,* 185–194.

Richmond, V., & Dickson-Markman, F. (1985). Validity of the writing apprehension test:

Two studies. *Psychological Reports, 56,* 255–259.

Riggs, J. (1992). Self-handicapping and achievement. In A. Boggiano & T. Pittman (Eds.), *Achievement and motivation: A social-developmental perspective* (pp. 244–267). Cambridge, MA: Cambridge University Press.

Robertson, D., & Keely, S. (1974, August). *Evaluation of a mediational training program for impulsive children by a multiple case study design.* Paper presented at the annual meeting of the American Psychological Association, New Orleans.

Rose, M. (Ed.). (1985). *When a writer can't write: Studies in writer's block and other composing process problems.* New York: Guilford.

Rosen, B., & D'Andrade, R. C. (1959). The psychosocial origins of achievement motivation. *Sociometry, 22,* 185–218.

Rosenbaum, M., & Drabman, R. (1979). Self-control training in the classroom: A review and critique. *Journal of Applied Behavior Analysis, 12,* 467–485.

Rosenfield, D., Folger, R., & Adelman, H. (1980). When rewards reflect competence: A qualification of the over-justification effect. *Journal of Personality and Social Psychology, 39,* 368–376.

Rosenholtz, S., & Rosenholtz, S. (1981). Classroom organization and the perception of ability. *Sociology of Education, 54,* 132–140.

Rosenholtz, S., & Simpson, C. (1984a). Classroom organization and student stratification. *Elementary School Journal, 85,* 21–38.

Rosenholtz, S., & Simpson, C. (1984b). The formation of ability conceptions: Developmental trend or social construction? *Review of Educational Research, 54,* 31–63.

Rosenholtz, S., & Wilson, B. (1980). The effect of classroom structure on shared perceptions of ability. *American Educational Research Journal, 17,* 75–82.

Rosenthal, R. (1974). *On the social psychology of the self-fulfilling prophecy: Further evidence for Pygmalion effects and their mediating mechanisms.* New York: MSS Modular Publications.

Rosenthal, R., & Jacobson, L. (1968). *Pygmalion in the classroom: Teacher expectation and pupils' intellectual development.* New York: Holt, Rinehart & Winston.

Ross, J. (1995). Effects of feedback on student behavior in cooperative learning. *Elementary School Journal, 96,* 125–143.

Ross, L. (1977). The intuitive psychologist and his short-comings: Distortions in the attribution process. In L. Berkowitz (Ed.), *Advances in experimental social psychology* (Vol. 10, pp. 174–220). New York: Academic Press.

Ross, L., & Nisbett, R. (1991). *The person and the situation: Perspectives of social psychology.* New York: McGraw-Hill.

Roth, K. (1992). Science education: It's not enough to "do" or "relate." In M. Pearsall (Ed.), *Scope, sequence, and coordination of secondary school science: Relevant research* (Vol. 2, pp. 151–164). Washington, DC: National Science Teachers Association.

Rotter, J. (1966). Generalized expectancies for internal versus external control of reinforcement. *Psychological Monographs, 1* (Whole 609).

Rotter, J. (1975). Some problems and misconceptions related to the construct of internal versus external control of reinforcement. *Journal of Consulting and Clinical Psychology, 43,* 56–67.

Rotter, J. (1990). Internal versus external control of reinforcement: A case history of a variable. *American Psychologist, 45,* 489–493.

Roy, P. (Ed.). (1982). *Structuring cooperative learning: The 1982 handbook.* Minneapolis: Cooperative Network.

Ruble, D. (1983). The development of social comparison processes and their role in achievement-related self-socialization. In E. T. Higgins, D. N. Ruble, W. W. Hartup (Eds.), *Social cognition and social development: A sociocultural perspective* (pp. 134–157). New York: Cambridge University Press.

Ruble, D., Boggiano, A., Feldman, N., & Loebl, J. (1980). A developmental analysis of the role of social comparison in self-evaluation. *Developmental Psychology, 16,* 105–115.

Ruble, D., Feldman, N., & Boggiano, A. (1976). Social comparison between young children in achievement situations. *Developmental Psychology, 12,* 192–197.

Ruble, D., & Frey, K. (1991). Changing patterns of comparative behavior as skills are acquired: A functional model of self-evaluation. In J. Suls & T. Wills (Eds.), *Social* comparison: *Contemporary theory and research* (pp. 79–113). Hillsdale, NJ: Lawrence Erlbaum Associates.

Ruble, D., Grosovsky, E., Frey, K., & Cohen, R. (1992). Developmental changes in competence assessment. In A. Boggiano & T. Pittman (Eds.), *Achievement and motivation: A social-developmental perspective* (pp. 138–164). Cambridge, MA: Cambridge University Press.

Ruble, D., Parsons, J., & Ross, J. (1976). Self-evaluative responses of children in an achievement setting. *Child Development, 47,* 990–997.

Rueda, R., & Moll, L. (1994). A sociocultural perspective on motivation. In H. O'Neil, Jr. & M. Drillings (Eds.), *Motivation: Theory and reearch* (pp. 117–137). Hillsdale, NJ: Lawrence Erlbaum Associates.

Rutter, M., Maughan, B., Mortimore, P., Ouston, J., & Smith, A. (1979). *Fifteen thousand hours: Secondary schools and their effects on children.* Cambridge, MA: Harvard University Press.

Ryan, R. (1982). Control and information in the intrapersonal sphere: An extension of cognitive evaluation theory. *Journal of Personality and Social Psychology, 43,* 450–461.

Ryan, R., & Connell, J. (1989). Perceived locus of causality and internalization: Examining reasons for acting in two domains. *Journal of Personality and Social Psychology, 57,* 749–761.

Ryan, R., Connell, J., & Deci, E. (1985). A motivational analysis of self-determination and self-regulation. In C. Ames & R. Ames (Eds.), *Research on motivation in education. Vol. 2: The classroom* (pp. 13–51). New York: Academic Press.

Ryan, R., Connell, J., & Grolnick, W. (1992). When achievement is *not* intrinsically motivated: A theory of internalization and self-regulation in school. In A. Boggiano & T. Pittman (Eds.), *Achievement and motivation: A social-developmental perspective* (pp. 167–188). Cambridge, MA: Cambridge University Press.

Ryan, R., Connell, J., & Plant, R. (1990). Emotions in nondirected text learning. *Learning and Individual Differences, 2,* 1–17.

Ryan, R., & Grolnick, W. (1986). Origins and pawns in the classroom: Self-report and projective assessments of individual differences in children's perceptions. *Journal of Personality and Social Psychology, 50,* 350–358.

Ryan, R., & Powelson, C. (1991). Autonomy and relatedness as fundamental to motivation and education. *Journal of Experimental Education, 60,* 49–66.

Ryan, R., & Stiller, J. (1991). The social contexts of internalization: Parent and teacher influences on autonomy, motivation, and learning. In P. Pintrich & M. Maehr (Eds.), *Advances in Motivation and Achievement* (Vol. 7, pp. 115–149). Greenwich, CT: JAI Press.

Ryckman, D. B., & Peckhan, P. D. (1987). Gender differences in attributions for success and failure. *Journal of Early Adolescence, 7,* 47–63.

Salili, F., Maehr, M., Sorensen, R., & Fyans, L. (1976). A further consideration of the effects of evaluation on motivation. *American Educational Research Journal, 13,* 85–102.

Sapp, M., Farrell, W., & Durand, H. (1995). The effects of mathematics, reading, and writing tests in producing worry and emotionality test anxiety with economically and educationally disadvantaged college students. *College Student Journal, 29,* 122–125.

Sarason, I. (1958). The effects of anxiety, reassurance, and meaningfulness of material to be learned on verbal learning. *Journal of Experimental Psychology, 56,* 472–477.

Sarason, I. (1961). A note on anxiety, instructions, and word association performance. *Journal of Abnormal and Social Psychology, 62,* 153–154.

Sarason, I. (1973). Test anxiety and cognitive modeling. *Journal of Personality and Social Psychology, 28,* 58–61.

Sarason, I. (1975). Test anxiety, attention and the general problem of anxiety. In I. Sarason & C. Spielberger (Eds.), *Stress and anxiety* (Vol. 1, pp. 165–187). Washington, DC: Hemisphere.

Sarason, I. (1978). The Test Anxiety Scale: Concept and research. In C. Spielberger & I. Sarason (Eds.), *Stress and anxiety* (Vol. 5, pp. 193–216). Washington, DC: Hemisphere.

Sarason, I. (1984). Stress, anxiety, and cognitive interference: Reactions to tests. *Journal of Personality and Social Psychology, 46,* 929–938.

Sarason, I.G., & Sarason, B.R. (1990). Test anxiety. In H. Leitenberg (Ed.), *Handbook of social and evaluation anxiety* (pp. 475–495). New York: Plenum.

Sarason, S., Davidson, K., Lighthall, F., Waite, R., & Ruebush, B. (1960). *Anxiety in elementary school children*. New York: John Wiley & Sons.

Scheffler, I. (1991). *In praise of the cognitive emotions and other essays in the philosophy of education*. New York: Routledge.

Schmitz, B., & Skinner, E. (1993). Perceived control, effort, and academic performance: Interindividual, intraindividual, and multivariate time-series analyses. *Journal of Personality and Social Psychology, 64*, 1010–1028.

Schunk, D. (1982). Effects of effort and attributional feedback on children's perceived self-efficacy and achievement. *Journal of Educational Psychology, 74*, 548–556.

Schunk, D. (1983a). Ability versus effort attributional feedback: Differential effects on self-efficacy and achievement. *Journal of Educational Psychology, 75*, 848–856.

Schunk, D. (1983b). Developing children's self-efficacy and skills: The roles of social comparative information and goal setting. *Contemporary Educational Psychology, 8*, 76–86.

Schunk, D. (1984a). Self-efficacy perspective on achievement behavior. *Educational Psychologist, 19*, 48–58.

Schunk, D. (1984b). Sequential attributional feedback and children's achievement behaviors. *Journal of Educational Psychology, 76*, 1159–1169.

Schunk, D. (1985a). Participation in goal setting: Effects on self-efficacy and skills of learning disabled children. *Journal of Special Education, 19*, 307–317.

Schunk, D. (1985b). Self-efficacy and school learning. *Psychology in the Schools, 22*, 209–223.

Schunk, D. (1986). Children's social comparison and goal setting in achievement contexts. In L. Katz (Ed.), *Current topics in early childhood education* (pp. 62–84). Norwood, NJ: Ablex.

Schunk, D. (1989a). Self-efficacy and cognitive achievement: Implications for students with learning problems. *Journal of Learning Disabilities, 22*, 14–22.

Schunk, D. (1989b). Social cognitive theory and self-regulated learning. In B. Zimmerman & D. Schunk (Eds.), *Self-regulated learning and academic achievement: Theory, research and practice* (pp. 83–110). New York: Springer-Verlag.

Schunk, D. (1990). Goal setting and self-efficacy during self-regulated learning. *Educational Psychologist, 25*, 71–86.

Schunk, D. (1991). Goal setting and self-evaluation: A social cognitive perspective on self-regulation. In M. Maehr & P. Pintrich (Eds.), *Advances in motivation and achievement* (Vol. 7, pp. 85–113). Greenwich, CT: JAI Press.

Schunk, D. (1994). Self-regulation of self-efficacy and attributions in academic settings. In D. Schunk & B. Zimmerman (Eds.), *Self-regulation of learning and performance* (pp. 75–99). Hillsdale, NJ: Lawrence Erlbaum Associates.

Schunk, D. (1995). Self-efficacy and education and instruction. In J. Maddux (Ed.), *Self-efficacy, adaptation, and adjustment: Theory, research, and application* (pp. 281–303). New York: Plenum.

Schunk, D. (1996). Goal and self-evaluative influences during children's cognitive skill learning. *American Educational Research Journal, 33*, 359–382.

Schunk, D., & Hanson, A. (1985). Peer models: Influence on children's self-efficacy and achievement. *Journal of Educational Psychology, 77*, 313–322.

Schunk, D., & Rice, J. (1989). Learning goals and children's reading comprehension. *Journal of Reading Behavior, 21*, 279–293.

Schunk, D., & Zimmerman, B. (Eds.). (1994). *Self-regulation of learning and performance*. Hillsdale, NJ: Lawrence Erlbaum Associates.

Schwartz, S. (1996, March). Hidden messages in teacher talk: Praise and empowerment. *Teaching Children Mathematics*, 396–401.

Schwarzer, R., & Jerusalem, M. (1992). Advances in anxiety theory: A cognitive process approach. In K. Hagtvet & T. Johnsen (Ed.), *Advances in test anxiety research* (Vol. 7, pp. 2–17). Amsterdam: Swets & Zeitlinger.

Sears, P. (1940). Level of aspiration in academically successful and unsuccessful children. *Journal of Abnormal and Social Psychology, 35*, 498–536.

Seligman, M., & Maier, S. (1967). Failure to escape traumatic shock. *Journal of Experimental Psychology, 74,* 1–9.

Selfe, C. (1985). An apprehensive writer composes. In M. Rose (Ed.), *When a writer can't write: Studies in writer's block and other composing process problems* (pp. 83–95). New York: Guilford Press.

Sexton, T., & Tuckman, B. (1991). Self-beliefs and behavior: The role of self-efficacy and outcome expectation over time. *Personality and Individual Differences, 12,* 725–736.

Shapira, Z. (1976). Expectancy determinants of intrinsically motivated behavior. *Journal of Personality and Social Psychology, 34,* 1235–1244.

Shapiro, E. (1984). Self-monitoring procedures. In T. Ollendick & M. Hersen (Eds.), *Child behavioral assessment: Principles and procedures* (pp. 148–165). New York: Pergamon Press.

Shapiro, E., & Bradley, K. (1996). Treatment of academic problems. In M. Reinecke, F. Dattilio, & A. Freeman (Eds.), *Cognitive therapy with children and adolescents: A casebook for clinical practice* (pp. 344–366). New York: Guilford Press.

Shapiro, E., & Cole, C. (1994). *Behavior change in the classroom: Self-management interventions.* New York: Guilford Press.

Sharan, S. (1980). Cooperative learning in small groups: Recent methods and effects on achievement, attitudes, and ethnic relations. *Review of Educational Research, 50,* 241–271.

Shell, D., Colvin, C., & Bruning, R. (1995). Self-efficacy, attribution, and outcome expectancy mechanisms in reading and writing achievement: Grade-level and achievement-level differences. *Journal of Educational Psychology, 87,* 386–398.

Sherman, J. (1979). Predicting mathematics performance in high school girls and boys. *Journal of Educational Psychology, 71,* 242–249.

Shirey, L. (1992). Importance, interest, and selective attention. In K. Renninger, S. Hidi, & A. Krapp (Eds.), *The role of interest in learning and development* (pp. 281–296). Hillsdale, NJ: Lawrence Erlbaum Associates.

Shirey, L., & Reynolds, R. (1988). Effect of interest on attention and learning. *Journal of Educational Psychology, 80,* 159–166.

Shultz, T., & Zigler, E. (1970). Emotional concomitants of visual mastery in infants: The effects of stimulus movement on smiling and vocalizing. *Journal of Experimental Child Psychology, 10,* 390–402.

Sieber, J., O'Neil, H., & Tobias, S. (1977). *Anxiety, learning, and instruction.* Hillsdale, NJ: Lawrence Erlbaum Associates.

Simpson, C. (1981). Classroom structure and the organization of ability. *Sociology of Education, 54,* 120–132.

Simpson, C., & Rosenholtz, S. (1986). Classroom structure and the social construction of ability. In J. Richardson (Ed.), *Handbook of theory and research for the sociology of education* (pp. 113–138). New York: Greenwood Press.

Simpson, S., Licht, B., Wagner, R., & Stader, S. (1996). Organization of children's academic ability-related self-perceptions. *Journal of Educational Psychology, 88,* 387–396.

Skaalvik, E., & Rankin, R. (1990). Math, verbal, and general academic self-concept: The internal/external frame of reference model and gender differences in self-concept structure. *Journal of Educational Psychology, 82,* 546–554.

Skinner, B. (1974). *About behaviorism.* New York: Alfred A. Knopf.

Skinner, E. (1990). Age differences in the dimensions of perceived control during middle childhood: Implications for developmental conceptualizations and research. *Child Development, 61,* 1882–1890.

Skinner, E. (1995). *Perceived control, motivation, & coping.* Thousand Oaks, CA: Sage Publications.

Skinner, E., & Belmont, M. (1993). Motivation in the classroom: Reciprocal effects of teacher behavior and student engagement across the school year. *Journal of Educational Psychology, 85,* 571–581.

Skinner, E., Chapman, M., & Baltes, P. (1988). Control, means-ends, and agency beliefs: A new conceptualization and its measurement during childhood. *Journal of Personality and Social Psychology, 54,* 117–133.

Skinner, E., & Wellborn, J. (1994). Coping during childhood and adolescence: A motivational perspective. In R. Lerner & M. Perlmutter (Eds.), *Life-span development and behavior* (Vol. 12, pp. 91–133). Hillsdale, NJ: Lawrence Erlbaum Associates.

Skinner, E., Wellborn, J., & Connell, J. (1990).

What it takes to do well in school and whether I've got it: The role of perceived control in children's engagement and school achievement. *Journal of Educational Psychology, 82,* 22–32.

Slavin, R. (1977). Classroom reward structure: An analytic and practical review. *Review of Educational Research, 47,* 633–650.

Slavin, R. (1980a). Cooperative learning. *Review of Educational Research, 50,* 315–342.

Slavin, R. (1980b). *Using student team learning* (rev. ed.). Baltimore: Johns Hopkins University, Center for Social Organization of Schools.

Slavin, R. (1983a). *Cooperative learning.* New York: Longman.

Slavin, R. (1983b). When does cooperative learning increase student achievement? *Psychological Bulletin, 94,* 429–445.

Slavin, R. (1984). Students motivating students to excel: Cooperative incentives, cooperative tasks, and student achievement. *Elementary School Journal, 84,* 53–63.

Slavin, R. (1987a). Developmental and motivational perspectives on cooperative learning: A reconciliation. *Child Development, 58,* 1161–1167.

Slavin, R. (1987b). Mastery learning reconsidered. *Review of Educational Research, 57,* 175–213.

Slavin, R. (1988). *Student team learning: An overview and practical guide.* Washington, DC: National Education Association.

Slavin, R. (1990a). Achievement effects of ability grouping in secondary schools: A best-evidence synthesis. *Review of Educational Research, 60,* 471–499.

Slavin, R. (1990b). *Cooperative learning: Theory, research and practice.* Englewood Cliffs, NJ: Prentice Hall.

Slavin, R. (1993). Ability grouping in the middle grades: Achievement effects and alternatives. *Elementary School Journal, 93,* 535–552.

Slavin, R., Sharan, S., Kagan, S., Hertz-Lazarowitz, N., Webb, N., & Schmuck, R. (1985). *Learning to cooperate, cooperating to learn.* New York: Plenum.

Smiley, P., & Dweck, C. (1994). Individual differences in achievement goals among young children. *Child Development, 65,* 1723–1743.

Smith, M. (1980). Meta-analysis of research on teacher expectations. *Evaluation in Education, 4,* 53–55.

Sohn, D. (1982). Sex differences in achievement self-attributions: An effect-size analysis. *Sex Roles, 8,* 345–357.

Spear, P., & Armstrong, S. (1978). Effects of performance expectancies created by peer comparison as related to social reinforcement, task difficulty, and age of child. *Journal of Experimental and Child Psychology, 25,* 254–266.

Speidel, G., & Tharp, R. (1980). What does self-reinforcement reinforce? An empirical analysis of the contingencies in self-determined reinforcement. *Child Behavior Therapy, 2,* 1–22.

Spielberger, C. (1972). Anxiety as an emotional state. In C. Spielberger (Ed.), *Anxiety: Current trends in theory and research* (Vol. 1, pp. 23–49). New York: Academic Press.

Spielberger, C., & Starr, L. (1994). Curiosity and exploratory behavior. In H. O'Neil & M. Drillings (Eds.), *Motivation: Theory and research* (pp. 221–243). Hillsdale, NJ: Lawrence Erlbaum Associates.

Spielberger, C., & Vagg, P. (1995). Test anxiety: A transactional process model. In C. Spielberger & P. Vagg (Eds.), *Test anxiety: Theory, assessment, and treatment* (pp. 3–14). Washington, DC: Taylor & Francis.

Stallings, J. (1985). School, classroom, and home influences on women's decisions to enroll in advanced mathematics courses. In S. Chipman, L. Brush, & D. Wilson (Eds.), *Women and mathematics: Balancing the equation* (pp. 199–223). Hillsdale, NJ: Lawrence Erlbaum Associates.

Stein, M., Grover, B., & Henningsen, M. (1996). Building student capacity for mathematical thinking and reasoning: An analysis of mathematical tasks used in reform classrooms. *American Educational Research Journal, 33,* 455–488.

Stevenson, H., Lee, S., & Stigler, J. (1986). Mathematics achievement of Chinese, Japanese, and American children. *Science, 231,* 693–699.

Stevenson, H., & Newman, R. (1986). Long-term prediction of achievement and attitudes in mathematics and reading. *Child Development, 57,* 646–659.

Stevenson, H., & Stigler, J. (1992). *The learning gap.* New York: Summit Books.

Stigler, J., & Stevenson, H. (1991). How Asian teachers polish each lesson to perfection. *American Educator, 15,* 12–20.

Stipek, D. (1981). Children's perceptions of their own and their classmates' ability. *Journal of Educational Psychology, 73,* 404–410.

Stipek, D. (1984a). Developmental aspects of motivation in children. In R. Ames & C. Ames (Eds.), *Research on motivation in education. Vol. 1: Student motivation* (pp. 145–174). New York: Academic Press.

Stipek, D. (1984b). Young children's performance expectations: Logical analysis or wishful thinking? In J. Nicholls (Ed.), *The development of achievement motivation* (pp. 33–56). Greenwich, CT: JAI Press.

Stipek, D. (1984c). Sex differences in children's attributions for success and failure on math and spelling tests. *Sex Roles, 11,* 969–981.

Stipek, D. (1997). Success in school—for a Head Start in life. In S. Luthar, J. Burack, D. Cicchetti, & J. Weisz (Eds.), *Developmental psychopathology: Perspectives on risk and disorder* (pp. 75–92). New York: Cambridge University Press.

Stipek, D., & Daniels, D. (1990). Children's use of dispositional attributions in predicting the performance and behavior of classmates. *Journal of Applied Developmental Psychology, 11,* 13–28.

Stipek, D., & Gralinski, H. (1991). Gender differences in children's achievement-related beliefs and emotional responses to success and failure in math. *Journal of Educational Psychology, 83,* 361–371.

Stipek, D., & Gralinski, H. (1996). Children's theories of intelligence and school performance. *Journal of Educational Psychology, 88,* 397–407.

Stipek, D., & Hoffman, J. (1980). Children's achievement-related expectancies as a function of academic performance histories and sex. *Journal of Educational Psychology, 72,* 861–865.

Stipek, D., & Kowalski, P. (1989). Learned helplessness in task-orienting versus performance-orienting testing conditions. *Journal of Educational Psychology, 81,* 384–391.

Stipek, D., & Mac Iver, D. (1989). Developmental change in children's assessment of intellectual competence. *Child Development, 60,* 521–538.

Stipek, D., & Tannatt, L. (1984). Children's judgments of their own and their peers' academic competence. *Journal of Educational Psychology, 76,* 75–84.

Stipek, D., & Weisz, J. (1981). Perceived personal control and academic achievement. *Review of Educational Research, 51,* 101–137.

Stodolsky, S. (1985). Telling math: Origins of math aversion and anxiety. *Educational Psychologist, 20,* 125–133.

Strein, W. (1993). Advances in research on academic self-concept: Implications for school psychology. *School Psychology Review, 22,* 273–284.

Sulzer-Azaroff, B., & Mayer, G. (1986). *Achieving educational excellence.* New York: Holt, Rinehart & Winston.

Swann, W., & Pittman, T. (1977). Initiating play activity of children: The moderating influence of verbal cues on intrinsic motivation. *Child Development, 48,* 1128–1132.

Swanson, H., & Scarpati, S. (1985). Self-instruction training to increase academic performance of educationally handicapped children. *Child and Family Behavior Therapy, 6,* 23–39.

Tang, S., & Hall, V. (1995). The overjustification effect: A meta-analysis. *Applied Cognitive Psychology, 9,* 365–404.

Thoresen, C., & Mahoney, M. (1974). *Behavioral self-control.* New York: Holt, Rinehart & Winston.

Thorndike, E. (1898). Animal intelligence: An experimental study of the associative processes in animals. *Psychological Review Monograph Supplements, 2* (4).

Thurlow, M., Christensen, S., & Ysseldyke, J. (1983). *Referral research. An integrative summary of findings.* Minneapolis: University of Minnesota.

Tobias, S. (1977). A model for research on the effect of anxiety on instruction. In J. Sieber, H. O'Neil, & S. Tobias (Eds.), *Anxiety, learning, and instruction* (pp. 223–240). Hillsdale, NJ: Lawrence Erlbaum Associates.

Tobias, S. (1980). Anxiety and instruction. In I. Sarason (Ed.), *Test anxiety: Theory, research, and applications* (pp. 289–309). Hillsdale, NJ: Lawrence Erlbaum Associates.

Tobias, S. (1986). Anxiety and cognitive processing of instruction. In R. Schwarzer (Ed.), *Self-related cognitions in anxiety and motivation* (p. 35–54). Hillsdale, NJ: Lawrence Erlbaum Associates.

Tobias, S. (1992). The impact of test anxiety cognition in school learning. In K.A. Hagtvet &

T.B. Johnsen (Eds.), *Advances in test anxiety research* (Vol. 7, pp. 18–31). Amsterdam: Swets & Zeitlinger.

Tobias, S. (1994). Interest, prior knowledge, and learning. *Review of Educational Research, 64,* 37–54.

Tobias, S., & Weissbrod, C. (1980). Anxiety and mathematics: An update. *Harvard Educational Review, 50,* 63–70.

Tobin, K., Kahle, J., & Fraser, B. (Eds.). (1990). *Windows into science classrooms: Problems associated with higher level cognitive learning in science.* London: Falmer Press.

Tollefson, N., Tracy, D., Johnsen, E., Farmer, A., & Buenning, M. (1984). Goal setting and personal responsibility training for LD adolescents. *Psychology in the Schools, 21,* 224–233.

Topman, R., Kleijn, W., van der Ploeg, H., & Masset, E. (1992). Test anxiety, cognitions, study habits and academic performance: A prospective study. In K. Hagtvet & T. Johnsen (Eds.), *Advances in test anxiety research* (Vol. 7, pp. 239–259). Amsterdam: Swets & Zeitlinger.

Trudewind, C. (1982). The development of achievement motivation and individual differences: Ecological determinants. In W. Hartup (Ed.), *Review of Child Development Research* (Vol. 6, pp. 669–703). Chicago: University of Chicago Press.

Tuss, P., Zimmer, J., & Ho, H. (1995). Causal attributions of underachieving fourth grade students in China, Japan, and the United States. *Journal of Cross-Cultural Psychology, 26,* 408–425.

Urdan, T., & Maehr, M. (1995). Beyond a two-goal theory of motivation and achievement: A case for social goals. *Review of Educational Research, 65,* 213–243.

Urdan, T., Midgley, C., & Wood, S. (1995). Special issues in reforming middle level schools. *Journal of Early Adolescence, 15,* 9–37.

Utman, C. (in press). Learning and performance goals effects on performance: A meta-analysis. *Personality and Social Psychology Bulletin.*

Vagg, P., & Papsdorf, J. (1995). Cognitive therapy, study skills training, and biofeedback in the treatment of test anxiety. In C. Spielberger & P. Vagg (Eds.), *Test anxiety: Theory, assessment, and treatment* (pp. 183–194). Washington, DC: Taylor & Francis.

Vagg, P., & Spielberger, C. (1995). Treatment of test anxiety: Application of the transactional process model. In C. Spielberger & P. Vagg (Eds.), *Test anxiety: Theory, assessment, and treatment* (pp. 197–215). Washington, DC: Taylor & Francis.

Vallerand, R., Gauvin, L., & Halliwell, W. (1986). Negative effects of competition on children's intrinsic motivation. *Journal of Social Psychology, 126,* 649–657.

Vanfossen, B., Jones, J., & Spade, J. (1987). Curriculum tracking and status maintenance. *Sociology of Education, 60,* 104–122.

Van Overwalle, F., Mervielde, I., & De Schuyter, J. (1995). Structural modeling of the relationships between attributional dimensions, emotions, and performance of college freshmen. *Cognition & Emotion, 9,* 59–85.

Varnon, C., & King, R. (1993). A tidal wave of change—OBE in the USA. *Outcomes, 12,* 16–19.

Vygotsky, L. (1962). *Thought and language.* Cambridge, MA: MIT Press.

Vygotsky, L. (1978). *Mind in society: The development of higher psychological processes.* Cambridge, MA: Harvard University Press.

Wade, S. (1992). How interest affects learning from text. In K. Renninger, S. Hidi, & A. Krapp (Eds.), *The role of interest in learning and development* (pp. 255–277). Hillsdale, NJ: Lawrence Erlbaum Associates.

Walker, D., Greenwood, C., & Terry, B. (1994). Management of classroom disruptive behavior and academic performance problems. In L. W. Craighead, W. E. Craighead, A. Kazdin, & M. Mahoney (Eds.), *Cognitive and behavioral interventions: An empirical approach to mental health problems* (pp. 215–234). Boston: Allyn & Bacon.

Wall, S. (1983). Children's self-determination of standards in reinforcement contingencies: A re-examination. *Journal of School Psychology, 21,* 123–131.

Wang, M. (1983). Development and consequences of students' sense of personal control. In J. Levine & M. Wang (Eds.), *Teacher and student perceptions: Implications for learning* (pp. 213–247). Hillsdale, NJ: Lawrence Erlbaum Associates.

Wang, M., & Palincsar, A. (1989). Teaching students to assume an active role in their learning. In M. Reynolds (Ed.), *Knowledge base for the beginning teacher* (pp. 71–84). New York: Pergamon Press.

Wang, M., & Stiles, B. (1976). An investigation of children's concept of self-responsibility for their school learning. *American Educational Research Journal, 13,* 159–179.

Webb, F., Covington, M., & Guthrie, J. (1993). Carrots and sticks: Can school policy influence student motivation? In T. Tomlinson (Ed.), *Motivating students to learn: On overcoming barriers to high achievement* (pp. 99–124). Berkeley, CA: McCutchan.

Webb, N. (1984). Student interaction and learning in small-group and whole-class settings. In P. Peterson, L. Wilkinson, & M. Hallinan (Eds.), *The social context of instruction: Group organization and group processes* (pp. 153–170). Orlando, FL: Academic Press.

Webb, N. (1985). Student interaction and learning in small groups: A research summary. In R. Slavin, S. Sharan, S. Kagan, R. Hertz-Lazarowitz, C. Webb, & R. Schmuck (Eds.), *Learning to cooperate, cooperating to learn* (pp. 147–172). New York: Plenum.

Weiner, B. (1979). A theory of motivation for some classroom experiences. *Journal of Educational Psychology, 71,* 3–25.

Weiner, B. (1980a). *Human motivation.* New York: Holt, Rinehart & Winston.

Weiner, B. (1980b). The role of affect in rational (attributional) approaches to human motivation. *Educational Researcher, 9,* 4–11.

Weiner, B. (1983). Some methodological pitfalls in attributional research. *Journal of Educational Psychology, 75,* 530–543.

Weiner, B. (1985). An attributional theory of achievement motivation and emotion. *Psychological Review, 92,* 548–573.

Weiner, B. (1986). *An attributional theory of motivation and emotion.* New York: Springer-Verlag.

Weiner, B. (1992). *Human motivation: Metaphors, theories and research.* Beverly Hills: Sage Publications.

Weiner, B. (1994). Integrating social and personal theories of achievement striving. *Review of Educational Research, 64,* 557–573.

Weiner, B. (1995). *Judgments of responsibility: A foundation for a theory of social conduct.* New York: Guilford Press.

Weiner, B., Graham, S., Stern, P., & Lawson, M. (1982). Using affective cues to infer causal thoughts. *Developmental Psychology, 18,* 278–286.

Weiner, B., Russell, D., & Lerman, D. (1978). Affective consequences of causal ascriptions. In J. Harvey, W. Ickes, & R. Kidd (Eds.), *New directions in attribution research* (Vol. 2, pp. 59–90). Hillsdale, NJ: Lawrence Erlbaum Associates.

Weiner, B., Russell, D., & Lerman, D. (1979). The cognition-motion process in achievement-related contexts. *Journal of Personality and Social Psychology, 37,* 1211–1220.

Weinstein, R. (1976). Reading group membership in first grade: Teacher behaviors and pupil experience over time. *Journal of Educational Psychology, 68,* 103–116.

Weinstein, R. (1985). Student mediation of classroom expectancy effects. In J. Dusek (Ed.), *Teacher expectancies* (pp 329–350). Hillsdale, NJ: Lawrence Erlbaum Associates.

Weinstein, R. (1989). Perceptions of classroom processes and student motivation: Children's views of self-fulfilling prophecies. In C. Ames & R. Ames (Eds.), *Research on motivation in education. Vol. 3: Goals and cognitions* (pp. 187–221). New York: Academic Press.

Weinstein, R. (1993). Children's knowledge of differential treatment in school: Implications for motivation. In T. Tomlinson (Ed.), *Motivating students to learn: Overcoming barriers to high achievement* (pp. 197–224). Berkeley, CA: McCutchan.

Weinstein, R., Madison, S., & Kuklinski, M. (1995). Raising expectations in schooling: Obstacles and opportunities for change. *American Educational Research Journal, 32,* 121–159.

Weinstein, R., & Middlestadt, S. (1979). Student perceptions of teacher interactions with male high and low achievers. *Journal of Educational Psychology, 71,* 421–431.

Weinstein, R., Soule, C., Collins, F., Cone, J., Mehlorn, M., & Stimmonacchi, K. (1991). Expectations and high school change: Teacher–researcher collaboration to prevent school failure. *American Journal of Community Psychology, 19,* 333–363.

Weisz, J. (1986). Understanding the developing understanding of control. In M. Perlmutter (Ed.), *Cognitive perspectives on children's social and behavioral development: The Minnesota symposia on child psychology* (Vol. 18, pp. 219–278). Hillsdale, NJ: Lawrence Erlbaum Associates.

Weisz, J., & Stipek, D. (1982). Competence, contingency and the development of perceived control. *Human Development, 25,* 250–281.

Wentzel, K. (1989). Adolescent classroom goals, standards for performance, and academic achievement: An interactionist perspective. *Journal of Educational Psychology, 81,* 131–142.

Wentzel, K. (1991). Social and academic goals at school: Motivation and achievement in context. In M. Maehr & P. Pintrich (Eds.), *Advances in motivation and achievement* (Vol. 7, pp. 185–212). Greenwich, CT: JAI Press.

Wentzel, K. (1992). Motivation and achievement in adolescence: A multiple goals perspective. In D. Schunk & J. Meece (Eds.), *Student perceptions in the classroom* (pp. 287–306). Hillsdale, NJ: Lawrence Erlbaum Associates.

Wentzel, K. (1993a). Does being good make the grade? Social behavior and academic competence in middle school. *Journal of Educational Psychology, 85,* 357–364.

Wentzel, K. (1993b). Motivation and achievement in early adolescence: The role of multiple classroom goals. *Journal of Early Adolescence, 13,* 4–20.

Wentzel, K. (1994). Relations of social goals pursuit to social acceptance, and perceived social support. *Journal of Educational Psychology, 86,* 173–182.

Wentzel, K. (1996). Social goals and social relationships as motivators of school adjustment. In J. Juvonen & K. Wentzel (Eds.), *Social motivation: Understanding school adjustment* (pp. 226–247). New York: Cambridge University Press.

West, C., & Anderson, T. (1976). The question of preponderant causation in teacher expectancy research. *Review of Educational Research, 46,* 185–213.

White, R. (1959). Motivation reconsidered: The concept of competence. *Psychological Review, 66,* 297–333.

Wigfield, A. (1994a). Expectancy-value theory of achievement motivation: A developmental perspective. *Educational Psychology Review, 6,* 49–78.

Wigfield, A. (1994b). The role of children's achievement values in the self-regulation of their learning outcomes. In D. Schunk & B. Zimmerman (Eds.), *Self-regulation of learning and performance* (pp. 101–124). Hillsdale, NJ: Lawrence Erlbaum Associates.

Wigfield, A., & Eccles, J. (1989). Test anxiety in elementary and secondary school students. *Educational Psychologist, 24,* 159–183.

Wigfield, A., & Eccles, J. (1990). Test anxiety in the school setting. In M. Lewis & S.M. Miller (Eds.), *Handbook of developmental psychopathology: Perspectives in developmental psychology* (pp. 237–250). New York: Plenum.

Wigfield, A., & Eccles, J. (1992). The development of achievement task values: A theoretical analysis. *Developmental Review, 12,* 265–310.

Wigfield, A., & Eccles, J. (1994). Children's competence beliefs, achievement values, and general self-esteem: Change across elementary and middle school. *Journal of Early Adolescence, 14,* 107–137.

Wigfield, A., Eccles, J., Mac Iver, D., Reuman, D., & Midgley, C. (1991). Transitions during early adolescence: Changes in children's domain-specific self-perceptions and general self-esteem across the transition to junior high school. *Developmental Psychology, 27,* 552–565.

Wigfield, A., Eccles, J., & Pintrich, P. (1996). Development between the ages of 11 and 25. In D. Berliner & R. Calfee (Eds.), *Handbook of educational psychology* (pp. 148–185). New York: Macmillan.

Wigfield, A., & Harold, R. (1992). Teacher beliefs and children's achievement self-perceptions: A developmental perspective. In D. Schunk & J. Meece (Eds.), *Student perceptions in the classroom* (95–121). Hillsdale, NJ: Lawrence Erlbaum Associates.

Wigfield, A., & Meece, J. (1988). Math anxiety in elementary and secondary school students. *Journal of Educational Psychology, 80,* 210–216.

Williams, T. (1976). Teacher prophecies and the inheritance of inequality. *Sociology of Education, 49,* 223–236.

Williams, B., Williams, R., & McLaughlin, T. (1991). Classroom procedures for remediating behavior disorders. *Journal of Educational Psychology, 80,* 210–216.

Wine, J. (1980). Cognitive-attentional theory of test anxiety. In I. Sarason (Ed.), *Test anxiety: Theory, research, and applications* (pp. 349–384). Hillsdale, NJ: Lawrence Erlbaum Associates.

Winfield, L. (1986). Teacher beliefs toward academically at risk students in inner urban schools. *Urban Review, 18,* 253–268.

Winterbottom, M. (1958). The relation of need for achievement to learning experiences in independence and mastery. In J. Atkinson (Ed.), *Motives in fantasy, action, and society*. Princeton: Van Nostrand.

Wood, D., Rosenberg, M., & Carran, D. (1993). The effects of tape-recorded self-instruction cues on the mathematics performance of students with learning disabilities. *Journal of Learning Disabilities, 26*, 250–258.

Woolfolk, A., & Hoy, W. (1990). Prospective teachers' sense of efficacy and beliefs about control. *Journal of Educational Psychology, 82*, 81–91.

Yussen, S., & Kane, P. (1985). Children's conception of intelligence. In S. R. Yussen (Ed.), *The growth of reflection in children* (pp. 207–241). Orlando, FL: Academic Press.

Zahorik, J. (1996). Elementary and secondary teachers' reports of how they make learning interesting. *The Elementary School Journal, 96*, 551–564.

Zatz, S., & Chassin, L. (1985). Cognitions of test-anxious children under naturalistic test-taking conditions. *Journal of Consulting and Clinical Psychology, 53*, 393–401.

Zeidner, M. (1992). Statistics and mathematics anxiety in social science students: Some interesting parallels. *British Journal of Educational Psychology, 61*, 319–328.

Zeidner, M. (1994). Personal and contextual determinants of coping and anxiety in an evaluative situation: A prospective study. *Personality and Individual Differences, 16*, 899–918.

Zeidner, M. (1995). Adaptive coping with test situations: A review of the literature. *Educational Psychologist, 30*, 123–133.

Zeidner, M., & Nevo, B. (1992). Test anxiety in examinees in a college admissions testing situation: Incidence, dimensionality, and cognitive correlates. In K. Hagtvet & T. Johnsen (Ed.), *Advances in test anxiety research* (Vol. 7, pp. 288–303). Amsterdam: Swets & Zeitlinger.

Zigler, E., & Harter, S. (1969). The socialization of the mentally retarded. In D. Goslin (Ed.), *Handbook of socialization theory and research* (pp. 1065–1102). Chicago: McNally.

Zimmer, J., Hocevar, D., Bachelor, P., & Meinke, D. (1992). An analysis of the Sarason (1984) four-factor conceptualization of test anxiety. In K. Hagtvet & T. Johnsen (Ed.), *Advances in test anxiety research* (Vol. 7, pp. 103–113). Amsterdam: Swets & Zeitlinger.

Zimmerman, B. (1995). Self-efficacy and educational development. In A. Bandura (Ed.), *Self-efficacy in changing societies* (pp. 202–231). New York: Cambridge University Press.

Zimmerman, B., & Bandura, A. (1994). Impact of self-regulatory influences on writing course attainment. *American Educational Research Journal, 31*, 845–862.

Zimmerman, B., Bandura, A., & Martinez-Pons, M. (1992). Self-motivation for academic attainment: The role of self-efficacy beliefs and personal goal setting. *American Educational Research Journal, 29*, 663–676.

Zimmerman, B., & Martinez-Pons, M. (1986). Development of a structured interview for assessing student use of self-regulated learning strategies. *American Educational Research Journal, 23*, 614–628.

Zimmerman, B., & Martinez-Pons, M. (1992). Perceptions of efficacy and strategy use in the self-regulation of learning. In D. Schunk & J. Meece (Eds.), *Student perceptions in the classroom* (pp.185–207). Hillsdale, NJ: Lawrence Erlbaum Associates.

Zimmerman, J., & Silverman, R. (1982). The effects of selected variables on writing anxiety. *Diagnostique, 8*, 62–70.

Zuckerman, M., Porac, J., Lathin, D., Smith, R., & Deci, E. (1978). On the importance of self-determination for intrinsically motivated behavior. *Personality and Social Psychology Bulletin, 4*, 443–466.

Author Index

Aber, L., 12, 156
Aboud, F., 83
Abrahams, S., 172
Abramowitz, A., 25, 31
Abrams, L., 128
Adelman, H., 128
Adler, T., 63, 81, 85, 142, 143, 144, 195
Ainley, M., 150
Airasian, P., 204
Alafat, K., 129
Alexander, K., 212
Alexander, P., 168, 169
Algaze, B., 198, 199
Alleman, J., 164
Allen, A., 114
Alschuler, A., 24
Amabile, T., 125, 128
Ames, C., 63, 112, 113, 146, 147, 148, 149, 152,
    154, 172, 173, 175
Ames, D., 122
Ames, R., 113, 172, 173, 175
Anderman, E., 84, 85, 86, 133, 150, 157, 159, 233
Anderson, L., 32, 111, 163
Anderson, R., 124, 128, 169
Anderson, S., 188
Anderson, T., 204
Anton, W., 193, 194
Appel, M., 188
Apple, M., 84
Archer, J., 146, 147, 148, 149, 152, 154
Arkes, H., 128
Armstrong, S., 82
Aronfreed, J., 82, 138
Aronson, E., 114
Arunkumar, R., 78

Asarnow, J., 48
Asher, S., 124, 169
Ashton, P., 206
Aspinwall, L., 104, 184
Atkinson, J., 11, 12, 53, 54, 55, 57, 58, 69, 138,
    140
Azuma, H., 63

Babad, E., 210, 215, 216
Bachelor, P., 189
Bachman, J., 86
Bachmann, M., 33
Baer, D., 46
Baker, D., 68, 81
Ball, D., 166
Ball, S., 187
Baltes, P., 59, 60
Bandalos, D., 43, 187
Bandura, A., 39, 40, 41, 42, 43, 48, 57, 97, 119,
    128, 138, 187, 191
Bangert-Drowns, R., 111
Barbar, B., 86, 87, 108
Barbaranelli, C., 42
Barden, R., 47
Barker, G., 211
Barnes, J., 63, 82, 90
Baron, R., 205
Barrett, M., 124, 125, 229
Barwick, N., 196
Basile, D., 196
Bates, J., 126
Baum, M., 32
Beamer, J., 43
Becker, J., 214
Bedell, J., 188

Beery, R., 30, 75, 77, 78, 80, 92
Belfiore, P., 45, 46
Belmont, M., 156, 157, 158
Bempechat, J., 74
Benjamin, M., 191, 197
Benson, J., 187
Benware, C., 124, 149
Berlyne, D., 122
Berry, J., 43
Betley, G., 128
Betz, N., 43, 81
Biermann, V., 33
Biggs, J., 50, 104
Birch, S., 157
Black, J., 47, 205
Blanck, P., 128
Blaney, N., 114
Blankstein, K., 191
Block, J., 109, 110
Bloom, B., 109, 110
Blue, S., 24
Blumenfeld, P., 76, 81, 82, 83, 84, 85, 90, 144,
   148, 166, 167, 168, 171, 177, 184, 214
Bobko, P., 43
Boggiano, A., 83, 121, 124, 125, 126, 128, 164,
   175, 229
Bootzin, R., 25
Borko, H., 213
Borkowski, J., 50, 104
Bornstein, P., 49
Bossert, S., 76, 84, 85, 106, 107
Bouffard-Bouchard, T., 43
Bracken, B., 88
Bradley, K., 45, 48
Bragonier, P., 83
Brattesani, K., 216
Brockner, J., 148
Brooks-Gunn, J., 18
Brophy, J., 31, 32, 84, 85, 163, 164, 169, 170,
   203, 204, 212, 214, 216, 219, 243, 251
Brown, A., 50
Brown, R., 50, 104, 168, 169
Brown, S., 43
Bruch, M., 192
Bruner, J., 167
Bruning, R., 82
Brush, L., 194
Bryant, B., 111
Buckholdt, D., 112
Buenning, M., 97
Burdick, N., 90
Burhans, K., 75
Burns, M., 147

Burns, R., 114
Butkowsky, I., 110, 111
Butler, R., 69, 83, 125, 147, 149, 174
Byrne, B., 73, 88, 90

Cain, K., 74
Cairns, L., 63, 82, 90
Cameron, J., 126, 128
Caprara, G., 42
Carpenter, T., 194
Carr, M., 104, 105
Carran, D., 48, 51
Cartledge, G., 109
Casady, M., 127
Chabay, R., 104, 184
Chapman, M., 59, 60
Chassin, L., 193
Chatman, C., 203, 204
Chen, C., 63
Chessor, D., 86
Childs, K., 46
Christensen, S., 204
Ciminero, A., 47
Clarke, S., 46
Clifford, M., 98, 104, 230
Cobb, P., 146, 149
Cochran, L., 109
Coe, K., 128
Cohen, E., 109, 112, 114, 223
Cohen, H., 24, 26
Cohen, P., 111
Cohen, R., 83
Cole, C., 45, 46, 48
Collins, F., 233
Collins, J., 44
Colvin, C., 82
Comer, J., 205
Cone, J., 233
Connell, J., 58, 60, 73, 121, 124, 125, 126, 127,
   128, 137, 138, 139, 140, 155, 156, 157
Cooper, H., 203, 205
Corbitt, M., 194
Cordova, D., 168, 177
Corno, L., 178
Cosden, M., 113, 115
Courtney, D., 81, 142
Covington, M., 12, 27, 30, 33, 69, 73, 75, 76, 77,
   78, 80, 92, 173, 190, 200
Cramer, J., 63, 67
Crandall, V. , 54, 59
Cravn, R., 86
Crawford, J., 32
Crockenberg, S., 111

Cross, D., 50
Csikszentmihalyi, M., 148
Culler, R., 191
Cunningham, J., 126

Daly, J., 196, 197
Damnjanovic, A., 31
Damon, W., 32, 99
D'Andrade, R.C., 54
Daniels, D., 82, 121
Danner, F., 119, 164
Danner, K., 26
Dauber, S., 212
Davey, M., 129
Davidson, K., 187, 188, 189, 192, 194
Davis, M., 188
Deaux, K., 64
Debus, R., 63
deCharms, R., 122, 123
Deci, E., 73, 119, 122, 123, 124, 126, 127, 128,
      129, 137, 138, 149, 156, 157, 172, 175, 177
Deffenbacher, J., 188, 198
Deffenbacher, T. L., 188
De Groot, E., 43, 50, 187
DeJong, W., 128
de la Torre, G., 26
Delgado-Gaitan, C., 151
Dembo, M., 206
Dendato, K., 198
De Schuyter, J., 68
Desiderato, O., 191
DeVries, D., 113
Dialdin, D., 133
Dickson-Markman, F., 196
Diener, C., 66, 67
Diener, D., 198
DiGangi, S., 46
Doane, K., 204, 206, 232
Dollinger, S., 128
Doubleday, C., 69
Drabman, R., 25, 49
Drake, M., 128, 133
Dubey, D., 47
Dulany, D., 39
Dunlap, G., 46
Durand, H., 194
Dusek, J., 191, 203, 204, 205
Dweck, C., 63, 66, 67, 74, 75, 81, 104, 107, 146,
      147, 148, 149

Earley, P., 42
Eaton, W., 201

Eccles, J., 12, 43, 56, 63, 73, 75, 76, 81, 82, 83,
      84, 85, 86, 87, 90, 103, 133, 137, 140, 142,
      143, 144, 145, 156, 158, 159, 178, 182,
      193, 194, 195, 198, 203, 204, 205, 214
Eckert, P., 215
Eder, D., 87
Edmonds, R., 203
Edwards, C., 177
Efthim, H., 110
Eisenberg, N., 138
Eisenberger, R., 28
Eisenhart, M., 213
El-Dinary, P., 104
Elliot, A., 146, 150
Elliott, E., 74, 146, 147, 148, 149
Emerson, H., 102
Emery, J., 124, 175
Engel, M., 214
Ensminger, M., 18
Entwisle, D., 81, 212
Estes, W., 39
Eswara, H., 76
Evans, K., 110
Everson, H., 190, 194
Evertson, C., 32, 84, 85
Eysenck, M., 191

Fagot, B., 181
Fantuzzo, J., 45, 90
Farmer, A., 97
Farnham-Diggory, S., 181
Farrell, W., 194
Feather, N., 79, 142
Feld, S., 188
Feldlaufer, H., 75, 83, 85, 159, 178, 182
Feldman, N., 83
Felker, D., 112, 173
Felson, R., 87
Feng, H., 109
Fennema, E., 81, 166
Fielding, L., 169
Fincham, F., 62
Finn, J., 18
Flanagan, C., 144
Fletcher, T., 199
Flett, G., 191
Flick, L., 167
Flink, C., 124, 125, 229
Folger, R., 128
Forsterling, F., 104
Fowler, S., 46
Fox, K., 196
Fraser, B., 214

Frederick, E., 43
Freedman, J., 126
Freitas, J., 46
Frey, K., 83
Frieze, I., 63
Fry, P., 128
Fuligni, A., 86, 87, 108
Furman, W., 47
Furstenberg, F., 18
Futterman, R., 12, 63, 81, 142, 143, 144
Fyans, L., 172, 189

Gaa, J., 97
Garbarino, J., 28
Garibaldi, A., 205
Garner, R., 168, 169
Gauvin, L., 128
Gavanski, I., 68
Gavin, D., 90
Gibbs, J., 114
Gibson, S., 206
Gillingham, M., 168, 169
Gitelson, I., 63
Goetz, T., 66
Goff, S., 12, 63, 81, 142, 143, 144
Golan, S., 149
Goldberg, M., 87
Goldberger, M., 163
Goldenberg, C., 218
Gonzalez, H., 198
Good, T., 102, 164, 209, 212, 216, 219, 251
Goodenow, C., 156
Goodlad, J., 194
Gordon, D., 181
Gorman, J., 45, 46, 48, 49, 51
Gottfried, A., 121, 130
Gourgey, A., 194
Gouvernet, P., 90
Graham, L., 51
Graham, S., 21, 50, 61, 62, 68, 69, 149, 210, 211
Gralinski, H., 63, 81, 150
Grant, L., 205
Graves, D., 100
Greene, D., 126, 128
Greene, J. C., 63
Greenwood, C., 22
Greenwood, G.E., 48
Grolnick, W., 124, 138, 178
Grosovsky, E., 83
Gross, T., 200
Grover, B., 166
Grundy, D., 196
Guarino, P., 69

Gullickson, A., 85
Guo, G., 18
Guskey, T., 109, 110, 111, 206
Guthrie, J., 27, 30
Guzdial, M., 167

Hackett, G., 43, 81
Haertel, G., 177
Hall, V., 126
Hallahan, D., 45, 48
Hallinan, M., 85
Halliwell, W., 128
Hamilton, H., 181
Hamilton, S., 109
Hamilton, V., 76, 82, 83, 84, 85
Hampton, V., 90
Handley, H., 214
Hanson, A., 42
Harackiewicz, J., 97, 128, 146, 150, 172
Harel, K., 102
Haring, T., 113, 115
Harnisch, D., 189
Harold, R., 81, 82, 90, 144, 203
Harris, K., 50
Harter, S., 28, 82, 85, 87, 88, 89, 119, 120, 121, 125, 130, 131, 132, 133, 134, 140, 142, 157, 172, 187, 201
Hartman, H., 194
Hastings, J., 110
Hattie, J., 50, 73, 82, 104
Hayduk, L., 85
Hayes, S., 49
Heckhausen, H., 76, 83
Hedl, J., 187, 188
Heimberg, R., 24
Heller, K., 81
Helmke, A., 193, 198
Hembree, R., 187, 190, 191, 194, 195, 198
Hempelmann, P., 33
Hennessey, B., 125
Henningsen, M., 166
Hertz-Lazarowitz, N., 112, 114
Hess, R. D., 63
Hicks, L., 85, 133, 150, 159, 233
Hiebert, E., 213
Higgins, E., 85
Hill, K., 85, 187, 189, 193, 194, 200, 201
Ho, H., 63
Hocevar, D., 189
Hoffman, J., 63
Hoge, R., 86
Hokoda, A., 62
Holahan, C., 191

Holinger, D., 191
Holloway, S., 63
Holmes, I., 90
Holroyd, K., 188
Holt, J., 30
Holt, K., 150
Holubec, E., 114
Hom, H., 79, 97
Hoy, W., 206
Hoyle, R., 148
Hughes, B., 128, 172
Hughes, C., 45, 46, 48, 49, 51
Hull, C., 10
Hulton, R., 113
Hunt, J. McV., 122
Hunter, M., 122
Hutchings, C., 188
Hutchinson, S., 187
Hymel, S., 169

Ichikawa, V., 63
Irvine, J., 205

Jackson, L., 128
Jackson, P., 207
Jacobs, J., 81
Jacobson, L., 203
Jagacinski, C., 77, 83, 149
Jerusalem, M., 187, 191
Johnsen, E., 97
Johnson, D., 112, 113, 114, 170
Johnson, R., 112, 113, 114, 170
Jones, G., 214
Jones, J., 213
Joseph, G., 204, 205
Junker, L., 177
Jussim, L., 16, 88, 203, 204, 205
Juster, H., 192
Justman, J., 87

Kaczala, C., 12, 63, 81, 142, 143, 144, 195, 204, 211, 214
Kaflowitz, N., 192
Kagan, J., 122
Kagan, S., 112, 114
Kahle, J., 81, 128, 144, 213, 214
Kamann, M., 48
Kamii, C., 32
Kane, P., 82
Karabenick, S., 79, 102
Karniol, R., 128
Kashiwagi, K., 63
Katkovsky, W., 59

Katz, P., 121, 124, 125
Kauffman, M., 229
Kazdin, A., 25, 46
Keavney, M., 128
Keely, S., 48
Keith, L., 88
Kellaghan, T., 204
Keller, F., 110, 111
Kelly, H., 61
Kepner, H., 194
Kermis, M., 191
Kern, L., 46
Kimball, M., 214
King, J., 110
King, N., 84
King, R., 110
Kirby, K., 46
Kleijn, W., 191
Klisch, M., 194
Koestner, R., 229
Kohn, A., 25, 28, 32, 126
Kolb, K., 16, 88
Koopman, R., 122
Korinek, L., 45, 46, 48, 49, 51
Korn, Z., 49
Koskinen, P., 191
Kowalski, P., 85, 121, 133, 174
Krajcik, J., 167
Kramer, N., 129
Kratochwill, T., 45, 46
Krismer, K., 126
Krohne, H., 193
Kuhn, D., 167
Kuklinski, M., 206
Kulik, C-L., 111
Kulik, J., 111
Kulikowich, J., 168, 169

Ladd, G., 157
Lalli, E., 46
Lampert, M., 166
Laosa, L., 151
Larivee, S., 43
Latham, G., 43, 47, 97
Lathin, D., 177
Lawson, M., 69, 210
Lazarus, M., 194, 195
Lee, C., 43
Lee, S., 63
Lefcourt, H., 58
Leggett, E., 74, 146
Leinhardt, G., 214
Lent, R., 43

Lenz, R., 48
Leonard, J., 26
Lepper, M., 104, 126, 128, 139, 146, 168, 177, 184
Lerman, D., 68
Levine, J., 83, 112
Lewin, K., 178, 181
Lewis, J., 188
Lewis, M., 68, 82
Licht, B., 63, 66, 67, 81, 90
Liebert, R., 188
Light, R., 108
Lighthall, F., 187, 188, 189, 192, 194
Lillibridge, E. M., 193
Lin, Y-G., 191, 197
Lindquist, M., 194
Lipinski, D., 47
Lippitt, R., 178, 181
Lipson, M., 50
Litrownik, A., 46
Little, T., 60
Lituchy, T., 42
Locke, E., 43, 47, 97
Loebl, J., 83
Lonky, E., 119, 164
Lotan, R., 109, 223
Lundberg, I., 43
Luria, A., 48
Luster, T., 18
Luthar, S., 187

Maag, J., 46
Mace, F., 45, 46
Mac Iver, D., 82, 84, 85, 121, 144, 174, 178, 194
Madaus, G., 110, 204
Madison, S., 206
Madon, S., 203, 204, 205
Madsen, C., 24
Maehr, M., 84, 86, 128, 133, 146, 150, 151, 157, 172, 233
Mahn, C. S., 48
Mahoney, M., 46
Maier, S., 65
Main, D., 121, 124, 125
Malone, T., 168
Manderlink, G., 97, 128
Manoogian, S., 128
Manz, P., 90
Marks, H., 204, 206, 232
Marks, M., 104
Marlowe, H., 188
Marsh, H., 63, 73, 82, 86, 88, 90
Marshall, H., 85, 216

Martinez-Pons, M., 43, 50
Marx, R., 167
Marzano, R., 110
Masset, E., 191
Mastenbrook, M., 200
Masters, J., 47
Matheny, K., 177
Maughan, B.,, 204
Mayer, G., 22
McAdoo, H., 18
McClelland, D., 54
McCombs, B., 155, 205
McCullers, J., 125
McDermott, P., 90
McDermott, R., 213
McGraw, K., 125
McKeachie, W., 191, 197
McLaughlin, T., 25
McMullin, D., 119, 164
Meece, J., 12, 43, 50, 63, 76, 81, 82, 84, 85, 142, 143, 144, 146, 148, 150, 169, 171, 177, 184, 194, 195, 204, 211, 214
Mehlorn, M., 233
Meichenbaum, D., 45, 47, 48
Meid, E., 33
Meinke, D., 189
Mendez-Caratini, G., 83
Mergendoller, J., 166, 171
Mergler, N., 191
Mervielde, I., 68
Meyer, J., 86
Meyer, W., 33, ;73, 211
Middlestadt, S., 215
Midgley, C., 12, 63, 75, 78, 81, 83, 84, 85, 86, 133, 142, 143, 144, 150, 159, 178, 182, 194, 233
Miller, A., 79, 82, 83, 211
Miller, C., 144
Miller, D., 75, 79
Miller, M., 42, 43, 196
Miller, S., 201
Millsap, R., 194
Miserandino, M., 73, 125
Mitchell, M., 130, 167, 170
Moll, L., 169
Mone, M., 68
Montessori, M., 32
Morris, L., 188
Morris, W., 83
Morse, L., 214
Mortimore, P., 204
Mosatche, H., 83
Mosley, M., 128, 172

Mossholder, K., 128
Mosteller, F., 103
Multon, K., 43
Mumme, D., 104, 184
Munk, D., 171, 177
Munt, E., 49
Murphy, M., 97
Mussen, P., 138

National Council of Teachers of Mathematics, 165
Naveh-Benjamin, M., 191, 198
Nelson, R., 47
Nelson-Le Gall, S., 103
Nemcek, D., 83
Nevo, B., 187, 188, 194
Newman, R., 18, 81, 82, 102, 144
Newmann, F., 164
Nezlek, J., 177
Nicholls, J. , 63, 77, 82, 83, 146, 147, 148, 149, 150, 152, 211
Niedenthal, P., 68
Nierenberg, R., 76
Nimetz, S., 156
Nisan, M., 125, 174
Nisbett, R., 126, 208
Nolen, S., 148
Nottelmann, E., 85
Notz, W., 126
Numi, J., 68

Oakes, J., 213
Oettingen, G., 60
Ogbu, J., 151
Oka, E., 50
O'Leary, K., 25
O'Leary, S., 25, 31, 47
O'Malley, P., 86
Omelich, C., 33, 69, 76, 78, 173, 190, 200
O'Neil, H., 187, 200
Oshima, T., 63
Ouston, J., 204

Pajares, F., 42, 43
Palardy, J., 214
Palincsar, A., 50, 167
Pallas, A., 212
Papay, J., 187
Papsdorf, J., 198, 199
Parent, S., 43
Paris, S., 50
Parker, J., 86
Parker, L., 81, 168

Parsons, J., 63, 81, 83, 85, 195, 204, 214
Pascarella, E., 177
Passaro, P., 106
Passow, A., 87
Pastorelli, C., 42
Patashnick, M., 149
Patrick, B., 58, 125, 139
Pearlman, C., 124, 175
Peckhan, P.D., 63
Pelletier, L., 127, 156
Pepitone, E., 107
Perkinson, H., 167
Petersen, A., 63
Peterson, P., 15, 147, 166
Phillips, B., 201
Phillips, D., 16, 88
Piaget, J., 118, 119
Pianta, R., 156, 157
Pierce, W., 126, 128
Pigott, T., 111
Pike, R., 82, 89
Pintrich, P., 43, 50, 76, 82, 83, 84, 85, 86, 90, 143, 148, 187, 190
Pitcher, G., 201
Pittman, T., 124, 126, 128, 129, 164, 175, 177
Plant, R., 124, 128
Plass, J., 201
Ploger, F., 33
Polite, K., 45
Porac, J., 128, 177
Powelson, C., 156
Prawat, R., 167
Pressley, M., 50, 104
Preston, A., 59
Purdie, N., 50, 104
Puro, P., 171, 177, 184

Quevillon, R., 49

Rainey, R., 177
Ramsey, B., 181
Randhawa, B., 43, 194, 195
Rankin, R., 88
Rashid, H., 163
Reed, M., 87
Reid, M., 104
Reis, H., 128
Relich, J., 63
Rellinger, E., 104
Renick, J., 87
Rennie, L., 81
Renzulli, J., 86
Repp, A., 171, 177

Reppucci, N., 63, 66
Rest, S., 76
Reuman, D., 85, 87, 144, 178, 194
Reyes, O., 26
Reynolds, R., 169
Reys, R., 194
Reznick, J., 128
Rheinberg, F., 173
Rice, J., 97
Richmond, V., 196
Riggs, J., 77
Robertson, D., 48
Roche, L., 86
Rodriguez, C., 194
Roeser, R., 43, 50
Rohrkemper, M., 163, 178, 212
Rollins, K., 157
Rose, M., 196
Rosen, B., 54
Rosenbaum, M., 49
Rosenberg, M., 48, 51
Rosenfarb, I., 49
Rosenfield, D., 128
Rosenholtz, S., 85, 106, 107
Rosenthal, R., 203
Ross, J., 83, 115
Ross, L., 208
Ross, M., 75, 128
Roth, K., 167
Rotter, J., 53, 57, 58, 59, 61, 62
Roy, P., 114
Ruble, D., 83, 124, 126, 128, 164, 175
Ruebush, B., 187, 188, 189, 192, 194
Rueda, R., 169
Russell, D., 68
Rutherford, R., 46
Rutter, M., 204
Ruzany, N., 83
Ryan, R., 73, 119, 122, 123, 124, 126, 127, 128,
        129, 137, 138, 140, 149, 152, 156, 157,
        174, 175, 177, 178, 229
Ryckman, D. B., 63

Sachs, J., 108
Salili, F., 172
Sanders, R., 62
Sansone, C., 97
Sapona, R., 45, 48
Sapp, M., 194
Sarason, B. R., 187, 188, 191, 199
Sarason, I., 189, 199
Sarason, I. G., 187, 188, 191, 199
Sarason, S., 187, 188, 189, 192, 194

Sauser, W., 188
Scarpati, S., 48
Scheffler, I., 122
Schiefele, U., 73, 81, 84
Schmitz, B., 58, 60
Schmuck, R., 112, 114
Schrauben, B., 50, 143, 148
Schunk, D., 41, 42, 47, 50, 97, 104, 105, 106, 149
Schwartz, A., 177
Schwartz, S., 32
Schwarzer, R., 187, 191
Sears, P., 79
Secada, W., 204, 206, 232
Seewald, A., 214
Selfe, C., 196
Seligman, M., 65
Sethi, S., 133
Sexton, T., 43
Shapira, Z., 124, 164, 175
Shapiro, E., 45, 46, 48
Sharan, S., 112, 113, 114
Shavelson, R., 88
Shea, M., 45, 46
Sheinman, L., 177
Shell, D., 82
Sherman, J., 81, 144
Shirey, L., 124, 169
Shultz, T., 119
Sieber, J., 187, 200
Sikes, J., 114
Silverman, R., 196
Simpson, C., 85, 106, 107
Simpson, S., 90
Skaalvik, E., 88
Skinner, B., 19, 20, 21, 23
Skinner, E., 58, 59, 60, 125, 139, 156, 157, 158
Slavin, R., 108, 111, 112, 114
Slavings, R., 102
Slusarcick, A., 90
Smiley, P., 147, 148
Smith, A., 204
Smith, I., 90
Smith, M., 212
Smith, R., 177
Smodlaka, I., 190
Snapp, M., 114
Snyder, H., 83
Sohn, D., 63
Soloway, E., 167
Sorensen, A., 85
Sorensen, R., 172
Soule, C., 233
Spade, J., 213

Spear, P., 82
Speidel, G., 49
Spencer, M., 156
Spiegel, N., 229
Spielberger, C., 122, 187, 188, 198, 199
Spiller, H., 33
Stader, S., 90
Stallings, J., 214
Stallings, W., 128, 172
Starr, L., 122
Steffen, J., 119, 164
Stein, M., 166
Stein, S., 104
Steinberg, M., 156, 157
Stephan, C., 114
Stern, P., 69, 210
Stetsenko, A., 60
Stevenson, H., 18, 63, 81, 144, 163, 164, 165, 170, 184
Stigler, J., 63, 163, 164, 165, 170, 184
Stiles, B., 178
Stiller, J., 127, 138, 149, 157
Stimmonacchi, K., 233
Stipek, D., 17, 33, 58, 59, 63, 81, 82, 83, 84, 121, 150, 174
Stluka, M., 212
Stodolsky, S., 195
Strein, W., 108
Suinn, R., 198
Sullivan, H., 128, 172
Sullivan, M., 68
Sulzer-Azaroff, B., 22
Swann, W., 128, 177
Swanson, H., 48
Swing, S., 15

Tang, S., 126
Tangney, J., 68
Tannatt, L., 17, 82, 83
Terry, B., 22
Tharp, R., 49
Thelen, M., 128
Thoresen, C., 46
Thorndike, E., 19
Thorndike-Christ, T., 43, 187
Thorpe, P., 50
Thurlow, M., 204
Tidman, M., 82, 90
Tobias, S., 121, 124, 125, 187, 188, 190, 191, 194, 195, 200
Tobin, K., 63
Tobin-Richards, M., 63
Tollefson, N., 97

Tom, D., 203, 205
Topman, R., 191
Tracy, D., 97
Trudewind, C., 54
Tuckman, B., 43
Tuss, P., 63

Urdan, T., 78, 150, 151, 233
Utman, C., 149
Uttal, D., 63

Vagg, P., 187, 188, 198, 199
Vallerand, R., 127, 128, 156
van der Ploeg, H., 191
Vanfossen, B., 213
Vangelisti, A., 196
Van Overwalle, F., 68
Varnon, C., 110
Vygotsky, L., 48

Wade, S., 124, 168
Wageman, R., 172
Wagner, R., 90
Waite, R., 187, 188, 189, 192, 194
Walberg, H., 177
Walker, D., 22
Wall, M., 82
Wall, S., 49
Walters, R., 40
Wang, M., 50, 178
Watson, M., 191
Webb, F., 27, 30
Webb, N., 112, 114, 115
Webb, R., 206
Weiner, B., 21, 53, 56, 61, 64, 65, 66, 68, 69, 76, 210, 212
Weinstein, R., 85, 87, 206, 212, 215, 216, 219, 233
Weissbrod, C., 195
Weisz, J., 58, 59
Wellborn, J., 138, 155, 156, 157
Wentzel, K., 13, 150
Wessels, K., 76, 82, 84, 85
West, C., 204
West, R., 43
Wetherill, K., 129
Weyhing, R., 105
Wheatley, G., 146
Wheatley, J., 214
White, C., 169
White, R., 12, 118, 119, 122, 123, 178, 181
Whitesell, N., 85, 121, 133

Wigfield, A., 43, 50, 56, 73, 76, 81, 82, 84, 85, 86, 90, 142, 143, 144, 169, 178, 187, 193, 194, 195, 198, 203
Williams, B., 25
Williams, R., 25
Williams, T., 205
Willows, D., 63
Wilson, B., 106
Wilson, P., 169
Wine, J., 191
Winfield, L., 205
Winterbottom, M., 54
Witte, S., 196

Wodarski, J., 112
Wolfert, E., 49
Wong, B., 48, 51
Wood, D., 48, 51
Wood, S., 233
Wood, T., 146, 149

Woolfolk, A., 206
Worsham, M., 201

Yackel, E., 146, 149
Yates, K., 43, 187
Yee, D., 144
Youssef, Z., 79
Ysseldyke, J., 204
Yussen, S., 82

Zahorik, J., 166, 167
Zatz, S., 191, 193
Zeidner, M., 187, 188, 191, 194
Zettle, R., 49
Zigler, E., 119, 201
Zimmer, J., 63, 189
Zimmerman, B., 41, 43, 44, 50
Zimmerman, J., 196
Zimmerman, M., 16
Zuckerman, M., 177

Subject Index

Ability grouping, 74, 85–88, 108, 205, 212–213, 234
Actor-observer effect, 208
Age differences
  in intrinsic motivation, 132–134
  in motivational problems, 17–18
  in perceptions of ability, 82–86
  in value formation, 144
Anxiety, 30, 48, 54, 79, 190–194, 249
  achievement anxiety, 43–44, 187–202
  gender differences in, 195
  math anxiety, 6, 143, 194–195
  measurement of, 188–190
  state anxiety, 187–188
  test anxiety, 187–189, 191, 194, 198–201
  trait anxiety, 187–188, 196–197
  writing anxiety, 195–197
Aspirations. *See* Performance standards
Assessment. *See* Measurement
Attainment value, 142, 144
Attributions, 11, 61–71, 77, 148–149, 211
  antecedents to, 62
  attribution retraining, 104–106
  attribution theory, 53, 61–69
  consequences of, 65–69
  cultural differences, 63
  dispositions, 62–64
  gender differences, 63–64, 67
  measurement of, 64–65
Autonomy, 15, 176–178, 228–230, 232–233
  and intrinsic motivation, 12, 122–123, 129–130. *See also* Personal responsibility

Capacity (agency) beliefs, 59
Challenge, 95–98, 122, 147, 183–184, 227, 231–232
  and intrinsic motivation, 124, 134, 163–165
  principle of optimal challenge, 119
Choice, 177–180. *See also* Autonomy
Cognitive behavior modification (CBM) 22–31, 34, 37, 44, 51
Competence motivation, 118–122, 129–130
Competition, 76–77, 84, 86, 128, 173
Cooperative incentive structure, 94, 112–115
Cooperative learning programs, 112–115
Creativity, 125, 134
Cultural differences, 204–205
  in attributions, 63
  in goals, 151
Curiosity, 125, 130, 168

Desensitization, 198–199
Differentiated task structure, 106–107
Discounting principle, 127
Discriminative stimulus, 21, 45
Drive theory, 10

Effectance motivation. *See* Competence motivation
Ego orientation, 147–150, 152, 174. *See also* Goals, performance
Enjoyment, 125, 142, 149–150. *See also* Pride
Entity concept of ability, 74–75, 195, 206, 234
Evaluation 84–86, 94, 98–102, 133, 161–162, 247. *See also* Grades

Expectations, 41, 53, 64, 94, 142–143, 156–157, 193, 196–197, 213. *See also* Attributions, consequences of; Expectancy *x* value theory
Expectancy *x* value theory, 11–12, 53–57, 137, 140–146
Extinction. *See* Reinforcement theory
Extrinsic motivation, 125, 127, 134
Extrinsic regulation, 138–140

Fear of failure, 15, 54–55
Flow, 148
Frame of reference, 86–88

Gender differences
    in anxiety, 194–195
    in attributions, 63, 67
    in perceptions of ability, 81–82
    in teacher expectations, 204–205, 211, 213–215
    in value formation, 143
Generalization, 21
Gifted children, 67, 81, 86, 121
Goals 13, 96–98, 128
    distal, 96–97
    goal theory, 13, 138, 146–153
    learning (task), 146–152, 169
    performance, 79, 146–152
    proximal, 96–97
    in social cognitive theory, 40–41
    social responsibility, 150
    teacher effects on, 47, 77
Grades, 20, 26–27, 57–60, 83–85, 98–102, 161–162, 171–176

Helping behavior, 102–103, 211
Helplessness. *See* Learned helplessness
High achievers, 16, 67, 106. *See also* Gifted children

Identification, 139
Impression management, 77–78
Incentive value of failure, 55–56
Incentive value of success, 55–56
Instrumental-incremental concept of ability, 74–75, 195, 206
Internalized motivation, 138–140, 142
Intrinsic motivation, 12, 117–135
    advantages of, 124–125
    age-related changes in, 132–134
    individual differences and, 129–134
    intrinsic motivation theory, 12, 117–135, 143

maximizing, 161–185
    perceptions of competence and, 121–122
Intrinsic value, 121, 142–144
Introjected regulation, 139

Law of effect, 19
Learned helplessness, 2–4, 65–68, 75, 104
Learning goals. *See* Goals, learning
Locus of causality, 58, 60–61, 123, 127–128
Locus of control (LOC), 58–62
    effects of classroom context on, 60
    measuring, 59–60

Mastery learning programs, 109–112, 164
Mastery motivation. *See* Competence motivation
Math anxiety. *See* Anxiety, math
Measurement, 130–133, 152, 157
    of anxiety, 188–190
    of attributions, 64–65
    of locus of control, 59–60
    of perceptions of ability 88–92
Metacognitive strategies, 45, 48–51, 148
Minimal but sufficient principle, 139
Motive to avoid failure, 54–56
Motive for success, 54–56
Multidimensional classrooms, 107

Need to achieve (Nach), 54
Novelty, 122, 168–170
    and intrinsic motivation, 117

Outcome-based education (OBE), 110

Parents, 13, 42, 54, 63, 67, 81, 120, 130, 138–139, 192–193, 212, 230
Peer relations, 26, 151, 155–156, 162, 185. *See also* Cooperative learning programs
Perceived probability of failure, 55–56
Perceived probability of success, 55–56
Perceptions of ability, 73–92
    age differences in, 82–86
    classroom effects on, 84–86
    measurement of, 88–92
Perceptions of competence, 18, 63, 73–74, 85–88, 90, 121–122, 142–144, 179
Performance goals. *See* Goals, performance
Performance standards, 41, 49, 79–80
Personal responsibility, 44–46. *See also* Autonomy
Praise, 23, 31–34, 128–129, 205, 207, 211, 214, 243
    effectiveness of, 31–35. *See also* Social reinforcement

Pride, 12, 53, 55, 68
Proximal goals. *See* Goals, proximal
Punishment. *See* Reinforcement theory

Reactivity, 46
Reciprocal determinism, 48
Reinforcement theory, 10, 13, 19–37, 39–40, 57,
    126
  extinction, 20
  negative reinforcement, 20
  partial reinforcement, 20
  positive reinforcement, 19–20, 27
  punishment, 11, 20–23, 25–26, 28, 30–31, 34,
      39, 45, 53, 78, 130, 139–140
  secondary reinforcement, 20
  shaping, 23, 40
  stimulus control, 21
Relatedness, 153–159, 182–185
Resultant tendency to approach/avoid achieve-
    ment activity, 55
Rewards, 11, 19, 57–58, 60, 128–129
  effects on intrinsic motivation, 126–129, 171–
      176
  negative effects of, 25–26, 28–29
  performance contingent, 128–129
  task contingent, 128–129
  use in behavior modification, 22–23, 25–30
Risk taking. *See* Challenge

Self-attribution theory, 127
Self-concept, 12, 142, 211, 214
Self-confidence, 6, 15, 32, 43, 73, 148, 195, 211.
    See also Perceptions of competence
Self-determination theory, 137–140, 142. *See also*
    Autonomy
Self-efficacy, 41–44, 82, 150, 191
  consequences of, 43–44
  of teachers, 206–207
  sources of, 42–43
Self-fulfilling prophecy, 203, 208, 217
Self-instruction, 47–48. *See also* Cognitive
    behavior modification
Self-management approach. *See* Cognitive
    behavior modification
Self-recording, 46–47
Self-regulation, 44–50, 138–140

Self-reinforcement, 48–49
Self-worth, 73, 75–81, 87, 89, 157
  self-worth theory, 12–13, 75–81
Shame, 12, 53, 54–56, 68–69, 76
Shaping. *See* Reinforcement theory, shaping
Social cognitive theory, 39–52
Social comparison, 33, 84–86, 94, 106–107
Social context, 16–17, 84, 86–87, 92, 127, 155,
    159, 193, 232
Social learning theory, 53, 57–60, 73
Social reinforcement, 20, 82, 85, 128–130. *See
    also* Praise
Social responsibility goals. *See* Goals, social
    responsibility
Stage-environment fit theory, 86
State anxiety. *See* Anxiety, state
Stimulus control. *See* Reinforcement theory,
    stimulus control
Strategy (means–end) beliefs, 59

Task orientation, 147–149. *See also* Goals, task
Task value. *See* Values, task
Teacher expectations, 203–220
  gender differences in, 204–205, 211, 213–215
Teacher-student relationships, 84–85, 138, 153,
    155–159
Token economy, 23–25
Tracking. *See* Ability grouping
Typical shifts, 65–69

Underachievement, 17
Undifferentiated academic task structure, 106
Unidimensional classroom, 106
Utility value. *See* Values, utility

Values, 11–13, 137–146, 151, 156–159
  age-related changes in, 144
  attainment value, 142, 144
  gender differences, 143–144, 195
  intrinsic value, 121
  task value, 56
  utility value, 142–144. *See also* Expectancy *x*
      value theory
Vicarious learning, 40

Work avoidance, 152